INSIDE THE MIND OF A VOTER

Inside the Mind of a Voter

A New Approach to Electoral Psychology

Michael Bruter

Sarah Harrison

PRINCETON UNIVERSITY PRESS
PRINCETON AND OXFORD

Copyright © 2020 by Princeton University Press

Requests for permission to reproduce material from this work should be sent to permissions@press.princeton.edu

Published by Princeton University Press
41 William Street, Princeton, New Jersey 08540
6 Oxford Street, Woodstock, Oxfordshire OX20 1TR

press.princeton.edu

All Rights Reserved

Library of Congress Control Number: 2020931097
ISBN 9780691182896
ISBN e-book 9780691202013

British Library Cataloging-in-Publication Data is available

Editorial: Sarah Caro
Production Editorial: Leslie Grundfest
Jacket/Cover Design:
Publicity: Kate Hensley, US; and Kate Farquhar-Thompson, UK

Jacket/Cover Credit: Shutterstock

This book has been composed in Adobe Text and Gotham

Printed on acid-free paper. ∞

Printed in the United States of America

10 9 8 7 6 5 4 3 2 1

TABLE OF CONTENTS

Preface and Acknowledgements   vii

Chapter Synopses   xi

1. *Homo Suffragator*   1
2. Mapping the Mind of a Voter: Anatomy of *Homo Suffragator*   24
3. A Day in the Life of a Voter   66
4. Personality and Morality   119
5. Electoral Memory   152
6. Electoral Identity and Individual–Societal Dynamics   184
7. Elections and Emotions   212
8. Electoral Ergonomics   240
9. Electoral Resolution and Atmosphere: From Hope to Hostility   263
10. Coda: Flipping the Electoral World Upside-Down: *Homo Suffragator* beyond the Age of Reason   291

Glossary of Concepts   315

Bibliography   335

Index   345

PREFACE AND ACKNOWLEDGEMENTS

For the authors, on so many levels, this has not felt quite like writing any of our other books. First, this book stems from the intellectual stimulation of some ambitious research projects we were able to conduct. We acknowledge below the sponsors who made these possible, but we must already point out that when it comes to ambitious research based on intellectual curiosity, generous open schemes such as European Research Council (ERC) Frontier grants and Economic and Social Research Council (ESRC) Standard grants are simply invaluable. Worldwide, research funding bodies are under pressure to impose research priorities, but any attempt to decide what researchers should study today—even based on researchers' input—is bound to highlight what we should really have been researching ten years ago. Open schemes, by contrast, allow researchers to convince peers that they have new ideas worth exploring.

Second, the work invited us to get out of our methodological 'comfort zone' and design new approaches that we had never explored before to collect and code an intimidating mass of heterogeneous data, in order to observe elections from more angles than we had ever previously imagined.

Third, there is something very odd in the feeling that the period in which you live is uniquely grave and momentous. To become scientifically excited, as academics, about something which, as citizens, we may often worry about or even deplore leaves a quasi-schizophrenic impression in the mind. We suspect that many of our peers have experienced similar feelings in this period.

For all these reasons, this is a book in which we have invested more time and thought than in any of those that we had written—be it together or separately—before. This is not so much because of the analytical scope and the mass of data to code, analyze, and ponder about, but rather because we wanted to be certain about what exactly we were trying to say. It had been our original intention to write a book that would revive our discipline's interest in psychological explanations of the vote that are, paradoxically, out of fashion at the very time that we need them most; but we started gradually to ponder whether we might have a more radical and more fundamental message (or two) to deliver. What if we were looking at elections entirely the wrong way round? What if it mattered a lot more to understand whether elections make people happy, and give them a sense of closure and resolution, than to focus on why they vote for Mr X or Ms Y? What if the universal assumption that the vote is the translation of a direct preference was actually wrong, and what if, in fact, voters do not enter the polling booth like spoiled children wanting the biggest ice cream, but rather like teachers about to grade an essay, with an implicit role to play? What if elections could bring, at the very same time, the best and the worst out of the same individuals, and how would such a thing even be possible? What, indeed, if the very existence of elections had changed the nature of mankind? These are some of the arguably provocative questions that we want to address in this book.

Such intellectual mountains would obviously be impossible to climb without considerable help, more in fact than we could possibly acknowledge; but to start, at least: we thank our projects' sponsors, the ERC, the ESRC, and LSE REFSC. Apart from thanks to the institution itself, we want to thank Frank Kuhn for being an exceptional research officer for our ERC project, always willing to talk about the science and the research rather than the technicalities of our grant management, as well as the whole Communication team at the ERC, which did so much to help promote the project. We also want to thank our long-time survey partners Opinium (in particular James Endersby, James Crouch, Adam Drummond, Olivia Playle, and Priya Minhas), who directly sponsored some of our later studies when we had no funds for them; the Falling Walls Foundation which organized and financed our visual experiment as part of the wonderful 2012 Falling Walls Conference; and Tony Langham, Clare Parsons, Rimmi Shah, and Ralph Jackson from Lansons, who organized amazing events to share our key findings.

We thank too the heads and senior staff from Electoral Commissions who have opened their doors and collaborated with us, hoping that our findings would enable them to deliver better electoral democracy to their citizens, notably Nomsa Masuku and Lonwabo Jwili (respectively Commissioner and Strategic Stakeholder Officer, Independent Electoral Commission of South Africa); Dean Logan (Registrar and County Clerk, Los Angeles County); Phil Thompson (Head of Research, UK Electoral Commission); Tamar Zhvania (Chairperson, Central Electoral Commission of Georgia); Natia Zaalishvili (Director of the Centre for Electoral Systems

Development, Reforms, and Training, Georgia); Tom Rogers, Anna Stewart, Andrew Trainer, and Dale Easterby (respectively Electoral Commissioner, Assistant Commissioner, Director of Research and Electoral Integrity, and Assistant Director for Research Coordination, Australian Electoral Commission); Hisham Kuhail (CEO, Palestinian Central Electoral Commission); and Anne-Julie Clary and volunteer polling observers throughout France.

We thank our wonderful team of researchers, Eri Bertsou, Sandra Obradovic, Erin Saltman, Annie Bird, Julie Vogt, Elena Pupaza, Eponine Howarth, Adele Scemama, Kelly Benguigui; our ECREP visitors, Sophie Lecheler (Vienna) and Soetkin Verhaegen (Stockholm); our Youth Participation Project colleagues, Bart Cammaerts, Shaku Banaji, and Nick Anstead; and our hosts at Columbia University, McGill University, and the ANUCES, Jacqueline Lo, Annmarie Elijah, Kasia Williams, and Jasmine Henkel. We also thank the wonderful staff from the LSE Research and Innovation Division and from the Department of Government for their unstinting help, and James Robins for helping to film our repeat visual experiment in the UK. Finally, we are immensely indebted to the four anonymous reviewers, to Charlie Allen, Hannah Paul, the entire Princeton University Press team, our copy editor Francis Eaves, and to our wonderful editor Sarah Caro, who helped us from the beginning to the end to improve this book.

Remaining limitations are undoubtedly ours alone, but we feel proud and happy that *Inside the Mind of a Voter* is the result of a true co-authorship, shaped by mutual trust and respect, many walks spent thinking out loud, and constant dialectic and discussion, rather than simply representing a division of labour. After six books and many articles and projects, we still feel privileged to work together.

Michael Bruter and Sarah Harrison, London, February 2020

CHAPTER SYNOPSES

Chapter 1: *Homo Suffragator*

What if resolving conflict and disagreements through elections have become an inherent part of the nature and conditions of contemporary human beings in democracies? What if elections have come to change something about our social interaction, rituals, expectations, ways of thinking and behaving, and our experiences, in a quasi-anthropological manner, like the grand stages of human evolution? In sum, what if, from a democratic point of view, it does not really matter who gets elected in a vote, compared to the much bigger question of whether elections make people happy, fulfil the functions citizens ascribe to democracy, give them a sense of control, or at any rate of democratic relevance, and bring them a sense of cyclical closure, which makes conflicts and disagreements manageable and tolerable for populations? Or what, for that matter, if elections have lost their capacity to provide some citizens with that sense of resolution?

Inside the Mind of a Voter aims to be a different and hopefully unique book about elections.[1] It asks questions with a potential to change fundamentally our understanding of the role elections serve in our societies. The first chapter explains our unusual perspective. Whilst most electoral science research takes it for granted that the relevant outcome of elections is citizens' electoral choice (or sometimes whether they vote or not), our book moves the goalpost to consider, instead, a trio of interrelated dependent

---

1. The research contained within this book was supported by three grants from the European Research Council (ERC): INMIVO (no. 241187), First Time (no. 680486), and ELHO (no. 788304); a grant from the Economic and Social Research Council (ESRC): First and Foremost (ES/S000100/1); and a contribution from a Research Excellence Framework Strategy Committee (REFSC) grant from the LSE. We also collaborated with the insight company Opinium to conduct surveys in 2016 and 2017 to study the feelings and expectations of the British public during the UK referendum on EU membership in June 2016 and the UK 2017 general election and jointly launched and run the Hostility Barometer series, starting May 2019.

variables: electoral experience (how people experience elections and their emotional consequences); electoral behaviour (participation and electoral choice); and electoral resolution (the capacity of elections to bring to individuals and societies a sense of democratic closure, and/or consequences such as electoral hostility).

Changing the dependent variable has seismic implications for the concepts, causal links, and methods needed to understand elections. Chapter 1 spells out some of those tectonic effects. At the heart of this argument is a fundamental paradox: historically, electoral behaviour research has developed around an eminently institution-centric, rather than a citizen-centric, vision, and correcting this displacement shakes the assumptions of electoral research and models.

The book's research question is the following. What are the effects of voters' psychology (notably their personality, morality, electoral memory, and identity) on citizens' electoral experience (including the emotions triggered), electoral behaviour (including participation and choice), and sense of electoral resolution (including perceptions of closure, hope, and hostility), and how are those effects impacted by electoral ergonomics?

To answer this question involves the generation of new concepts, including electoral atmosphere, electoral hostility, empathic displacement, projected efficacy, electoral resolution, longitudinal projection, electoral identity, and electoral ergonomics (the interface between voters' psychology and electoral organization). These oblige us to reconsider the way the relationship between self, groups, and society plays out in elections, and how hope and hopelessness can be central to an experiential vision of elections, and to rethink the nature of electoral cycles.

We also innovate in our combination of methods. Over 90% of what we think and do (electorally or otherwise) is subconscious, yet much electoral research is intrinsically based on self-reporting. Our new perspective rethinks that constraint by combining panel studies, election diaries, and in-depth and on-the-spot interviews with non-self-reporting methods, including visual experiments, direct observation, and implicit measures. Finally, our first chapter focuses on the implications of our new perspective for electoral science and its sub-disciplines, on the definition of the model that will be developed and tested in the book, including the effects of electoral atmosphere and electoral ergonomics, and on the five key ambitions—conceptual, analytical, methodological, narrative, and historical—of the volume.

Chapter 2: Mapping the Mind of a Voter: Anatomy of *Homo Suffragator*

This second chapter describes where our book fits in the electoral science field and how it will set out to answer our complex research question. The chapter starts by exploring the ambition of electoral psychology as a scholarly approach, and grounds our work theoretically and analytically in relation to the many disciplines that have puzzled over elections and electoral behaviour. We consider the contributions of models of electoral socialization (including early socialization and later habituation), research on electoral memory, the various attempts made at uncovering the effects of personality and the vote, and pscyho-political research on the impact of morality. We then switch to studies of emotions, particularly in the context of the vote, the increasing interest of the political science literature in the role of electoral context, and how we can stretch our parameters in order to study an individual dimension of context and the atmosphere of elections.

We look at political-theory controversies regarding the function of elections, and at the analytical grounding of our concept of electoral ergonomics based on both general ergonomics research and studies of electoral management and administration. The chapter proceeds to explore analytical insights into the relationship between individual and society, starting with sociotropic and egocentric perceptions, to question the role of voters, introducing to this end our proposed concepts of empathic displacement, projected efficacy, electoral identity, (our electoral take on) hopelessness, and electoral hostility.

The chapter then describes how the book will set about testing our complex model with its three interrelated dependent variables (each of which is itself complex), role for intervening elements such as electoral ergonomics, and distinct set of electoral psychology predictors. We introduce our overall methodological architecture and research design, explain how we operationalize the different components of the dependent variables, and discuss the unusual comparative scope of the book, including its audacious choice to include both established and recent democracies.

The chapter finally discusses the individual components of the methodology: the surveys and panel studies, the interviews, diaries, and family focus groups, the experiments (both traditional and visual), the elements of self-observation and direct observation. Finally, as complexity also has costs, we ponder the methodological limitations of our approach, and some of the potentially controversial implications of some of the choices that we have made in order to provide what we believe to be a multifaceted and multidimensional understanding of the mind of a voter.

Chapter 3: A Day in the Life of a Voter

There is a paradox of artificiality inherent in much of the data we use in electoral science. The moment when a voter casts his/her vote is shrouded in a taboo of secrecy, so we recreate the experience and decisions of this supposedly cathartic moment on the basis of self-declared answers obtained after the election. This apparently benign distortion has crude consequences, for Election Day is probably in fact the most democratically dense day in the life of democratic creatures. It is made up of multiple sequences, some wholly unconnected with the election itself, while others constitute successive layers of voters' electoral experience: thinking about the election, getting into an election mood (just as being on the way to an exam, a sports game, or one's wedding is part of the event's build-up), and experiencing proto-electoral parasitic thoughts when one is in the polling station, queueing, or exposed to other citizens arriving for the same reason as oneself. Then comes the moment of the vote (in a booth or remotely), the release of tension that follows, the wait for and anticipation of the results, and finally Election Night: the discovery of the outcomes, and chance to react and potentially experience closure.

Election Day is also a tale of multiple interactions. An election is eminently societal, and likely to be at the forefront of the news and of many people's conversations, but is also often played out in more intimate spheres. Many report it to be a family affair, involving taking their children to the polling station, going to vote with family, or bumping into neighbours, or because Election Night is often shared and ritualized. Then, within this, there is the individual sphere, because democratic systems aim by design to isolate voters, on the pretext of privacy, organizing the voting experience effectively to mimic a sense of solitude.

Finally, we must also ask how Election Day and Night differ for on-the-day voters, people who voted earlier, and those who do not vote at all, and for those who vote for 'winners' or 'losers'.

In this chapter, we systematically and by narrative unfold the ultra-dense fabric and sequences of that period of twenty-four hours, its layers of societal inclusion and exclusion so often conflated into one amalgamated account. We disaggregate the concept and nature of electoral experience. We disentangle the sequences of Election Day to show how the electoral atmosphere builds up, and how people live the day, the moment of their vote, and Election Night. We also offer an unprecedented account of the thoughts that go through people's minds as they cast their vote.

The research reported in the chapter uses a unique methodological dialectic, combining intimate accounts from election diaries, accounts from on-the-spot interviews conducted outside polling stations, responses to a mixture of closed and open questions relating to the logistics, thoughts, and feelings voters experience on Election Day, in the polling booth, and on Election night, and also, crucially, direct observation in collaboration with polling station observers in France who systematically reported on the demeanours and appearance of voters.

Chapter 4: Personality and Morality

The question of the role and impact of personality, including the 'Big Five' dimensions, on the vote, has been an important but often disappointing staple of the political psychology literature. In this chapter, we reopen the question of what a notion of 'personality' entails. We start by focusing on eight discrete personality traits: sensitivity, anxiety, alienation, freedom aspiration, extraversion, risk aversion, care, and confrontation, to see whether they may allow us to go beyond the limitations of Big Five research, which has been somewhat controversial in psychology. We then assess whether personality derivatives such as favourite colours and animal resemblances also help to explain differences in electoral behaviour.

Next we introduce a twist to the question of morality. Much research on morality in relation to politics focuses on the impact of caring more, or less, about moral principles. We suggest instead that while different people may be more, or less, vocal about their sense of morals, the most relevant variation in electoral politics pertains rather to moral hierarchization: different citizens prioritizing differently some moral principles over others. We look at the relationship between those moral hierarchies and the vote—be it in terms of left/right or of moderate/radical variations.

We reintroduce the notion of egocentrism and sociotropism in the vote, but unlike much of the existing literature, we focus on egocentrism and sociotropism as personality components, rather than as evaluations, and move away from thinking in purely economic terms, to identify instead four dimensions of sociotropism: economic, social, safety, and misery. We measure these implicitly and using truncated measures to test for curvilinearity.

Finally, we bring in the notion of projection—that is, voters' arbitration between short- and long-term sacrifices and benefits.

The chapter comes up with important findings. First, we find that the belief found in the literature that older voters are more sociotropic is an artefact of an undue focus on sociotropism's economic dimension. In fact, sociotropism is conditioned by citizens' vulnerabilities: whilst the old are more sociotropic economically, because generally less worried financially than the young, the young show higher sociotropism with regard to housing and safety. Second, we find that sociotropic citizens have more positive electoral experiences than others, and are more likely to feel closure from elections. We also show that moral hierarchies have strong effects on the vote. Those who mostly resent laziness and sexual and family 'sins' are more likely to support the right, whilst those who particularly condemn aggression and deprivation (of life or property) are more likely to vote for the left. We furthermore suggest that divergence in moral hierarchies explains electoral hostility, because citizens mistake other voters' preparedness to sacrifice some moral principles in favour of others they feel to be of even of even greater worth for oblivion towards the values that they themselves accept the need to sacrifice.

Ultimately, the chapter shows that personality elements make significant contributions to explaining electoral choice, the nature of electoral experience, and electoral resolution. It relies on quantitative evidence from our survey and panel studies, but uses a mixture of traditional and implicit measures in order to paint a more coherent picture of the impact of personality, morality, sociotropism, and longitudinal projection on the vote.

Chapter 5: Electoral Memory

Much of the existing electoral behaviour literature has assumed that citizens have no reliable memory of past elections because they often fail to remember how they voted in recent elections and rationalize their past behaviour instead. In this chapter, however, we revisit psychological models of visual, auditory, and haptic memory, in order to derive new hypotheses regarding what we could expect citizens to remember from past elections, and how we can imagine those memories to influence their future behaviour.

We show that reliable recollections of how people have voted in the past is the least likely component of electoral memory, and that even when this is absent, voters may rather be crucially influenced by a whole range of memories of their interaction with the system and with others. In many ways, this reinforces the centrality of electoral experience in our model, because it shows that whilst institution-centric academic expectations of electoral memory have been disappointed, their absence does not mean that citizens have no memory at all, but instead that it is precisely the accumulation of their electoral experiences over time which builds up into a (reinterpreted and dynamic) memorial collage.

We thus see that citizens internalize electoral experience, and in turn electoral memory, from elections that constitute vivid experiences for them—from their childhoods and their first votes, to discussions and arguments about elections. This chapter thus reframes the concept of electoral memory by posing questions pertaining to what type and which aspects of elections voters remember, and how that cumulative memory influences their future electoral experiences, perceptions, and behaviour.

In the course of that thinking, special attention is devoted to the first (and to an extent the second) election in a citizen's life. We show how first- and second-time voters differ from more experienced citizens in terms of their approach to and experience of elections.

The chapter relies on a mixture of quantitative and qualitative data, including survey and panel study questions, but also in-depth narrative interviews.

Chapter 6: Electoral Identity and Individual-Societal Dynamics

In this chapter, we develop our model of electoral identity. Our starting point is that virtually all electoral science is based on a silent assumption: that the vote is a direct translation of electoral preference. This corresponds to an intrinsic tenet of representative democracy, the idea that elections are intended to aggregate citizens' preferences, which representative institutions will thereby reflect. There is, however, nothing to suggest that those original intentions are necessarily confirmed by how citizens behave in elections. The chapter therefore asks a question which has the potential to invalidate the single most important premise of electoral research: what if citizens do not go to the polling booth to register a raw preference, but instead inhabit a certain role when they go to vote? What if voters approach the vote much as a teacher sets about grading a student's exam: not according to whom or what they personally like, but instead constrained by largely subconscious and implicit conceptions of their role as voters, which they inhabit in every election?

We hypothesize that the vote is not a straightforward measure of spontaneous preference, but that instead, citizens' behaviour is shaped by how they perceive the function of elections, and in turn their role as voters. This makes function a form of cognitive disturbance. Using the analogy of sports events, whereby parties and candidates represent the competing teams, we identify two key alternative perceptions of the role of voters: 'referees' and 'supporters'.

At the heart of voters inhabiting of an electoral identity is the idea that elections test a unique form of relationship between citizens and others; that voters assume a form of responsibility through their vote, considering not only the interest of others (sociotropism), but also the way their own behaviour ascribes itself in relation to that of others. This introduces the notion of 'empathic displacement': the idea that when they go to vote, voters make assumptions about what the rest of the country is thinking, choosing, and doing, which can make them feel either integrated or alienated. In turn, a critical consequence of empathic displacement is projected efficacy. For a long time, rational-choice-inspired models have stumbled against the notion that most citizens know that their vote is unlikely to alter electoral outcomes, seemingly making it irrational to vote unless by virtue of the so-called 'expressive value' of the vote. Here, we suggest that citizens project the effect of their own behaviour as part of a broader trend. Most people tempted to throw rubbish on the street intuitively realize that theirs is not just an isolated dirty paper flying around, and that if everyone threw their rubbish about, the world would soon become unlivable in. Projected efficacy reflects the same idea: that, even though an individual vote is unlikely to make a difference, if people like ourselves mobilize, together we will make a difference. Finally, the chapter explores long-term projections and sacrifices for future generations. Throughout it, we explore the logic and characteristics of electoral 'referees' and 'supporters', and the consequences of those diverging roles for citizens' experience and perception of elections. We assess the stability of electoral identity over time, at both aggregate and individual levels. The chapter is based on panel study closed and open questions, measuring in particular perceived functions of elections and roles of a voter.

Chapter 7: Elections and Emotions

One of the three interrelated dependent variables in our model is what we term 'electoral experience', and in the perspective of this work, the emotions that voters (and non-voters) feel during an electoral event are a direct reflection of that experience, and in particular of our two operational measures of electoral experience: the emotionality and the happiness associated with the vote.

Do elections make citizens feel happy, anxious, excited, emotional? Electoral emotions also matter because human beings only develop emotions if they care, and one of the core suggestions of this book is that many citizens care far more about elections—that they are far more important in their lives even when they are not actually interested in politics—than they might themselves typically assume.

In this chapter, we decipher the emotions that citizens experience during elections, and in particular when they are in the polling booth. We do so relying not only on their self-perceptions, but also on implicit measures whereby we consider the words that occur to them in electoral contexts, and even directly observing the emotions that citizens physically display as they vote, by filming their shadows in the polling booth and interpreting the emotions that these display.

The chapter first shows that elections are indeed highly emotional experiences, to the point of potentially bringing many citizens to (happy or sad) tears. We also show that the emotions elicited by elections are overwhelmingly positive, on the whole. In many ways, elections make people happy even when politics leaves them frustrated or annoyed.

The chapter also considers how electoral emotions vary across types of voter, and notably how elections are typically much more emotional for first-time voters than for the rest of the population, thereby shedding new light on the crucial nature of the first vote.

Chapter 8: Electoral Ergonomics

One of the most important concepts that we propose in this book is that of electoral ergonomics. We define it as the interface between every aspect of electoral organization and the psychology of the voters, and, importantly, conceptualize that interface as being affected by the specific function of a given election (see chapter 7) for a given voter.

In short, our claim is that every small detail in the organization of the vote—what we refer to as 'electoral ergonomics'—matters not only mechanically (as it is usually considered to in the case of electoral systems), but also because of the way it may trigger different psychological mechanisms and emotional reactions (something, in fact, that was already suspected by

Duverger (1954), and that as a result (an implication that was not necessarily considered in earlier work), the ergonomic interface will have different effects on different types of voter, such as 'referees' or 'supporters'.

Electoral ergonomics is a critical variable in our model. It affects the way citizens experience the vote (what they think about and for how long, the emotions that may be mobilised at the time they cast their vote), their attitudes (sense of efficacy, democratic satisfaction, trust, etc.), their likeliness to vote in elections, and their actual electoral choice.

In our global model, we have tested the concept, notably by running separate models of electoral experience (emotions), electoral behaviour (turnout, electoral choice), and likelihood of experiencing a sense of closure for in-station and remote voters respectively; but in this chapter, we unpack the theoretical and empirical logic behind the influence of electoral ergonomics, both in general and through specific case studies, including the impact of the use of remote voting on electoral experience in the general population, its influence on the electoral choice of young voters, and the effect of ballot-paper design (including paper vs electronic ballots) on the electoral experience.

Chapter 9: Electoral Resolution and Atmosphere: From Hope to Hostility

If elections are not only about selecting governments or representatives, as much of the literature implicitly assumes they are, and which this book questions, then what are they about? In our model, their psychological purpose is also to give citizens a sense of democratic control, and, through their cyclical nature, a sense of resolution of emerging or persistent political and ideological conflicts.

This concept of electoral resolution is one of the three interrelated dependent variables in our model because we believe it to be so central in citizens' logic of elections. It is also a concept which, by its nature, generates others—such as electoral hostility, democratic frustration, or even the centrality of hope and hopelessness in electoral behaviour. Electoral resolution additionally forces us to redefine yet other notions, such as election cycles and electoral honeymoons, which take on a whole new meaning once we consider them through the prism of elections as resolution mechanisms.

After empirically revisiting the notion of electoral atmosphere using two UK case studies (the 2016 referendum on EU membership, and 2017 general election), this chapter examines those concepts one by one. Crucially, it focuses in particular on what comes after the vote in an election. It addresses the centrality of hope and hopelessness in elections, proposing a new theory of the long-observed 'electoral honeymoon' on the basis of our theory of electoral resolution and of democratic legitimization. We introduce the concept of electoral hostility: that is, the extension of citizens' critical attitudes towards democratic politics to encompass voters as well as political personnel and institutions, and relate this to the other recent concept of 'democratic frustration'. Finally, we consider how electoral resolution as a variable—in other words, elections' capacity to bring closure to individual voters or society as a whole, or lack thereof—affects the very definition of election cycles as experienced by voters themselves rather than their institutions.

Chapter 10: Coda: Flipping the Electoral World Upside-Down: *Homo Suffragator* beyond the Age of Reason

This final chapter summarizes what we have learned about *Homo Suffragator* and the psychology of voters. Do personality, memory, and identity shape citizens' electoral experience and behaviour, and elections' capacity to bring democratic resolution; and what are the main determinants of each model? Has our attempt to turn electoral science upside-down by switching the dependent variable been successful? We effectively suggest that it may be of greater consequence to know whether elections make people happy, and whether they offer a continuous peaceful resolution to divergent preferences and beliefs, than to know whom people and nations vote for, and that we need such reconsideration to clarify an electoral 'chicken-and-egg' situation. Beyond summarizing the results of the static models explored so far, this chapter also reintegrates our original dynamic expectations into the model, and assesses the reciprocal causality between our three interrelated dependent variable sets—behaviour, experience, and resolution—using the panel study design in the US case.

The chapter also reconsiders the full and far-reaching implications of our finding that citizens do not express a direct preference when they vote, but instead assume and inhabit a function, a role, and reach the verdict dictated by this function regardless of whether or not it corresponds to their spontaneous electoral preference.

We revisit key questions we uncovered: paradoxes of internalization, the nature and behavioural logic of election cycles, the tension between hope and hostility, atmosphere and projection, the fact that sociotropism is multidimensional and that different citizens are in fact sociotropic in diverging ways, paradoxes of populist victimhood, and how contradictory moral hierarchizations lead voters to misunderstand one another and foster electoral hostility, not out of selfishness or brute preference, but because they mutually feel that others, through their choices, are proving less socially-minded and morally virtuous than themselves.

And this leads us to a paradoxical conclusion. Something has changed with regard to hope and hopelessness in electoral democracies, and whilst elections, in many ways, bring the best out of citizens, that very moral righteousness carries the risk of those same citizens increasingly challenging whether electoral democracy is fit for purpose and capable of bringing democratic closure to societies. Citizens who do not even care much about politics increasingly dismiss electoral outcomes as illegitimate and we risk opening a new uncertain and worrying chapter in our history.

INSIDE THE MIND OF THE VOTER

1

Homo Suffragator

Homo What?

It is not every day that political scientists introduce categories derived from a classical language, which may put off even the most sympathetic of readers. Nevertheless, if we are talking of a *Homo Suffragator* in this book, it is because voting—conferring the ability to take democratic responsibility for influencing one's community—might constitute a turning point in the evolution of mankind. It allows for peaceful and negotiated power organization, and creates specific habits, functions, and behaviours. Indeed, we will come to argue that voting may even 'bring out the best' in human beings, not only by defining their understanding of their relationship with their society and political system and their own role as citizens and voters (conceptualized as 'electoral identity' in chapter 6), but by making them feel ownership for democratic organization and decisions, thus making them more likely to accept and comply with democratic outcomes, even when these do not match their own preferences.

We also talk about *Homo Suffragator* because our journey inside the mind of a voter is interested in understanding how elections influence and permeate our lives, how, despite their occasional nature, they might through experience, memory, ritualization, and anticipation come to define who we are, how we grow and transmit, how we fit within our societies and relate to various categories of others within them, even how we live.

At the same time, considering elections as changing the nature of mankind requires us rethink how we study them. Thus, if elections affect our lives, then we need to understand them not only as an institutional mechanism to choose representatives or leaders, but as a human experience. Conversely, if the ability to resolve conflict peacefully through elections is so critical, we must understand how and when elections deliver that sense of resolution.

This chapter will thus briefly explore the scope and historical context of the book, introducing some key new concepts (and their articulation with the existing concepts and literature of electoral behaviour) that will be developed in chapter 2 and used throughout the book. It will also highlight how we can borrow from the combination of physiological, anthropological, and psychological insights traditionally applied to understand the stages of evolution of mankind similarly to comprehend the psychology, functioning, personal/societal relationships, and behaviour of *Homo Suffragator*.

Why *Homo Suffragator*?

Homo Suffragator means literally 'person who can vote'. What this power entails, what it changes with regard to man's condition and social interaction, and what the psychological mechanisms are that determine whether or not one exercises this power are all questions central to the puzzles our study aims to resolve. Throughout the book, we explore the relationship between human nature, personality and morality variations, cognitive and emotional elements, and systemic choices and determinants which constrain and shape our electoral power.

The construct of *Homo Suffragator* also mirrors the labels of the stages of human evolution (*Homo Habilis, Homo Erectus, Homo Heidelbergensis, Homo Neanderthalensis, Homo Sapiens*). These stages of evolution have been identified not only with physiological developments, but also with the nature of the new conditions, skills, and behaviours that have characterized humans. For example, the ability to create tools was acquired by *Homo Habilis*; *Homo Erectus* learned to master fire and cook; *Homo Heidelbergensis* was the first to hunt and to bury the dead; whilst *Homo Neanderthalensis* learned to build housing and wear clothes. Finally, it is *Homo Sapiens* (the current stage of evolution of mankind) who first mastered language and transmitted knowledge.

Of course, we are not suggesting that shaping how our community is ruled through elections is similar to those fundamental skills and behaviours, or that man has reached a new stage of evolution through the foundation and practice of mass democratic politics. However, it is perhaps a fair intellectual exercise to enquire as to how democracy has modified the human condition.

In this sequential vision, the very nature of man is always partly defined by his/her interaction with others and with his/her environment. In our conceptualization of a *Homo Suffragator*, this takes the form of a reference to the concepts of 'empathic displacement' and 'electoral ergonomics' which we discuss in chapters 4 and 8 respectively. The idea behind the first concept is that citizens approach elections subconsciously projecting how their behaviour will fit vis-à-vis others. The second notion is even simpler: every small detail of electoral arrangements and organization will interact with voters' psychology, influencing which aspects of their personality, memory, and emotions will be triggered to influence their electoral behaviour, experience, and sense of resolution, and even lead to different interpersonal relations between citizens, thereby restricting or reinforcing the emergence of 'electoral hostility' (chapter 9).

Even more importantly, there may be value in mirroring the broad-minded approach scientists have adopted when characterizing stages of human evolution. Indeed, they have habitually combined quasi-anthropological narrative and descriptive analyses of how the various stages of *homines* lived and acted, quasi-biological assessments of their nature, activities, and reactions, and attempts to decipher the foundations of their psychology, preferences, emotions, and motivations. There could be worse inspirations for a book aiming to understand both how political beings experience elections, and also how elections come to interact or interfere with their lives, psychological functioning, and habituation.

Finally, from the point of view of macro-history, stages of human evolution are never straightforward or clear-cut. Not only are there multiple controversies within the scientific community regarding some stages of human transformation, but evolution is also, by its nature, progressive and fluid. It is thus only in retrospect—often centuries after a crucial articulation in the history of the species, that scientists have been able to conclude that a new stage had been achieved. From that perspective, the resolution of societal regulation and coexistence through electoral democracy is a startlingly recent event, especially if we focus on universal suffrage, which in many countries only dates back to the mid-twentieth century for men and women, in some cases even later. To figure out what exactly this new societal *modus operandi* will have changed in terms of our modes of interaction—the social, moral, and economic outputs of mankind—and how durably they will have been shaped by it, may thus take centuries or millennia.

All this makes the *Homo Suffragator* metaphor inspiring, and we hope that it will intrigue readers rather than put them off, stimulate rather than confuse them, give them a flavour of why we argue that, to an extent, we need to deconstruct some of the basic premises of electoral research and turn its usual perspectives upside-down. We realize that this is an unusual approach, but we believe that it can make our attempted journey inside the mind of a voter stand out and excite for the right reasons, and we hope that the reader can find some worth in our thought-provoking 'evolutionary' parallel. We apologize to those who, by contrast, suspect that this is merely a pedantic (or worse, megalomaniac) choice by two scholars predictably and admittedly over-excited by the object of their research, and only hope that by the end of the book, such readers might at least partially have changed their minds.

What Is a *Homo Suffragator*?

If, as according to Aristotle, 'man is, by nature, a political animal', then perhaps we should consider the democratic citizen to be, whether by nature or institutional construction, a voting person, or at the very least, a person who can vote—literally, a *Homo Suffragator*.

From the very beginning of Athenian democracy, the possibility to vote has emerged as the central entitlement of democratic citizens. In fact, arguably, the entitlement to vote may be the sole characteristic shared by ancient and modern democracies, and is thus the foundation of our understanding of what democracy is.

With voting playing such a critical role in the definition of the democratic citizen, there arises a need to understand how the act of voting shapes our thinking, our habits and even some of our physiological reactions. On the face of it, elections are merely 'snapshot' moments, occurring relatively infrequently, and as such are unlikely candidates to define our nature. However, we know from psychological research that rare events can, in the right circumstances, structurally irradiate our existence. Elections can affect the life of nations well beyond their temporal limitations; maybe the same is true of their effects on voters' personal lives. Elections can also weave into a thread of sequential but nearly continuous history, where the hopes, regrets, joys, or disappointments stemming from a given election will frame the context of the next. At the collective but also at the individual level, elections have a potential for ritualization and sequential continuity, such as to weave a thread that will sustain a life fabric. Collective and individual memories, meanwhile, be they happy or traumatic, can punch above their weight: the once-a-year childhood holiday may be remembered with more vividness than the two hundred days of school that separated it from the next.

The claim that voting makes us *Homo Suffragator* also rests on the idea that voting alters our perception of our own function, role, and responsibility in a civic context, and conversely that a democratically shaped civic context imposes itself upon us regardless of our preferences.

Thus, political science has long noted the existence of 'honeymoon periods' welcoming most newly elected leaders, but the way in which the mechanics of these seems to clash with the known logic of electoral behaviour deserves our attention. Indeed, the existence of honeymoon periods suggests that democratic victors effectively benefit, mere days after an election, from the support of people who did not vote for them. The electoral process itself seems to lead to democratic legitimation of the winner by citizens whose electoral choice was initially contrary.

In this book, we claim that this shows that our nature as *Homo Suffragator* goes beyond our preferences as a voter, and that citizens do not approach an election as a mere opportunity to weigh in with their pure preference but rather as a context in which they inhabit a specific function. This invested voter role may vary across times, systems, individuals and even, for a given individual, across elections. *Homo Suffragator* is thus defined not only by his/her nature—let alone preferences—but also by his/her 'electoral identity', which is at the heart of our model (chapter 6), which he/she embraces, whether consciously or sub-consciously, and which radically differs from partisanship, relied upon by much of the political behaviour literature since the publication of *The American Voter* (Campbell et al., 1960).

Homo et Homines

In the various evolutionary stages of mankind, the *Homo* is defined in relation to his/her environment, but also systematically by the relationship between the individual and his/her fellow *homines*. The interaction between the individual and his/her society is a complex emotional, intellectual, and physical web which is also shaped by evolution as the species' needs, means, tools, and regulation of interaction and communication transform (Maslow, 1943). As mentioned earlier, ritualized interactions, such as the burial of the dead, and language are seen as defining moments of evolution in their own right by evolution scientists.

Along the same lines, we are interested in understanding what the act of voting changes in terms of the relationship between the individual *Homo Suffragator* and others. This pertains to direct interaction (e.g., discussing or arguing about elections—see Huckfeldt and Sprague, 1987; McPherson et al., 2001), but also to the definition of his/her role as a voter in egocentric and sociotropic terms. It even involves projecting his/her electoral behaviour onto that of other citizens, to redefine efficacy, strategic behaviour, feelings of inclusion or marginality, and sense of positive or negative affect towards fellow voters, including developing electoral hostility in reaction to actual or perceived differences in electoral preferences and behaviour (chapter 9).

It is crucial to remember what democratic elections are: a specific mechanism intended to arbitrate between conflicting preferences of individuals and resolve conflict between them. There is thus an intrinsic rationale to the notion of *Homo Suffragator* being a 'true' stage of evolution when it comes to regulating societal conflict. That ability to bring about a sense of resolution also becomes a key criterion of the effectiveness of elections in making citizens happy. Furthermore, elections have the potential profoundly to change the fabric of intra-social interaction, creating a framework for collaboration and coalition, or designing democratic 'waiting times', all of which differentiates them from the mechanisms of other forms of power structure. They also create a unique logic of representation—and thus of sociotropism and empathy—which adds another dimension to political power. Finally, elections open the door to different dynamics of human evaluation, projection, and accountability, not only towards those competing for citizens' votes, but between voters themselves. These mirror effects between individual, group, and society lead to specific patterns, some well delineated in the literature (representation, coalition, partisanship, etc.), but others deserving of the new conceptual attention at the heart of our book.

A first concept is *empathic displacement*. This refers to individual citizens considering how the rest of the electorate concurrently behaves—with has important implications in terms of strategic voting, which requires assumptions about others' electoral behaviour. Empathic displacement thus also pertains to how individual voters may feel that they engage in a collective event. It may be shaped by whether or not they vote, the manner in which they vote (e.g., attending a polling station surrounded by many other voters, or remotely), their electoral choice, and their direct human environment. Conversely, empathic displacement may itself shape a voter's sense of inclusion or alienation.

One derived aspect of this sense of inclusion is the concept of *projected efficacy*. Whilst external efficacy relates to an individual's perceived ability to influence the political direction of his/her community, it is often confronted by the rational reality that in practice, individual behaviour is extremely unlikely to affect electoral outcomes. By contrast, however, individuals have a capacity for projection in relation to their behaviour, which leads them to consider the effect of their actions if others were to behave similarly (see, e.g., Krueger and Acevedo, 2005). This is a key mechanism of civic behaviour (if 'everyone' threw their litter on the street, or played music loud on public transport, or jumped the queue, life would become miserable for all, so you do not do these things); we suggest, however, that such projection may powerfully redefine efficacy, and that when deciding whether to vote, and for whom, projected efficacy means many voters will consider what may happen if people like them emulate their behaviour.

At the opposite end of the spectrum, alienation may lead to *electoral hostility*, which we define as negative feelings towards others because of their actual or perceived vote. There is an abundant literature on polarization (e.g., Baldassarri and Gelman, 2008; Fiorina et al., 2008), but it largely relies on the concept of partisanship, and sees polarization as an extension of increasingly drifting competing partisan identification, such as that between US Democrats and Republicans. The concept of electoral hostility differs analytically from this in assuming instead that hostility represents further deterioration of citizens' already negative attitudes towards their political personnel and institutions. Thus, citizens who develop negative feelings towards politicians and later towards institutions will, in a third phase, englobe opposing voters in that same negativity. Consequently, unlike polarization, hostility need not, firstly, mirror partisan rifts, but may instead follow non-partisan divisions and even split parties; and, secondly, will affect not the most partisan people, but potentially those who do not feel close to any party and may even not be politically interested or involved. We develop the concept of electoral hostility in chapter 9, and show how it becomes a feature of *Homo Suffragator* when elections fail to bring a sense of resolution and citizens lose faith in the ability of electoral democracy to deliver closure.

Finally, we aim systematically to analyze better-known aspects of the relationship between *Homo Suffragator* and fellow *homines*—notably sociotropism (towards both group and society as a whole) and egocentrism, horizontal and vertical socialization, and political discussion.

A Russian Doll of Long and Short Cycles

How would *Homo Suffragator* as a stage of evolution, a cycle within the history of mankind, combine with the (sometimes much) shorter cycles within electoral history? Political science is awash with models of electoral change (Inglehart, 1971; Franklin et al., 1992; Dalton, 1996, etc.) which look at how the bases of electoral behaviour have undergone durable changes throughout the history of electoral democracy, using models such as realignment and dealignment. They add to a significant literature on the nature of electoral cycles, which usually follow an 'institutional' logic; whilst this book, by contrast, aims to understand how election cycles may reflect a *voter's* perspective.

Some models, such as that of second-order elections (Reif and Schmitt, 1980 implicitly acknowledge that election cycles have an impact on political behaviour, notably in terms of lowering support for ruling parties after a first-order election, before their fortune turns shortly before the next first-order vote. How far backwards and forwards will an election irradiate, however, and how is this affected by its ability to bring closure? If we think in terms of relative weights of (one or multiple) previous elections and (one or multiple) forthcoming votes in a voter's or country's mind, until the weight of the previous votes subsides, the next election will struggle to impress its mark on the electoral cycle, lengthening the transition between two fluid and interdependent conflicting cycles. Would the resulting balance and turning point depend on the country, electoral system, electoral term, or the political nature of elections and the sense of closure that they convey?

Here, we introduce the concept of *electoral atmosphere*. We propose that voters associate a certain atmosphere with an election, which evolves over the election cycle but is remembered holistically. In chapters 3 and 9, we show that 'atmosphere' is a feature voters frequently discuss in relation to an election. We aim to understand how they pick it up, and how it affects them, as systematically as possible. The intuition of many is that atmosphere is a hopelessly impressionistic and fluid concept; but many scientific and technical fields, including architecture, design, lighting, and marketing have learned to capture it in rigorous frameworks, and these can be adapted to the analysis of electoral atmosphere. We will explore how voters describe this atmosphere, and relate those observations to key attributes of electoral organization, campaign, and political contexts.

This can then illuminate micro-dynamics of electoral atmosphere: when do voters start being 'in the mood' of the election? What are the crystallizing moments when electoral atmosphere 'sets'? We expect the breaking down of electoral atmosphere into its components and phases to shed light upon elections' capacity to radiate beyond the instant of their occurrence, and upon their nature as defining events in a person's civic life.

The Obscure but Fascinating Nature of the Psychology of Voters

At a time when many citizens shun the vote, either occasionally or permanently, the question of what voting means to citizens, what emotions it triggers and what goes through citizens' minds at the very moment when they exercise their voting right feels more crucial than ever. *Homo Suffragator* is a democratic citizen with a right to vote, and this book is entirely dedicated to trying to put ourselves inside that citizen's mind to understand his/her psychology, emotions, experiences, and personality, and the progressive emergence of his/her identity as a political creature. We are interested both in the single act of voting, that unique moment of civic communion between a citizen and his/her political system, and in the long-term development of a voter's psychology and identity: the way it acquires its consistency and logic throughout a citizen's life, from childhood to death.

The study of voting behaviour is rich in exciting contributions. However, while political scientists have long perceived the essential need to understand the psychological mechanisms behind voters' attitudes (Lazarsfeld et al., 1944; Campbell et al., 1960), recent developments in political science have dedicated proportionally more attention to political sociology and political economy approaches, and to electoral context, than to psychological analyses of the vote. In the 1950s, Lane (1955) thought that the influence of individual personality on the vote was somewhat overlooked, and he would likely reach similar conclusions today. Furthermore, our understanding of psychological models of the vote differs from sociological and economic alternatives. In sociological and economic terms, we recognize 'dominant' models, whilst having to account for exceptions. In electoral psychology, by contrast, we often study exceptions, but lack dominant models delineating the psychological leitmotiv behind citizens' electoral behaviour. The cognitive and emotional processes underlying the vote have often been oddly neglected, compared to social and demographic determinism or rational electoral preferences. Perhaps the frontal opposition between cleavage-based and rational-choice theories has left little space for distinct psychological models to develop.

Whilst psychological approaches to elections do not undermine the usefulness of sociological and economic approaches to the vote, they introduce crucial elements—personality, cognition (for instance memory), emotion, and identity in models of political behaviour—and dramatically filter, condition, and modify the impact of sociological or rational predictors.

Shifting the Dependent Variable?

Despite the combined efforts of electoral research in the past sixty years, there is no doubt that a certain 'unknown side' of the vote remains a frustratingly hard nut to crack; and the limits to our collective understanding are worth spelling out. We have just evoked (and will explore in detail in chapter 2) some types of independent variable used in electoral research in the past sixty years, but this is only a small part of how our field has developed its own habits and approaches. Perhaps the biggest paradox we face is that, ultimately, the core dependent variables of electoral behaviour research—Will people vote or not? Who will they vote for?—or variations thereof at both the individual and aggregate levels—Who will win elections? What will turnout be?)—are in fact intrinsically institution-centric in the way that they are framed. It is almost as though we were not interested in people as people, but rather in what people do to institutions; in how people will answer the question that is put to them by the system. Crucially, almost all the relevant academic literature is written from the premise that what one ultimately tries to explain by any electoral model is the actual outcome of the election, or an individual's contribution to it. Does this really go without saying?

Inside the Mind of a Voter boldly questions that perspective, and claims that whilst we have come intuitively to accept electoral choice as the 'be all and end all' of electoral research, this applies a paradoxically institutional logic to behaviour (in which an election is an obvious end point), which may become wholly counter-productive if we assume instead a truly behavioural logic, with the citizens at its heart. In such a context, electoral attitudes, behaviour, and experience all compete for dependency, becoming endog-

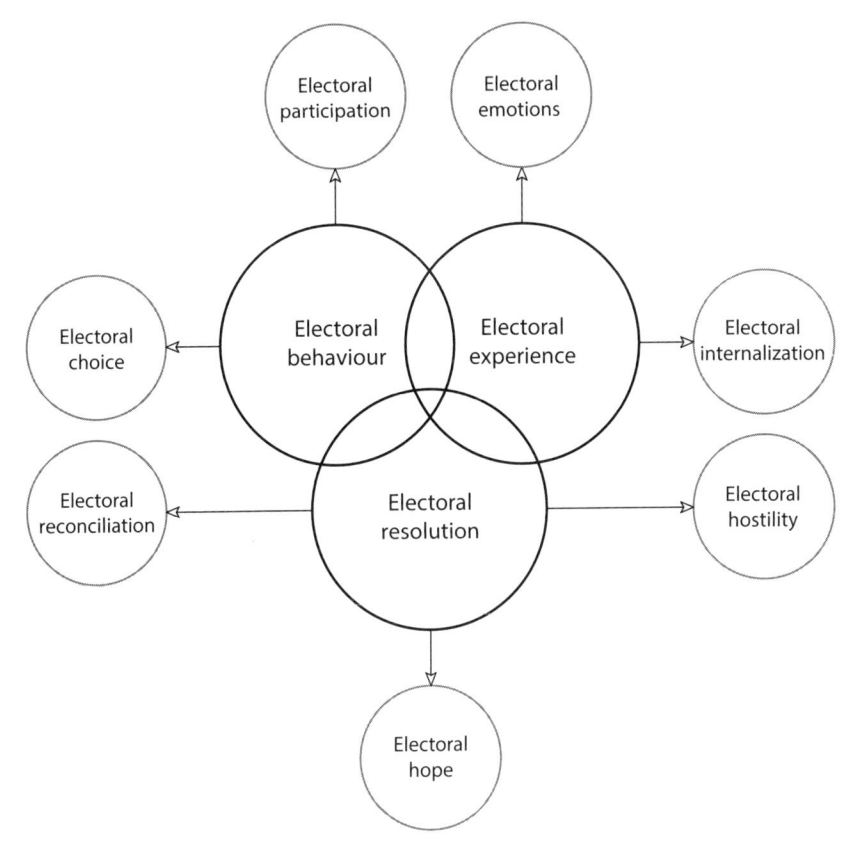

FIGURE 1.1: Dependent variable

enous in dynamic cycles that are not monolithic. What is more, these factors also interact with the capacity of elections to serve as peaceful resolution mechanisms—to bring closure—to determine the starting 'baggage' of the next cycle.

In fact, it is even possible that the existing literature has failed fully to understand electoral choice precisely because it focuses on it as an ineluctable end in itself, largely ignoring what is actually a far more meaningful contribution of elections to voters. This in turn may have led to looking at the logic of voters' choice from the wrong perspective, seeing this choice as in itself the endgame of voters' behaviour, whilst in truth it may just be a route to an end, a by-product of something much bigger. Thus, we propose that to truly understand the nature of the psychology of voters, we must consider a triple interrelated dependent variable: electoral behaviour, electoral experience, and electoral resolution, illustrated in figure 1.1. These aspects of the voter's engagement are intrinsically interrelated, both statically and dynamically.

In turn, the three interrelated dependent variables are themselves complex. As discussed, when considering electoral behaviour, we focus on both electoral choice and participation. Conversely, with regard to electoral experience, we explore the emotions triggered by elections as a critical measure of that experience. That is, we ask ourselves if (and under what circumstances) elections make citizens happy, worried, emotional, or excited. Additionally, we question how elections shape and affect citizens' daily lives: what we label *electoral internalization*. These are not very traditional ways for political scientists to look at why elections matter, but across social science there would be no hesitation in considering that understanding what makes people happy (or for that matter worried) is more critical than understanding their choice in any given short-term decisional situation.

Indeed, intuitively, from a human-centric (rather than institution-centric) perspective, is it not more important to understand when elections make people happy than when they will vote for a left- or right-wing candidate? Even for representative democracy and its legitimation, is it not more crucial that elections should help citizens to feel fulfilled, rather than that they lead them to choose candidates of whatever persuasion? Finally, when it comes to the electoral resolution, should it not be bigger news for electoral democracy to find out under what circumstances elections will fail to lead to reconciliation and feed hostility, damaging societal peace and harmony, than to know when they might produce left- or right-wing victors?

Beyond the normative question of what matters, there is a chicken-and-egg question involved in our triple dependent variable. As we discuss in chapter 9, in many cases, it may make more sense to think of people's behaviour in a given election as a predictor of their future electoral attitudes than to think of the electoral experience as a mere predictor of electoral choice. Thus, because of the dynamic nature of voters' electoral life, we suggest that if voters have a positive and fulfilling electoral experience in election 1, they will be far more likely to participate in election 2. What makes our research question and model complex, therefore, is that we relax possibly the most universal assumption of electoral causality in the literature (that it all ends with electoral choice): an assumption which seems unreasonable from an electoral-psychological perspective.

Reintegrating the question of what elections mean to citizens and their lives explicitly seeks a voter-centric change of paradigm. It comes with its own need for new concepts, labels, lenses; but also methods and tools aimed at visualizing how people experience elections—rather than how they express electoral preferences.

Balancing Rooting and Innovation—Navigating Charted and Uncharted Territories

This optical shift indeed requires us to pioneer methods that focus on the specific electoral 'mirror' we are interested in, approaches that betray a focus on the voter per se as opposed to his/her completed ballot paper, and to move from self-reporting to seeking to capture the subconscious process of electoral engagement. This involves both crafting new ad hoc methodological approaches and adapting some from other disciplines.

Given our geographical and historical scope, we could have embraced either of two different approaches. Traditionally, a simple research design would be applied consistently throughout the six countries investigated. However, given the organizational, financial and practical limitations of (even large) research projects, this would have minimized our methodological breadth. Thus we maintain instead a limited core research design spanning all six countries, including a panel study survey, in-depth interviews, and Election Day spot interviews, and add an array of innovative components, each conducted in one country or only certain countries. This methodological choice has a cost in terms of data homogeneity, with some research only tested in sub-parts of the book's universe, and the truly fully specified model only tested in the US; but we gain an ability to zoom in on an unusual range of important questions and puzzles and retain cross-validation.

Thus, we offer insights into young people's pre-voting age electoral experience, election officials' perceptions of voters' demeanour and behaviour in their polling station, vertical and horizontal family transmission, in-depth election diaries, and captures of the facial and body language of voters inside the polling booth. Had we restricted ourselves to methodologies feasible across our six countries, the research would have excluded most of the above.

Challenges and Puzzles

Our conceptual and methodological endeavour to rethink what matters about and explains the nature of a citizen's electoral experience also raises new challenges and puzzles involving both the specification of our model and comparability across citizens, elections, and countries.

First, not all elections are created equal. There is an abundant literature on the difference between first- and second-order elections (e.g., Reif and Schmitt, 1980; Marsh, 1998; Carrubba and Timpone, 2005), suggesting that voters typically see one type of election as primarily about choosing who will govern them, whilst the rest only take on meaning in reference to that cycle of first-order votes. These differences will likely affect citizens' electoral experience, memory, and emotions. Furthermore, we consider the possibility that electoral experience will differ fundamentally between candidate-centric elections, party-centric ones, and referenda.

By extension, considering differences in electoral traditions, the scope of voting may differ across systems. In France, the UK, South Africa, and Georgia, voters typically cast one vote in a given election, but in Germany, they cast two, and in the US, elections are typically an opportunity for voters to cast dozens of different votes on a single electoral occasion and in a single ballot. Beyond our case studies, preferential voting in Australia or Ireland, or compulsory voting in Australia or Belgium, could similarly affect voters' experience. As an illustrative consequence, we study the time voters spend casting their vote, but the definition of that decision—and by extension that moment—will largely depend on what the vote is about and what it comprises, and the impact of different types of ballot design is likely to be substantially different in a single vote election in the UK from in multi-vote elections in California. Furthermore, the length and complexity of a typical US ballot may trigger different psychological mechanisms from simpler votes elsewhere, require higher levels of information and sophistication, and even change the incentive structure of choosing between in-person and remote voting. In fact, as we shall show, the whole notion of electoral ergonomics involves a reference to the function of elections, which is itself affected by those differences.

Effects may similarly differ between countries with fixed term and open term elections. Campaign timings and dynamics will change, the notion of closure may subtly differ and, ultimately, the sense of control and democratic ownership by voters and the emotions these entail (tension, excitement, solemnity, etc.) may be affected by the ability of voters to prepare for an election and their perception of the degree to which elites control the process.

Similarly, in chapter 3, we explore when people vote and with whom, but this will be heavily affected by whether elections are organized on a work day (US, UK), on a Sunday (France, Germany), or on a weekday specifically deemed a national holiday (Israel). On a work day, voters will likely time their presence in the polling station around work commitments, whilst for Sunday or national holiday voting, this will be more likely to follow family and leisure commitments. Opening hours and seasonality will also matter. Weekday voting also means voters would likely bring their children along to vote by design, whilst with Sunday or national holiday voting, a family electoral experience may well be a default solution in the absence of easy childcare options. All these systemic differences will compound into differences of practice and, beyond that, of atmosphere and experiential routine.

A third challenge is path dependency between the choices that citizens make and their electoral experience. Let us consider the decision as to whether to vote in a polling station or remotely, an increasingly available option across political systems. While much existing literature on remote voting focuses on whether 'convenience voting' brings additional voters, we claim, in chapter 8, that the experience itself will vary significantly and may thus affect a voter's electoral experience, choice, and long-term turnout. However, path dependency kicks in when, in a polling station, the 'moment of the vote' (a major focus of our research) is clearly defined as the time the voter is in the polling booth, whilst for geographically remote voting, at home, that moment of the vote may be much more diffuse. The home voter controls his/her ballot for a long time, and may fill it in over multiple moments, contexts, and circumstances. The actual moment of voting is thus harder to identify, both absolutely and in the minds of the voters themselves. 'Election Day' itself may become extended, and last days or weeks as opposed to the single day it is for others.

Furthermore, under temporally remote voting, citizens may not just vote at different times from others in abstract terms, but effectively in the light of different information (key campaign events or debates may follow their vote), and in a different atmosphere. (As we show, 20–30% of traditional voters make up or change their minds during the week of the vote, about half of these on Election Day itself—see, e.g., Lord Ashcroft Polls, 2016. Temporally remote voters' vote is typically cast well before that crucial final week or day). How do we assess the consequences of such fundamental differences?

Ultimately, Election Day may mean very different things for different citizens. For traditional voters, this is the day when both they and their country vote, creating an overlap in agenda, a presumption of communion between the focus of the individual and that of the collective. However, temporally remote voters will reach Election Day having already cast their ballot, and be waiting for others to catch up. They may be engaged, but diachronically and perhaps passively. As for non-voters, Election Day may highlight the divergence between their own agenda and situation and those of the society in which they live, likely focused on an event they are excluded from, be it by choice or accident.

That differentiation is critical well beyond the question of Election Day. To understand how elections affect citizens, intrude on their lives, emphasize integration or alienation, we must raise the question of differentiated penetration for those who are technically part of the process, and those who abstain from and are out of a substantive part of it. Indeed, much literature has largely ignored non-voters, who are seemingly irrelevant to election results except as 'lost potential', but our redefined object of study requires us to fully consider the paradoxical nature of the electoral experience (and perceptions of resolution) of non-voters, because if being part of an electoral process may affect our feelings, attitudes, and behaviours, then conversely, being excluded from this event will likely also have implications.

This leads to perhaps the most crucial challenge that we face: the notion that most political experience and behaviour obey largely subconscious mechanisms. Lakoff and Johnson (2003) underline the immense preponderance (over 90%) of subconscious effects in political communication, and beyond, in human behaviour. Consequently, even perfectly honest respondents cannot accurately tell us how they feel when they vote, why they vote as they do, or what dominates their electoral experience, because they are bound by the limits of their own knowledge and beliefs, unaware of their preponderantly subconscious logic. The difficulty of tapping into the subconscious part of the human iceberg is a quasi-universal problem in the social sciences, if often ignored in practice, but it is perhaps an abnormally critical factor in our endeavour. We need to distinguish the influence of and interaction between various electoral and non-electoral thoughts, events, and experiences which defy consciousness. Moreover, we need to differentiate between 'elections' and 'politics', which are inextricably linked in citizens' conscious minds, despite negativity towards politics being potentially compatible with a positive contribution from elections, if only because elections offer an opportunity (whether notional or real) for citizens to change the course of politics.

Altogether, our investigations will need to develop methods and approaches that encroach upon this subconscious territory and reach beyond conscious accounts. In chapter 2, we explain how we triangulate self-expressed methodologies with observational ones, including visual experiments and direct observation, and decouple explicit narratives from implicit measures.

Research Question and Operational Questions

The question that *Inside the Mind of a Voter* primarily addresses is this. What are the effects of voters' psychology (notably their personality, morality, electoral memory, and identity) on citizens' electoral experience (including the emotions that they trigger), electoral behaviour (including participation and choice), and sense of electoral resolution (including perceptions of closure, hope, and hostility), and how are those effects conditioned by electoral ergonomics?

We have explained how we intend to shift the traditional dependent variable in electoral behaviour research—or least question its universal primacy by replacing it with three interrelated dependent variables: electoral behaviour, experience, and resolution. As discussed above, we see these as interrelated both statically and dynamically (that is, experience at t1 impacts behaviour at t2, behaviour at t1 affects perceptions of electoral resolution later in the cycle, electoral resolution at t1 impacts electoral experience and behaviour in the subsequent cycle, etc.)

We have also explained that each of the three dependent variables is intrinsically complex. Everyone knows that participation and choice are two critical pillars of electoral behaviour, but equally, we claim that electoral experience is made up of both the way in which citizens live and internalize the election and the emotions that they consequently experience. We also suggest that to assess the ability of an election to bring resolution and closure to both individuals and societies, we must assess its effects on appeasement, hope, and hostility alike.

Relatedly, this book will address four subsets of operational questions. First, regarding the implications of electoral psychology: how do voters' personality, morality, memory, and identity affect, respectively, their electoral attitudes, behaviour, experience, and sense of electoral resolution? Second, regarding the nature of electoral experience: how do voters experience elections, Election Day and Election Night, what emotions and memories are elicited, how do electoral cycles start, gain momentum, climax, overlap, and end? Third, regarding the consequences of electoral ergonomics: how do elements such as ballot paper design and remote voting choice affect voters' experience, emotions, and behaviour and trigger different personality traits, memories, and emotional relations? Finally, questions relating to the dynamics of electoral resolution: what conditions the atmosphere of an election and how does it develop; under what circumstances do elections generate hope or closure among given voters; when do they generate hostility; and what has changed about the psychology of voters through the 2010s?

A key specificity of the research reported in this book is that its dependent variables were conceived as moving targets. At times, we explain, very traditionally, the electoral attitudes and behaviour of voters. In other sections, we dissect electoral experience itself, and what shapes and determines it. Finally, in other investigations, we look at how elections have differing capacities to produce democratic hope, appeasement/resolution, or, on the contrary, hostility. In some cases, we look at those effects statically; at other times, we are interested in their dynamics. Sometimes, we aim to derive generalizable insights into the psychology of voters; at others, to understand what is happening in a very specific period of our history. We try to disentangle complex causalities, the interface with electoral arrangements through electoral ergonomics, and how this interface is mediated by such deceptively simple notions as electoral atmosphere. Ultimately, this book asserts a need to reinvent our understanding of the nature of electoral causality, from a citizens' point of view, redefining the logic of electoral endgames, by-products, and cycles not from the point of view of democratic institutions, but instead as a voter-centric logic with a dynamic of its own.

Model

This approach leads to a dynamic and multifaceted model, depicted in figure 1.2. The model does not shy away from complexity, in at least four different ways. First, there is our focus on not one but three interrelated dependent variables: electoral behaviour, electoral experience (including emotions), and electoral resolution. Second, each dependent variable and each independent variable is itself multifaceted. Third, the model does not stop at static causality, but aims to integrate a dynamic element that mirrors the logic of how election cycles are conceived and domesticated by voters. Fourth, a complex initial set of psychological independent variables is additionally conceived in interface with systemic design, to create electoral ergonomics, then further mediated by electoral atmosphere. Let us unfold the detailed logic of the model.

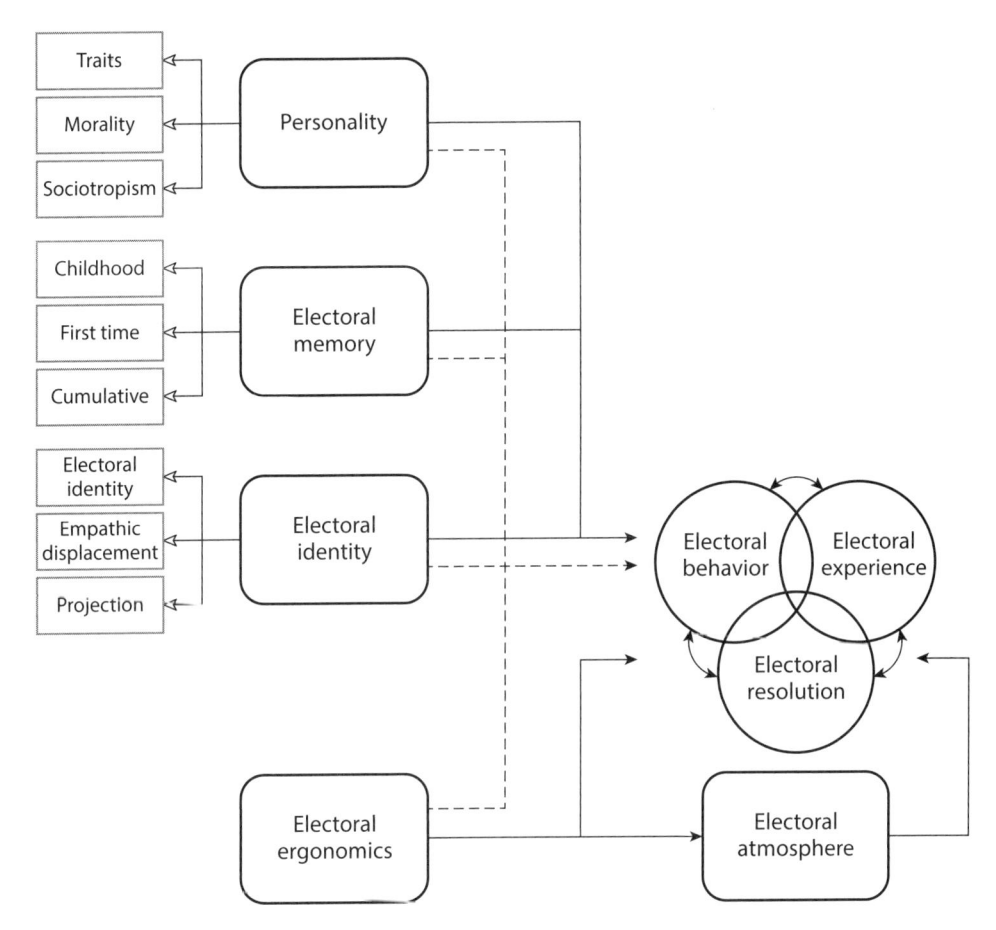

FIGURE 1.2: Model

On the independent variables side, the model includes several psychological predictors. First, personality, which encompasses traits, personality derivatives, morality, and sociotropism. Second is memory, the accumulated baggage of sensorial perceptions and experiences from our childhood and first vote to recent elections in which we did or did not participate. Third is electoral identity, our largely subconscious understanding of our role as a voter, including the referee/supporter model and empathic displacement (that is, the articulation between the individual, collective, and societal dimensions of the vote).

There is then an interface between these initial psychological variables and the infinitely nuanced aspects of electoral design and organization, to create electoral ergonomics which will trigger specific aspects of our electoral personality, memory, and identity as we vote. A further potential mediating variable is the perceived atmosphere of the election, which is itself affected by voters' personality, electoral memory, and identity, and by electoral ergonomics. It is also affected by exogenous contextual factors such as campaigning elements.

Next, fundamental psychological determinants, ergonomics, and atmosphere all affect voters' electoral attitudes (sense of efficacy, representation, etc.), behaviour (turnout, electoral choice, etc.), and experience, including the emotions that people feel during and as a result of an election, and the capacity of those elections to bring resolution. Crucially, these dependent variables are all endogenous, and further affect one another. Thus, whether a citizen votes, and whether it is for a winning or losing side, will affect his/her experience of the election, and the emotions triggered during the election and its aftermath. Further, positive or negative electoral experience will affect a citizen's likelihood of voting again at the next opportunity.

A special note pertains to how electoral ergonomics, atmosphere, emotions and the attitudes, behaviour, and electoral experience of voters will affect the quality of the election as a resolution mechanism, leading to hope and reconciliation (including a potential honeymoon period) or, conversely, to fracture and hostility. This resolution highlights our model dynamics, as it will shape the 'starting point' of the next election cycle and colour the spirit in which voters will approach the new election and understand its function (for instance, to achieve representation, policy change, or accountability, egocentrically or sociotropically, with greater or lesser concern for the hypothetical behaviour of others, etc.). Implicit in the dynamic path dependency of our model is thus further complexity, leading us to revisit the notion of election cycle and question the assumption that institutionally defined cycles match their behavioural perceptions.

We shall explore in the book the nature, determinants, and consequences of some of these new concepts (electoral atmosphere, hostility, ergonomics, identity, etc.), dissect the experience of voters, first-time voters, and non-voters, and their thoughts and demeanour, but also test overall models of electoral behaviour (left/right vote, extremist vote, turnout), electoral experience (when does the vote make citizens happy, and when does it make them emotional?), and resolution, introducing our predictors by stage: first, personality (traits, morality, sociotropism, etc.); second, memory (including first-time voting effects and childhood and first-time memories); and third, identity (electoral identity, projection, empathic displacement, and projected efficacy). The overall models will also account for ergonomics effects by splitting the model between in-station, advance, and absentee voters.

The Essence of the Book

Inside the Mind of a Voter invites the reader on a unique journey into electoral psychology. It shows how citizens' personality and memory affect their vote. It dissects the electoral experience and what constrains the capacity of elections to bring democratic resolution. It explores what voters think about in the polling booth, how they inhabit a role as they cast their vote, and how electoral arrangements trigger specific memories and emotions, which in turn influence electoral atmosphere and voters' democratic perceptions and behaviour. The book analyses the psychology of voters in the US, UK, Germany, France, South Africa, and Georgia between 2010 and 2017, and uses a complex combination of innovative and traditional methods, from filming the shadows of voters in the polling booth and election diaries, to five-year panel study surveys, polling station observation, and in-depth and on-the- spot interviews.

The book pursues five key ambitions. First, conceptually, it explores a new model of electoral identity, and the emotions citizens experience when they vote, but also key new concepts: electoral identity, empathic displacement, and projected efficacy (chapter 6); electoral ergonomics (chapter 8); and electoral atmosphere and hostility (chapter 9). Second, analytically, it assesses the impacts of personality, memory, identity, and the ergonomics of electoral arrangements on electoral behaviour, experience, and sense of resolution. Third, methodologically, it combines quantitative and qualitative, static and dynamic, self-reported, and externally observed methods to uncover the hidden story of electoral-psychological effects beyond conscious perceptions. Fourth, narratively, it offers unprecedented findings on how voters experience elections (unique moments of civic communion with their political systems), what they think as they vote, and how they perceive the atmosphere of elections. Fifth, historically, it looks at changes in electoral psychology through a unique period, which saw the world desert the centrist dominance of New Labour, Obama, and Mandela and move to the shock victories of Brexit, several extremist and populist parties and Trump, the 2019 UK general elections with their unprecedented levels of suspicion and acrimony, and Macron's new moderate-politics fightback.

Structurally, this results in nine consecutive chapters (summarized in greater detail previously) fulfilling those five ambitions. After this introductory chapter, chapter 2 develops our model and methodology. Chapter 3 explores (both narratively and systematically) a day in the life of a voter, and how citizens (including both voters and non-voters) experience Election Day and Election Night. Chapter 4 then analyzes the importance of the personalities of citizens, as well as their moral hierarchizations, for their electoral behaviour, experience, and sense of resolution. Chapter 5 turns our attention to the nature and impact of electoral memory. Chapter 6 focuses on a third key independent variable: electoral identity and the articulation between the individual and societal dimensions of the vote. Chapter 7 offers a study of voters' emotions, which we use as our main proxies to measure the experience of voters. Chapter 8 then introduces the concept of electoral ergonomics (the interface between electoral psychology and electoral design), analyzing a number of case studies that are symptomatic of its nature and effects. Chapter 9 is concerned with on our third key dependent variable—electoral resolutionas well as a number of concepts that are indispensable to understand it, such as electoral atmosphere, electoral hostility, and how elections can generate hope or hopelessness amongst voters and non-voters alike. Finally, chapter 10 concludes the book and assesses the full and dynamic nature of our models. In addition to our ten chapters, we include an analytical glossary of the new concepts that we develop throughout this work, as well as of some more traditional ones. The material presented in the chapters is further complemented by four online appendices, available to readers on the website of our Electoral Psychology Observatory: www.epob.org.[1] Appendix 1 presents sample questionnaires from our quantitative panel studies. Appendix 2 presents samples from our qualitative work, including in-depth interviews, polling station observation, family focus group themes, and election diaries. Appendix 3 presents supplementary tables and figures that we did not include in the main text because of its already considerable empirical density. Finally, appendix 4 (on our website) considers how the electoral history of the six countries studied in this book illustrates or validates the broader conceptual and analytical contributions it contains. In addition to these four appendices, the website supplementary material includes a full electoral psychology bibliography, complementing the list of works cited that comes at the end of the volume.

---

1. This information is correct at the time of publication. Whilst we intend to maintain this website for as long as possible, the material may be moved at a later date.

This is a tale of three analyses. One involves a unique insight into how citizens experience an election, a campaign, Election Day, and Election Night, and the thoughts and emotions that characterize these occasions. Another involves the use of an ambitious arsenal of quantitative and qualitative methods to investigate systematically what goes on in the minds of voters and non-voters, and test a complex model of electoral behaviour, experience, and resolution. Finally, there is the story of a unique period of electoral change, and an attempt to explain results which had been deemed 'impossible' mere days before they occurred.

2

Mapping the Mind of a Voter

ANATOMY OF *HOMO SUFFRAGATOR*

Unveiling Electoral Psychology

Chapter 1 unveiled the far-reaching scope of this book, but we must now more finely describe its analytical framework and its complex and ambitious research design, and ground it in our field. This chapter will also introduce and delineate both existing and novel key concepts used throughout the book, from 'personality', 'memory', and 'emotions' to 'electoral identity', 'electoral atmosphere', 'ergonomics', and 'hostility'. Finally, we explore each component of our research design and methodology.

Electoral behaviour research has produced a dense and insightful literature alongside an ever growing list of unanswered puzzled and complex paradoxes. This book is grounded in this rich literature, of which it inherits the collective knowledge, but also the doubts and questions. Awkwardly, the psychology of voters sometimes seems to remain mysterious and perplexing, 227 years after the 1793 French-revolutionary Jacobin constitution first stipulated a right of universal suffrage for adult males, and more than a century after Finland entrenched universal suffrage and the right to run for office for both men and women (1906).

Surprisingly, psychological models of voting remain more enigmatic than sociological or economic ones, although human psychology is presumably more constant than economic and social realities. On the one hand, the vote is a unique opportunity for civic communion between citizens and their political system; on the other hand, it is an act surrounded by secrecy and intimacy. Citizens value the secrecy of the ballot, and worldwide, Election Management Bodies implement strict rules and guidelines to ensure its protection and shield voters from undue pressure, disruption, and manipulation. These solemn secrecy and privacy measures place a certain taboo on the vote, and capturing citizens' condition as they cast it represents a complex methodological conundrum. Confidentiality ensures that direct observation of the act of voting is impossible, whilst relying on voters' accounts raises a double problem of, firstly, selectivity—not everyone is comfortable talking about his/her vote, and those who do so are unlikely to be random—and secondly, credibility: citizens can of course misreport their behaviour, either purposefully or in good faith. As numerous neurological studies show, well over 90% of human decision-making is subconscious (e.g., Dewey, 2002), so taking self-reports at face value is intrinsically problematic.

While these limitations affect sociological, economic, and contextual electoral models, they are radically more problematic for psychological models because the determinants we study—such as personality, emotions, memory, and identity—are as hidden from the researcher as the electoral decision. These challenges have discouraged many scientists from deciphering the psychology of voting at all. Yet, arguably, no approach could prove as fundamental and generalizable as one that exploits the psychology behind the vote, and it is the psychological implications of electoral experience that may have greater impact than any others on citizens themselves.

Beyond methodological difficulties, electoral psychology research may have suffered from being associated with party-centric approaches from the 1960s that were dismissed as dated by many. Arguably, modern studies of political behaviour can be traced back to the research by Lazarsfeld and the Columbia school in the 1940s (Lazarsfeld et al., 1944; Berelson et al., 1954). The Columbia model promoted the use of surveys as the obvious method of electoral investigation, and quickly tailored their model towards a sociological understanding of the vote. Another resounding triumph for the political psychology approach came with the Michigan model and *The American Voter* (Campbell et al., 1960), a seminal work which many still recognize as one of the most influential books in the history of political science. These authors put partisan identification at the heart of citizens' political behaviour. Their model suggests that, for reasons including socialization, social class, and environment, voters identify with a political party. This partisan identification is the 'baseline' of the vote, and combines with voters' evaluations of short-term factors (candidates' personalities, incumbent's record, issues, etc.) to produce an electoral decision.

The centrality of partisan identification in psychological models of political behaviour persisted in further influential studies such as Butler and Stokes (1969), who refined the Michigan model of socialization, environment, and electoral change. Partisan identity remained the centerpiece of all behaviour, capable of absorbing most psychological and sociological paths to electoral choice. In both works just cited, the electoral identity of a citizen is equivalent to (or effectively superimposed upon) his/her partisan identity. However, this approach very possibly overlooks essential questions about what elections represent. Partisan identification models limit the concept of electoral consistency to the relatively 'superficial' level of partisanship. While this might—at a stretch—have made sense in an era of aligned politics, identity and consistency could register at a much deeper level (a certain 'conception' of politics, values, the relationship between citizens and the state, or, as we shall see, the role of a voter) which may be entirely dissociated from partisanship, notably in dealigned contexts (Franklin et al., 1992; Dalton, 1996).

Is a citizen who votes for the left in the 1980s and switches to the extreme right in the 2000s necessarily incoherent? Could there instead be internal consistency that is not accounted for by party-centric models? Is it not possible that a floating voter who chooses new parties, or switches back and forth with every disappointment in an incumbent, may express a coherent electoral identity (unrelated to partisanship), and exhibit a form of systematic behaviour? Even Campbell and Miller (1957) had to consider the possibility that split-ticket voting may be intentional and part of a purposeful coherence, a theory that has gained ground since (Alvarez and Schousen, 1993; Lewis-Beck and Nadeau, 2004; Bruter and Harrison, 2017).

It would be inconceivable to consider dealigned voters as an anomaly or unexplainable (Arcuri et al., 2008; Schoen, 2014; Dalton and Flanagan, 2017). While partisan identification might still work in the simplified US party system, research into European electoral behaviour faces complex definitions of electoral choice itself, often replacing party choice by propensity to vote (van der Eijk and Franklin, 1996; Harrison and Bruter, 2011; van der Brug et al., 2007, etc.), and most scholars agree that Brexit divisions have created stronger attachments in the UK than parties. In this context, the psychological consistency of voters must be sought beyond partisanship.

In the Michigan model, partisan identification is considered a deeply held psychological trait (indeed, an 'identity'), a position largely questioned by the literature. It is hard intuitively to imagine partisanship as a foundational identity, and citizens only exceptionally refer to parties in their identity discourse (Bruter, 2005). Moreover, observational dependency occurs between partisan identity and party choice, as respondents asked about these may rationalize their answers to both questions, creating a 'snapshot effect' of partisan identification.

Psychological approaches to behaviour have thus been progressively emancipated from partisan identity models, though many struggle to dissociate electoral psychology from this iconic heritage. Consequently, despite political psychology's increasing popularity in recent years, elections have become a minor focus within that approach. Yet new knowledge in the field of campaigning and persuasion (Gidengil et al., 2002; Norris et al., 2018), transnational identity (Díez Medrano and Gutiérrez, 2001; Meinhof, 2003; Bruter, 2005), citizenship (Déloye and Bruter, 2007), multi-level governance and globalization (Puntscher-Riekmann and Wessels, 2006), and cues and communication (de Vreese, 2004; Schuck et al., 2013) abounds. This book builds on these insights, in fields including socialization, emotion, cognition, communication, and persuasion.

Models of Electoral Socialization

Much research has studied socialization. Whether in the context of partisan identification, political interest, efficacy or participation, authors such as Greenstein (1965) show that early childhood socialization has a dominant impact on future behaviour. However, his findings demonstrate that partisanship is a minor and uncertain element of transmission compared to deeper conceptions of politics and social responsibility. Indeed, for Greenstein, children's mimicking of parents' partisan choices is more fragile and shallow than parental transmission of political openness and interest. While children can free themselves from their parents' preferences, their interest in and conception of politics are deeply rooted in their childhood experience. Butler and Stokes (1969) found, however, that children were more likely to replicate parental partisanship if both parents were aligned than when parents have diverging partisan identification. They also found that a vote for the same political party in someone's first two elections led to an over 90% chance of continued voting for the same party throughout life.

Bruter and Harrison (2009a; 2009b), meanwhile, show that the link between electoral and other forms of political participation can be complex, and the way they are shaped by family and personal influences can be alternatively symbiotic or negative.

These findings raise important questions about socialization beyond partisanship, with implications for our role-centric electoral identity model. An interpretation consonant with the Butler and Stokes parental congruence model is that children may derive a capacity for critical electoral assessment from partisan divergence. Conversely, a young voter who chose different parties in his/her first two elections may become habituated to dealigned voting, and one who does not vote at all could become a chronic abstentionist. At the same time, we might question whether mechanisms that worked in the 1960s and 1970s are still effective in the twenty-first century. Another critical question relates to how socialization effects may sketch models of electoral memory, and the impact of the cumulative memory from childhood onwards that voters carry with them into the polling booth.

Electoral Memory and the Vote

Our model of electoral memory is indeed grounded in ample social psychology research literature on memory and identity (Tulving and Schacter, 1990; Breakwell, 2004) to provide an understanding of how memory and experience likely shape future behaviour. Memory research is comprehensive and vibrant (Atkinson and Shiffrin, 1968; Squire, 1992; Schacter and Tulving 1994; Baddeley, 2013). Studies show how memory is constructed, mobilized, and able to affect human behaviour consciously and subconsciously. The Atkinson and Shiffrin (1968) model suggests that memory stems from three different types of register: visual, auditory, and haptic: we remember the things we see, hear/say, or 'touch' (physically experience). This distinction is important to understand potential sources of electoral memory. In the short term, memories are stored through a sequence of rehearsal, coding, decision, and retrieval before potentially being transferred into the long-term memory. Squire (1992) argues that long-term memory can be expressed in either a declarative (explicit) or a nondeclarative (implicit) manner. The former relies on remembering facts and events, while the latter relates to the assimilation of skills and habits, priming effects, classical conditioning, and non-associative learning. Electorally, we thus dissociate between explicit memories (what voters recall from the past) and implicit mechanisms (unconscious habits and conditionings that voters reproduce). Finally, Baddeley (2013) highlights three memory stages: the encoding (registration) of information, its storage (maintenance over time), and its retrieval (access through recognition, recall, or implicit reproduction). These insights capture the complex itinerary of an electoral image from experience to memory, and its retrieval and mobilization in future elections.

Historically, political scientists have focused on memories of electoral choice (Himmelweit et al., 1978; Granberg and Holmberg, 1986; Shachar and Shamir, 1996, etc.), finding that 10–20% of respondents misreport it (Himmelweit et al., 1978), and Price et al. (1997) suggest that misrepresentation and rationalization based on expected future vote is actually far more frequent. Many political scientists thus believe that citizens do not remember past elections. However, the memory models we have just discussed suggest that vote choice is actually an unlikely basis for electoral memory. In terms of the Atkinson and Shiffrin model, electoral decision is neither an auditory, a visual, nor a haptic stimulus. Memories of past thought processes exist if they are salient, but not otherwise, and not when the mental process is subconscious. Visual memory of election adverts or Election Night, auditory memory of discussions or arguments, and haptic memories of the polling station experience, on the other hand, could all persist. Consequently, if in citizens' minds electoral experience is not limited to electoral choice, but also involves rituals, feelings, and democratic interaction, and if the election is an infrequent act of communion with the political system, one's vote is a most unlikely candidate for memory when compared to more experiential and atmospheric aspects of the process.

Furthermore, given the distinction between short-term and long-term memory, our memory of first elections may matter far more than that of recent electoral events. Similarly, and referring to the Squire model of declarative and non-declarative memory components, an electoral memory we cannot spontaneously phrase can still emphatically influence future electoral behaviour. We thus reconsider here which past elections voters may remember best (early childhood election, first vote, 'key' realignment elections, recent elections) and which aspects of them (vote, outcomes, discussions or arguments, images or slogans, atmosphere of the polling station or Election Night) voters may remember best, resulting in our model of electoral memory in figure 2.1.

The model depicts both a chronological and a substantive 'hierarchy' of elections that is essential to the creation and consolidation of our electoral

30 CHAPTER 2

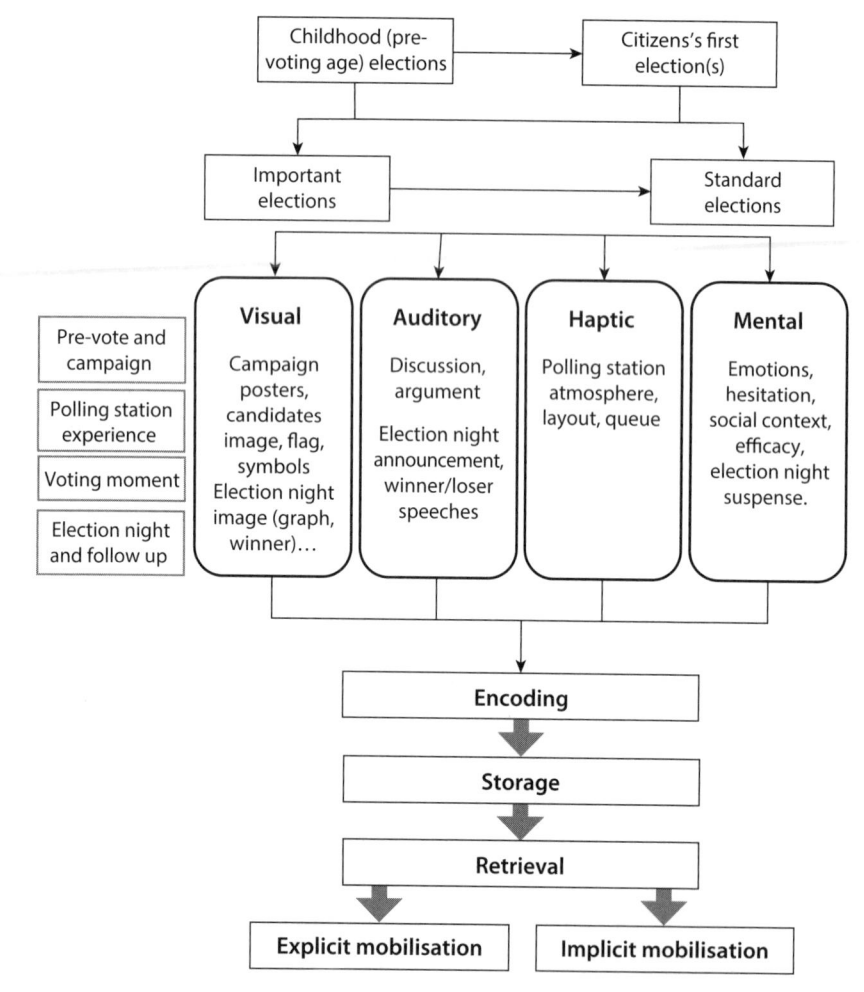

```
                    Childhood (pre-          Citizens's first
                    voting age) elections ──▶ election(s)
                           │                       │
                           ▼                       ▼
                    Important ──────────────▶ Standard
                    elections                  elections
                           │
          ┌────────────────┼────────────────┬──────────────┐
          ▼                ▼                ▼              ▼
       Visual          Auditory          Haptic         Mental
```

	Visual	Auditory	Haptic	Mental
Pre-vote and campaign	Campaign posters, candidates image, flag, symbols Election night image (graph, winner)…	Discussion, argument Election night announcement, winner/loser speeches	Polling station atmosphere, layout, queue	Emotions, hesitation, social context, efficacy, election night suspense.
Polling station experience				
Voting moment				
Election night and follow up				

```
                    ▼
                 Encoding
                    ▼
                 Storage
                    ▼
                 Retrieval
                 ╱      ╲
     Explicit mobilisation    Implicit mobilisation
```

FIGURE 2.1: Make up of electoral memory

memory. Thus, memories of childhood elections will constitute the starting ground of cumulative electoral memory, followed by our (potential) first vote, and then 'historic' elections. The political science understanding of 'key' elections has centred on the notion of realignment, such as in Anderson's (2000) study of the 1932 election which realigned US politics. Other elections may be deemed historic because they are highly disputed (e.g., the 2000 US presidential election and Florida counting fiasco; or symbolic (e.g., the first non-racial election in South Africa); or traumatic (e.g., 'le 21 avril' 2002 in France, when Jean-Marie Le Pen succeeded in progressing to the second ballot run-off for the first time, or the Austrian 1999 elections which saw the FPÖ enter a coalition government with 26.9% of the vote, or, for many, the 2016 US presidential election and UK referendum of the same year).

Electoral memory may, however, not be homogeneous, and electoral events may have idiosyncratic historical importance for given individuals. An election may be remembered primarily because it is a voter's first, because of a noteworthy argument with a parent or partner, or because it matches unique life circumstances for the individual. This echoes our original claim that elections permeate and intermingle with the lives of citizens such that 'small' and 'big' history overlap to impact upon one's electoral perceptions, memories, emotions and behaviour.

We thus model sources of electoral memory along two dimensions: type of registration, and electoral cycle. We could almost call these the 'psychological' and 'political' dimensions of electoral memory formation. In terms of registration, we adapt the Atkinson and Shiffrin model, retaining visual and auditory registration, but expanding haptic memories to include electoral atmosphere impressions alongside physical perceptions. In chapter 3, we show that citizens recall 'physical' sensations, such as shaking, feeling the heart beat, the urge to laugh, and so on, while chapter 9 details their characterization of electoral atmosphere. We also add a fourth 'mental' source of memory, covering unexpressed thoughts and feelings (efficacy, excitement, suspense, pride, shame, etc.) related to the vote. Meanwhile, we highlight four periods of interest: the pre-vote period, the polling station/place of vote experience, the vote, and finally Election Night and the electoral outcome. Thus, a voter's remembering of an argument with a friend during the campaign constitutes an auditory pre-election memory; recalling queueing outside the polling station is a haptic polling station memory; and reference to the BBC 'swingometer' switching from blue to red on election night is a visual post-election memory.

Finally, the model describes the emergence, consolidation and impact of electoral memory. The registration phase identifies the memory creation and its encoding. The storage phase occurs if the short-term memory is transformed into a long-term memory. The retrieval is the recapturing of this 'stored memory' and is divided into explicit (narrative and conscious) and implicit (sub-conscious and potentially automatic) mobilization. Memory mobilization does not preclude the possibility of memory transformation, misrepresentation, or rationalization through storage and retrieval. In particular, explicit mobilization may be wholly mistaken, and different memories may accumulate, contradict, or interact. A voter may 'believe' that he/she first voted in 1974 while in fact having done so in 1977, or may create a false memory of participating in an election when he/she abstained, and may rationalize past electoral choices over multiple elections. Memory is not understood as a pseudo-photography of historical truth, but rather as a seed that becomes real inside the mind of a citizen. Notwithstanding original reality, electoral memories will potentially influence long-term perceptions, experiences, emotions, and behaviour.

Memory is also not limited to self-contained stored 'snapshots', but is constituted by a progressive accumulation of experiences, which become increasingly complex and defining over time. Our extant memory at time t shapes our next experience, then adds to it and retrospectively affects the meaning for us of what precedes. Memory is cumulative and perpetually transformative, with older elements shaping the new, and newer elements redefining the old. The resulting portfolio of thoughts, experiences, and narratives becomes increasingly complex, and its components potentially confused through subconscious connections as they are retrieved in specific contexts and situations. A word, a smell, will unexpectedly reignite a memory we had all but forgotten, just as in the case of Proust's famous madeleines. The resulting dynamic—almost dialectical—accumulation continuously shapes who we are, how we think, and how we react in elections, thereby closely interacting with another critical component of identity: personality.

Opening the Pandora's Box of Personality and the Vote

In the 1960s and 70s, as traditional alignment models such as Lipset and Rokkan (1967) were progressively confronted with the notion of electoral change, a number of scholars started questioning the impact of personality on behaviour. Greenstein (1965; 1967) dedicated a significant part of his work to the impact of personality on politics and the limits of 'political personality' studies within political science, though focusing on leaders' (US presidents) rather than voters. He recognized both that personality must matter in politics, and that many of the studies conducted on the matter were under-delivering, often appearing 'arbitrary and subjective' (1967: 629) and insufficiently systematic (or even rigorous).

'Personality' is a complex and diffuse concept, and studying it with scientific rigour and economy is of course notoriously difficult. Sniderman et al. (1974) note the way in which a given personality element apparently leads to different attitudes, doubting the benefits of such investigations as regards causal explanation. On the complex relationship between personality and environment, both Greenstein and Sniderman et al. suggest that regardless of the individuals (citizens, activists, leaders) concerned, environment tends often to take precedence over personality. This has largely justified the contemporary trend to focus on context and its impact on elections. However, the dichotomy between context and personality is less straightforward than it appears, and in this book we argue that there may be an *individual* component of electoral context, which cannot be captured if we ignore personality, memory, or experience.

Psychologists frequently argue over what to include under the heading 'personality'. Smith et al. (1956) consider 'opinions' to be part of personality and Caprara et al. (2006) include 'values'. Some psychological anthropologists focus on national personality characteristics and the interaction between societal habits and psychological mechanisms (Riesman et al., 2001), whilst Di Palma and McClosky (1970) highlight conformity, and Sniderman et al. (1974) and Lane (1955) see ideology as an extension of personality. Most political scientists, including DeYoung et al. (2007) and Gosling et al. (2003) use the so-called 'Big Five' (extraversion, agreeableness, conscientiousness, emotional stability, openness to experience: collectively 'OCEAN') as measures of personality in their analyses, but these categories are contested in psychology. Some authors prefer the 'Big Three', or 'Alternative Five' (Zuckerman et al. 1993), and Caprara et al. (2006) use discrete traits (friendliness, openness, energy, and conscientiousness) alongside specific values. Boyle et al (1995) suggest that the Big Five account for only about half of normal personality traits, whilst Zillig et al. (2002), Paunonen and Jackson (2000), and McAdams (1995) all highlight some key—and often deeper—personality traits that the Big Five do not address. Paunonen and Ashton (2001) and Paunonen (1998), meanwhile, show that primary traits are typically much better predictors of human behaviour than are the Big Five.

The Big Five psychological model was never intended for application to political science, but rather to diagnose specific personality disorder pathologies in clinical psychology. It is not clear that these five categories would necessarily be most relevant to understand political behaviour in general or electoral psychology in particular. Some of them may simply not matter in electoral contexts, and conversely, personality traits which may have little to offer in terms of understanding psychopathic or sociopathic profiles may have immense relevance to voter types or behaviour. This book therefore chooses to consider specific personality traits and how they shape us as voters. Elements of the Big Five, such as openness to experience, are included, alongside discrete traits such as personal rigidity, aversion to risk, aversion to change, sense of alienation, empathy, individualism, and long-term projection.

We also incorporate personality derivatives, such as favourite colour and most similar animal. Indeed, in our model, with its interrelated dependent variables, personality not only causes electoral behaviour, but also shapes citizens' outlook, emotions, and attitudes towards elections, all of which transpire through derivatives. For example, Gelineau (1981) identified how colours adapt to contexts and situations rather than corresponding to 'pure' personality features, whilst Birren (1973) illustrates how colour preferences in such situational contexts are impulsive and emotional rather than being sheer personality markers. Walters et al. (1982) relate colour preferences to the colours' arousing or relaxing qualities, making them implicit shortcuts for stress, excitement or serenity—that is, telic or para-telic states. For elections, to which excitement and stress (Waismel-Manor et al., 2011) have long been identified as key emotional reactions, this is a crucial notion, making personality derivatives such as colour preferences, animal or landscape shortcuts, or the sort of drink a person thinks that he/she needs, meaningful products of personality and emotionality in electoral contexts.

From Personality to Morality

A particularly important aspect of personality, beyond character traits, is that of individual conceptions of morality, a unique combination and hierarchization of values which may often conflict internally and challenge life experiences and priorities. Studies of morality encompass many approaches, including explicit or implicit references to religious canons in shaping conceptions of right and wrong (King, 1967). We thus use two popular references: the Mosaic Ten Commandments (moral commandments only) and the Seven Deadly Sins of Christian tradition. Whilst both lists derive originally from specific religions, they have long permeated popular culture through films, fiction, and the legal orders of all six countries studied here. They also serve as a reference point in the scientific literature (Vrabel, 2018), and Veselka et al. (2014) link 'Vices and Virtues Scales' (VAVS) to the Deadly Sins.

Much morality literature focuses on whether some people put more emphasis on moral values than others, and how important these values are to them, and indeed their political attitudes (Baumeister and Exline, 2000; Peterson and Park, 2009; Kraft, 2018). Other research compares alternative morality belief systems at individual or aggregate levels (Ziv, 1976; Lutzer, 1989; Forgas and Joliffe, 1994; Miles and Vaisey, 2015). Our model highlights a different question: whether citizens' hierarchization between often conflicting moral priorities shapes their electoral stances. This approach departs from most morality research, which typically takes morality as a 'bulk' and considers its importance in individuals' minds; we argue, however, that the idea of 'more or less moral' citizens is likely a fallacy deriving from artefacts of self-reporting. Thus, Baumeister and Exline (1999) stress how morality internalization enables human beings to live together beyond impulse and selfishness, which makes us question how citizens prioritize such common rules to lay the ground for that elusive coexistence, if not harmony. Alternatively, Vrabel (2018)'s focus on individual differences in attitudes toward the Deadly Sins implies that different personality types react more or less strongly to different sins. Ultimately, our approach is constrained by the nature of elections, which are inherently about prioritization, and the resolution of potential tensions, externalities, principles, and resource control. It thus seems sensible to allow expressions of morality to follow that inbuilt tension system just as elections are, themselves, about institutionally inbuilt tensions between competing political priorities.

The Emotional Act of Voting

Despite significant efforts (Neuman et al., 2007) to bring emotions into political analysis, the study of emotions and elections within the political science literature is limited. In psychological models, affect remains one of the three key components of the human mind, alongside cognition and conation (Neuman et al., 2007: 9), to shape human behaviour. Marcus et al. (2000) criticize the normative tendency of studies of emotions in the democracy literature and question emotions' role in politics (Kuklinski et al., 1991; Bruter and Harrison, 2017). By contrast, the political identities literature recognizes the intrinsically emotional nature of political experiences and behaviour, with identities anchored in strong emotions (Britt and Heise, 2000; Bruter, 2005; Neuman et al., 2007). The role of emotions is also well established in the study of electoral campaigns and communication (Brader, 2006; Neuman et al., 2007), and authors such as Banerjee (2017) show how emotional and personal the experience of voters can be in a country like India.

While emotions and reason are often described as the heart and head of a voter (Kinder, 1994), research has moved away from perceiving emotion as purely affective (Kuklinski et al., 1991; Neuman et al., 2007) and opposed to reason, to suggest permanent interaction between them (see chapter 7). Together, they affect all stages of political judgement and decision, through complex neurological processes. Behavioural models have devoted attention to specific emotions—notably hope, pride, sympathy, disgust, anger, fear and uneasiness (Kinder et al., 1980)—and are used by the National Election Study to assess respondents' characterization of US presidential candidates. Lazarus (1991), meanwhile, focuses on six fundamental emotions: anger, guilt, fear (anxiety), sadness, hope, and happiness. In our analyses, we use some of the key emotions listed in the two models, such as happiness/sadness and fear/anxiety, but also include feelings of belonging, of importance (both individual and collective), shame/pride, optimism/pessimism, and excitement/boredom. We also consider emotionality as an experiential measure per se. Marcus (2010) suggests that emotions are affected by memory, beliefs, values, and conscious awareness of context, and impact behavioural outputs. We derive insights from this model to highlight the important role of emotions as symptoms of electoral experience. In the context of this book, we focus on emotions felt by citizens throughout the electoral process, and notably in the polling station; casting their vote (in the polling booth or remotely); and during Election Night.

Critically, unlike in much of the literature, we see electoral emotions not as exogenous causes of electoral choice, but instead as markers of electoral experience, our second dependent variable. Thus, feeling happy, excited, emotional, or worried in the election is part of the electoral experience itself, an outcome of the democratic process, likely to both shape and be shaped by electoral behaviour and closure. Our model is thus one of contextualized emotions affected by a voter's identity, memory, and personality, and by electoral ergonomics and atmosphere. It assesses how conscious and subconscious emotions are mobilized through the election cycle, characterize electoral experience, and impact behaviour and resolution.

The Individual Dimension of Context, Echo Chambers, and the Atmosphere of Elections

Emotionality is implicit in another concept frequently mentioned by citizens, yet often dismissed as overly fluid, which this book aims to characterize academically: electoral atmosphere. While social scientists may intuitively consider that electoral atmosphere is too impressionistic to deserve much scientific attention, there are three critical points to consider. First, conceptual fluidity is common in social sciences. Many of the realities and perceptions that we study could be described as highly subjective—from happiness to efficacy, empathy, and inequality—yet happen to be immensely important, as these broad perceptions are often more meaningful to citizens than narrower, specific alternatives. Second, while it may seem difficult to reduce atmosphere to a subset of positive perceptions, its crucial impact on human behaviour (notably consumption, aggression, and social participation) has already been demonstrated by disciplines including architecture, marketing, commercial ergonomics, psychology, and education science (see respectively Pallasmaa, 2014; Donovan et al., 1994; Rigby et al., 2001; Brugman et al., 2003; Miller et al., 2005, among others). In fact, its study has led to specific technical changes to patterns of shop lighting, theatre staging, and educational planning: so why not electoral democracy too? Third, in chapters 3 and 9, we show that atmosphere is explicitly meaningful to and spontaneously mentioned by citizens in electoral contexts. Ultimately, there is an even greater need to understand the meaning ascribed to categories that many use spontaneously than to try to confront respondents with concepts considered critical by scholars but which are not immediately intuitive to the subjects that they study. 'Tense', 'exciting', 'nerve racking', 'anxious', 'solemn'—these feature among the plethora of striking adjectives used by the media to characterize the atmosphere of elections and referenda that took place in the UK, US, and France between mid-2016 and mid-2017. They complement an even longer list of words citizens use to describe the atmosphere of those elections (see chapter 9).

In this book, we state that electoral atmosphere comprises both individual perceptions and an overall societal reality, likely to be shaped by the organization of elections and what the electoral literature overwhelmingly refers to as 'context'. Studies of context have provided remarkable insights into the impact of specific aggregate-level elements. Van der Brug et al. (2007) assesses the impact of domestic context on participation and electoral choice in European elections, Kitschelt (2003) the impact of economic context on German elections, and Powell and Whitten (1993) the interactive effects of context on economic voting.

Whilst these analyses help us to understand an aggregate-level definition of context that can determine, mediate, or interact with individual behaviour in elections, the natural focus of this book leads us to ask whether context also has an individual-level dimension. A major economic crisis will obviously have significant impact on an election, but it can be losing a job, being victim of a crime, or experiencing the hospital system a few days before an election that may have an even stronger contextual effect on a voter's behaviour. Huckfeldt and Sprague (1987), Pattie and Johnston (2001), and McClurg (2006) touch upon the notion by evaluating the importance of social networks with regard to political behaviour. However, their work does not pertain to specific electoral contexts, but rather to the formation of social capital, conceived as a permanent rather than a contextual feature. Fournier et al. (2004) may bridge this gap, by studying the effects of voting-decision time on individuals' permeability to campaign effects. Additionally, a recent trend in the literature focuses abundantly on the role of social media in, effectively, diffusing context (Aral, 2012; Kushin and Yamamoto, 2013) particularly amongst young people (Loader et al., 2014; Cammaerts et al., 2016). It is clear that social media use alters the way in which electoral phenomena diffuse (though primarily amongst politically involved minorities) and contextual perceptions spread, but ample evidence of echo-chamber effects (Colleoni et al., 2014; Boutyline and Willer, 2017) reinforces our claim of contextual individualization. The individual component of context can indeed condition or interact with societal context. We focus on electoral experience to tease out more specifically when the individual layer of context is mobilized, its interface with societal realities, and the way it permeates the electoral mind throughout the election cycle.

The Function of Elections

At first sight, many would argue that the function of elections is to elect representatives or leaders (already two very different functions!); but in this book, we argue that this vision is very institution-centric (the functions elections are 'supposed' to have), and that elections can do much more: notably, validate the premise of representation, offer an acceptable and effective substitute for direct democracy and make citizens feel they control their political system. The notion of the function of elections entails whatever gives citizens a sense that the system works for them—an arduous task amidst unprecedented levels of worldwide political distrust and cynicism (Cappella and Jamieson, 1996; Mishler and Rose, 1997; de Vreese, 2004; Bertsou, 2016).

When it comes to democratic processes, function is never obvious. Democratic theory amply questions representative processes and mandate conceptions (Mayo, 1960; Sartori, 1965; Katz, 1997; Dahl, 2013). It finds election type, separation of powers, electoral systems, and representational models (Eulau and Karps, 1977) to affect the function of elections. Dennis (1970) concludes that elections really have a triple function of 'giving majority approval to the exercise of leadership' (choice of leadership), indicating 'public choice among government policies' (policy representation), and 'legitimation of a regime', in particular through the 'public endorsement—or occasionally . . . repudiation—of the system of government' (legitimation).

Competing functions have behavioural consequences: voting for a government is not the same as using a ballot as an accountability mechanism to overthrow poorly performing incumbents, as illustrated by the contrasting retrospective and prospective models of voting (MacKuen et al., 1992), the literature on accountability (e.g., Przeworski et al., 1999; Berry and Howell, 2007), protest and expressive voting (Bowler and Lanoue, 1992; Carter and Guerette, 1992; van der Brug et al., 2000), strategic voting (Blais and Nadeau, 1996; Cox, 1997; Alvarez and Nagler, 2000), and sincere (or insincere) voting (Rosema, 2004). Even the distinction between egocentric and sociotropic voting underlines that between the functions of maximizing one's position within society and enhancing public well-being (Meehl, 1977; Kinder and Kieviet, 1981; MacKuen et al., 1992). Other models show functions of elections to include ritualization (Déloye and Ihl, 2008) and identity building, well-being, and more (Horowitz, 1990; Bruter, 2005; Emmanuel, 2007; Thomassen, 2014).

These distinctions have comparative implications. Many British or French citizens likely see elections as a tool to choose government, whereas Dutch or Israeli citizens may refer to selecting congruent representatives. Democratic frustration (Harrison, 2018; 2020) emphasizes accountability functions by enabling voters to 'replace' disliked incumbents. Beyond institutional constraints, any citizen may privilege the executive, representative, or accountability functions of their vote. However, all three alternatives remain institution-centric; instead, a main function elections could be to give citizens a symbolic sense of relevance within a system that increasingly escapes them, or, equally, to force political leaders to listen to—perhaps fear—the citizens they supposedly serve, once every few years. What if the function of elections was to validate the principle of representative democracy by creating a moment of ritualized civic communion between citizens and their political system, and between citizens themselves?

Multiple competing functions may vary by political system, by election, or indeed across citizens, and a given citizen might use different elections to perform different functions over contexts. Yet, the design and ergonomics of elections always assumes a particular function, and improves the process to perform it at the likely expense of alternative democratic functions. Furthermore, such functional assumptions are made by stakeholders (parties, institutions) whose own interests and needs will inevitably bias their perceptions , and by technological gatekeepers with another agenda of their own. The only group excluded from that discussion is citizens themselves: they have no vote to decide what elections should be about, no chance to give a running commentary on the meaning of their own behaviour, no opportunity to question the assumptions of democratic processes, as opposed to their outputs.

The Concept of Electoral Ergonomics

This leads us to consider the concept of electoral ergonomics (Bruter and Harrison, 2017), defined as 'the interface between electoral arrangements and voters' psychology'. We will develop the concept further in chapter 8, but in this section, we discuss its basics and how it relates to some key debates such as those on electoral management, convenience voting, the use of electoral technology, and electoral integrity, particularly in new democracies.

Existing research has shown that voting in churches or schools can impact electoral choices (Berger et al., 2008; Rutchick, 2010) and that traditional election rituals affect the vote (Déloye and Bruter, 2007; Déloye and Ihl, 2008). Electoral arrangements have attracted increasing scholarly attention with the diversification of voting procedures and efforts to make the vote more accessible to citizens. Attempts to reverse turnout decline have focused on making voting 'easier', notably remotely, through advance voting, mail-in ballots/postal voting or, in some cases, e-voting. We suggest that electoral ergonomics seeks to optimize electoral organization based on voters' psychology and the function citizens ascribe to elections.

Systemic attempts to improve democratic ergonomics based on a mistaken or biased understanding of electoral functions is not merely a risk, but an necessity inbuilt at the heart of systems tailoring technology to democracy. This paradox of dysfunctionality is confirmed empirically, notably where political institutions use technology to facilitate democratic participation—for instance through postal and internet voting based on the underlying assumption that participation stems from an arbitration between the benefits of voting (policy outcomes, or expressive benefits) and its cost (collecting and processing information, and the actual cost of going to vote) (Downs, 1957). A prominent use of rules and technology in politics has thus attempted to increase mechanically citizens' political participation by reducing its cost. ('If citizens do not bother to register or go to the polling station to vote, surely if we register them automatically and allow them to vote from home using postal or internet voting, there is no reason why they would not?')

A growing body of literature focuses on how electoral arrangements impact voting conditions, including their safety and electoral choice. Scholars have studied in particular the role of electoral administration in facilitating or impeding democratic transition in new democracies (Jinadu, 1997; Pastor, 1999; Schedler et al., 1999; Lyons, 2004; Wall et al., 2006; Atkeson and Saunders, 2007; and the works of IDEA and the Electoral Integrity Project, notably Karp et al., 2018; Norris et al., 2018, on the causes and consequences of election failure to meet international standards of electoral integrity).

The introduction of Direct Recording Electronic (DRE) voting machines since the 1990s, and the recent use of remote electronic voting using internet or mobile devices, notably in Switzerland and Estonia, have led to an increasingly rich literature on the impact of electronic voting compared to paper voting. Much literature on electronic voting systems has focused on its possible impact on turnout and electoral choice. Norris (2003) compared turnout under remote e-voting and all-postal voting in the British context, based on experimental evidence. Cammaerts et al. (2014; 2016) used an experiment on teenagers to compare remote electronic voting with in-station paper voting, and found a negative impact on turnout, electoral choice, voters' emotions, and efficacy. This last result matches a large parallel body of literature dealing with non-electoral paper and electronic prompts, such as the research into paper and electronic modes for surveys. Shannon and Bradshaw (2002) showed that electronically delivered surveys are answered significantly faster than their paper-delivered equivalent, while Kiesler and Sproull (1986) looked at the impact of the electronic survey medium on response effects and Boyer et al. (2002) assess data characteristics and notably data integrity under the two methods. These findings feed the models we test in chapter 8.

Approaching Elections as an Interface between Individual and Society

In chapter 1, we highlighted the fact that elections may have changed the condition of mankind, by offering a unique way of resolving differences in preferences and interests across individuals. There are well-known implications within collective action theory (Riker and Ordeshook, 1973; Olson, 2009). In this book, however, we aim to spell out further consequences, in terms not just of the way elections shape collective action, but also of how, through their individual–societal dialectic and winners–losers framing, elections can exacerbate or enhance citizens' sense of exclusion or inclusion within society and redefine their place within the polity.

In the next few sections, we analyze elections as a permanent dialectic between self and society, preference and projection, personal rights and duties, societal roles and responsibilities. We explore this dialectic under four successive angles: the egocentric/sociotropic dichotomy; the question of empathic displacement; the concept of projected efficacy; and the concept of electoral identity, defined as 'the role voters espouse and enact'.

Sociotropic and Egocentric Perceptions and Projection

The tension between individual and societal interests in electoral motivations was established in the literature by Kinder and Kiewiet (1981), who opposed egocentric voters who (in effect) ask candidates, 'What have you done for *me* lately?' to sociotropic ones who ask, instead, 'What have you done for *the country* lately?' As early as 1977, Meehl identified a paradox of the selfish voter, which, in his view, reinforces the hypothesis that sociotropic evaluations must dominate electoral choice. Similarly, MacKuen et al. (1992) show that sociotropic economic evaluations better predict future voting behaviour than egocentric ones. Other authors have further looked at the impact of sociotropic economic evaluations in interaction with context in dealigned polities (Anderson, 2000), or suggested an egocentric framing of sociotropic evaluations (Acevedo and Krueger, 2004), based on an illusion of relevance and importance of one's vote rather than an egocentric evaluation of electoral outcomes.

We note three elements. First, the egocentric–sociotropic literature is mostly limited to economic voting. Yet, other evaluations can affect electoral choice—security, crime, housing, social cohesion, for example. What is true of economic evaluations is not necessarily replicated in social, safety, or other evaluations, so we will propose an alternative four-dimensional model.

Second, whilst egocentric perspectives are relatively straightforward, sociotropic ones are complex. Kinder and Kiewiet (1981) focus on the national polity, but group interests have been the object of much behavioural research, and a focus in studies of empathy (Hayes, 2010). More broadly, sociotropism can be asymmetric, and in this book, we particularly wish to evaluate the extent to which sociotropism and notably altruism (Johnston et al., 2000; Zettler et al., 2011) may lead different voters to accept electoral sacrifice in favour of specific generations, such as the elderly, or younger generations.

Third, economic voting models suggest that many citizens consider the greater social context and see themselves as depositories of a vote on behalf of their nation, rather than one aimed at protecting their own individual interest. This predominance of sociotropic evaluations is compellingly demonstrated, but suggests that beyond evaluations, citizens feel a sense of societal duty and responsibility, the precise nature and implications of which require attention. It is difficult to reconcile these findings with rational-choice models based on the maximization of *individual* utility functions through the vote (Downs, 1957). Yet, the notion of a sociotropic utility function would question the basis of significant aspects of experimental research in the field, not least when it uses personal gain as incentives.

Altruism has long permeated participation models. Rational choice has incorporated the 'expressive value of the vote', the infamous 'D term', which comes in addition to the (minimal) value of the vote in deciding government. However, this term is mostly conceived as a 'disturbance' (e.g., Riker and Ordeshook, 1973; Barry, 1975; Mueller, 2003; Dowding, 2005). Many authors remain sceptical about the lack of specificity of the term, while others note that duty to vote influences turnout (Lane, 1955; Knack, 1992; Blais, 2000), or take altruism into account per se (Fowler, 2006; Blais and St-Vincent, 2011). Our model, however, makes a blunter claim: that the implications of sociotropism go beyond altruism, and that its main relevance is not so much about *who* voters think about when they vote (or decide to vote), but more about what the *role* is that they explicitly or implicitly assume and inhabit throughout the voting process, and which will colour all of their electoral experience and behaviour.

Above, we noted that a specific form of sociotropism could lead citizens to accept sacrifices for different—in particular younger—generations. This relates to another form of arbitration, which differs subtly from sociotropism, and which pertains to the concession of short-term sacrifices for the sake of the long-term benefit of our own and future generations–a particularly relevant choice in the context of the prominence of debates on climate change and sustainability. We label this sense of a responsibility to use elections as long-term investment *projection*, in view of the geometric nature of the concept, and conceive it as an important feature of electoral identity.

Voters' Roles and the Question of Empathic Displacement

We thus broaden our understanding of how voters consider society in their vote, not through the impact of their vote, but by implicitly inhabiting a role as voter which they aim to fulfil. We claim that the person entering the polling booth is not merely an individual asserting what they do or do not want, but rather someone 'wearing a cap', performing a function, almost a job, in the same way as teachers or a doctors are there not to decide whether they like a student or a patient, but to act in a certain capacity that goes beyond their individual choices and preferences and brings out the best in them.

On Election Day, that role is potentially shared with millions of others who presumably, in their view, wear a similar cap as they synchronically decide for whom (and whether) to vote. Considering these other voters as we evaluate, decide, and vote is what we label *empathic displacement*. It encompasses the implicit perception that our vote is 'in sync' or at odds with the rest of the population. It pertains to the crucial question of how we incorporate the way the rest of the country is feeling and behaving on Election Day into our own actions, and of how it makes us feel part of a solemn, important, and momentous Election Day. In essence, empathic displacement is about the dual individual and societal reality of the vote.

Notwithstanding the methodological difficulties of 'navigating' between individual-and aggregate-level realities, the dichotomy, however misperceived, likely permeates the voter's mind. Many behaviour models assume that voters only express individual preferences, without querying the behaviour of millions of fellow voters who effectively determine the election result; but this does not do justice to human intelligence and sophistication. Frameworks like strategic voting assume such displacement without ever naming it, in acknowledging that voters can differentiate between wasted and effective votes, but they still presume voters to be 'selfish' and merely focused on their own influence. There are many other ways in which the (expected) vote of others may frame our own electoral thought process, experience, and behaviour.

Projected Efficacy

A particularly noteworthy perception is that one's vote may be aligned with that of many other citizens, part of a societal trend of sorts. Feeling in tune with the rest of the population could have contradictory implications. Negatively, rational-choice theory has always covertly considered it an oddity that citizens should vote when their vote is least likely to make a difference, thereby invoking the expressive value of the vote. Positively, we claim that voters may project perceptions of efficacy based not on the sole effect of their own vote, but considering that if many people like them vote accordingly, collective impact will be achieved. This is the phenomenon we label *projected efficacy*.

Projected efficacy can generate a sense of inclusiveness, of being in tune with fellow citizens and integrated within a national (or local) polity. It can emphasize a sense of being part of a collective experience, a solemn and symbolic national movement. Equally, feeling electorally at odds with others may lead to alienation. Knowingly casting a minoritarian vote may feed feelings of social marginalization from national trends and collective satisfaction. We noted earlier that people resist the urge to throw rubbish on the street because they feel that if others did the same, the results would be appalling. We ask them, conversely, whether they think that if people like them go to vote, they will make a difference: our measure of projected efficacy.

The Concept of Electoral Identity—Referee or Supporter?

We earlier referred to the concept of partisan identity (Campbell et al., 1960), which has shaped much electoral research since the 1960s but has been widely contested. This book argues instead that citizens may have an electoral identity which is foundational and constant, but entirely distinct from partisanship. We relate it to the roles citizens subconsciously embrace as voters and which will shape their perceptions, interaction with the system, experience, and behaviour. We use a sports analogy to illustrate the role that voters inhabit. Thinking of parties or candidates as players in a sports game—say, the final of the football (soccer) World Cup or Super Bowl—we claim that voters may see their own role as either 'referees', arbitrating between the two teams, or 'supporters', cheering for one of them.

We argue that electoral identity on the referee–supporter scale has an enormous impact not only on voters' interaction with the campaign and their electoral attitudes (efficacy, sense of duty, and so on), but also on electoral emotions and experience and the conditions under which elections will bring a sense of resolution. We also believe that being a supporter in this sense does not equate to being partisan. Referees will evaluate which of the candidates competing for their vote is most convincing. They will see themselves as *external* to the election, and act as fair and independent assessors, voting in an election as they would adjudicate a popularity contest such as *The X Factor*. For referees, efficacy will stem from the evaluative power they have, and their level of excitement during the election will replicate that of a spectator watching a tense and exciting sporting event. Abstention is plausible if no candidate seems better than others.

Supporters, by contrast, will see themselves as projective participants in the election. The election becomes a competition between alternative camps, making supporters involved insiders in the electoral process. The emotions associated with the vote will derive their intensity directly from the fortunes of 'their' camp, and their efficacy will be directly dependent upon the result of the election, as will their sense of integration. Abstention would be defection.

The referee/supporter dichotomy has direct consequences for the psychological experience of the vote and subsequent electoral behaviour. For instance, supporters would be more likely to be strategic, whilst this would serve little purpose for referees. Protest voting, however, would be a far more likely from unimpressed referees. The perceived responsibility of voters will also be radically affected by their nature as referees or supporters, as will perceptions of electoral atmosphere and other emotions and memories triggered on Election Day and Night.

Electoral Hopelessness, and Hostility

We highlighted electoral resolution as one of the three interrelated dependent variables this book aims to explain. In ideal terms, when elections function well, they bring citizens a sense of closure after a period of potentially intense political disagreement, and restore legitimacy and hope in the system. By contrast, hopelessness could result from a resolution failure, especially where voters cannot foresee any electoral route to change.

In our model, we suggest that hopelessness is a route to hostility. For years, voters' trust and confidence in institutions and their political personnel has declined across Western democracies (Bertsou, 2016). More recently, however, many voters have seemed to extend this dislike to fellow voters, simply on account of the way they believe them to vote. This is the phenomenon we refer to as *electoral hostility*. While an abundant literature focuses on partisan polarization (Abramowitz and Saunders, 1998; Fiorina et al., 2008) and notably affective polarization (Huddy et al., 2015; Iyengar and Westwood, 2015), our concept of hostility obeys a different analytical logic.

Indeed, the polarization literature suggests that negative feelings towards political opponents stems from hardening partisanship. Thus, the more partisan a person, the more polarized he/she would become and the more antagonistic towards opposite partisans. Parties (and party identity) are at the heart of the polarization phenomenon. By contrast, the (dis)trust and cynicism literatures (e.g., Bertsou, 2016) suggest that those with least hope in electoral democracy are the most likely to democratically disengage. The likely antagonistic 'target group' is thus almost opposite to that envisaged in the partisan polarization model, with those who believe least in any parties being the most likely to distrust. Additionally, parties need not play any role in these citizens' negative emotional responses. In the electoral hostility model, we expect negative feelings towards groups of voters, rather than the radicalization of partisanship, to represent a further deterioration of political trust (and thus affect potentially apartisan citizens).

We thus decouple electoral hostility from partisanship and relax any assumption as to whether hostility is more likely to be based on parties, values, or issues, or experienced by partisans or non-partisans. We also explore the combination and hierarchy of negative emotions that citizens may feel towards those they either know or perceive to vote differently from themselves. Feeling distrust towards someone is different from feeling contempt, frustration, anger, disgust or enmity. We claim that those emotions represent increasingly 'hard' forms of hostility, which can transform and degenerate over time.

A critical challenge is to translate this ambitious conceptual framework and complex model into a research design and methodological strategy which can fit the research question introduced in chapter 1.

Methodological Challenges and Conditions

In chapter 1, we discussed embarking upon this study of the mind of a voter and noted that exploring models of electoral behaviour, experience, and resolution would mean facing some exceptional challenges. We highlighted the complexity of tapping into the 'hidden part of the iceberg', as well over 90% of our behaviour stems from subconscious rather than conscious motivation, thereby discrediting approaches that would solely rely on self-reporting; we noted too that not all elections are 'created equal', and that comparative differences, order differences, and the divergence between party-, candidate-, and issue-centric vote could lead to different mobilization of personality, memory, and identity predictors. We underlined the difficult position of electoral ergonomics in our project, and notably its nature as a psychology–system interface, which effectively suggests that ergonomics is not just about entering organizational variables as independent predictors, but rather about expecting psychological predictors to function differently across key ergonomic conditions such as traditional, temporally remote, and geographically remote voting. We also introduced a whole range of new concepts, many of which are complex and fluid, and which also require us to offer citizens 'space' and freedom to confirm them narratively rather than impose too rigid a deductive framework from the onset.

Finally, our model, which focuses not only on behaviour but also on experience and resolution, involves an element of 'micro-dynamics'. It is not content with an estimation of the vote that citizens will ultimately cast, but suggests a need to disaggregate the extremely dense period of the vote, and notably to isolate the specific moment when a citizen casts his/her vote, which is shrouded in secrecy. Legally and symbolically, the polling booth is arguably the most guarded public place in political life. In a technological age, when citizens' actions are increasingly scrutinized, recorded, and traced, casting a ballot is conceivably the only civic act subject to an absolute and permanent interdiction upon intrusion by anyone. Within this protective framework, how can we capture precisely a moment that is designed not to be observable?

Ultimately, as we will see, our entire methodological approach is therefore one of balance and triangulation—between quantitative and qualitative, self-reported and observed, deductive and inductive, static and dynamic, real and experimental approaches. To shed light on different facets of the vote, we combine approaches of which each has its limitations, hoping that through their superimposition, their different strengths and weaknesses (for instance high internal but low external validity vs high external but limited internal validity) will 'cancel out'.

Another key challenge pertains to the temporal heterogeneity of electoral psychology cycles. Citizens do not speak about elections all the time, elections do not take place all the time and not all elections are created equal. In this book, we tackle the challenge of time heterogeneity at two levels: within life cycle, and within election cycle. We thus integrate dynamic elements both by including panels lasting several years (beyond exploring citizens' recreated memory) and by asking citizens to keep election diaries combined with the immediacy of on-the-spot interviews conducted immediately after they voted. With this in mind, regarding life-cycle dynamics, we disentangle, first, early electoral memories from, second, the first election and, third, adult elections. In terms of electoral cycle dynamics, we focus particularly on, first, the run up to the election (including identifying who either decides how to vote or changes his/her mind within a few minutes, hours or days of casting a vote), and second, the electoral experience (polling station, polling booth, early or postal or electronic vote), including, third, the voting moment (when the ballot is cast) and fourth, Election Night.

Altogether, embarking upon a journey inside the mind of a voter will be no easy task. However, the book's research design combines multiple approaches, triangulation of methodologies, and comparative confirmation in order to approach our object of study rigorously and multilaterally.

Overarching Research Design

The comparative research design that we use in the book has deliberately aimed to combine a large number of different methods to compensate for their individual constraints and limitations. It seeks balance between quantitative and qualitative methodologies which enable us to cross-validate internally valid (experiment, in-depth interviews, diaries) and externally valid (mass survey, spot interviews) elements, static and dynamic approaches, experimental, observational, and self-reported modes, retrospective and prospective components, static and dynamic data. Sometimes, we analyze information emanating from large representative samples of the general population; elsewhere, we collect narratives from narrower samples with depth; in third cases, we systematically gather information pertaining to sub-samples of more specific population categories such as first-time voters and non-voters.

We see these combinations as a scientific necessity rather than just a palette of technical gimmickry. The relative advantages of quantitative and qualitative data have been amply discussed in the social sciences. Quantitative evidence typically makes systematic comparison easier, which has enormous value in large comparative endeavours, but qualitative evidence affords greater narrative granularity and reduces the risk of missing important realities, which may occur when over-constraining responses with strictly deductive response models. In this research, we use a twist on the quantitative/qualitative debate because part of our data is both qualitative and generalizable, using open questions in systematically sampled surveys and panels to allow analytically driven coding and validation.

The choice between survey and experimental approaches is often summarized as being arbitration between external and internal validity. Surveys are based on robust samples from which general trends are safer to infer, but experimental designs enable researchers to isolate specific causal processes whilst maintaining all other conditions constant, thereby offering 'cleaner' conditions to test causality. Here, we also use quasi-experimental approaches when it comes to remote voting in the US, as opportunities for absentee or early voting are directly determined by state decisions on remote voting options. We also compare the use of in-person and remote voting in the context of survey data in other countries, including the UK, but this is not a quasi-experimental setting, as unlike the availability of specific remote voting processes, choosing remote or in-person voting (whether in the US or elsewhere) is not random.

The need to balance self-reported and observational data is less frequently discussed, but arguably even more important. It relates to the importance of subconscious mechanisms in human (and electoral) behaviour. Whilst there is a generic case to be made for the exploration of the immerged subconscious part of the 'human iceberg', the risk of conscious distortion is particularly strong in electoral studies, if only because most citizens only know of electoral opinion research in the context of election polls, the measurement of citizens' preferences, and the prediction of electoral results. While this is a respectable field, its goals, foci, and methodological requirements differ from those of academic research, and over decades of electoral polling, democratic citizens have undoubtedly developed a strong sense of how polling results get interpreted by eletes and affect their behaviour. As for the balance between static and dynamic, it enables us to entangle cyclical effects and look at their durability and consistency over time. In many cases, it also enables us to compare effects across contexts, for instance in presidential and mid-term elections in the US, or in elections and referenda in the UK.

Finally, focusing on specific sub-groups beyond the general population by means of sub-samples or additional surveys allows us to zoom in on unique cases of some specific categories such as first-time voters, pre-voters aged 15–17, and non-voters. These categories may have unique and different experiences of elections, but also, through their uniqueness, shed light on mechanisms that clarify hidden effects amongst the entire democratic population.

The methodological architecture of the book merges panel studies, time series, single surveys, including of specific categories, in-depth interviews, 'on-the-spot interviews', visual experiment of voters in the polling booth, quasi-experimental setting direct observation in polling stations, election diaries. The combination is summarized in table 2.1.

Approaching and Operationalizing the Dependent Variable(s)

This multimodal research design seeks to address the need for some level of sophistication imposed by a triple interrelated dependent variable. Shifting the paradigm of behavioural research by questioning the largely unchallenged supremacy of electoral choice as its arch-dominant dependent variable has methodological consequences. Escaping this paradoxically institutionalist approach to behaviour requires a rethinking of elections from the point of view of the voters, so the ways in which elections matter may suddenly change radically; hence our focus on electoral behaviour, experience, and resolution. We noted that each of the three dependent variables is itself complex. Electoral behaviour divides into participation and electoral choice; electoral experience comprises the way citizens practise and internalize elections and the emotions that elections elicit; while electoral resolution and the ability to bring closure to both individuals and systems subdivides into elections' potential to generate appeasement, hope, and hostility.

This triple complex dependent variable means that different questions approached in the book may be better suited to different methodological approaches. We saw how the Columbia School showed that participation and electoral choice are naturally captured quantitatively; however, to explain how citizens experience and internalize the election within their lives, it seems essential to tap into qualitative observations and narratives. As for the emotions that citizens consciously and subconsciously experience throughout the electoral process, these lend themselves to experimental observation. Finally, electoral resolution, and how elections bring closure, hope, and hostility, require an exploratory understanding of citizens' perceptions.

We thus capture aspects of our dependent variables and components of our model using different layers of research design. The survey component

TABLE 2.1. Methodological Components of the Research Design

Component	Sub-Comp.	Specification	Highlights
Surveys	Panel study	All six countries, two to five waves and up to five years. Starting samples of over 2,000 respondents in all countries (UK: 2,020, Germany: 2,735, US: 2,004, France: 2,029, Georgia: 2,021, South Africa: 1,006). Mixture of face-to-face and internet mode.	Panels of up to five waves and years depending on number of elections in each country. Includes coded and factor-analyzed open questions, and over 200 items comprising implicit emotional measures, five discrete personality traits, electoral memory, electoral identity, separate items for non-voters, etc. Quasi-experiments on the impact of electoral ergonomics.
	Ad hoc survey	Ad hoc surveys for the EU-membership referendum (three-wave panel, sample size: 3,008), the Scottish independence referendum (sample size: 522), the UK general election 2017 (sample size: 2,008), and young people in France (two waves, two sub-samples: 15–17 and 18–25 year-olds, sample size: 1,990), internet only.	Surveys focusing on specific electoral contexts or groups: voting in referenda, focus on pre-voters (.5–17) and young voters, new battery of items on egocentric and sociotropic voting, projection of referendum outcome, impact of voting arrangements and campaigning, etc.
Experiments	Visual experiment	Germany and UK only. Filming the shadows of voters behind the curtain when in the polling booth, comparing thinking time under three types of ballot and analyzing emotions displayed through facial and body language, using psychiatric insights from kinesics. Sample: 145.	Unique experiment run with professional film crews to capture the shadows of voters in the polling booth and analyze facial and body language using kinesics, a body of research grounded in psychiatry and originally intended to decipher the emotions of patients with limited verbal communication, such as autistic children, and also used in anthropology. Multiple blind coding and additional physiological measures using Apple watches.
	Lab experiments	Young people aged 15–17 only, two comparative lab experiments on in station vs remote e-voting, and traditional campaigning vs social media campaigning. Sample size: 425 per experiment.	Experiments conducted with young people who have never voted before, on the impact of social campaigning and remote e-voting on turnout, engagement, electoral choice, efficacy, and electoral satisfaction.

Interviews	In-depth interviews	Four countries (all except Georgia and Germany). In-depth interviews on electoral memory, history, habits, experiences, and emotions.	Narrative interviews with focus on memory of childhood elections, first electoral experience, habits and behavior during election campaigns, Election Day, Election Night, perception of electoral identity, the function of elections, role of voters, emotions associated with vote.
	Spot interviews	Four countries (all except Georgia and Germany). Spot interviews asking voters to explain what they thought about in the polling booth, in one sentence only, as they exit the polling station.	Hundreds of voters being asked to explain in one sentence what they thought of when they were in the polling booth immediately after they exit the polling station.
Diaries		Four countries (all except Georgia and Germany). Diaries completed daily by respondents for a period starting three weeks before the election and ending one week after the vote.	Election diaries with four daily sections and additional twice-weekly sections capturing citizens' daily experience of elections in terms of thoughts, discussions, campaign exposure, family interaction, habits, etc.
Direct Observation		France. Partnering with election officials to observe behavior of voters in the polling station throughout election day. Total: 17 polling stations. Also direct observation in US and UK.	Partnership with election officials or observers for full day reports and to record the way people come to vote (with whom, how they dress, how they behave, etc.), their questions, comments, etc.

tests our model on some quantified aspects of the three dependent variables: firstly, for electoral behavior, turnout, and electoral choice (main left- or right-wing party or both, continuous left/right and/or extreme right vote, depending on the system); secondly, for electoral experience, happiness and emotionality resulting from the election; and thirdly, for electoral resolution, feeling closer to fellow citizens as a result of the election. Depending on the dichotomous or continuous nature of these operationalized dependent variables, we test those models using OLS regression or logistic regression, each time entering independent variables (personality and morality, memory, identity) in a step-wise manner to understand the contribution of each category to variance beyond a control variable baseline. Moreover, due to the interface nature of electoral ergonomics, we test the models separately for non-voters, in-person voting, and main modes of remote voting (except turnout, obviously). We use the US case study as our principal test, because it includes all of the variables in the model, but also analyze the model for other countries whilst specifyng the missing predictors in each case. The multivariate model is progressively tested across chapters 4, 5, and 6, and discussed again in chapter 10.

Similarly, qualitative approaches (interviews, diaries, and observation) and experiments are used throughout the model testing. To capture electoral experience and internalization, we use evidence from election diaries, in-depth interviews, on-the-spot interviews, and direct electoral observation (chapter 3). To avoid relying solely on self-perceptions to capture the emotions experienced by citizens as they vote, we use a unique visual experiment whereby the reactions of voters in the polling booth were captured by filming their shadows (chapter 7), and to study electoral atmosphere and electoral resolution, notably the possibility for elections to increase electoral hostility, we privilege open questions (chapter 9). We also look at the dynamic effects of electoral resolution by considering episodes of electoral hope and hostility across the electoral decade this book investigates.

Comparative Scope

It is sometimes hard for those who have only ever voted in one country to realize how different a vote may 'feel' across contexts. In the UK, voters do not need identification to vote. Voters enter the polling station, provide their name, confirm the address read out to them, proceed to a curtainless booth, and drop their completed ballot in an unmanned ballot box. In France, voters surrender identification to the station manager who reads their name out loud before handing them an envelope. The voter collects individual papers with the names of each candidate from a table before entering a fully curtained booth. The envelope with the ballot enclosed is returned to the station official, who lifts the Electoral Code (strategically placed over the ballot box slot) before exclaiming '*a voté*!' ('has voted!') as the voter drops the envelope. Only after the voter signs the register are identification documents returned.

The book's fieldwork focuses on six countries: the US, the UK, France, Germany, South Africa, and Georgia. The US receives more attention in the literature than any other democracy. This will enable us to evaluate how our model complements, or possibly contradicts, our knowledge in the field. Moreover, the decentralized US electoral structure means that most aspects of electoral management and organization vary by state or county, providing quasi-experimental settings to test key electoral ergonomics questions. The UK, France, and Germany are also much-studied democracies. They differ considerably. The UK represents the origins of modern parliamentary democracy, France is an example of complex system and rules changes, and Germany, whilst associated historically with some of the most atrocious crimes in the history of humanity, has been largely hailed as a most effective example of democratization post-1945. South Africa and Georgia represent two cases of recent democratization, South Africa since the end of apartheid, and Georgia in the wake of the collapse of the Soviet Union.

Each of these six countries plays a part in our analysis of the psychology of voters and their experience of elections across contexts. However, part of the methodological originality of our book lies in not treating them similarly across methodological components. Instead, beyond a common comparative survey core, some methods are implemented in a core of three countries, with additional unique ones in each of the six cases. The core composed of the USA, the UK, and France encompasses most of the empirical components. These include dynamic data collection for the surveys (multi-year panel in the US, time series in France, both multi-year panel and non-panel time series in the UK), in-depth interviews, and on-the-spot interviews. Election diaries are also run in all three countries, as well as in South Africa.

Finally, as mentioned above, certain components were run in one or two countries uniquely. These included, in the US, family focus groups and quasi-experimental analysis based on remote voting options. In the UK, we conducted two referendum studies, and exploratory analyses of electoral hostility and electoral atmosphere. In France, we partnered with polling station officials to conduct direct polling station observation in a country-wide sample of polling stations, and conducted specific panel surveys of pre-voters and first-time voters. In Germany, we ran a unique visual experiment, filming the shadows of voters in the polling booth. Finally, in Georgia, we ran our survey on a large-scale face-to-face basis, using direct sampling of the electoral register in each region within the country.

Our case selection is based not only on countries important in their own right, but mostly too on countries which together represent a mixture of contexts and features. The US and UK are old democracies, France and Germany have had relatively tumultuous regime changes, and South Africa and Georgia represent consolidating democracies. The US has a presidential system, the UK and Germany parliamentary systems, whilst France, South Africa, and Georgia have semi-presidential systems. The US and the UK both use plurality in their elections, South Africa uses closed list proportional representation, Germany and Georgia use slightly different forms of mixed electoral systems (both mixing proportional representation system and plurality in single member districts for parliamentary elections, while Georgia also uses a two-round run-off electoral system for presidential elections), and France achieves the quasi-miracle of using six different electoral systems in its various elections: two-round run-off presidential elections with plurality and majority, two-round run-off legislative elections with plurality in both, proportional representation with different majoritarian bonuses (50% and 25% respectively) in municipal and regional elections, two-member-district majority in county elections, and proportional representation in European Parliament elections. The US and Germany have federal systems, the UK has asymmetric devolution, South Africa has strong regional decentralization, and France and Georgia have unitary systems. Finally, the countries range as regards their economic and social situations from South Africa's largely developing economy with a majority of the population living in poverty to Germany's position among the world's wealthiest countries. Let us now explore the individual components of our research design.

First Component: Surveys and Panel Studies

The first foundation of our research design is a combination of large-scale surveys and multi-wave panel studies. The surveys and panel studies vary in time scope and methodology. The shortest fieldwork took place in South Africa and Georgia, where we ran single-wave surveys. In Germany, we ran a two-wave panel study during a federal election. In France, we ran two separate two-wave panel studies, one of the general population during a presidential election, and one with two sub-samples of pre-voters (aged 15–17) and first-/second-time voters (aged 18–25) across consecutive municipal and European Parliament elections. In the US, we ran a three-wave panel study spanning consecutive presidential and mid-term elections. Finally, in the UK, we ran a six-year five-wave panel study, including two general elections plus local elections and referenda. We ran a separate three-wave panel study on the EU-membership referendum, and two separate surveys on the Scottish independence referendum and the 2017 general election. These arrangements offer different scopes for longitudinal analysis, individually over periods of up to five years (UK and US) or over the course of an election period (France, Germany, EU-membership referendum), and over eight years at the aggregate level (UK). Additionally, the French case enables us to look specifically at the electoral experience of pre-voting teens and first/second time voters longitudinally and using specific representative samples (as opposed to sub-parts of national samples).

Regarding mode and sample size, our fieldwork in Georgia was the most ambitious, with a face-to-face survey of a random sample based on the full electoral register and conducted in each of the country's constituencies. Elsewhere, the surveys were conducted online with representative samples. Online surveys have both supporters and detractors in the literature, but apart from being an increasingly frequent choice, including in national election studies, they offer by far the best long-term response rates for panel studies, which was critical given our design. Sample sizes and panel response rates are presented in table 2.2. The sample size for main national surveys varied from 1,006 respondents in South Africa to 2,743 in Germany. It was around two thousand respondents in other countries. Additional studies had samples ranging from 522 in Scotland to 3,010 for the EU referendum. In France, the categorical survey had samples of 972 for 15–17-year-old respondents, and 1,018 for 18–25-year-old ones.

The panel response rates, predictably, vary, notably in relation to wave gaps, and are reported in the same table. In the UK, the response rate by wave 2 was 96.7% and five years later was still 48.5%. In the same country, for the referendum on EU membership, the response rate in the final wave was 70.2%. In the US, however, whilst the response rate in wave 2 was 73.7%, by wave 3 it had dropped to 28.9%. However, our checks confirmed that the churn did not overwhelmingly affect the balance of respondents.

TABLE 2.2. Samples and Response Rates across Panel Waves

	Starting sample	No of waves	Resp. rate wave 2 (%)	Resp. rate final wave (%)	Total time-span (months)
UK general	2,020	4	96.7	48.5	61
UK (EU ref.)	3,010	3	70.1	70.2	4
UK (Scot. ref.)	322	1	—	—	—
USA	2,017	3	73.7	28.9	25
France (presidential)	2,029	2	76.8	—	2
France (local+EP 15–17)	972	2	60.4	—	4
France (local+EP 18–25)	1,018	2	42.5	—	4
Germany	2,743	2	89.2	—	2
South Africa	1,006	1	—	—	—
Georgia	2,021	1	—	—	—

In France, the response rate at wave 2 was 76.8%, and 89.2% in Germany. The retention rate in the French panels of pre- and young voters was over 60% for pre-voters but slightly below 50% for young voters. On balance, these figures make it possible to analyze longitudinal dynamics across cases, though caution is essential, particularly for the US.

The first wave of the election survey was fielded approximately three weeks before a major election (presidential/general/legislative). This questionnaire included questions on personality, morality, memory, voting habits and rituals, electoral attitudes, and emotions associated with voting and not voting, in addition to voting intentions and sociological, demographic, cultural, and political controls. The second wave was conducted on Election Night and featured electoral experience, decision, and behaviour, and the roles, emotions, thoughts, perceptions, attitudes, and behaviour associated with the vote. Further waves were on Election Night of subsequent elections. Appendix 1 (see www.epob.org) presents sample questionnaires.

In the corresponding survey, we also included specific questions pertaining to pre-voters' and first-time voters' socialization, experience, habits, and projected participation, as well as their perception of politics and politicians and their nascent electoral memory. The survey also included a question module about the respondents' (actual or projective) first election, and items exploring possible ways to encourage interest in elections, positive voting experience, efficacy, and turnout. Respondents were asked about the likely effects of such measures on themselves and on their generation in general.

All questionnaires included both closed and open questions. Several open questions asked respondents about Election Day thoughts and experience: for example, 'What are the first three words that come to your mind when you think of the day of the election?', or, 'In one sentence, what are the thoughts that went through your mind when you were in the polling booth about to cast our vote?' Others target feelings during Election Night, perceptions of the role of a voter explained to someone about to vote for the first time, words associated with 'election', and the atmosphere of the election. Most surveys limit the use of open questions, on account of the complexity and expense involved in back-translating and coding respondents' answers. However, open questions were critical to understanding electoral experience and key concepts introduced by our model—such as electoral identity, experience, atmosphere, empathic displacement, and polling booth thoughts—and chart new conceptual territory. Our team conducted all the open-question coding in-house, using analytically driven coding frames that we designed based on our model.

Unlike qualitative evidence collected from interviews, these answers are generated from fully representative samples, and are amenable to generalization and inference after coding. It may be presumptuous to claim that we aimed for the best of both worlds; certainly, however, there was an ambition to collect data from representative samples, yet uncontaminated by restrictive question and response phrasings on key issues such as thoughts in the polling booth (or elsewhere, when citizens vote from home), perceptions of the role of a voter, and electoral atmosphere. We also used implicit questions to go beyond respondents' conscious self-reporting of electoral perceptions, thoughts, and processes. Our traditional and innovative implicit questions included personality derivatives, word-stem completion, and emoji prompts. We repeated many of these across waves to compare emotions in pre- and post-electoral contexts.

Finally, to assess the multivariate models comparatively, we should note that we can only test a completely fully specified model in the US case, where the full range of independent variables was included. In other countries, some of the question modules are not included—for instance, morality in the UK, and electoral identity in France. This is discussed in more detail in chapter 4, when we introduce the models' specifics. As a result, the US dataset is our 'flagship' model for the multivariate analysis, though we also include the results for the other four relevant countries at each stage of the model testing, whilst reporting on missing predictors which worsen the coefficients.

We should note that in terms of overall performance, the process of entering independent variables step by step is inherently 'unfair', in that it gives optimal credit to the control variables and the early stages of the model (notably personality), whilst leaving little unaccounted variance for later sets of variables (notably identity) to explain; so we then ran the models with all the variables, which is the procedure we use when crediting individual variables in the model.

Second Component: In-Depth Interviews, On-the-Spot Interviews, and Diaries

The second—qualitative—pillar of our methodological toolkit comprises in-depth interviews, on-the-spot interviews, and election diaries. The in-depth interviews lasted one to two hours and were semi-structured, with respondents of different ages, backgrounds, and ethnicities, selected from geographically diverse areas. These narrative interviews aimed for in-depth insight into electoral memory, experiences, habits, emotions associated with the vote, and into how citizens approach and conceive elections, including their perceived identity, role, and responsibility

By contrast, on-the-spot interviews were conducted outside polling stations, where volunteers were asked volunteers to answer one question: 'Can you tell me what went through your mind when you were in the polling booth about to cast your vote?' This immediate intervention sought to capture an immediate, unpolluted account directly following citizens' vote. As noted above, a similar question was asked in the panel study to get generalizable data from representative samples, but the on-the-spot interviews benefited from immediacy. These interviews were conducted by our team at various polling stations throughout Election Day.

Finally, diaries were kept daily by approximately fifty respondents per country/election, starting about two weeks before Election Day and ending two days after it. Each diary page included four open fields: first, hearing about the election; second, discussing the election,; third, thinking about the election; and lastly, any other element related to the election. About twice a week and on special days (such as major television debates, Election Day, or the day after the election), respondents received separate diary questionnaires with other entries combined with shorter questions. Examples of the qualitative fieldwork, including in-depth interviews and diaries are presented in Appendix 2 (see www.epob.org).

Note that in reporting respondents' answers in all interviews as well as diaries and open-ended survey responses, we chose to report all quotes verbatim, only correcting for obvious spelling mistakes in the context of written material, and transcribing non-verbal reactions in the oral material whenever possible.

Third Component: Visual Experiment

A key issue of behaviour studies is that they often rely on respondents self-reporting their decisions and the processes and motivations behind them. Even most experiments in the field are survey-based, implying a self-reporting component. The exception to this rule is physiological experiments which, while very useful in allowing precise clinical measures of citizens' reactions in given conditions, frequently expose participants to highly unnatural and sometimes uncomfortable conditions, which may, in themselves, affect their reactions and behaviour. We have thus developed a different experimental method, intended to serve as a potential alternative for specific research questions, whereby the dependent variable is an observable experience: visual experiments when we film the shadows of voters in a polling booth. Because of the taboo surrounding the polling booth, ethical precautions are particularly critical: hence the development a system based on filming shadows, to offer extremely strong guarantees of anonymity and secrecy of the electoral choice made.

Visual observation allows us to capture accurately and directly the act of voting, including how long people think before casting their vote, and what emotions they display. By contrast, questionnaires only inform researchers about voters' self-perceptions of their own behaviour, with a necessary element of approximation and inbuilt error. Moreover, unlike the typically invasive protocols of physiological experiments, visual experiments, whilst also artificial (featuring as they do a simulated election), involved visual capture not interfering with the subjects' voting experience, nor any physical anomaly in their environment.

Visual experiments have their own limits. Beyond known experimental issues of external validity, the format cannot target the two dominant dependent variables of electoral analysis: electoral participation (which does not vary here) and electoral choice (which is not measured); but focus instead on electoral experience, process, and emotions. Visual experiments are relatively complex to set up to ensure realistic and unobtrusive conditions for the participants, and they impose rigorous ethical and technical safeguards to ensure full respect of subjects' privacy and consent, while interfering as little as possible with their natural behaviour. Finally, there is an element of interpretation of the visual evidence, involving strong coding guidelines and multiple coders to ensure reliable data. Nevertheless, we argue that this type of experiment, long used by biologists, psychologists, and anthropologists, can shed a different light on key aspects of the highly secret world of voters' behaviour within the polling booth.

In collaboration with professional camera crew, we captured the shadows of voters to decipher emotions during the act of voting. The experiment was conducted in Germany and replicated in the UK, with a total of two hundred volunteers. The participants were randomly assigned to three groups based on different types of ballot paper (UK-style paper ballot, French style poly-paper ballot, and electronic). We then identified the effect of the ballot paper type on the time that they spent thinking about their vote before casting it and the emotions visually displayed in the polling booth. We analyzed these using insights from clinical psychiatry and the kinesics approach to interpreting physical displays of emotions (Birdwhistell, 1970; Fast, 1988), which was originally used by psychiatrists to analyze the emotions of patients unable to verbalize them easily, such as autistic children, and later in anthropology.

Fourth Component: Direct Observation

The fourth component of the research design focuses on accounts of direct observations of Election Day from officials inside the polling stations, supported by additional polling station observation by our team. Direct observations inside polling stations were conducted during the French presidential elections by election officials in seventeen stations across the country, mixing rural, city, and metropolitan predominantly left- and right-wing wards in four different regions. After the partnership was confirmed and we had selected the seventeen polling stations to be included, we sent one official in each of these a short questionnaire that asked him/her to provide an account of Election Day as it happened inside the station throughout the day. This afforded a rare insight into the intimate and usually off-limits environment of the polling station. Observations were made, for example, of people coming in and out, entering the polling station on their own or with others (partner, children, friends, as a larger family or group, and so on), atmosphere, emotions, facial expressions, clothes, questions, discussions, and electoral material such as flyers or ballots. The questionnaire mixes specific and fairly impressionistic questions. An example of a completed questionnaire is reproduced in Appendix 2 (see www.epob.org).

Additionally, our team made extensive observations of polling stations in the US, the UK, and France whilst conducting the on-the-spot interviews. This provided extensive notes on polling station arrangements, how people arrived and left, who were coming and going (families, couples, friends, etc.), the appearance of voters, the questions asked, conversations, and more. These impressionistic micro-portrait observations, whilst not directly analyzed, served as a background used to refine our theoretical model and survey and interview instruments, and made invaluable contributions to the fascinating insights gained into the hearts and minds of voters.

Methodological Trade-Offs

We have described a complex and modular design, which uses multiple components to bring complementary perspectives on electoral behaviour, experience, and resolution. This richness of approaches has a cost. It implies comparative heterogeneity, some contextual diversity, a certain descriptive emphasis when we validate our myriad proposed new concepts, and limits to how much we can control for traditional predictors, given survey limits.

As discussed above, whilst surveys ran in all six countries observed, other empirical elements focused instead on subsets of cases, due to legal, financial, and practical constraints. Polling station observation is restricted across countries, and we could only obtain the required partnership in France. The technical nature of visual experiments meant that we could only conduct these in two countries. The expense involved in a nationwide face-to-face survey, and its incompatibility with the panel element, limited it to Georgia, and some questionnaire items were not allowable there. Despite these variations, we believe that the complex research design is a valuable contribution. First, there are anyway limitations to the types of inference that one can make from non-survey data, and therefore experiments or in-depth interviews do not claim to be 'representative' of national populations. Second, most research components were conducted in at least two countries to avoid wholly idiosyncratic findings. In an ideal world, every aspect of the research design would be conducted throughout, but realistically, we believe that methodological innovation and diversification deserved precedence over a 'lowest common denominator' approach.

We also conducted the visual experiment and in-depth interviews in non-electoral contexts. The visual experiment used mock elections, as no country currently allows the filming of polling booths in real elections, despite the guarantee of anonymization, privacy, and confidentiality our design ensured. The in-depth interviews were held between elections, meanwhile: a simple pragmatic choice for a small team conducting all research directly. However, we combined these components with fieldwork conducted at the heart of the electoral process. On-the-spot interviews ran literally as people left the polling station; the panel study included started about three weeks before Election Day, with further waves on Election Night. Diaries covered the same period, and direct observation was on Election Day. The quasi-experimental panel setting for traditional, advance, and absentee voters, combined with control for original voting intention pre-vote, enables us to compare the impact of remote-voting options in true electoral contexts, offering a unique insight into citizens' electoral psychology.

Let us now consider new concepts and measurement. Our unique approaches to the measurement of personality and memory and our attempts to structure the concepts of electoral identity, atmosphere, and hostility both analytically and operationally may be unusual, but we hope will intrigue readers. They require an element of exploratory (first qualitative, then descriptive) analysis which most research, typically preferring to use standard established measures that have long been validated, has little time for. Researchers will know that descriptive statistics or correlations have their obvious limits, and feel like a crude first take on a new variable, but somehow, giving our field a sense of how those new variables 'behave', how they are distributed across ages, countries, or gender, how they correlate with known variables that constitute our bread-and-butter in the field, whilst requiring caution, is an indispensable step.

We cannot guarantee that the variables we wish to put on the behavioural map will share the successful future of the likes of efficacy, sociotropism, or trust; but all canons of current research have had to start somewhere, and establishing a variable one believes to be meaningful and necessary is rarely a glamorous affair. We fully accept that not everyone will be convinced, but hope that some will espouse the principle and help find even better operationalization strategies in due course. In short, we accept that not everyone will agree with our answers, but hope to ask central questions and stir fundamental discussions.

Additionally, the breadth and depth of our research draws upon an impressionistic portrait of voters' psychology, which cannot always be tested with purely theoretically derived hypotheses. The nature of the exploratory research questions obliges us to leave 'space' for voters to narrate their experience, to describe the atmosphere of elections, to explain the role they inhabit as they vote. We cannot continue to claim to focus on the nature, life, and actions of humans and not put people at the heart of our research strategies, inviting them to feed, refine, or indeed contradict our models, and we believe that both that stage of openness, despite the risk it carries of disorderly findings, and the second step, when we translate them into rigorous quantitative measures that we test, are equally necessary.

Finally, the conceptual richness of the model also limits how many existing variables we can bring in as controls. There is only so much time you can ask a respondent to spend on a survey, and multiplying phrasings corresponding to largely overlapping concepts increases the risks of rationalization and multicollinearity. So we just could not, for instance, both test our suggested role of personality traits and also control for the lengthy 'Big Five' though all major social, demographic, and political controls featured in our multivariate models. Those models are also complex. We chose the US as our flagship test, and we chose to express changes in explained variance by stage, though as noted, this is inherently 'unfair', as the original controls and the first stage (personality) have a much easier task in explaining virgin variance than the last (identity) stage, which can only improve an already well-explained model at the margin. As mentioned, individual coefficients are not stage-based, however, so are equitable across variables.

Ultimately, our research design combines numerous complementary methods, be they quantitative (surveys, experiments) or qualitative (interviews, on-the-spot interviews, diaries, observation), static and dynamic components (panel study survey, observation), foci on the general population or specific groups (e.g., first-time voters). In the next chapter, we start using them to retrace the way citizens experience Election Day and Election Night, and paint an impressionistic picture of that 'day in the life of a voter'.

3

A Day in the Life of a Voter

Election Day

ELECTORAL INTIMACY

One of the clichés most universally and endurably conveyed by political commentators across democracies is that people do not care about politics. There may be a certain paradox in such comments coming from people who are themselves unashamedly interested in the topic, but are frequently persuaded that their fellow citizens differ. Yet, regardless of the political situation of a country, the state of opinion polls, and the level of (dis)satisfaction or (dis)trust in the system, it seems that millions of citizens do consider Election Day to feel a little different from all others.

In this chapter, we explore how Election Day penetrates citizens' daily lives, and thus picture how citizens experience Election Day and Election Night. We dissect the routines, tensions, thoughts, and feelings that they go through. We explore how the atmosphere of an Election builds up, and what citizens actually do and how they do it, from waking up, and their time in the polling booth, to the discovery of the results in the aftermath of the vote.

To draw an impressionistic but accurate portrait, we rely on a mixture of approaches, some of which are unusual. We use closed and open survey questions and in-depth interviews, but also capture the instantaneous thoughts of hundreds of respondents immediately after they had exited the polling station by asking them to explain, in one sentence, what went through their minds when they were in the polling booth. We also asked citizens to keep election diaries every day for a period of three weeks, and complemented self-reported narratives by partnering with election observers in France, asking them to report on what they saw, noted, and heard throughout their day in the polling station, using a questionnaire to assess elements ranging from the proportions of people coming to vote alone, as couples, or with children to what voters wear to vote or asked in the polling station.

Mounting Atmosphere

As discussed above, political science has typically thought of electoral cycles in terms of their institutional logic—the time the election is called, possibly including a primary, the official campaign, the date of the election, and when the results are announced. There is, however, little reason to believe that this is the dynamic that imposes itself on voters in their experience of elections. A country may be 'in the mood' for an election well before it is called—perhaps because of the crisis which will ultimately precipitate an early election, or because some leader will invariably have an incentive to start signalling his/her candidacy or win voters over well before an official campaign starts. An election can therefore invite itself—or indeed invade— the life of the voter at a time when it is neither expected nor desired, just because stakeholders will attempt to circumvent institutional cyclical logics to their own strategic advantage, or because events create windows of opportunity—or risk—which someone will exploit. Equally, an election could be a 'slow starter', the electoral mood only setting in well after the campaign officially starts, in the absence of cathartic debate, discourse, or campaigning. Election polls consistently show that public opinion does not react continuously to campaigning, and instead that campaign effects may 'go crescendo' sometimes late in the pre-electoral period.

When an electoral cycle ends, from voters' perspectives, is likewise variable. Political scientists conventionally use Election Day as an end point in the process, but that convenient approximation does not fool anyone. Election Night and the direct aftermath of a vote are clearly an integral sequence in virtually any democratic election. History makes it obvious that the mood of the election may sometimes linger much longer than that—for days, weeks, or even months after a vote ends and its result is known. Anecdotally, the prolongation of the electoral mood after a vote may depend on its result (whether the resulting system is 'governable' or not), procedural controversies (such as fraud claims), and the reactions of politicians, journalists, or citizens themselves. We suggest that elections have a potential for democratic *closure* which may or may not be achieved, depending on institutional, political, and human circumstances.

Augmented Reality

Attempting to capture the reality of the campaign period and the crucial twenty-four hours of Election Day in the life of citizens emphasizes the distortion associated with any given method of depiction. Citizens asked about the election period in a survey or interview may rationalize their narrative according to what they know to be the conclusion of the 'story'. As time goes on, only the 'important' aspects of the voter's electoral experience—or worse, those that they feel may be considered important by researchers—may persist. Inconsistent feelings or experiences may be redacted in one's memory (see chapter 5), and their recollection contaminated by response bias and agreeableness (Furnham, 1986). Focusing on feelings and experiences at specific points in time—the polling booth experience, when results are revealed, or even Election Day in general—can become confusing as time elapses, especially where multiple potentially intensive moments succeed each other, creating a risk of mental harmonization and confusion. Very intense but varying emotions may overwhelm a voter successively as he/she goes to vote in the late afternoon, returns home, gets ready for Election Night, discovers first estimations of the outcome, and then a different, corrected result, before witnessing the reactions of family and friends. Mere hours later, the sequence may become confused or uncertain in the voter's mind.

We partly address this problem by using two strategies: time disaggregation through election diaries, and immediacy through on-the-spot interviews of voters exiting the polling station. The diaries enable individuals to log their experience of the election every day, thereby being less likely to be selective in what they report' or to rationalize experiences that may be inconsistent across time. Of course, keeping a diary will undoubtedly prime a voter to be unnaturally attentive to the election. We circumvent this issue to an extent by asking questions relating not to the voter him/herself but to his/her family and friends, as displacement is less subject to response bias. The answers can thus be used to control for the possible artificial oversensitization that could directly emanate from diary-keeping. Furthermore, to avoid relying solely on voters' own narratives, with their dramatic potential, we use external observation in partnership with election officials (and, as discussed later in the book, our visual experiment). These observation strategies help us to triangulate visions of electoral experience, using methods whereby voters' demeanour and behaviour are captured independently of their own perceptions.

A Special Day

In chapter 1, we noted the fact that 20–30% of voters typically either make up or change their minds during the week of an election, half of them on Election Day itself. Even though aggregate effects tend to 'hide' this movement, because voters changing their minds in different directions largely cancel each other out, it suggests that there is something about the atmosphere of the day when people vote which is prone to triggering specific emotions and memories and 'switching on' electoral identity. In fact, for less salient votes, the effect may be even more marked: Bruter and Harrison (2017) showed that in the 2012 Irish referendum on children's rights, 80% of voters had made up or changed their minds in the last week, which underlines the need to understand the mood and the sequence of Election Day—the focus of this chapter. In this section, we explore how Election Day is anticipated, how it unfolds, and whether citizens develop repetitive routines or habits they reproduce for every election.

We should remember that Election Day can, technically, entail different things. For many, it is the day when both they and the country as a whole will vote, thereby fusing individual and societal agendas. However, temporally remote voters (see chapter 8) will already have voted when the rest of the country goes to the polls, and, for non-voters, Election Day may be the day which epitomizes the divergence between their political situation and that of most other citizens.

At the Polling Station

Polling station queues may be the greatest worry of Election Management Bodies worldwide. Organizers assume that queueing will put voters off and generate dissatisfaction and distrust. Yet, the evidence we gathered suggests that queues of reasonable length inspire pride rather than complaint. Like those at major concerts or sports games, queues at the polling station demonstrate that it is 'the place to be', and that voters are participating in a meaningful and enthusing collective event. Excessive queueing generates complaints, but moderate queues are subconsciously perceived as a symptom of shared experience rather than as wasting time.

Curiously, there is arguably no such thing as a polling station. Unlike schools, supermarkets, churches, or city halls, no piece of architecture is ever designed with the function of being a polling station in mind. Instead, buildings used for a whole variety of purposes (schools or public buildings in France and Georgia; churches, supermarkets, garages, or even caravans and laundromats in the US and the UK) temporarily become hosts to polling stations once every few years. Yet, in the eyes of citizens, polling stations are often the primary location of democracy, and where they interact with their political system. Thus, despite assuming its civic function for mere hours, the polling station has an unquestionable reality throughout Election Day and indeed throughout citizens' electoral experience(s), election after election. Polling stations are 'electoral Cinderellas', whose political princessdom is no less real for ending at midnight (or rather 6, 8, or 10 pm), once every few years.

The Cinderella dress of polling stations also varies significantly across and within countries. France uses Sunday voting, whilst the UK and the US use weekdays. This means that the French are more likely to be *en famille* on Election Day and to adapt their electoral experience accordingly, whilst in the US or the UK, people often go to vote on their way to or from work. Polling stations also vary. In France, all are located within public buildings (schools, city halls, fire stations, community halls), though urban and rural environments differ. For the US, locations are far more heterogeneous, and the impact of school and church voting has been widely studied. One polling station we observed was a large downtown public library where people often went during their lunchbreak. Another was located in a lifeguard hut on a beach, ideal for visits as part of a leisurely walk. Other settings we observed included private garages, a home gym, a women's association headquarters, and many schools, some of which organized parent–teacher meetings on the day. In the UK, the polling stations we observed varied immensely in both location and style, ranging from city-centre schools and public libraries to pubs, a laundromat, and a portacabin at a train station, which was often visited in the early morning or late evening as an extension of voters' commuting journey. Another was housed in a bowling-green clubhouse, attracting more voters with their children and elderly relatives on a late afternoon walk. In fact, polling station locations even seem to have an impact on how people dress, and how special or indeed solemn the occasion seems to feel, as do the day and season of a vote.

It is impossible to understand the day of a voter without understanding what happens inside a polling station, and unrealistic to ignore the variety of settings we have just illustrated. Our direct observation protocol in partnership with French election observers from seventeen polling stations across the country aims to sketch that necessary impressionistic portrait. In France, observers nominated by political parties sit throughout the day in each polling station across the country, to ensure the transparency of electoral operations and help with routine operations. These officials agreed to observe voters coming to the polling station all day and to complete on our behalf a questionnaire which systematically assessed how, with whom, and when people come to vote, what they say, and how they interact with polling station personnel, and endeavoured to gain an impressionistic sense of the emotions that they betray, according to observers. The stations were selected in four regions, and included urban, suburban, and rural settings. We triangulated our findings by conducting direct observation of polling stations the UK and US, although these results are not reported here.

How Do People Come to Vote?

As already noted, how people go to vote is constrained by the systemic choice of a voting day, as well as by the location of polling stations themselves. Nonetheless, in terms of experience, going to vote alone has a very different symbolic meaning from going as a family, bringing children along, or making it a collective social outing with friends or neighbours. We thus asked what proportion of voters went to vote alone, or with different categories of others. The results are reported in figure 3.1 and in appendix 3.[1] In France, only a minority of voters goes to vote alone—43.8% on average across the polling stations observed. A majority uses the polling station visit as a family or social outing, coming to vote with a partner (32.1%), children (17.1%), and older relatives (16.8%). Voting is therefore first and foremost a family affair and an opportunity to socialize French children into electoral experience. Additionally, 6.2% of voters visited the polling station with friends or neighbours,[2] making the occasion a broader social outing.

---

1. Appendices referred to in this chapter are to be found online at www.epob.org.

2. It can be extremely difficult for observers to decide how to interpret whether the people accompanying a given voter are family members or friends/neighbours. Whilst some asked openly, others reported difficulty in ascribing people arriving to vote together who were clearly not spouses or children. Moreover, observers were inside polling stations, so there is a risk that some people who went to vote separately but saw each other outside were seen as entering the polling station together, even though that was not their initial intention. Conversely, people

How do people go to vote (France, observed %)

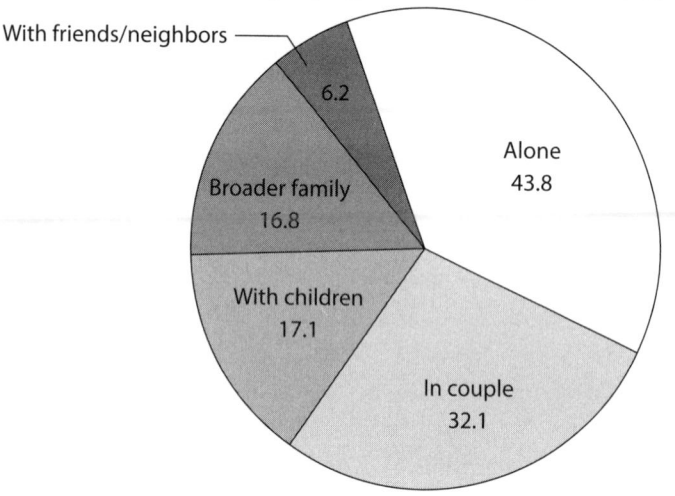

- With friends/neighbors: 6.2
- Broader family: 16.8
- With children: 17.1
- In couple: 32.1
- Alone: 43.8

Note: Totals exceed 100% as voters could come accompanied by more than one type of friend or relative

FIGURE 3.1: With whom people go to vote

When Do People Go to Vote?

Polling station opening times also vary considerably. Weekday-voting countries typically offer longer voting hours (07.00–22.00 in the UK and Ireland, 7.30–22.30 in Hong Kong, typically 08.00–20.00 in the US) compared to those which use Sunday voting. Countries with compulsory voting often limit voting hours more strictly (08.00–14.00 in Luxembourg and 08.00–16.00 in Belgium and Colombia. In France, voting hours vary by election type and size of municipality (usually 08.00–18.00 for secondary elections and all elections in rural areas, and 08.00–20.00 for first-order elections in large cities). The shortest opening hours are in Indonesia (07.00–13.00), Nigeria (08.00–14.00), and Luxembourg, and the longest in Israel (07.00–23.00).

With those differences in mind, the times of voting reported by polling station observers are reported in figure 3.2. Voting is largely concentrated around morning and lunchtime, accounting for 35.5% and 25.9% of voters respectively, according to the observers. Afternoon and evenings only at-

---

coming to the polling station together may have been identified as voting separately because one may have dropped relatives before parking a car.

When do people go to vote (France, observed %)

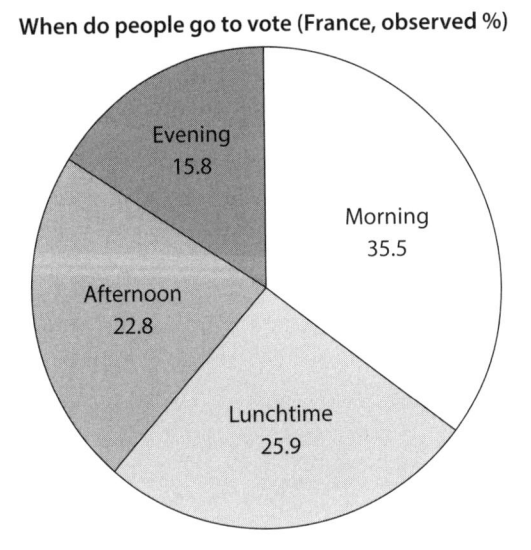

- Morning 35.5
- Lunchtime 25.9
- Afternoon 22.8
- Evening 15.8

FIGURE 3.2: When people go to vote

tracted 22.8% and 15.8% of observed voters respectively. These distributions are also affected by season and weather. By contrast, in the US and the UK, with weekday voting, mornings and particularly evenings are more significant voting times, and afternoons less busy. In both countries, the longest queues are observed in the last hour of the vote, and include people taking advantage of the fact that those joining the queue by the closing hour are allowed to vote; such late queues do not occur in France.

The time spent voting varies significantly across systems. In chapter 8, we show that the choice of electronic or paper, or single or poly-paper ballots can cause thinking time to vary by a factor of three (twenty to sixty seconds, in terms of the specific choice we selected in our experimental design). However, these effects compound substantive ones deriving from the number and complexity of votes. Typically, in the UK, South Africa, Georgia, and France, an election corresponds to one choice. In Germany, a number of votes are typically organized simultaneously. In the US, however, ballots typically involve dozens of individual votes that a citizens has to cast at a given time. As a result, whilst the presence of citizens in the polling booth lasts seconds or up to a couple of minutes in most countries, the time we observed a voter to spend in the polling booth in the US typically ranges from three to four minutes for the fastest voters to well over half an hour for many, with a median of approximately fifteen minutes in the case of California.

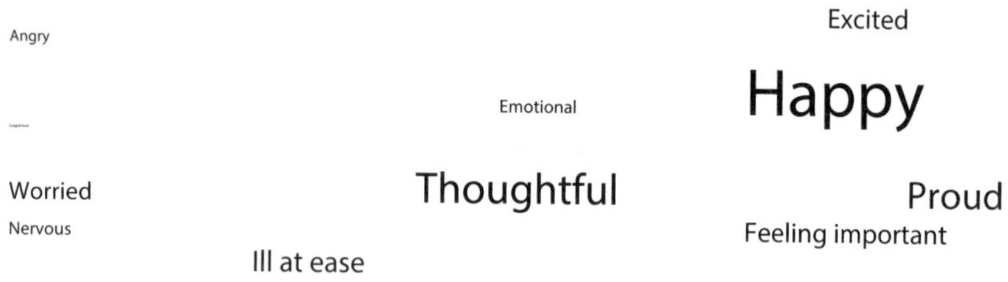

Angry   Excited

                          Emotional   **Happy**

Worried   **Thoughtful**   Proud
Nervous   Feeling important
                     Ill at ease

Note: the font size is directly proportional to frequency of mentions

FIGURE 3.3: How people appear when they vote

An Emotional Moment

We also asked polling station observers to describe the emotions and demeanour of voters they faced throughout the day. Unlike our rigid kinesics protocol (see chapter 7), these results are informal observers' perceptions, but are telling nevertheless (figure 3.3). Overall, voting predominantly appears a fairly cheerful affair. 'Happy' is the emotion polling station observers noted most frequently by far (29.3% of the total). This was followed by people who appeared 'thoughtful' (18.5%), 'proud' (17.4%), and, more negatively, 'ill at ease' (13.1%), followed by excited (12%), 'feeling important' (11.5%), and 'worried' (11.2%).

Voters' conversations inside the polling station, meanwhile, both between themselves and with polling station staff are also telling. Figure 3.4 and results in appendix 3 highlight that over half of voters engage in conversation in the polling station (48.5% do not). Approaching one-third (29.1%) talk to people with whom they arrived in the polling station, 22.9% with polling station personnel, and 12.9% with other voters who did not accompany them into the polling station but were met there instead. Additionally, many voters interact with polling station personnel: mostly (59.9%) to greet them politely, but 23.6% to ask questions about the voting process, including about the polling station, the booths, the ballot paper, and the voting procedures. Finally, 18% asked questions which were unrelated to the voting process and regulations themselves—for instance about turnout so far, the atmosphere of the polling station, or about the polling station observers themselves—including whether they had been provided with any food!

Overall, the emotional and conversational atmosphere noted by the observers is typically one of positivity and friendly demeanour, whereby voters

Polling station talk (France, observed %)

- Silent: 48.5
- Talked to other voters met at the station: 12.9
- Talked to polling station staff: 23.0
- Talked to people who came to vote with them: 29.1

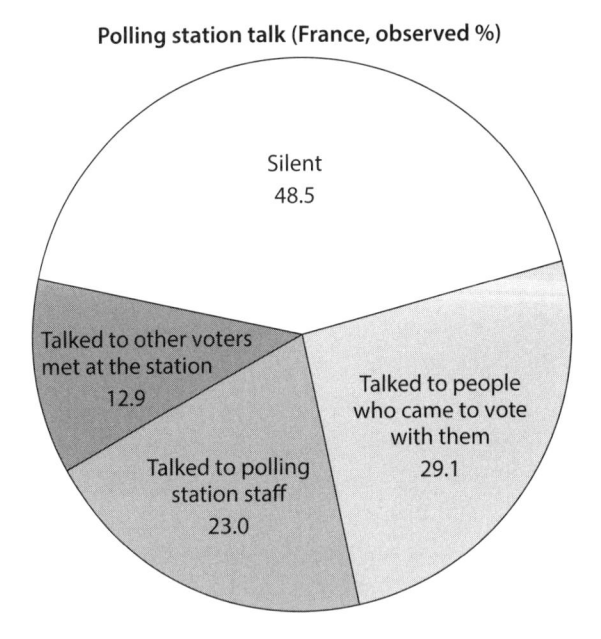

FIGURE 3.4: Talking at the polling station

implicitly express a sense of shared experience and sympathy with both fellow voters and polling station personnel, as well as openness and curiosity throughout their polling station experience.

What Do People Think About When They Are in the Polling Booth?

The climax of a polling station voting experience is undoubtedly the moment when citizens are in the polling booth, ready to cast their vote. With the increasing use of geographically remote voting, an ever-growing proportion of citizens do not experience this moment and, instead, the moment they cast their vote from home or other non-traditional electoral location is the more diffuse climax of their electoral experience. Voting in a polling station or using geographically remote voting specifically affects the locus and time of the vote. Combined, they wholly alter the voter's experience. For polling station voters, the place and time they cast their vote is well delineated by the polling booth visit. The actual 'vote' of a citizen is but an instant, and represents what happens during that crucial time point when a voter is alone with his/her conscience and choices. However, for geographically remote voters who cast their vote from home, both the geographical and temporal location of the vote may be impressionistic and diffuse. The voter may well consolidate a decision over time and space without the clear symbolic limit of a polling booth curtain to crystallize his/her vote.

The moment of casting one's vote is possibly the most intimate in the political life of a citizen, and the ultimate taboo of electoral behaviour, protected by a shroud of mystery and intimacy relating to the secrecy of the vote. As noted above, the time spent in a polling booth by individuals varies significantly, for both systemic and individual reasons. Often, it this is the moment when electoral choice is either made, changed, or ultimately confirmed and implemented. However, it is also the one locus where voters are protected by an absolute right to secrecy and privacy, making it extremely difficult to validate and test any theory regarding how people feel at that specific point in time, what (or who) they think about, or even whether they basically merely rubber stamp electoral decisions that they have already made or actually decide, at least in some cases, how to vote there and then and under what circumstances.

As political scientists, we understand the need to capture this moment, yet typically we are left either assuming some temporal continuity based on what we knew to be true before voters enter that democratic equivalent of a confessional, or recreating the reality of the polling booth experience retrospectively by interviewing voters after the vote. Despite the limits of self-reporting noted earlier, focusing on what happens when citizens are in the polling booth—getting as close as possible to this crucial moment without relying on earlier expectation or later reconstruction and rationalization—is critical. In the next section, we thus look at spontaneous answers regarding what people thought about in the polling booth (or at the time they cast their vote remotely), and at their answers to the survey closed question on the same.

One Vote, One Thought

POSITIVITY IN THE BOOTH

'In one sentence, could you please tell us what went through your mind when you were in the polling booth casting your vote?' We asked this question in hundreds of on-the-spot interviews in the US, the UK, and France, and in our survey of representative samples across countries, with a comparable alternative phrasing for geographically remote voters. Before ex-

TABLE 3.1. Main Polling Booth Thought in One Sentence—Spontaneous Themes

	USA	France	SA	UK	EU ref.	EU ref. Remain	EU ref. Leave
Accountability	4.8	7.2	5.6	3.0	0	0	0
Alienation	5.7	5.2	0.9	3.8	12.5	2.6	18.8
Anger/frustration	4.6	7.4	4.1	5.7	6.1	3.3	10.2
Despair/fatalism	5.9	8.9	6.9	8.2	0.8	0.5	0.9
Doubt/confused	4.8	6.5	11.4	13.3	6.5	6.0	6.4
Excited/curious	4.1	3.4	4.4	4.0	2.6	1.5	3.6
Fed up	4.4	0.7	0.7	6.2	1.6	0.8	0.5
Happy	11.4	7.8	6.3	5.9	3.0	3.6	2.3
Hatred/disgust	2.6	3.2	0.1	0.4	5.5	1.5	9.3
Hope	23.6	24.5	17.9	17.1	20.2	20.7	19.7
Nostalgia/atmosphere	1.2	1.1	1.4	1.3	2.0	1.6	2.6
Power	10.3	3.0	11.3	5.0	5.0	2.4	7.8
Prayer	5.0	0.4	2.3	1.5	1.3	1.6	0.7
Proud	4.8	1.8	2.1	1.5	1.2	1.1	1.1
Reassured	0.7	0.1	0.4	0	0.4	0.5	0.2
Responsibility	10.6	25.7	10.3	7.9	17.6	25.7	9.7
Resolution	6.0	4.3	2.9	2.0	11.0	17.5	4.3
Worry/nervous	13.4	10.8	11	15.8	15.8	16.6	14.8

Note: Entries are percentages of total respondents.

ploring the narrative details of the answers, we present trends from the survey open question. Results in appendix 3 map the thoughts expressed by voters using two different dimensions: valence (positive, neutral, or negative), and reference (personal, systemic reference, societal reference, or empathic displacement), and constitute a range of the thoughts, emotions, and feelings most frequently referred to by voters about the time they cast their vote.

We code most frequent thoughts in table 3.1. A clear trend emerges of the types of response provided. The first striking finding, however, relates to the answers that are *not* forthcoming. Notable by their absence are references to issues. Similarly, very few voters claim to think of candidates whilst in the polling booth, and if they ever mention thinking of the campaign and campaign promises, it is usually in generic terms and disparagingly. In contrast to well-known disillusion towards politics, the valence of the polling booth thoughts is overwhelmingly positive or neutral (figure 3.5). Negative thoughts only account for 8.1% (EU referendum) to 17.9% (South Africa), followed by 15.3% (the US) of respondents' spontaneous answers. Positive references account for 49% (South Africa) to 68.6% (France).

a. **Valence of spontaneous polling booth thoughts**

	S. Africa	UK	EU ref. leave	USA	EU ref.	EU ref. remain	France
Positive	49.0	50.5	53.0	54.8	57.9	62.8	68.6
Neutral	33.7	37.6	38.1	29.9	34.0	30.0	20.6
Negative	17.3	11.9	8.9	15.3	8.1	7.2	10.8

b. **Empathic displacement in spontaneous polling booth thoughts**

EU ref. leave	France	UK	USA	EU ref.	S. Africa	EU ref. remain
10.3	11.2	11.7	15.2	19.3	20.3	28.2

c. **Family projection in spontaneous polling booth thoughts**

France	USA	EU ref. leave	UK	S. Africa	EU ref.	EU ref. remain
2.0	2.3	2.5	2.7	3.3	4.9	7.2

d. **Change reference in spontaneous polling booth thoughts**

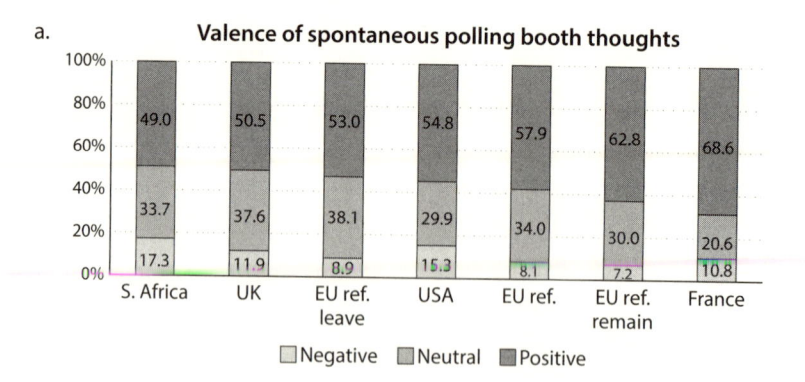

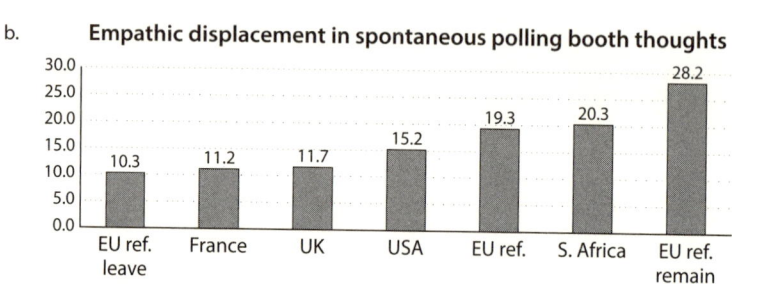

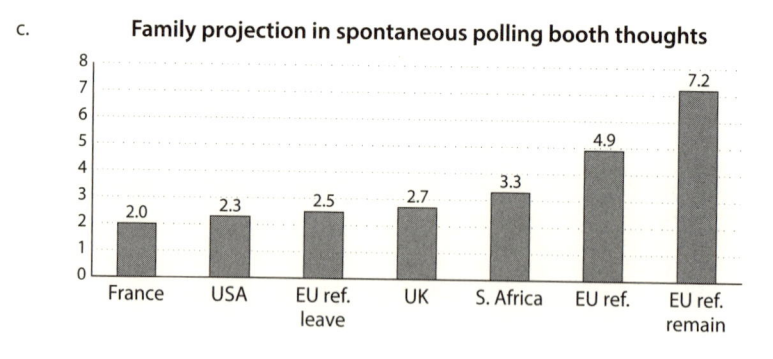

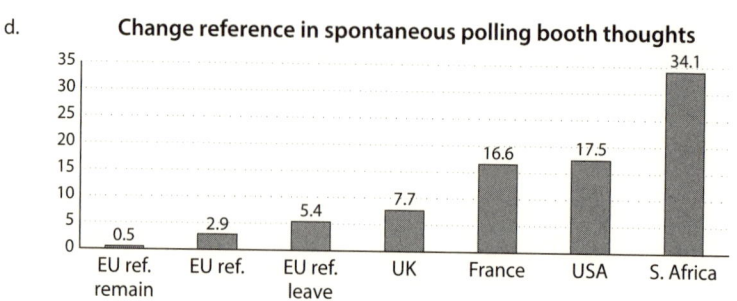

EU ref. remain	EU ref.	EU ref. leave	UK	France	USA	S. Africa
0.5	2.9	5.4	7.7	16.6	17.5	34.1

FIGURE 3.5: Scales of spontaneous one sentence polling booth thoughts

A DAY IN THE LIFE OF A VOTER 79

e. **Doubt references in spontaneous polling booth thoughts**

EU ref. leave	EU ref.	EU ref. remain	USA	France	UK	S. Africa
13.7	13.7	13.8	17.7	23.0	25.7	31.8

f. **Ergonomics references in spontaneous polling booth thoughts**

France	EU ref. leave	EU ref.	EU ref. remain	S. Africa	USA	UK
4.9	9.9	10.0	10.1	11.2	20.8	22.5

g. **Hope and hopelessness—spontaneous polling booth thoughts**

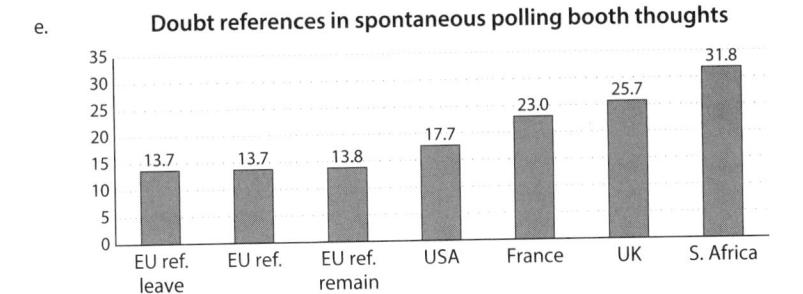

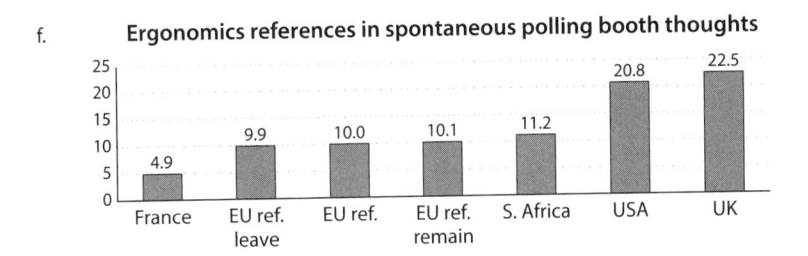

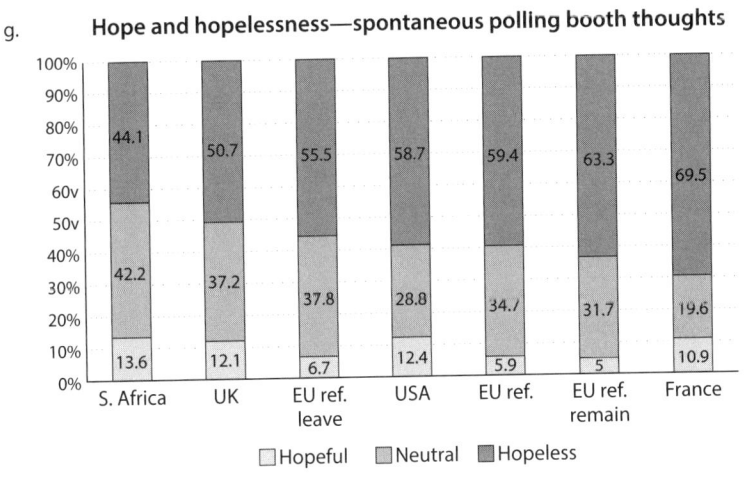

	S. Africa	UK	EU ref. leave	USA	EU ref.	EU ref. remain	France
Hopeless	44.1	50.7	55.5	58.7	59.4	63.3	69.5
Neutral	42.2	37.2	37.8	28.8	34.7	31.7	19.6
Hopeful	13.6	12.1	6.7	12.4	5.9	5	10.9

☐ Hopeful ■ Neutral ■ Hopeless

FIGURE 3.5: (*continued*)

HOPE AND PRAYER

In terms of references, we first coded answers on a scale from 'hopelessness' to 'hope'. Interestingly, the UK's EU-membership referendum had the lowest proportion of 'hopeless' answers (5.9%), and South Africa the highest (13.6%), followed by the US (12.4%) and UK general elections (12.1%). By contrast, 'hopeful' answers represented 69.5% of the total in France and 59.4% in the EU-membership referendum, but only 44.1% of responses in

South Africa. Qualitatively, hope is the positive feeling spontaneously evoked by the greatest proportion of respondents—24.5% in France, 23.6% in the US, 20.2% in the EU-membership referendum, 17.9% in South Africa, and 17.1% in British general elections. In some cases, hope is related to specific outcomes:[3]

> I closed my eyes and made a wish that the election would turn out as I wanted. FR482[4]

> I hope that 'remain' wins—I am European as well as a Briton. EU2126

> I hope that my vote will help Mitt Romney get elected. US1337

Elsewhere, it pertains to broader political directions, or a positive effect of the election on the country and society, such as ideological change or a pacification of society:

> I hope that our country sees this as a mandate to follow traditional American thinking. US1338

> How much I was hoping that this would lead to some political change for France. FR342

> Hope—that we can get past our history and get rid of our complacency. SA765

> Hoping others were as optimistic as me. UK1543

Alongside hope, many respondents refer to prayer and religion in their polling booth thoughts. Whilst references to religion are minimal in very secular France (0.4% of total answers), they occur frequently in the US (5%) and to a lesser extent in South Africa (2.3%). Religious references are often to God or prayer in general.

> Prayer—I just pray to God. US4ZF038

> Please God please God. US6ZF018

> A silent prayer. SA477

> I prayed and asked God for guidance. SA1

> That the hand of God protect this country. US1865

---

3. As noted in chapter 2, we have chosen to report all quotes as verbatim, except for the correction of obvious spelling mistakes where using written material.

4. Respondent numbers are coded differently for interviewees, diaries, and references to open-ended responses from the surveys. See appendix 2.

Sometimes, they are more specific, and God is asked for a particular outcome.

> Please God let this election be fair. SA369

> Hoping and praying my candidate would win and we'd get our country back. US1193

> God, help us make Hollande win! FR997

> God help us if the result is to leave. EU1945

> I was praying that we would continue to belong to our great European Union of nations. EU2255

> I was praying we would be exiting EU. EU2256

Finally, there are a few obscure references to heaven and hell, as in this rather gloomy US example:

> That the individual's vote no longer counts and our country is going straight to hell. US1866

There are, however, besides hope, other positive feelings and emotions associated by voters with their polling booth thoughts. Note that proportions are out the total respondents' answers and thus driven down by the many respondents not expressing emotional thoughts.

HAPPINESS

In chapter 7, we will see that most citizens say that they feel happy when they vote. This is confirmed by the thoughts they report from the polling booth. Answers connoting happiness represent 3% of the total in the EU-membership referendum (though much higher amongst Remain voters than Leave voters), and up to 11.4% in the US. Qualitatively, expressions of happiness, relaxation, and well-being include the following:

> I'm happy to be here. US1619

> I was very happy happy! [sic] SA689

> When I am in this polling booth I feel relaxed. FR658

> It feels good! FR783

> I have great pleasure sliding the ballot inside the envelope [. . .] FR675

I enjoy voting. US1252

I was euphoric and actually certain of changes to come! FR1184

I was simply delighted to vote. FR1195

Happiness is also expressed in references to other occasions, such as the best day of one's life or a particular vote such as one's first vote.

I was thinking, this is the best day of my life! US1579

It was as if I voted for the first time. SA318

Finally, happiness is also expressed in terms of it being a privilege to vote, either in general or in reference to other countries or generations who do not or did not enjoy the same rights:

I'm just glad to be an American and that we get a change at the banquet of life. US4ZF023

This is such a privilege as a woman, being able to cast a vote. There are thousands of woman in this world that does not have the privilege of expressing an opinion. SA492

EXCITEMENT

A little different from references to happiness and emotionality are those to excitement. Quantitatively, these represent between 2.6% (EU-membership referendum) and 4.4% (South Africa) of open-ended answers. Again, in the case of the EU referendum, there was a strong difference between Remain (1.6% only) and Leave (3.6%) voters (though the balance is reversed compared to references to happiness). Elections represent momentum for many citizens, increased tension and emotionality which electrify their experience. Indications of this were already present in many 'happiness' references ('euphoric', 'happy happy', etc.), but it is also framed as 'pure' excitement by many:

I was pretty excited! SA593

I was excited to make my mark. SA1005

In some cases, citizens trade the 'excitement' frame for that of 'emotionality', which is just as strong, but focuses on depth of feeling rather than its mobilizing effects:

This was a very emotional moment. FR1067

I felt a great moment of emotion. FR653

So emotional! FR974

Finally, in some other cases, excitement is expressed as optimism in the booth:

Optimistic! SA1004

POWER AND PRIDE

The next two interrelated feelings expressed in many respondents' thoughts are pride and a sense of power. Pride is not as frequent as one might expect—varying from 1.2% of answers in the referendum on EU membership to 2.1% in South Africa, except for 4.8% in the US. By contrast, many express power and efficacy in their polling booth thoughts—from 3% in France and 5% in the UK (both in the general election and the 2016 EU referendum) to 10.3% in the US and 11.3% in South Africa. Once again, in the context of the EU referendum, the sense of power more than triples between Remain voters (2.4%) and Leave voters (7.8%). A first set of pride references relates to the act of voting per se:

Pride! I just feel proud. US7ZM027

I felt extremely proud. SA609

I was proud to cast my vote. SA50

Being seventy-eight years old, I have always voted, today I still choose liberty for France. FR736

I felt that I contributed to the future of France. FR677

In other cases, pride relates to the specific vote the citizen cast:

I felt proud to cast my vote that can make a difference. SA273

I hope my vote helps. UK1319

Proud and sure who I wanted to vote for. UK1849

Interestingly, pride is sometimes framed as defiance towards a hypothetical shame associated with a voter's choice, or a switch from pride to shame when it comes to the voter's electoral decision, as illustrated by, respectively, French and British quotes below:

> Why should I hide? FR1660

> At the time I felt proud, now ashamed. EU1777

Sometimes, pride is framed in regard to nation or society rather than the individual, be it because of the democratic character it confirms, or national pride and patriotism:

> Proud to live in a democracy. UK39

> I felt proud to be a South African walking out of that booth. SA34.

> I felt proudly South African. SA868

In the two cases below, a variation on the same consists of voters expressing pride in being part of the democratic process, emphasizing empathic displacement, which we discuss later.

> Feeling proud to be part of something bigger than myself. UK1474

> I was proud to be part of a democratic process. SA274

References to power are a little different. Initially, they typically reveal a sense of external efficacy and importance:

> In my hands, I have the power to change things. FR700

> I felt empowered. US1261

> I felt like my decision mattered and made a difference. UK545

> With this ballot I can make a difference, however small it may be. SA14

> Every vote counts. EU1868

> Every vote counts, I want mine to make a difference US1074

In some cases, this sense of empowerment is merged with excitement or happiness:

> I was excited to cast my vote as I knew it will make a difference. SA23

> It is exciting to be important enough that my vote can make a difference. SA542

I was excited, knowing my vote would make a difference in such a close race. US1486

It is awesome to live in a country where every vote counts. SA19

It would be so wonderful if a presidential election could change everything. FR722

Frequently, however, power is associated with pride in potentially making a difference in one's country's—or even the world's—future, sometimes in very metaphorical ways:

The future of my country depends on the vote that I will cast on this day. SA281

Make my mark for posterity. UK873

This action is why I love to live in the USA. US1989

I can't believe I have the right to vote and elect who I want to represent our country. US1245

The moment of truth had come—would my vote be the one that made sure Obama got elected? US1880

To give me the right to vote gives me the sense that I can change the future and make it a little better. FR827

A very solemn moment and the feeling my vote could change everything. FR1970

That this was probably the most important matter on which I would ever vote. EU2794

The fate of the world would be decided that day . . . US1876

This pencil is blunt. EU2887

Finally, in some cases, citizens' sense of power relates to a sense of accountability and of becoming noticeable by the powerful, the thought that this is their one chance to be heard by politicians they largely consider unreceptive to their needs and frustration:

My opportunity for someone to listen to me. SA272

To be able to give my verdict on the five years that have elapsed. FR1713

A sense of history. [multiple]

Given such references to pride, power, and efficacy, notably those with national connotations, it is perhaps unsurprising that many citizens express historical or 'nostalgic' ideas in the polling booth. Quantitatively, these references only account for only from 1.1% (France) to 2% of total open-ended answers in the UK EU-membership referendum (and even 2.6% amongst Leave voters). However, they are striking references. They first pertain to a sense of historic occasion:

> This is to be one of the most momentous days in UK history. UK994

> Being part of a momentous, historical event in which I was hoping to regain sovereignty for my country. EU1781

In some cases, the historical importance is experiential and relates to the voter's life specifically:

> That this is one of the most important moments of my lifetime. UK1946

> There are only so many presidential elections you can vote in during your life, so I was determined to make it happen and make it count. US1893

> About time after forty years of waiting. EU1752

In further cases, respondents refer to historicity with regard to respecting the heritage of historical leaders or their fight for democracy. This is particularly salient in South Africa, where references to Madiba (Nelson Mandela) are very common, as are memories of apartheid. In France and the US, references to the heritage of the French Revolution and to the Forefathers are frequent:

> That I fight for the freedom that Mandela fought for! SA705

> I deserved to vote since many people died for us to have this opportunity, Mandela went to prison for this, it was a way of appreciating what they had done for us. SA617

> My forefathers sacrificed for our right to vote, so we have to vote in honour of them. SA963

> To think that there was a time when I was not allowed that privilege. SA30

> My vote matters and people fought very hard to make sure I'm able to do this so I feel that it is my duty and I'm honored to do it. US1710

This is America—people have died to allow us this privilege—everyone needs to let their voice be heard. US1908

It took a Revolution to get that right to vote, and now some morons would like to deprive us of it! FR983

As in every election, I think of those who fought for us to have the right to vote. FR759

People fought for me to enjoy the right to vote. I have to be here, and I have to play my part in changing things. FR803.

Some female respondents made gender references, connecting their vote to generations of women who fought for equal electoral access and the fair representation of women in elections.

A sense of history linking me with generations of women voters and the hard won right to vote. UK1384

Women who were prevented from voting for so many years. UK2013

In some cases, it is the substance of the vote which is seen as historical, rather than the right to vote, with history—be it national or personal—said to impose a given choice upon voters, for positive or negative reasons.

I hoped that the past will not be repeated. SA275

To cast a vote to put America back to what its founders had hoped for, all are equal. US1927

Solidarity with my comrades all over Europe and my grandfather's sacrifice during World War 2. EU2696

All the benefits the EU has provided the UK. EU1753

Doing the right and sensible thing rather than pretending we have an empire and are superior. EU1848

I felt that I wanted to return to the France of my childhood, the France of my parents and grandparents. FR1096

Finally, in some rare cases, voters invoked history to suggest that elections are precisely *not* the right way to settle a major political question, notably EU membership:

This is not how such a monumental question should be decided. EU2882

SENSE OF DUTY AND RESPONSIBILITY

There is an obvious link from history to one's duty as a citizen and responsibility in the election. Quantitatively, references to a sense of responsibility in the polling booth are amongst the most frequent positive references, accounting for only 7.9% of total references in the UK general election, but 25.7% in France. In the context of the EU referendum, the overall figure of 17.6% of total references hides a great schism between a low focus on responsibility amongst Leave voters (9.7%) but a very high one among Remainers (25.7%). Below, we illustrate how citizens envisage their duty and responsibility inside the polling booth. A first set of thoughts refers to the duty to vote and citizens' function in a democracy:

> Doing my citizen's duty. US3ZF051
>
> I thought about being proud about doing my civic duty. US3ZF064
>
> I am merely doing my civic duty as a citizen. FR329
>
> Sense of doing my duty. UK1129
>
> Performing the most important duty of a citizen of the USA. US1772
>
> I felt a sense of duty fulfilled as I tried to cast an intelligent vote. US1257

In other cases, citizens go further, to the extent of feeling entrusted with a democratic electoral mission:

> In a way, I felt entrusted with a mission. FR1741
>
> I've gotta do this, for the sake of America. US1627
>
> In my constituency this vote doesn't matter, but the gesture and act of voting is very important. UK11
>
> I felt like I was a needed part of my country and was feeling very wanted and proud to vote. SA51
>
> I felt responsible. FR1258
> Sometimes, responsibility is expressed under openly 'referee' frames:
>
> Who is the best? UK1072
>
> Who is most competent to continue this country's recovery and stability? UK1212

> Performing a civic duty based on personal beliefs and thorough research of the candidates and issues. Non-partisan obligation to choose who can best lead and serve our country. US1801.

Finally, some respondents see voting as a privilege or a prerequisite to being allowed to complain about democratic outcomes:

> This is a privilege. US1904

> That I was part of something bigger and privileged to have my say. UK1906

> I am only allowed to complain if I vote. SA570

Many voters thus think of their duty and responsibility as voters, often with positively connoted thoughts: it is part of the process through which elections connect us to our political system and to others around us. But one particular aspect of positive projection deserves its own category: thoughts of projected efficacy.

PROJECTED EFFICACY

We defined projected efficacy as the feeling that even if our individual vote may not matter much on its own, if like-minded citizens mobilize, the combined effect will be significant. This form of efficacy is spontaneously mentioned by many voters as a key polling booth thought. Two metaphorical formulations seem particularly noteworthy. One respondent compared voters to the 'hummingbird of the African tale', and one effectively reconceives projected efficacy as marginality, seeing his/her ballot as 'the last digit' of a much larger number:

> I felt like the hummingbird of the African tale. I do my bit hoping that so will the others. FR726.

> My vote will be registered as the last digit in the final figure. EU2443

Others see their vote as a matter of collective power, through adding it to that of other like-minded voters:

> That a single vote may not make a difference, but if everybody exercised their right to vote, collectively we could make a difference. SA574

> In the booth you are just hoping everyone else sees it the way you do. US2ZF048

That my ballot join millions of others who also want change. FR818

The hope that many others are currently doing the same as me. FR838

I hoped my vote would add to the millions who thought the same way as I did. EU2153

Let's hope many of us are making the same choice. FR1488

Together we'll succeed. FR857

SOCIOTROPISM

Arguably, the flip side of one's feeling of responsibility towards others is our sense of sociotropism. This frequently sits at the heart of citizens' thoughts inside the polling booth. Many citizens openly express a desire to do what is best for their country:

I hope I'm doing the right thing for America and the world, not just for me, but for humanity. US4ZM060

I felt a responsibility on my shoulders, think again of who would be best as I have to ensure to make the choice that will improve things for France. FR623

I want my vote to help to support the country. UK842

Will this actually help this country? SA852

I am an American about to express my opinion and attitude toward candidates I believe will best serve my nation, not necessarily me. US1213

In some cases, respondents' thoughts pertain to specific social categories that may be affected by the vote, notably young generations and vulnerable or exposed groups:

Protecting the younger generation. EU2632

The single farm payment from Brussels that farmers need to pay bills in the winter. EU2864

The young of the UK as I am not going to have to deal with the exit. EU2869

How to make this country more human and fairer? FR757

My European colleagues, and my desire to live lives like theirs. EU2430

Additionally, citizens' often merge personal and sociotropic concerns, as in the cases below:

> The future for myself, my country, younger people and the whole of Europe. EU2837

> Effect of the vote on me, my family and the UK. EU1861

FAMILY PROJECTION

Beyond sociotropism and society as a whole, voters often think about those close to them in the polling booth, notably their family. Those references represent 2% of total mentions in France, compared to 3.3% in South Africa and 4.9% in the UK EU-membership referendum. In the referendum, family thoughts represented only 2.5% of the focus of Leavers, but 7.2% of the thoughts of people who voted to remain. Qualitatively, citizens mainly express four types of family reference: to family in general, to ancestors, to children or grandchildren, and specific mention of the presence of family members in the polling station. References to family often express worry about their future, and a sense of responsibility and connection:

> The future of my family depends on this ballot. FR850

> This is important for my family. UK1915

> That I was not doing it for me, but for my family's future and security. EU2755

> I felt a connection to family that fought for my right to be there. US1256

By contrast, thoughts of parents predominantly emphasize the 'connection' side, though some respondents also thought about decisions their parents or grandparents made decades ago, notably in the 1975 EEC-membership referendum, as in the last example below.

> Just thought of how our parents and grandparents when everyone else could vote but not then and again when they went to cast their vote for the first time. SA2

> My nan. UK1743

> That I was righting a mistake that my parents made, and regretted for the rest of their lives. EU2759

By contrast, thoughts of children and grandchildren are typically associated with their future well-being, rights, or how they will be affected by current decisions. There were dozens of respondents who, when asked what thoughts went through their minds in the polling booth, merely answered 'my children' or 'my grandchildren'. Less curt examples include:

> I thought of my daughter and that I needed to do the right thing by her. FR615

> Make the right choice for the future of our children. FR774

> This is my chance to vote for what I believe in, my opportunity to ensure my children have a better future. SA165

> I was thinking of my children's future. SA885

> I am doing this for a better South Africa, so my children can enjoy freedom. SA568

> I thought about my baby boy's future. SA908

> I feared for the future of my country—for my children and grandchildren. US1253

> This is the most important vote I have ever cast for our country's and my children's future. US1920

> What kind of future were my grandchildren going to have? US1976

> I was thinking that my vote must protect my children and grandchildren. FR1080

> I was thinking of my daughter, thinking I was doing that for her. FR1295

> I was thinking of the future of my grandchildren. FR1304

> A secure future for my daughter. EU1746

> How to help my children and grandchildren remain happy and successful in the future. EU2067

> Scared for the future for my children. EU2684

> That it will be my children and grandchildren who will be most affected. EU2771

Many also refer to specific rights they want to protect for their children and future generations:

Ensure the future of my children in a free and secular country. FR638

A future where reform and negotiation will still be a possibility for my children and grandchildren. EU1742

My children and their future and the freedom of movement and right to live and work abroad. EU2426

A number of people, meanwhile, also refer to coming to vote with their family:

I was thinking of my family. I travelled by train to come and vote with them. FR1294

Just happy to vote with grandma. US2ZM029

A particular case pertains to voters bringing their children along to vote. This is usually a source of happiness and of an urge to communicate the importance of voting to them. Occasionally, it is also a source of stress. Both cases are illustrated below:

Happy I voted with my daughter for the first time. US6ZF025

It's great for my child to be with me and watch my vote count. US1651

Voting is a huge responsibility, which I was trying to communicate to my young daughter. US1948

I was nervous Obama was not going to win and my husband would not have a job, I had my kids with me and stressed to them how important it is to vote, it is their duty as citizens. US1541

Nothing, my eight-year-old was talking to me so I was just struggling to concentrate! SA90

In some cases, family is present not in person, but in the form of proxy voting (notably in France, where this remains the dominant procedure for remote voting, although the following example is from the UK):

I thought about what I would want for me irrespective of having to vote to leave by proxy for two members of my family. EU2200

Finally, many respondents stress the importance of polling stations as a neighbourhood focal point on Election Day, and thought of friends and family they encountered at the polling station:

Surprised to find a friend in the polling station. UK509

Glad to run into friends and neighbors voting, carefully and thoroughly marking the ballot I anticipated not learning the results until the next day. US1120

Overall, thoughts of close ones—notably family—and cross-generational references represent a prominent aspect of citizens' thoughts inside the polling booth, from first-time voters referring to their parents and grandparents to adults thinking of their children and grandchildren whilst voting. This represents a first layer of empathic displacement well before citizens start considering the electoral experience of those citizens who are far less intimately known to them.

EMPATHIC DISPLACEMENT

Earlier in this book, we highlighted empathic displacement as a critical part of the projective dimension of the vote. This, crudely, consists of thinking of the rest of the country voting as we consider our own vote, thereby underlining the collective nature of elections and projecting our own individual behaviour into that collective event. We already addressed projected efficacy as the 'positive side' of empathic displacement, whereby the vote becomes meaningful because of the syntonic behaviour of like-minded voters (or voters one assumes to be like-minded), and we will later look at references to hostility, that is, negative feelings relating to perceived divergence in electoral preferences and choices. In this section, we consider empathic displacement as the neutral consideration of (or curiosity as to) how the rest of the country may be voting, an acknowledgement of the layer of electoral behaviour taking place concomitantly with ours. This sentiment is exemplified succinctly by the following series of quotes:

I need to do my bit to get the right government. UK475

Hoping that everyone voted the same as me. UK1603

Hoping Americans think as I do. US1192

I hope that my vote and my desire represent the desire of a majority of others. FR1064

I hope and pray that there are a lot of people voting right now making the same choice that I am. US1290

I hope that all those who hadn't made up their minds would choose the right party. UK1126

> I hope everyone change the government. [sic] UK1778

In many cases, respondents think specifically about the way their family or friends are voting:

> In 2000, I assumed my parents were voting for Gore, but found out they both were voting for Bush. Now I can't talk to them. US36F015

> I'm interested in what my friends have to say about a candidate. It might impact me—I can't be a close friend with someone who voted for Romney. Politics are so much a part of how I interact with people. These issues are personal. I don't understand how people separate politics from relationships. Say you're friends with someone who supports a genocide. You choose your friends based on values. US34M016

> I usually talk in-depth with my mom and I know we are on the same team. When talking about things with friends, I try to talk to like-minded friends just because I don't feel like debating or angering people with differing agendas. US3ZM017

> I have a strict rule not to discuss politics with my parents. But in the last election, I threw the first punch and then my dad started sending all these anti-Obama emails. It gets too emotional speaking in person. They hate Obama. I told a friend not to make out with someone because he was an undecided voter. US28F004

In quantitative terms, empathic displacement is present in the thoughts of a range from 11.2% of French voters to 15.2% of US presidential election voters and 20.3% of South African ones. The 2016 UK EU-membership referendum is simultaneously responsible for the lowest and the highest levels of empathic displacement in respondents' answers: only 10.3% of total thoughts for Leave voters, but 28.2% for Remain voters, by far the highest total. This is perhaps one of the most interesting differences between Leave and Remain voters overall, with the latter recurrently expressing deep concern about the rest of the country and what they may be thinking and doing during the vote, whilst Leave voters were unlikely to do so, and were far more focused on their individual electoral decision. This is mirrored in terms of thoughts of resolution, expressed by 2% of UK general election voters, 4.3% of French presidential election and UK EU referendum Leave voters, and 6% of US presidential election voters, but by 17.5% of Remain voters: a clear outlier.

Narratively, empathic displacement references range from acknowledgement of others to curiosity, enthusiasm, and excitement about the collective movement an election represents. Thoughts of the nature of others' vote also vary from hope of synergies to a sense of marginalization and alienation. A first type of empathic displacement denotes symbiosis within the polity through the shared experience of voting, a sense of resolution and collective excitement which may involve assumptions about fellow voters' electoral choice:

> I felt at one with fellow Americans [multiple]

> I'm glad so many people are voting and that I'm able to be one of them. US1628

> I was happy and proud to be there with my fellow citizen most of whom, I was quite sure, voted for the same candidates as I did so there was a sense of unity too. US1500

Often, even in the absence of a sense of resolution, a connotation of delight or excitement at the mobilization of others remains, either because it underlines the momentous nature of the election, or because citizens consider civic mobilization and electoral turnout inherently positive. In chapter 1, we suggested that voting may well 'get the best out of' citizens, and in many ways, many respondents seem to agree:

> I was delighted to see so many people going to vote and it made me feel that I was living in interesting times. UK1729

> Great to see other people that were really enthusiastic and eager to vote. US6ZF058

> The wait was much shorter than last time. And it's great to see so many people out today. US3ZF062

> Yes! I can see people with positive, friendly attitude! SA478

> This is a very important election and I am pleased to see so many people voting—more than I have seen in a long time. US1905

> Pleased that a young man, who had spoken to me in queue, was interested but sad that turnout high—as latter indicated people might be voting through fear and/or personal interest only. UK1842

> Excited and proud that so many people were queueing at the polling station in a small rural village. EU1873

In some cases, positive connotations are entirely absent, but respondents descriptively think of others voting at the same time, or wonder about their experience, turnout, and choice, as in the quotes below. They may try to double guess what others do, such as the French respondent trying to infer the state of the vote from the piles of remaining ballots (which legally have to be kept equal), or another trying to interpret voters' preferences based on their way of dressing, or how different they seemed compared to her usual experience of the same station.

> I was thinking of all the people waiting in line behind me, and of all the others who would be voting today. FR1297

> I was thinking that as I was casting my vote, most other French people had already decided how they would vote themselves. FR1251

> What the turnout was like. EU2989

> I wondered if the high density suburbs were lucky enough to have such a quick and organised polling station as I was. [sic] SA831

> What the person in the next booth was voting for. EU2988

> Who are the others voting for? UK1813

> I was wondering who others were voting for. US1589

> Who others were voting for. UK1992

> I was wondering which party will get the most votes. SA367

> I was counting the ballots people had left in the polling booth to try and guess who others voted for. FR1891

> I was wondering why today the people in the polling stations were not the ones I am used to seeing when I come to vote. A lot of unknown faces, too many jackets and ties, this was not normal. FR655

In other cases, respondents' curiosity is not about fellow voters per se, but rather about how they compare to them specifically, notably in their own polling station or local area:

> I wonder if the people from my town will have voted like me? FR1708

> What proportion of people locally would be voting the same as me? EU2985

Curiosity about others' behaviour may also be framed as hope, rather than uncertainty:

> I was hoping for a large turnout. US1525

> Thank god this ghastly campaign is over and hope the GB public get it right this time. UK283
>
> I hope that all those who hadn't made up their minds would choose the right party. UK1126
>
> I hope many will vote like me. FR1147
>
> Hoping that more people make an informed choice. SA955
>
> That people would make honest and sensible votes. UK1914
>
> I hope that my vote and my desire represent the desire of a majority of others. FR1064
>
> All the people I know vote to remain. EU1754
>
> I hope that lots of other people are voting the same as me! EU2127

By contrast, it may also denote apprehension or even an anticipation of alienation and of being at odds with the greater part of the voting public:

> I was thinking that I was apprehensive of other people's verdict. UK748
>
> I was questioning the vote of other French people because unfortunately, change scares many. FR830
>
> I hope other people don't mess this up. UK1814
>
> I was regretting that friends and neighbours often behave quite secretly about political opinions. FR1124
>
> My vote will be negated tenfold. US1714
>
> I thought I was voting against most other locals' viewpoint. EU2202
>
> Since I live in an area with a high proportion of Leave voters, I wondered if I might be the only one voting to remain. EU2695
>
> That the UK was about to make a dreadful mistake. EU2784

The idea that we can understand the vote as a simple expression of a citizen's preference is contradicted by projective narratives and consistent testimonies of citizens thinking of other citizens' vote at the time that they cast theirs. To some degree, this perception is already present in our understanding of phenomena such as strategic voting, but the projective narrative is broader than that. It is not merely about citizens trying to 'compute' the weight of others' votes in order to optimize their own decision. Rather, and more often, it involves feeling part of a broader and relevant collective event, taking pride in others' sense of civic behaviour, or trying to understand how they themselves fit within a communal decision, either emphasizing synergy with the majority, or marginalization and alienation. Taken to the extreme, that very sense of marginalization itself can lead to another set of references: that is, to electoral hostility.

HATRED AND HOSTILITY

We define 'hateful' as referring to violently negative thoughts (insult, aggression, etc.), and 'electoral hostility' overtly as negative feelings—notably frustration, anger, contempt, or disgust—specifically towards fellow citizens believed to vote differently. These are the most negative forms of projective reference. Hateful and hostile references inside the polling booth were very weak in South Africa (0.1% of total answers) but account for 2.6% of answers in the US, 3.2% in France, and as much as 5.5% of answers in the UK EU-membership referendum (1.5% among Remain voters, but 9.3% among Leave voters). Openly hateful political conceptions include:

I hope Hollande gets killed. FR1539

I hate politics. SA715

Hopefully, Romney will win. Obama is a murderer and liar. US1190

Hope we would get that asshole out! US1179

I could only hope that the misogynistic, bigoted, theocratic, plutocratic, and backwards looking GOP could be defeated. US1247

I can't believe Americans can't see the wolf in sheep's clothing that Obama is! He does NOT respect America let alone love her and yet the majority of her people don't see that and elected to follow one of the most deceitful humans on earth?? Sad. US1242

I need to let the tea party know that they are way off base. We are an open live and let live civilized society. No to racism, sexism, bigotry. US1401

This shocking level of anger and hatred towards politicians and institutions is now known about and expected across democracies. What is more intriguing, and perhaps even more frightening, is that a significant proportion of respondents reported polling booth thoughts that are openly hostile towards fellow voters. The 'mildest' such references consider opposite voters stupid:

> I hope I make the right choice, even though my choice won't really make a difference, since corruption and the uneducated majority will decide. SA665

> How can people be so stupid to even consider re-electing Obama? US1205

> That the masses are asses and would be taken in by Mitt Romney's lies and flip flopping. US1868

> How one can be so stupid as to want to leave the EU. EU2060

> That it was silly to hold a referendum when the country hadn't a clue what it was actually voting for. EU2769

> Only the intelligentsia should be allowed to vote. US1765

Opposite voters are also accused of being dishonest, corruptible, egocentric, and focused on 'sponging off' (to quote some respondents) their country for their own selfish benefit. Again, the wording used is sometimes fairly violent—'parasites' and 'takers':

> I was hopeful that the people of the US would vote for the right candidate, however, they only want to sponge off of the government and be lazy and get free stuff, the middle class is doomed and this is the beginning of the end of capitalism. Our kids' lives are forever ruined by Obama. US1522

> Property and business owners are outnumbered by government employees and those receiving 'entitlements'. US1806

> That our country would once again be bought by those who give free stuff to those who earn nothing and never work. President wins by carrying the big city welfare people and the unions who only vote to protect themselves not caring whether the country is in trouble. US1864

> The takers now outnumber the makers because of the deceivers. US1887

> French voters have not understood anything. They are selfish and cowardly parasites. What was the point of all those wars to reach that point? It's pathetic. I'm ashamed of being French. FR1512F

A third variation follows the theme of marginalization and generalization. Voters develop their own categorization as to which groups represent opposite voters—pensioners, rich people, Muslims, immigrants, xenophobes, and so on—and feel that those voters will prevent their own vote from being efficacious. A respondent refers to 'obvious Democrats', and others make similar references due to the tradition of being electorally marginalized within their own polling station:

> I was thinking that to be Christian in a country which is becoming Muslim is making me sick. Persecution will come soon and my vote will be drowned, but so many people fought for this country, we cannot let them win. FR1079

> I'm really not sure how to vote. Voting one way is adding one's vote to that of rich people, voting the other way is adding one's vote to that of immigrants. FR1281

> Hoping that xenophobic stupidity wouldn't influence too many people to vote 'leave'. EU2035

> Worried about the huge numbers of pensioners driving so badly in the car park, and clearly all voting leave. EU3038

> My vote for Romney will be negated by all of these obvious Democrats! US1709

Finally, one respondent turned hostile towards himself, resenting what he deems his stupidity:

> God, I'm so fucking stupid! FR821

Hatred and hostility are frequent in polling booth thoughts. In chapter 9, we analyze the increased personalization of negativity and hostility towards fellow voters through the period under review.

ANGER AND ALIENATION

This transformation comes alongside growing anger and a sense of alienation from society and others. References to anger, frustration, and social alienation (we consider systemic alienation separately) characterize 4.1% of total references in South Africa and 4.6% in the US, but 5.7% in UK general elections, 7.4% in France, and 10.2% of responses from Leave voters in the UK EU-membership referendum. Here are examples of such despair and hopelessness:

> We are in deep shit. FR1032
>
> That it was hopeless. UK243
>
> Same old crap. UK257
>
> How it felt to vote out of hopelessness. FR399
>
> That it cannot be worse than before anyway. FR513
>
> This is ridiculous. US1917
>
> It cannot be worse than before anyway. FR717
>
> This is enabling a farce and I shouldn't be here. UK1930
>
> Just a great fear of the next day. FR1965

Many references to hopelessness emphasize time-wasting.

> This is useless. SA159
>
> Why am I wasting my time? SA854
>
> Why am I wasting my time with this, when I could be spending it with my family or playing games or even counting my toes? SA728
>
> This is pointless, we're screwed either way. US1916
>
> I don't give a shit. US4ZF031

Hopelessness can also relate to equally uninspiring choices:

> Temptation to put a 'bad' ballot in the envelope [. . .] FR910
>
> I voted not for a party but out of despair. FR1086
>
> I don't like either one. I am not happy but I vote anyways. US6ZM037
>
> How the hell do I pick one of this awful lot? UK285

Finally, it is sometimes associated with dishonesty, corruption, or dislike for a given politician:

> What can deliver us from this corrupt government? SA174

May this end in a change of leadership and an honest and morally upstanding person that our people can look up to with pride and that we would be happy for our children to emulate. SA180.

I have to help stop these thieves. SA989

Adieu Sarkozy! FR625

Bye bye, little Napoleon! FR693

May Sarkozy be crushed. FR1710

Protest about the politicians failing this country about the immigration. EU2633

Thoughts in the Polling Booth—Complex Scales

We proceed with a second level of recoding of polling booths thoughts, focusing on such dimensions as positivity, electoral identity, sociotropism, emotionality, and temporal outlook (retrospective or prospective). This enables us to draw more vivid comparisons about polling thoughts in the US, the UK, and France, correlating them with age, electoral identity, and gender. The results are presented in figure 3.6. They show significant comparative differences. The positivity highlighted earlier is notably far greater in France and the US than in the UK. In terms of electoral identity, however, voters in the US and the UK are more likely to think as supporters in the polling booth, whilst this is not the case with French voters.

Comparative differences persist on two dimensions. Voters are more sociotropic than egocentric in their thoughts in both the US and France but the opposite is true in the UK. Likewise, citizens' thoughts are often emotional in the US and France, but emotionally detached in the UK. Everywhere, voters' thoughts are predominantly prospective. The dimensionality of polling booth thoughts also varies by gender, age, and the electoral identity of voters (referees or supporters), as illustrated in appendix 3. Each set of characteristics shapes polling booth thoughts in certain ways. Women tend to be more emotional (in the UK and the US), less likely to think like referees in the US, and more likely to feel like supporters in the UK. They are more prospective in the UK and less retrospective in France. Women also have more positive thoughts in the US, but more negative ones in the UK and France. Age-wise, as people grow older, they increasingly think like supporters. Older people are also more retrospective in the US, and more

Nature of polling booth thoughts

☐ Negative ☐ Supporter ☐ Sociotropic ☐ Emotional ☐ Prospective
■ Positive ■ Referee ■ Egocentric ■ Detached ■ Retrospective

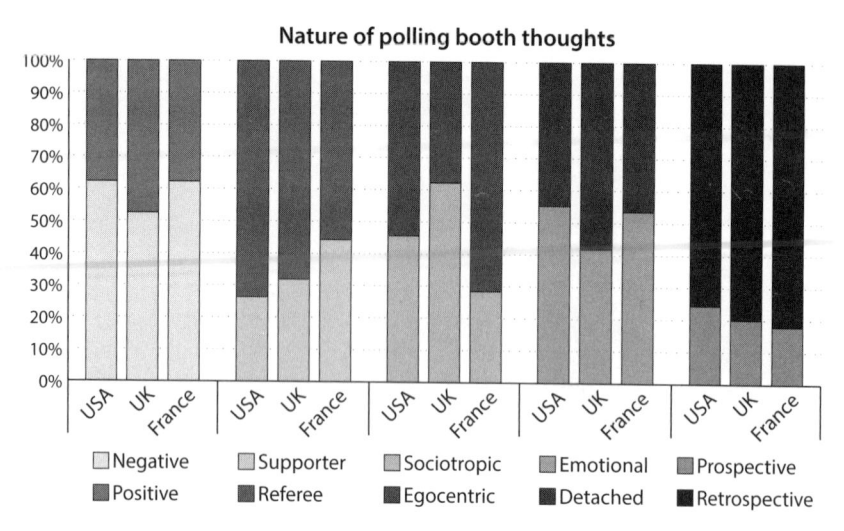

FIGURE 3.6: Citizens' thoughts in the polling booth

emotionally detached in the UK. Finally, with regard to electoral identity, the identity connotations of citizens' polling booth thoughts are coherent with their electoral identity as directly measured. In other words, referees think like referees and supporters think like supporters. Additionally, supporters are more likely to be positive, and, in the UK—though not the US, where they show the opposite tendency—more likely to have emotional polling booth thoughts. In short, recoded polling booth thoughts prove predominantly positive, prospective, sociotropic, emotional, and supporter-oriented, with significant differences across countries, gender, age, and electoral identity.

Comparing the Thoughts of In-Person and Remote Voters

We now want to compare systematically what voters think about as they cast their vote, using closed lists of possible thoughts distributed between in-person and remote voters and based on their demographic features. We saw that voters' thoughts are very diverse, from the technical to the emotional and intimate; but ultimately, they can also be divided into a number of key 'strands' of reference, which we use in the closed questions. These include possible election-centric thoughts (thinking of the candidates, something said the debates or campaign), internalized references (family, discussions or arguments with others), and projective elements (how others will vote). The findings for in-person and remote voters are in appendix 3.

On the whole, four key types of thought seem to dominate voters' minds: a sense of their own responsibility (related to issues of electoral identity); how the rest of the country would vote (empathic displacement); the candidates (the choice); and their own family (the internalization element). These four elements are at the forefront of many voters' minds.

Significant national differences and idiosyncrasies emerge from the table. Projective elements are very strong in France, but weak in the UK, where this is only the fourth reference amongst voters' main thoughts, for both polling station and postal voters. Candidates, meanwhile, are a major focus for US voters (again, voting traditionally, using absentee ballot, or advance voting), but not in Germany. Family is more salient in people's minds in the US and in South Africa. In the UK, Germany, and South Africa, future members of government are a concern for many voters, while the sense of a historic election is prominent in France. Many voters also refer to happy and/or emotional thoughts as they vote. That pre-eminence of emotionality and positivity mirrors spontaneous answers to open questions.

There are a few notable differences between traditional and remote voters. Most thought values seem to be higher for the latter. However, as discussed earlier, this may be an artefact of the way in which the 'moment' of casting one's vote is much more diffuse (and indeed much longer) for geographically remote than for polling station voters. They have no urgency to complete the process, which may last minutes, hours, or days. For remote voters, the equivalents of the polling station and polling booth experiences merge into one fluid sequence. This is to be compared to polling station observations of the time spent voting across countries, which averages one minute in France, and less in the UK, but over fifteen minutes in the US polling stations that we monitored.

An exception to the greater thought concentration when people vote from home, however, is that empathic and projective elements are less pronounced for remote voters compared to polling station voters. This confirms our other findings throughout the book showing that the polling station experience is far more conducive to empathic displacement than geographically remote voting. Similarly, the sense that the election may be historical is not higher amongst remote voters, which suggests it is a less obvious feeling than for polling station voters. By contrast, technical thoughts (relating to previous elections, debate promises, and campaign images) are far more likely to occur to remote voters who have more time to cast their ballot.

Differences by Age and Gender

Across the countries analyzed, age differences, shown in appendix 3, are significant. First, voters tend to think about fewer things as they grow older, suggesting that voting becomes more automatic, whilst the desire to make it a conscious and reflective decision is high amongst young people. This is particularly true of personal interaction preceding the election. Thus, younger people are far more likely to think of a discussion (for instance −0.16** in the UK, −0.12** in France) or an argument (−0.21** in the UK and Germany, −0.16** in the US, −0.15** in France, and −0.13** in South Africa) when they are in the polling booth. Older people are also less likely to think of the campaign, be it substantive campaign elements (−0.15** in South Africa, −0.14** in the UK) or images (−0.15** in Germany, −0.14** the UK, −0.13** in the US and South Africa). Happy (−0.13** in the UK, −0.09** in the US), angry (−0.19** in Germany, −0.09** in the US, −0.06* in the UK), and emotional (−0.09** in the UK) thoughts all decline with age. Strangely, some thoughts evolve more unevenly with age. For instance, thinking of one's family becomes more likely with age in France (0.08**) but less so in Germany and the UK (−0.12** and −0.08** respectively). Thinking of one's responsibility increases with age in the US (0.10**), as do thoughts about the historical character of elections and about possible ministers in France (0.07** and 0.06**). Citizens' thoughts only vary minimally by gender.

A Day in the Life of a Non-Voter

Finally, one cannot consider 'a day in the life of a voter', and its experiential and emotional meaning, without exploring how it compares to the same day in the life of a non-voter. Across our six countries, between 15% and over 50% of eligible citizens abstain in any given election, and some of them chronically. It thus seemed crucial to assess how those people who are—by habit, inertia, or choice—excluded from an electoral process experience Election Day, and the extent to which the electoral atmosphere still shapes their day and their lives. We thus looked at the thoughts reported by non-voters on Election Day, using the answers to both closed and, for UK respondents, open questions, comparing them to polling station voters. In the next section, we run similar comparisons on Election Night experience. We first measure occurrence of the main words that come to non-voters' minds

a. **Open-ended thoughts of nonvoters on Election Day (UK)**

[Bar chart with categories: Boring (~31), Nothing (~20), Exciting/interesting (~9), Uninterested (~8), Lies (~7), Overrated (~6), Crap/rubbish (~6), Farce/ridiculous (~6), Tension (~5), Anxious/worry (~5), Who/can't decide (~5), Curious (~5), Confusing (~5)]

b. **Open-ended thoughts of nonvoters on Election Day (US)**

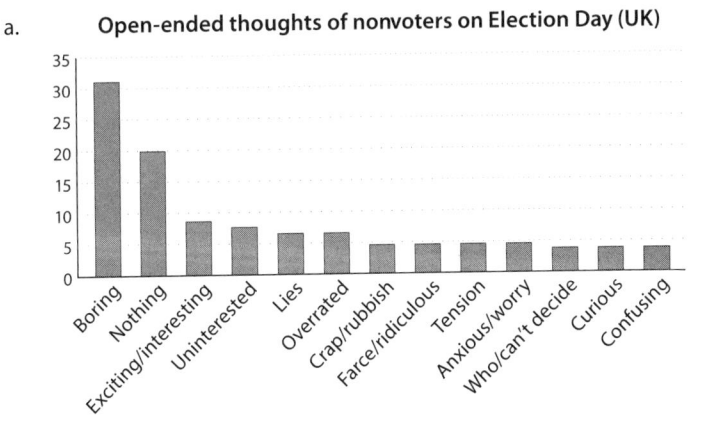

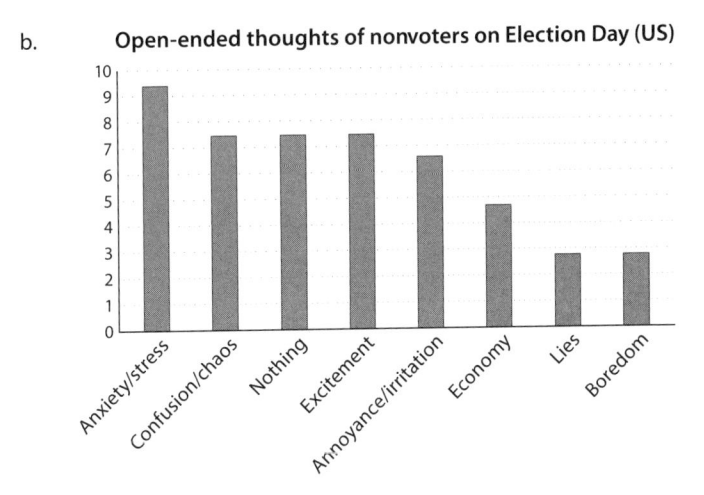

[Bar chart with categories: Anxiety/stress (~9), Confusion/chaos (~7.5), Nothing (~7.5), Excitement (~7.5), Annoyance/irritation (~7), Economy (~5), Lies (~3), Boredom (~3)]

FIGURE 3.7: Thoughts of non-voters on Election Day

on Election Day, focusing on the UK and the US case studies. Their main references are shown in figure 3.7.

As we can see, UK answers overwhelmingly express apathy. 'Boring' and 'nothing' being their most frequent answers, it seems that most non-voters think of elections as uninteresting and overrated. The third most frequent reference is positive, framing the election as 'interesting', whilst a smaller number admit to being curious about them. Overall, however, such positive connotations pale compared to aggressively negative references to lies or rubbish (or often ruder words), or to ridicule. Finally, a number of non-voters have thoughts about their inability to choose, or the fact that they find the election worrying or at times confusing.

Feelings of non-voters on Election Day

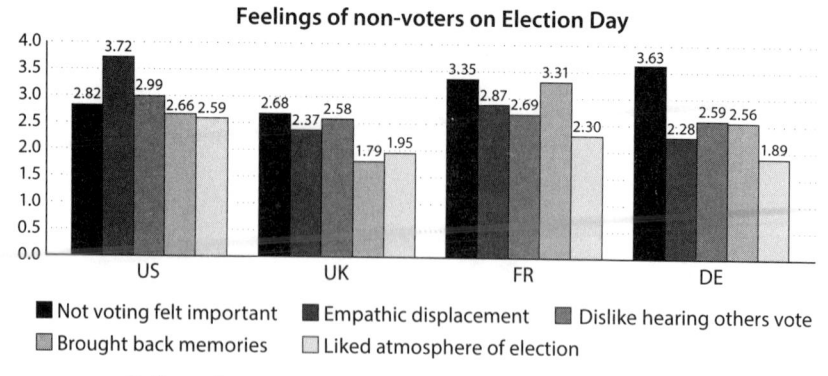

	US	UK	FR	DE
Not voting felt important	2.82	2.68	3.35	3.63
Empathic displacement	3.72	2.37	2.87	2.28
Dislike hearing others vote	2.99	2.58	3.31	2.59
Brought back memories	2.66	1.79	2.69	2.56
Liked atmosphere of election	2.59	1.95	2.30	1.89

FIGURE 3.8: Feelings of non-voters on Election Day

The comparison with the answers provided by polling station voters is striking. For the latter, the top answer is 'exciting', the third 'hope', the fifth 'change', and the sixth 'duty'. 'Boring' admittedly appears in second place, but with less than half the number of references to elections as 'exciting', and 'nothing' only comes seventh, with roughly a quarter of the number of references to excitement. For US non-voters, references are a little different, most frequently to stress and anxiety, and then to chaos and confusion, before voters mention 'nothing' and boredom, but also excitement. For voters, references to anxiety are also frequent, but references to hope and excitement are dominant, alongside other themes such as duty, anticipation, freedom, pride, and importance, and technical references, such as to crowds.

We next look at non-voters' responses regarding how they felt on Election Day in the US, UK, France, and Germany. The findings are presented in figure 3.8. First, not voting is actually a 'big deal' for many non-voters, who feel that this choice is important to them, particularly in Germany and France. Nevertheless, many non-voters explain that they think of other citizens, notably those voting. Non-voters' empathic displacement is particularly high in the US and France, though typically lower than for voters. Many non-voters also dislike hearing others talk about the election, and at the same time reminisce about previous elections on Election Day, despite not voting. However, very few non-voters claim to like the atmosphere of the election.

On all counts, there are significant differences between voters and non-voters. In the US, the differential for the perceived importance of voting is very substantial (+3.38), and so too for liking the Election Day atmosphere (+1.54), empathic displacement (+0.91), and memories of past elections (+0.71). Except as regards the importance of (not) voting, standard deviations are comparable across the two groups, and high in both cases.

On the whole, being a non-voter changes citizens' perspectives on Election Day and significantly emphasizes a sense of marginalization and alienation from the voting majority, who are sharing an electoral experience from which the non-voter is excluded. 'Others'—notably voters—are thus important to the mindset of non-voters on Election Day, but the differentiation between the two groups entails, for the latter, some unhappiness, resentment of the electoral atmosphere, or even, at times bitterness towards voters. We will see below how those differences evolve during Election Night.

Election Night

A SPECIAL NIGHT

In the final section of this chapter, we look at voters' experience of Election Night, and reactions to election results. We have so far considered the moment of casting one's vote as, within the experiential cycle of elections, the natural climax of the electoral experience; but societally, it is arguably Election Night and the discovery of election results which can claim to end an electoral sequence and potentially reconcile citizens to the democratic cycle. When it comes to voter-centric electoral cycles, Election Night is thus likely to crystallize post-election happiness, worry, shock, or the development of new political expectations, assessments, worries, and hopes which will open the transition from the old to the new cycle.

We must understand in narrative terms how citizens experience and ritualize Election Night: whether they develop habits and practices, individual and local traditions. Does Election Night become a special night for electoral 'believers' and 'non-believers' alike, just like New Year's Eve or Super Bowl Night? This is the 'experiential' quest of this section, based on answers from election diaries and in-depth interviews. Citizens overwhelmingly portray Election Night as a critical moment of the election cycle. Whilst we cannot infer statistics from the non-representative diaries, the immense majority of diary keepers (over 80%) reported following all or most of Election Night, especially in France and the US (less so in the UK and South Africa). Most think of Election Night as a ritualized experience, something that they always approach in the same way or with the same people over the years.

> I always watch election night. I usually do it at my house, and call people on the phone after the results come in. USF62IDI

> On election night—I get together with friends and family and stay up way too late. USF38IDI

> On election night, I'm glued to the TV. I go to a friend's house and watch it on TV. I have to know the results. I couldn't possibly go to sleep without knowing. USM35IDI

> On election night, I'm sure there will be a party going on with food and drinks. USM28IDI

> I'm sure election night is going to be a party. [. . .] I remember 2008 was a massive ordeal. I was a sophomore in college then. People rushed out to the streets. There was a huge outpouring of feeling. I don't anticipate that happening this time. But I'm sure we'll have a good time. USF23IDI

> I always watch election results on TV. [. . .] I'm one of those people that starts yelling at the TV—'You're lying—you can't say that!' USF53IDI

For many interviewees, Election Night is an intimate shared experience with family or friends:

> I'm organizing something. I'll watch with friends. [. . .] I need to be in a supportive environment. USF28IDI

> I sat up all night one election to see the results with my brother. UK72M007

> On election night, I made dinner with my boyfriend and watched TV. I didn't watch until the end. I was avoiding it until I knew everything was in the clear. USF33IDI

> I was watching the numbers come in. I was with my partner and two other friends. We had dinner and watched the results. I was slightly nervous. USM28IDI

> My husband sits up to watch it all, but I don't, I am usually fed up with it all by around 10 pm and I go to bed. I can honestly say that I don't get excited about it all, and he will tell me in the morning what happened and what is going on. UK75F010

> On election night, I watched the TV with friends. It was interesting to watch the TV broadcasting. It was so much more partisan than I remembered. [. . .] I didn't like that it was so partisan. USM30IDI
>
> I watched the election results with some people. It was fun. USF24IDI

A smaller number of interviewees engage in broader Election Night celebrations involving parties or election night outings in bars or in town, as they would approach a major game:

> We went to a bar in NYC. USF32IDI
>
> I had an election party. I had twenty-five friends over. It was enjoyable hanging out with everyone. USF36IDI
>
> I went to one of my best friend's house on election night. She's really plugged into lots of news sources. So we watched several channels, CSPAN and MSNBC, and NPR in the kitchen [. . .] My friend invited a lot of people over to her house, but a lot of people didn't show up. Maybe because people thought it was going to go well. USF31IDI
>
> We first went to a bar, but it was too crowded and small. So we went somewhere else where we could watch different channels. I was getting excited about issues that other people weren't. USF28IDI
>
> It was really memorable from the last election staying up late, drinking wine, good memories. I asked people to come for the election and my birthday. USF28IDI
>
> I went to my college roommate's house for election night. She made food, and we played election night bingo with cards. Two kinds of cards. If they mentioned gay marriage, or 2004, or when a state was called, we got bingo. USF28IDI

A sub-group of citizens approach Election Night as 'experts', obsessed with figures and media:

> I pay a lot of attention on election night. I'm usually listening in the weeks ahead. I always watch it. USF50IDI
>
> I read blogs on election night. My wife and housemate tried to get people over, but they had plans. It was stressful and exciting. USF36IDI

112 CHAPTER 3

> I came home and tried to watch the results, but it was going on so late that I went ahead and went to asleep. USM31IDI

> I was listening to the results in the car on the radio. I found myself getting really nervous about it. I have a portable radio in the car, so when I went to the grocery store I took around the radio so I could keep listening. USF70IDI

> Nice not to argue on election night. Low-key enough to watch screens, check twitter feeds. USF28IDI

Finally, many citizens refer primarily to their emotionality, excitement, or even happy or sad tears in the context of Election Night, echoing our internalization model:

> On election night, I get nervous that my people are going to lose or that my issues won't pass. USM29IDI

> I get excited before I watch it but once I'm watching it, it becomes boring. UK67M008

> [Election night] depresses me. USM33IDI

> I cried all night and most of the next day. USM34IDI

> A lot of crying. A Ghanaian taxi driver bear-hugged me and lifted me up. It was an amazing feeling. USM34IDI

> I didn't watch the election that night but I got up at 5 am to find out who had got in, and then saw all the news reports about the election. I kept turning from one channel to another to try to find out. UK47F009

Election Night Roller-Coasters

The emotions just mentioned are at the heart of what we tested in our panel survey, asking respondents how they felt during Election Night, considering differences between voters and non-voters (and those who voted on Election Day or remotely), and between those who voted for a winning or a losing candidate. These compared emotion registers are reported in figures 3.9 and 3.10

Election Nights carry a sense of importance in the eyes of citizens. Beyond that solemnity, they make citizens feel excited and emotional, and, to

a.

**Election night emotions for in-person voters, remote voters, and abstentionists
United States and United Kingdom**

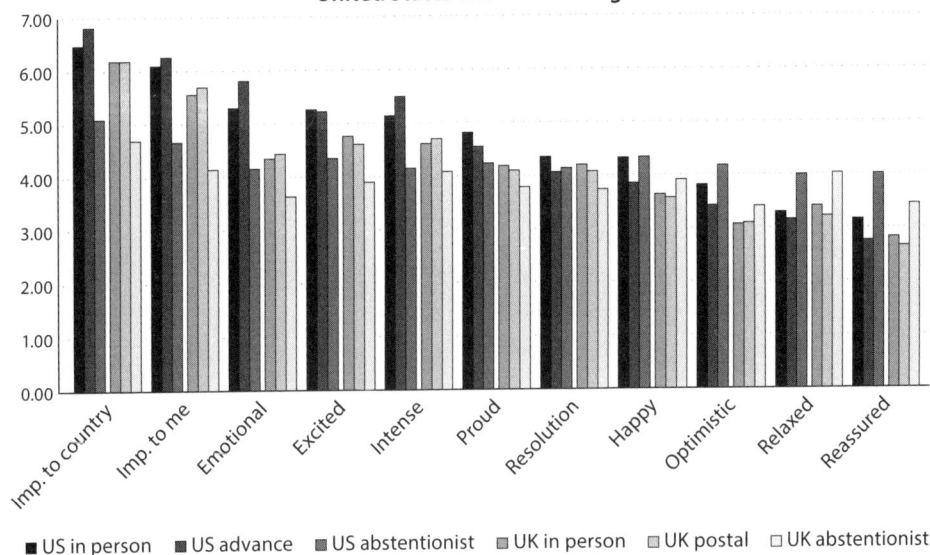

■ US in person ■ US advance ■ US abstentionist ▨ UK in person ▨ UK postal ☐ UK abstentionist

b.

**Election night emotions for in-person voters, remote voters, and abstentionists
France and Germany**

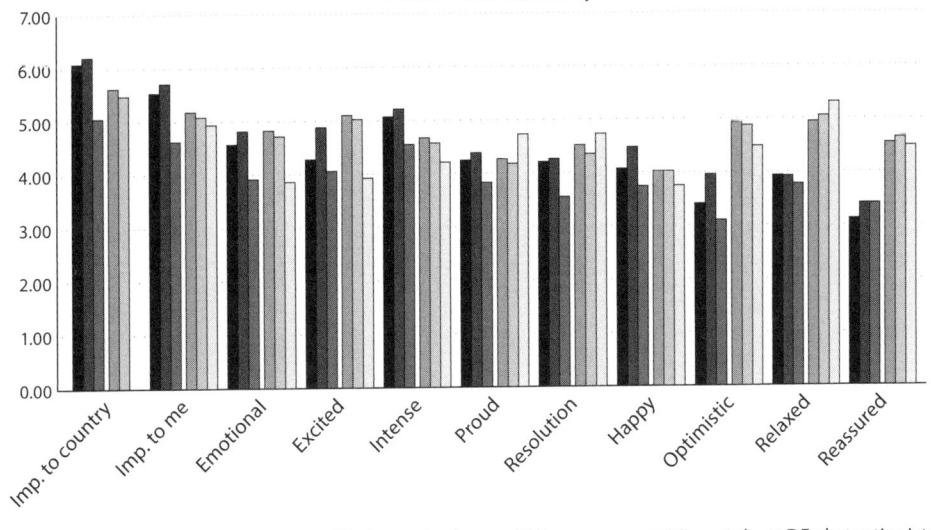

■ FR in person ■ FR proxy ■ FR abstentionist ▨ DE in person ▨ DE postal ☐ DE abstentionist

FIGURE 3.9: Election night emotions for in person voters, remote voters, and non-voters

a lesser extent, close to others and happy. We can infer that this is unrelated to the result, as few citizens feel optimistic or relaxed, let alone reassured, during Election Night. There is generally little difference in the way Election Night is experienced by those who voted earlier on the same day and those who voted remotely in advance, with the exception that those who vote on Election Day feel significantly happier during Election Night than remote voters do (save in France, with its proxy voting). By contrast, however, there are significant differences between the experience of Election Night of voters and non-voters. This is particularly true of the sense of importance, emotionality, and excitement of citizens, all of which decline significantly amongst non-voters. However, non-voters are also less worried and tense during Election Night. We report the compared Election Night emotions of winning- and losing-party voters in figure 3.10.

Differences are very country-specific. In the US and France, citizens' emotions during Election Night vary significantly in terms of happiness, excitement, pride, optimism, reassurance, and resolution. In Germany, winners and losers differ in happiness, optimism, reassurance, and resolution, but in the UK, there is virtually no difference at all, except for optimism and happiness. Across countries, perceived importance (both for oneself and for one's country) and the emotionality of the night are unanimous regardless of electoral choice, and in France and Germany, those who voted for a losing party or candidate even declare a more intense Election Night experience than those who voted for the winners.

Overall, Election Night is a reassuringly ritualized occasion for many, as well as an emotionally intense experience. Its connotations are largely positive, though with important differences. First, it is far less emotional (if less worrying) for abstentionists than for voters. Second, being in the winning or the losing camp clearly makes a difference in terms of citizens' sense of happiness and of optimism. Perhaps the most critical difference, however, is that voting or not, and having supported the winners or not, have a very direct impact on the extent to which Election Night, as a cathartic instant in the cycle, makes people feel closer to those estranged from them, our definition of electoral resolution. This sense of inclusion—or alienation—at the end of an electoral episode indeed emphasizes the role of Election Night as an essential ingredient in elections' success at bringing resolution and closure for different categories of voter.

a. **Election night emotions for in-person voters of winning and losing parties/candidates United States and United Kingdom**

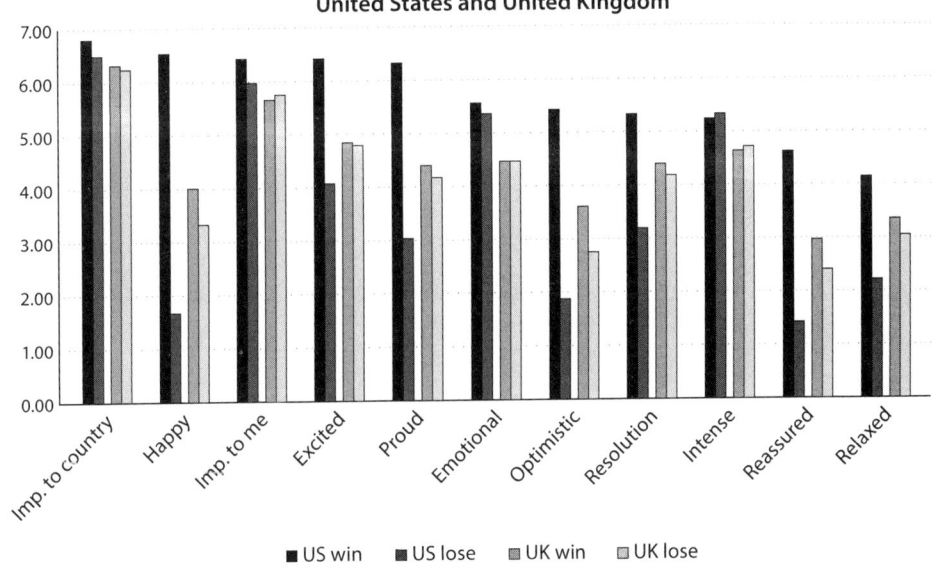

■ US win ■ US lose ☐ UK win ☐ UK lose

b. **Election night emotions for in-person voters of winning and losing parties/candidates France and Germany**

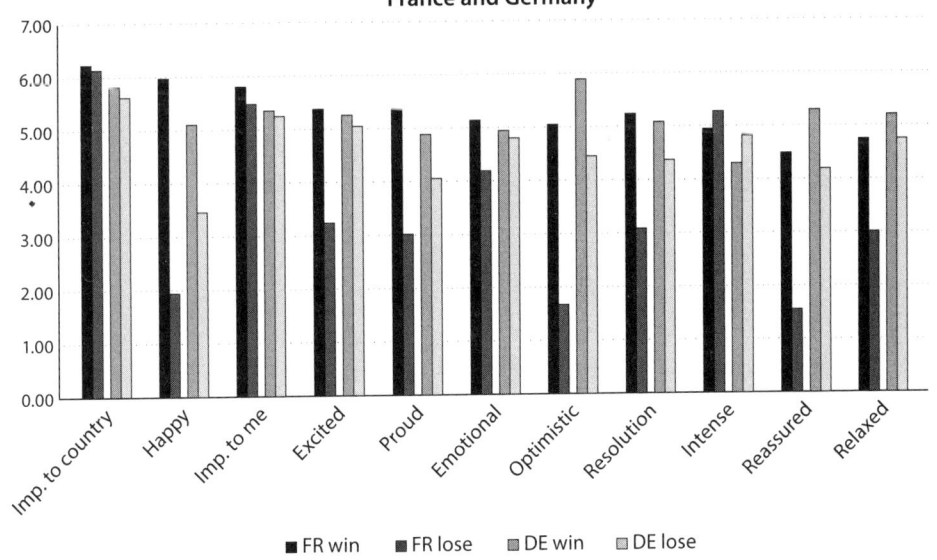

■ FR win ■ FR lose ☐ DE win ☐ DE lose

FIGURE 3.10: Election night emotions for voters of winning and losing parties/candidates

116   CHAPTER 3

TABLE 3.2. The Election Night of "Referees" and "Supporters"

	US	UK	FR*	GE
Reassured	0.01	−0.12**	−0.10**	0.02
Relaxed	−0.05	−0.15**	−0.12**	0.00
Optimistic	0.07**	−0.12**	—	0.02
Excited	0.19**	0.09**	0.08**	0.03
Happy	0.08**	−0.09**	0.12**	0.03
Emotional	0.19**	0.11**	0.11**	0.05*
Intense	0.18**	0.16**	0.11**	0.02
Important	0.21**	0.13**	—	0.02
Projected important	0.21**	0.15**	—	0.00
Proud	0.11**	−0.01	—	0.04
Resolution	0.10**	−0.05	—	0.03

Notes: * = sig<0.05; ** = sig<0.01. French data based on the first-time voters survey, with a number of different emotions proposed.

Referees and Supporters after the Game

We similarly consider differences in the Election Night experience of referees and supporters. The correlation between electoral identity and citizens' emotionality on Election Night are summarized in table 3.2. The intensity of supporters' emotions is usually higher than for referees, except in the case of Germany. For supporters, Election Night is typically more exciting, more intense, be it for all in the US and the UK, or for first-time voters in France. However, they are also more anxious than referees throughout the night.

Differences in valence-based emotions (happiness, optimism) are less clear. Supporters are generally happier in the US and France, but less happy in the UK. Unsurprisingly, being on the winning or losing sides affects valence-based emotions more for supporters. These differences affect elections' ability to bring democratic closure, end an election cycle or not, generate hope or hostility. They constitute the 'baggage' that the next election cycle will carry.

A Chance for Closure

For individuals and for the polity as a whole, Election Night may serve as a symbolic and emotional ending of the election cycle, a 'debriefing' episode which highlights and crystallizes the intellectual and emotional electoral experience. It is symptomatic of accumulated tensions and emotions, and path-dependent on people's electoral attitudes and behaviour throughout the period. In turn, this may or may not enable an election to bring closure to citizens.

The symbolic nature of Election Night as the cherry on the emotional cake of the election period in general and climactic Election Day in particular is obvious from citizens' narratives, the description of their habits and feelings. The emotional and cathartic potential of Election Night is illustrated by the abundant electoral tears which we analyze in chapter 7. In the context of the referendum on Britain's membership of the European Union, 28% of citizens felt tearful at the time they discovered the result of the vote. That proportion increased to 39% amongst young voters aged eighteen to twenty-four. These percentages are extremely high, and beg the question of how and why a specific vote may generate a tearful nation.

Ultimately, Election Day and Election Night are crucial in understanding the unique identity of a given election's atmosphere, and its ability to bring closure to citizens. These occasions contain the ingredients that may result in an electoral honeymoon, hope, convergence, and legitimation, or on the contrary to frozen fractures and possible spirals of electoral hostility. We will return to the nature of those cycles, and the link between electoral experience, elections, hope, hostility, resolution, and closure in chapter 9. Electoral resolution, however, is a crucial concept. In recent years, we have found frequent examples of elections unable to bring closure and apparently failing to renew the legitimacy of the social contract. Examples include the aftermaths of the UK EU-membership referendum and US presidential election in 2016, which saw virtually no convergence or resolution between the pre-election camps.

We also return in chapter 9 to this 'morning after the night before', to go beyond citizens' satisfaction or dissatisfaction with an electoral result, and assess voters' ranges of emotion (happiness, anger, disgust, empathy, worry) and the role of these in the transition between old and new election cycles, as well as the question of whether something has changed in elections' ability to bring resolution through the 2010s. In the meantime, however, our next chapter moves away from narratives of electoral experience, to assess how citizens' personalities and morality shape them as voters.

The question of the impact of personality on the vote, notably of the 'Big Five', has been an important but often disappointing staple of the political psychology literature. In this chapter, we reopen the question of what 'personality' entails, focusing in particular on specific discrete personality traits, including optimism, sensitivity, anxiety, alienation, risk aversion, empathy, and balance between freedom and order. The chapter also looks at the interaction, noted earlier, between those personality traits and context, efficacy, and projected efficacy. Our findings explore especially the complex logic of sociotropic behaviour, the role of projection in electoral behaviour (including long-term projection, generational sacrifice, and empathic displacement), and, more broadly, the way in which individual and societal perceptions interact.

4

Personality and Morality

A Personal Contract

Rousseau's (1762) influential work on politics as a social contract has had an enormous influence on our understanding of how citizens accept the surrender of some of their freedom to the state in order to get, in return, social order, peace, and a functional society. Beyond this original societal consensus, however, how do citizens enact a personal contract with their democratic system? How will their personality, sense of morality, and conception of their relationship with others affect their relationship to electoral democracy, and beyond, their electoral experience and behaviour? For years, political scientists have believed that citizens' personality must impact electoral behaviour. They have intuitively focused on the impact of the 'Big Five' personality traits (openness, conscientiousness, extraversion, agreeableness, and neuroticism—or 'OCEAN' model) on electoral behaviour (e.g., Bakker et al., 2015; Fatke, 2017), but their attempts to find patterns of voting on such a basis have met with uneven success, with some breakthroughs, but also a sense that Big Five-based models may not fully account for the true nature of electoral personality.

Anyone who has been on a safari will know about another 'Big Five': wildlife enthusiasts seek these out and feel that their trip is only complete if they have seen at least one specimen of each of the animals featured on that list. In practical terms, however, a cheetah is harder to see than a buffalo, a zebra more attractive than a leopard, a giraffe more elegant than an elephant, and a hippopotamus more dangerous than a rhinoceros. Thus the focus on the Big Five, however dominant in the field of wildlife-spotting, may not be the most appropriate for tourists, regardless of whether their main preoccupation is rarity, beauty, elegance, or danger, and their interest in African wildlife may well be better served by some alternative priorities. Similarly, while the psychological Big Five—which as we mentioned were originally proposed in order to diagnose certain key personality disorders, rather than political behaviour—are undoubtedly important, they do not account for the whole of an individual's personality. There is no reason necessarily to assume that all personality aspects influence electoral behaviour: kindness, for example, may be an important personality trait in a whole range of situations, but it need not influence our taste in arts, or our opinions about GMO or international trade. Our model, therefore, draws rather upon the insights of personality research to test the impact of specific personality markers on the electoral experience of citizens and their behaviour. Based on observation and pilots, we measure seven critical primary psychological traits, and assess their impact on key aspects of electoral behaviour such as electoral participation, left/right electoral choice, and extremism.

In our daily lives, our personality is expressed both in terms of fundamental traits and through attitudinal and behavioural consequences, such as what we like and dislike, how we see ourselves, how we feel others perceive us, and so on. This intuitive sense, that is hard to characterize, often guides our perceptions. When meeting people for the first time, we often perform instinctive, subconscious evaluations of them. Do they smile a lot, laugh a lot, or look serious? How do they dress, decorate their house, or act with others? Are they quiet or loud, and what do they like to do in their free time? None of these personality consequences is easily associated with a single raw personality trait, but we intuitively know that each and every one of them is the product of personality, if in ways that might be too complex to characterize analytically. This subtle and complex outcome of personality traits is known as 'personality derivatives', and we study the relationship with the vote of these too, in the second part of this chapter—considering, for example, whether citizens who favour a certain colour behave differently from others, or citizens who choose a specific type of animal to represent themselves behave in similar ways to each other? Finally, we look at a third important consequence of personality: moral hierarchization.

Eight Discrete Personality Traits

The rich narrative insights and impressionistic voters' portraits that we collected through qualitative fieldwork enabled us to identify a number of primary personality dimensions that seemed systematically meaningful in citizens' perceptions, evaluations, and behaviour throughout the electoral cycle. Those traits may not be the most important in defining an individual either politically or in general, but they are specific traits and scales that seem to be associated with distinct narratives of electoral experience. Using a number of self-declared characterizations and factor analysis (these measurement approaches are the most widely used for personality traits in the existing literature), we defined measurement scales to capture them. These eight discrete personality traits are: sensitivity, anxiety, sense of alienation, freedom aspiration, gregariousness, risk aversion, care, and confrontation.

Sensitivity is a fundamental personality aspect, which entails in particular compassion and understanding. It is expressed both inwardly (how we react to the behaviour of others, notably towards us) and outwardly (empathy). It is related to fundamental psychological measures such as affective intelligence (Marcus et al., 2000; Redlawsk et al., 2007). Sensitivity can be conceptualized as the feeling of understanding others and taking their interests and feelings into account, feeling understood by them, and the extent to which our self-image and behaviour are affected by their opinions of and attitudes towards us (Ajzen, 2005). The rationale behind expecting sensitivity to matter in our context relates to the emotionality of the vote, and key role of individual–societal articulation in voters' thoughts, in particular through empathic displacement. We include two operational items to capture the inwards and outwards components of sensitivity, reflecting respondents beliefs that they understand others, and are understood by them.

Anxiety is a fundamental personality trait, related to several psychological pathologies. Whilst associated with sensitivity, it entails in particular negative valence and demobilizing reactions. The former of these involves a propensity to a pessimistic outlook and to worry; the latter result in self-doubt (Marcus and MacKuen, 1993), which can have a 'paralyzing' effect. We saw in chapter 3 that voters' tendencies towards optimism/pessimism, or self-satisfaction/self-doubt, can strikingly permeate their spontaneous answers as respondents: some are eminently optimistic and others systematically pessimistic; some worry a lot about elections and others never; some citizens are unquestionably satisfied with their own decisions, whilst others doubt and self-criticize. Moreover, anxiety seems a likely cause of introspection and a more passive electoral engagement. Our anxiety measures encompass three elements: pessimism, propensity to worry, and self-satisfaction or lack thereof.

Alienation is also related to sensitivity, but taps into feelings of social inclusion or isolation. Some citizens feel spontaneously part of broader viewpoints and societal trends, while others feel different from the crowd and marginalized by it (Robinson et al., 2013). We noted that electoral resolution phenomena and empathic displacement can both lead to a sense of inclusion or, conversely, marginality and alienation, and that different voters may react differently to feeling part of a 'winning' or 'losing' trend, so assessing personal predisposition to alienation is essential. We use a single-item measure that simply asks respondents the extent to which they feel that their values and beliefs are different from anyone else's.

Freedom aspiration is a scale of arbitration freedom and order, two of the fundamental psychological needs of human beings (Lanyon, 1997). It is particularly relevant to political contexts. For example, models of tolerance such as Gibson's (1992) measure it in terms of arbitration between the freedom of disliked groups and public order or public morals. Law and order policies also reflect trade-offs on the same scale. Here, we do not measure freedom/order 'beliefs', but rather whether aspiration to freedom, vis-à-vis need for reassurance and order which may affect those beliefs, is a defining personality trait for respondents. Freedom and choice is also a quasi-permanent theme in many election narratives, while others emphasize fear of chaos and disorder. We measure freedom aspiration, based on self-descriptions (two behavioural one attitudinal), in terms of whether individuals prefer to stick to what they know or innovate, seek improvisation or tend to follow guidelines (in the specific context of cooking), and prefer explanations over decisiveness.

Extraversion is closely related to gregariousness and collective aspirations. It pertains to seeking physical, emotional, and intellectual interactions with others, the contrary being a preference for solitude and seclusion (Eysenck, 2012). We have highlighted perceptions of elections as a collective events, including polling station excitement or even—seemingly paradoxical—positive reactions to queues, and, in chapter 3, the fact that many voters also emphasize the collective social aspects of Election Night. We measure gregariousness by two items: preference to be with others, and sense of being a 'party animal'.

Risk aversion is a major psychological trait in many economic models. Individuals have varying appetites for high-risk, high-gain, or conversely for risk-averse, situations. This impacts insurance and investment behaviour (Zaleskiewicz, 2001), but could also affect degree of preference for unknown candidates or incumbents, or of willingness to put faith in the proposals of radical parties or radical change (e.g., populist models or Brexit). Our measure indexes two items, based on tendencies to plan and to arrive early, which capture both advance and present efforts to protect against risk or seek the thrill of improvisation.

Care, at worst, results in obsessiveness, but at best, in rigour and thoroughness. It is a crucial personality attribute that affects our approach to all cognitive situations. Caring people think preponderantly of processes, whilst less caring ones focus primarily on outcomes and outputs. The arbitration between these shapes radically different approaches to ideology and electoral thinking. Differences in degree of focus on processes vis-à-vis outcomes is especially apparent in respondents' descriptions of their electoral experiences, and may also impact the time scale of voters' evaluations, notably as regards projection and generational sacrifice. We measure care by indexing two items, respectively measuring the arbitration between fairness of process and efficiency of outcome, and patience, thereby highlighting both the process-oriented and the projective sides of care.

Finally, *confrontation* refers to the extent to which individuals are comfortable with initiating or responding to confrontation with others in cases of disagreements or incompatible interests, or prefer, on the other hand, to accept apparently sub-optimal outcomes to avoid tension. This trait is related to assertiveness and to the arbitration between belief and peace. We measure it by means of an item focusing on stimulation from arguments.

Throughout the book, we assess how these eight discrete personality traits affect citizens' electoral experience, behaviour, and resolution, in both bivariate and multivariate models.

The Impact of Personality Traits

We first look at the impact of personality traits on turnout and electoral choice (both mainstream and extremist) in the US (presidential and midterm elections), UK (EU-membership referendum), France, Germany, and South Africa, by assessing correlations for turnout, electoral choice, and extremism. The results are detailed in appendix 3.1

1. Appendices referred to in this chapter are to be found online at www.epob.org.

First, the impact of personality on turnout is limited. Anxious citizens are less likely to take part in elections (in the US, France, and Germany) and alienated citizens vote more in the US, France, and South Africa. Sensitivity also has a negative impact on turnout in South Africa, as does risk aversion in the UK referendum. Other traits have no impact. When it comes to left/right voting, effects are more complex. Sensitive citizens were more likely to support Remain in the UK, and less likely to vote for the CDU in Germany. Anxious citizens were also more likely to be Remainers, but less likely to support the ANC in South Africa. Perhaps predictably, those who value freedom over order shy away from the Republicans in the US and CDU in Germany, as do extraverts. Risk-averse people typically favour left-wing (and Remain) options. Conversely, alienated voters favor the CDU in Germany, and confrontational ones the Republicans in the US and opposition parties in South Africa.

Finally, there is a strong link between personality and extremism in Germany, France, and the UK. Typically, extreme right voting is higher amongst sensitive citizens (except in the UK) and less strong amongst anxious citizens and those who favour freedom over order. At the same time, extraversion and risk aversion are associated with greater propensities to vote for the extreme left and, perhaps unexpectedly, caringness entails a lower propensity to do so.

Personality Derivatives—Personality in Electoral Context

Having looked at the relationship between meaningful discrete personality traits and electoral behaviour in bivariate models (multivariate models follow later in this chapter), we turn to personality derivatives. Respondents were asked to consider real or hypothetical situations, to specify their self-image and preferences that we know to be broadly but complexly affected by personality, in order to reveal some of their latent characteristics. Instead of asking respondents directly about their personalities, these questions dispassionately capture personality symptoms which individuals are acutely aware of, such as their favourite colour or the animal they think they most resemble. Human beings are typically far more aware of such derivatives (people know what colours they like) than of underlying traits (we are not objective in describing our own nature), and their answers are far less tainted by response bias. Personality derivatives thus enable us to capture consequences of personality foundations that may influentially shape electoral experiences, perceptions, and perhaps even behaviour.

These questions were asked prior to any electoral questioning, to avoid framing effects, in particular with regard to colours or animals that may be associated with given parties. They referred to favourite colour, fruits, and flowers, and to animal 'alter ego' and artistic preferences. Let us take the example of voting preferences in relation to respondents' favorite colours. The results of the analysis for the US, UK, France, and Germany are presented in appendix 3. At first sight, a striking finding is that citizens sometimes seem to embrace the iconography of their political preferences. In the UK, for instance, people who claimed red as their favorite colour were more likely to vote Labour than any other group (33.7% against an average of 25.2%), while in the US, those preferred red were the group most likely to vote Republican (again, a party symbolized by that colour). Back in the UK, those choosing blue were second most likely of all colour groups to vote Conservative (41.2% against an average of 35%). Similarly, in Germany, people whose favorite colour is black were more likely to vote for the CDU (represented by black in the media) than those favouring any other color (43.9% against an average of 38.3%).

Some trends are harder to understand, and may represent false positives. For instance, people whose favorite colour is grey were most likely to vote for the Socialist party in France, but least likely to vote for the SPD in Germany—two relatively similar parties, in neighbouring cultures. Lovers of white are the most polarized group in the monarchic UK, showing the highest propensity to vote Conservative and the lowest to vote Labour. The colour is also associated with right-wing preferences in Germany, and to a lesser extent France, but in the US, white-lovers are the second least likely group to favour the Republicans. Finally, choosing purple as one's favorite colour is associated with the lowest propensity to be right-wing in the US, but some of the highest scores for extreme right parties in Germany and the UK (where it is UKIP's colour).

The detailed results in appendix 3 and figure 4.1 highlight other differences stemming from the personality-derivative analysis, notably when comparing respondents' patterns of electoral support according to the animals they claim to resemble most, their favourite fruit, and their favourite flower. In figure 4.1, we depict propensity to vote Conservative in the UK according to respondents' animal 'alter ego'. The more respondents compare themselves to an animal exuding power and stability, the more likely they are to vote Conservative, with lions, horses, and dogs first, third, and fifth in the league. Citing animals associated with cleverness, audacity, and insolence also corresponds to a higher likelihood to vote Conservative, with

Proportion of conservative voters by most similar animal

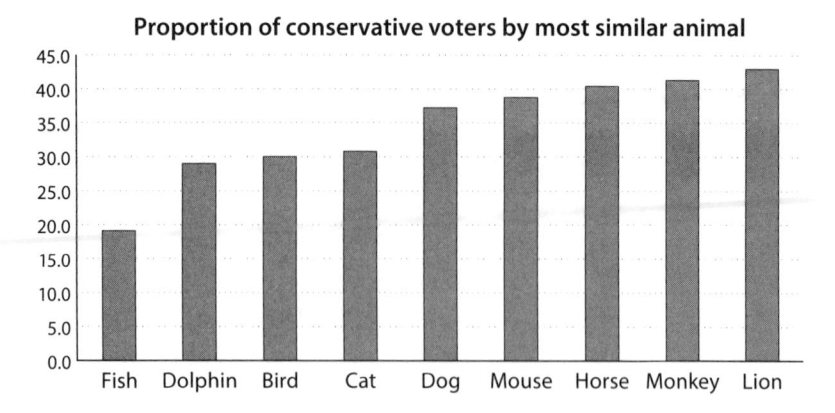

Fish	~19
Dolphin	~29
Bird	~30
Cat	~31
Dog	~37
Mouse	~39
Horse	~40
Monkey	~41
Lion	~42

FIGURE 4.1: Party animals in the UK
Note: figures represent the average proportion of Conservative voters in the General Election according to the = animal respondents declare to resemble them most

monkeys and mice coming second and fourth respectively. By contrast, respondents comparing themselves to animals associated with freedom (fish, dolphin, bird) are the least likely to vote Conservative.

We return to preference in other results in appendix 3, and consider French respondents' voting propensity according to their favourite flowers. Choosing a rose—the official logo of the French Socialists—entails a very strong likelihood of voting for that party, as does a preference for hyacinths. By contrast, voters who like ephemeral spring daisies are the least likely to vote for the two main traditional parties. Extreme right voters are overrepresented among daisy and crocus fans, but particularly weak among lovers of cherry blossoms, a tree associated with the French Resistance during the Second World War. Finally, those who claim carnations and lilies as their favourite flowers were the most likely to support the extreme left. The red carnation is an iconic flower for trade unions and the workers' movement in France, and frequently worn for Labour Day celebrations, though it is also true that lilies and white carnations are typically associated with the monarchy.

Finally, we consider respondents' favourite fruits in relation to voting patterns in the US and Germany. In both countries, those who love mangos, figs, and cherries are unlikely to support the right (in the US) and the extreme right (in Germany). By contrast, summer peach and strawberry lovers are amongst the main supporters of those types of party. Historically, the strawberry was held to be a symbol of purity and the peach of opulence. However, of all voter categories, by far most likely to support extreme right parties in Germany are lovers of bananas, a fruit associated with money and energy and which remains the country's most popular exotic fruit amongst less wealthy citizens.

Claimed relationships between personality derivatives and the voting preferences are to be taken with a pinch of salt, and serve most of all to indicate the scope of unexplained personality effects in our model. Correlations may be plentiful, but are not always easy to interpret, and patterns vary across countries; they nevertheless underline the need for more systematic personality research. We now return to a highly theorized consequence of personality: the impact upon the vote of hierarchies between potentially conflicting moral principles.

From Personality to Morality

Closely related to fundamental personality traits are defining conceptions of morality. We are talking here not just of traditional beliefs, but of the underlying moral conceptions that guide and constrain our principles, thoughts, and behaviour in life, and which are related to multiple psychological personality models, in the manner of the super-ego in Freudian psychoanalysis. There is ample debate in the literature on whether moral foundations are universal or culturally connoted, but either way, there is unanimous agreement that within any moral framework, yardsticks and prioritization will vary by individuals. For instance, when it comes to assessing different types of moral transgression, individuals may be more tolerant of 'bad' actions stemming from understandable motivations, or of 'bad' thoughts and motivations as long as these do not result in acts of which they disapprove. They might be more, or less, likely to tolerate transgressions affecting others or those pertaining to one's own beliefs, errors stemming from weakness or those stemming from power, those grounded in narcissistic or in aggressive motivation. Measuring moral prioritization is very difficult. Because our 'moral compass' is largely subconscious, its expression may be infinitely idiosyncratic—or indeed wholly non-verbalized—and because the desire for social acceptability encourages respondents to claim stricter moral norms than they may truly embrace, we need measures that tap 'pure' prioritization as opposed to unilateral intensity.

In our model, we use two renowned sets of criteria to disentangle moral prioritization: the Ten Commandments of the Old Testament (or more specifically, the six 'moral' commandments, excluding the four strictly religious ones), and the Seven Deadly Sins of Christian tradition. We asked respondents to rank each list of moral precepts from the most to the least important. The choice of rank ordering as a technique aims to limit the impact of the desire for social acceptability (since respondents are forced into a 'zero-sum game') and focus solely on individual hierarchies of moral norms. We explore moral dimensions deductively, and confirm them using exploratory factor analysis. We subdivide the commandments into three types of morality offence: deprivation (murdering and stealing from others); family (respecting one's parents, adultery, and coveting); and truth (perjury). We similarly recode the deadly sins into five different types of moral breach: aggressive (wrath, greed), lazy (sloth), narcissistic (pride, envy), sexual (lust), and self-indulgent (gluttony) sins. In most countries, these models are confirmed by the exploratory factor analyses. We use factor scores to operationalize moral prioritization and assess its impact on turnout, voting for mainstream left- and right-wing parties, and voting for extreme left and extreme right parties. Results are detailed in appendix 3.

Morality and Turnout

We are first interested in the effects of morality on electoral participation. Findings suggest strong comparative variations. While moral priorities have no statistically significant effect on turnout in Germany and South Africa, they are a major predictor in the US, and have specific but meaningful impact in the UK and France. Narcissism prioritization has statistically significant effects in the US, UK, and France, though interestingly enough in opposing directions: in the two English-speaking democracies, the less one cares about narcissistic sins, the more likely one is to vote; in France, it is the other way round. Causality is equally paradoxical with regard to aggressive sins: prioritizing these lowers propensity to vote in France, but increases it in the US. In the US, a moral emphasis on family-related commandments decreases turnout, whilst a primary moral condemnation of deprivation of life or property increases it. A moral focus on lies and on laziness increased turnout propensity only for the 2014 US mid-term elections. Finally, it is only in the UK that prioritization of sexual sins increases turnout; whilst in France, a focus on self-indulgence decreases it.

Morality and Left/Right Vote

Whilst citizens' moral hierarchization affects their likelihood to vote to an extent, its effects on electoral choice are significantly stronger. Left/right voting patterns show some such effects for all of the countries analyzed, though they are substantially stronger in the US and South Africa than in others like the UK and Germany. Certain findings travel best: almost everywhere, those who most strongly condemn aggression favour the left, and those who take particular offence at sexual and family deviation vote for the right.

In the US, almost every single aspect of prioritization between the Seven Deadly Sins and Six (out of Ten) Commandments has (often very) strong effects on a citizen's likelihood to vote Democrat or Republican. The strongest effects pertain to the emphasis on sexual and aggressive sins, and on family- and truth-related commandments. In particular, those who see lust as a major sin and family-related commandments (such as avoiding adultery and not coveting a person's partner) as central are far more likely to vote Republican. By contrast, seeing aggression and lies as particularly morally reprehensible is associated with a significantly greater likelihood to vote Democrat, as do a primary condemnation of depriving others of their life or property through murder and theft, and of self-indulgence. Rejecting narcissism, however, is predominantly a Republican moral positioning.

In other countries, the relevance of moral hierarchies to predicting left/right choice is limited to specific vices. In South Africa, taking a strong moral stance against deprivation of life or property and aggression correlates with a higher propensity to vote for the opposition, whilst taking offence at breaches of traditional sexual and family morality is associated with pro-ANC voting. In France, in a quasi-caricature of expectations, those who focus strongly on condemning aggression are likely to vote for the left (right-wing voters, conversely, worry less about aggression), and those who condemn laziness vote for the right (whilst, conversely, left-wing voters find it more forgivable). In the UK, Tory (Conservative) voters are again proportionally less worried about aggression.

Morality and Extremism

The link between moral hierarchies and voting tendency can also be seen in relation to extremism in Germany, France, and Britain. Effects on the extremism scale are in fact stronger than as regards left/right choices. Correlations between moral hierarchy and support for left- and right-wing extremist and populist parties are analyzed in appendix 3. In France, a strong condemnation of self-indulgence typically correlates with a higher likelihood of voting for extremist parties in general, echoing condemnation of 'fat cats'. Supporters of extreme right parties focus strongly on 'family' sins (Germany), laziness (Germany), and self-indulgence (France). However, they also tend to be less worried by deprivation (murder, theft) in (Germany), aggression (UK, France), and self-indulgence (Germany—unlike the

French case). In the UK, the moral priorities of (right-wing) English Democrat voters are, unexpectedly, similar to those of left-wing extremists elsewhere.

In all three countries, extreme left supporters are united by comparatively high tolerance for laziness. They also focus strongly on deprivation of life and property, as well as self-indulgence (Germany), and on aggression and narcissism (France), compared to the rest of the population. However, they tend to be more forgiving when it comes to sexual morality (France) and traditional family morality (Germany). Tolerance of sexuality and hatred of self-indulgence are in fact most closely associated with populist left voting in France, though the latter is shared with extreme right voters. These results echo traditional perceptions of extremist priorities. For those on the extreme right, aggression is an understandable fault, but there is little tolerance of people perceived as lazy, who are in turn tolerated on the extreme left, unlike the self-indulgent. This adds to criteria more broadly symptomatic of left/right differentiation. People on the right are far more likely to be bothered by a breach of traditional sexual or family values, whilst those on the left are more likely to care about the truth.

The relationship between morality, religiosity, and electoral psychology tells us something important about the moral order of electoral politics. Fundamentally, it highlights the complexity of moral trade-offs in the vote. Central to the hostility discourse we analyze in chapter 9 is that many cannot understand how opposite voters could possibly endorse positions which they themselves see as obviously and heinously immoral. The truth seems to be that voters may resent the moral sacrifices associated with their own choices, but see them as necessary to avoid what they consider even worse evils. They are not oblivious to the complexities, but simply pick their battles.

The results of allowing citizens to express a care for any moral priority tend to suggest, wrongly, that right-wing voters focus more on morality. However, using rank ordering (in practice, an implicit tension scale) to force prioritization, suggests instead that right-wing, and particularly extreme right-wing, voters can occasionally tolerate breaches of seemingly universal moral priorities (such as not killing others, not stealing from them, or not being aggressive) to ensure the maintenance of other priorities such as the sanctity of the family or work ethic. By contrast, left-wing voters who consider injunctions against violence and theft as more sacred, and hate self-indulgence, may tolerate laziness or family betrayal in return. Neither camp is at root immoral; subconsciously, however, most voters have long assimilated the idea that to protect the vision of morality they cherish, they will have to accept ugly compromises; which in turn gets them labelled as hostile by voters whose own hierarchies profoundly differ.

The Psychology of Egocentric and Sociotropic Voting

If the hierarchy of moral perceptions tells us how voters believe they should treat others, another critical distinction in the personality debate has long been made in the literature between egocentric and sociotropic attitudes and behaviour. However, as noted in chapter 2, this discussion has typically been limited to economic terms and relied upon explicit self-placement.

In this book, we develop indices for egocentric and sociotropic measures which go much further. First, we are interested in understanding the balance between egocentric and sociotropic perceptions on the way citizens approach their vote not just in economic terms, but on four dimensions: economic, social, and with regard to safety and to misery. We also wish to modify the strictly dichotomous nature of egocentric and sociotropic motivation to include intermediate potential beneficiaries, such as specific subgroups, family members, or specific generations. In particular, with regard to younger generations, we introduce a crucial distinction between short-term sacrifice and long-term benefits, which we label *projection*. We thus suggest that aspects of the egocentric/sociotropic assessment and group identity literatures overlap in sociotropism scales, disentangle these into multiple substantive dimensions, and introduce a new concept of arbitration between immediate benefits and long-term sustainability. Finally, we measure all of these aspects of sociotropism and projection with quasi-implicit measures independent of citizens' own perceptions of their own selflessness.

Variations in Egocentric and Sociotropic Attitudes

Our measurement of egocentric and sociotropic attitudes differs from usual survey instruments in three ways. First, in addition to self-placement measures, we include implicit sociotropism items. Second, instead of focusing on economic sociotropism only, we assess egocentric and sociotropic attitudes not only in economic terms, based on income, but also socially, based on pensions (arguably the main solidarity challenge in many advanced economies), regarding safety, based on crime (one of the most individualized policy worries of citizens), and in terms of misery, using the example of housing the homeless (a highly emotional solidarity principle in tension with neighbourhood situations). We also test, in addition to these four thematic dimensions, attitudes towards the interests of other generations vis-à-vis one's own, thereby introducing the concept of *generational projection*. Third, we mix both full egocentric–sociotropic scales and truncated scales: from egocentric change to the status quo, and from sociotropic change to the status quo. We can thereby test possible asymmetries and curvilinearity in the effects of egocentric and sociotropic tendencies on electoral behaviour.

We first explore egocentric and sociotropic attitude distributions on the basis of our unique measurement. The literature suggests that older voters are more sociotropic than the young (Kinder and Kiewiet, 1981). We find instead that older and younger citizens tend to be sociotropic in different ways. Economic and social sociotropisms are positively correlated with age (0.10* to 0.13** in the US and 0.09** to 0.13** in the UK on the economic dimension, 0.11** for the social dimension in the US only), echoing perceptions that young people are more egocentric. However, on the safety and misery dimensions, younger generations prove more sociotropic than their elders, and more willing to accept a share of the burden for the greater good (0.12** in the US, 0.07* in the UK). Gender has little impact in the US, except in so far as women are slightly more sociotropic with regard to misery. However, in the UK, women are slightly more sociotropic than men on all four dimensions: economic (0.09**), social (0.07*), regarding safety (0.08*), and regarding misery (0.07*).

Thus it seems that sociotropism does not increase with age, but rather mutates, and proves to be a function of generosity, but also of vulnerability. Young and old are equally likely to be egocentric where they feel more threatened and vulnerable: in terms of income for the younger generations, and of crime and mixing with feared communities for the older ones. These differences also echo some generational divisions in electoral events covered by our research, such as the UK EU-membership referendum, wherein young people were particularly worried about losing opportunity and prosperity through Brexit, whilst older voters prioritized control of migration, seen by more of them as a threat.

Sociotropism Scales

Based on the data collected, we created the five sociotropism scales used in various parts of our model. First, for each of the four substantive sub-dimensions (economic, social, safety, misery), we develop a mean index based on each of the indicators (i.e., the sociotropism indicator and negative of the egocentrism indicator). We then factor-analyze all dimensional scores to produce an overall sociotropism factor. For the US and the UK, this results in single factor solutions with Eigenvalues of 1.74–1.79 explaining 43.5–44.8% of total variance. However, because of the granularity of the dimensions, in overall models we enter separately the economic and social dimensions of sociotropism, the effects of which differ in bivariate tests.

Sociotropism, Turnout, and Electoral Choice

We now turn to the electoral consequences of sociotropism detailed in appendix 3, and find that sociotropic citizens are far more likely to vote. This is particularly true in the US, whilst the correlation is rather weaker for the UK. The overall sociotropism index correlates with cumulated turnout at 0.10** to 0.15** in the US, and 0.07* to 0.08* in the UK. Regarding individual dimensions, economic sociotropism is most highly correlated (0.16** in the US and 0.12** in the UK) followed by social sociotropsim (0.14** in the US and 0.08** in the UK), misery (0.12** in the US and 0.10** in the UK), and safety (0.09** in the US and 0.10** in the UK).

Sociotropic attitudes are even more strongly associated with electoral choice, once again particularly in the US, though in the UK they also affect the propensity to vote for extremist parties. In terms of left/right vote, overall sociotropism indices do not correlate, but individual dimensions do. In the US, this is most true of the misery dimension (0.26** to 0.34**). This is followed by the economic dimension (0.11** to 0.23**). Note that the relationship is not monotonic. Instead, arbitration between egocentrism and the status quo is far more meaningful than that between sociotropism and status quo. Finally, the safety dimension is only statistically significant in 2014 (0.11**) and the social dimension for 2012 (0.10**). In the UK, the misery dimension is related to Labour and Conservative votes, with correlations ranging from 0.11** to 0.22**. In the case of Labour, the social and economic dimensions (up to 0.10** and 0.09** repectively) are also relevant, but safety is not. The social (and safety dimensions (0.08* and 0.07* respectively) are correlated with the Conservative vote in 2010 only, whilst misery is only relevant for 2015.

Critically, in the UK, sociotropism is strongly related to propensity to vote for extremist parties. The overall index is significantly correlated with the propensity to vote for various populist-right parties (up to 0.10**), as are some items from all of the safety and social dimensions (between 0.09** and 0.13**). However, in some cases, voting for the English Democrats gets directions of correlation which would be expected for the far left rather than the far right.

In a twist to traditional sociotropic studies, we also explore the impact of inter-generational solidarity on the vote. In both the US and the UK, reluctance to increase fiscal pressure on the middle-aged to benefit the young is strongly correlated with right-wing voting (0.32** to 0.38** in the US, in the UK, 0.14** to 0.17** for greater likelihood to vote Conservative, and 0.10** to 0.15** for lower likelihood to vote Labour). It is also positively associated with voting for the extreme right BNP (0.07*). In the US, favouring low fiscal pressure on the middle-aged over the welfare of the elderly is also positively associated with voting Republican (0.22** to 0.27**), but this has no equivalent in the UK. When it comes to directions of intergenerational solidarity, privileging the elderly is more widespread amongst right-wing voters (0.14** to 0.16** in the US, and in the UK, 0.08* for increased propensity to vote Conservative and 0.08* to 0.10** for decreased propensity to vote Labour). In the UK only, privileging the interests of the middle-aged is also associated with lower turnout (0.09**).

Projective Citizens: The Power of Longitudinal Projection

In addition to sociotropism, a potentially important outlook feature when it comes to voters is what we term 'projection': the arbitration between short-term enjoyment and long-term good and sustainability. Within debates on the environment, pension systems sustainability, or EU membership, these arbitrations are key; but before becoming a policy preference, projection—expressing the balance between immediate and more distant future focus—is first of all a feature of personality. We devised three items to measure this projection in terms of short-term benefits/sacrifices and long-term vulnerability/safety. In both the US and UK, projective citizens are more likely to vote (0.09** in the US, 0.07* to 0.08* in the UK). In the UK, they are also more prone to vote Conservative (0.07* to 0.22**) and less to vote Labour (0.09** to 0.19), with no equivalent left/right effect in the US.

Overall, we show that sociotropic and projective citizens are more likely to vote. They also have a higher propensity to support the left, and a lower one to vote for extremes. We have also debunked the myth of older citizens being more sociotropic, showing this be an artefact of a sole focus on income, as both younger and older citizens are more likely to be sociotropic with regard to areas where they feel less vulnerable: income for the old, housing and crime for the young.

Having considered the relationship between personality, morality, projection, and the vote, we have made important findings. First, several personality traits such as anxiety and a sense of alienation seem to be associated with turnout, whilst others, such as the arbitration between freedom and order, risk aversion, confrontation and care, are correlate with citizens' left/right vote. Sensitivity, anxiety, and the arbitration between freedom and order also predict propensity to vote for the extreme right, and risk aversion and caringness propensity to vote for the extreme left. The role of moral hierarchies in predicting turnout and electoral choice is also critical, notably in the US, South Africa, and France. Condemnation of sexual and family-related sins and laziness is associated with a right-wing vote, outrage at aggression and deprivation of life or property with a left-wing vote. Moral hierarchies are also strong predictors of extremism. Extreme right voters often tolerate aggression, but not laziness, which is, conversely and unlike self-indulgence, tolerated on the extreme left. We concluded that these differences shed light on the logic of electoral hostility, as citizens perceived opposite voters as morally uncondonable, because the moral sacrifices each side is willing to make to prioritize what it deems essential are incompatible.

Finally, the chapter explored the influence of egocentric and sociotropic predispositions on the vote. It disentangled different dimensions of sociotropism (economic, social, and with regard to safety and misery) to avoid an exclusive focus on the economic, and considered generational solidarity and projection (the arbitration between short- and long-term goals), whilst adding implicit measures and truncated scales to test for asymmetry. We found not only that sociotropism and projection increase turnout and the left-wing vote, but that they are not monotonic (egocentrism outweighs sociotropism), and that sociotropic profiles inversely mirror perceived vulnerabilities.

Personality, morality, sociotropism, and projection are not just direct agents of human behaviour, but also shape the way citizens see the world. They affect what we look at in a given person or situation, what we notice, how we react, and ultimately what we remember.

First Model Stage: Do Personality, Morality, and Sociotropism Matter?

We next test the effects of personality in multivariate models of electoral behaviour, experience, and resolution using multivariate OLS and binary logistic regression models. These tests are mirrored in the next two chapters, on memory and electoral identity. With regard to electoral behaviour, we look at turnout and components of electoral choice (Republican vote in the US, vote in favour of Scottish independence in the UK, votes for the CDU-CSU, the SPD, and the AfD in Germany, left/right vote in France, and vote for the ANC in South Africa). Regarding electoral experience, we assess how our sets of independent variables contribute to making a citizen's electoral experience emotional and happy. Finally, in terms of electoral resolution, we consider effects of the election in making citizens feel closer to or conversely further away from—fellow citizens. Each time, we look at the contribution of each set of independent variables: stage 1: personality, morality, and sociotropism; stage 2: electoral memory and first-time vote; stage 3: electoral identity and empathic displacement, looking both at individual variables and change in R^2 or pseudo-R^2 from a control model. We primary focus on the US case, which alone comprehensively includes every item in our model, and compare it to equivalent models in the UK, Germany, France, and South Africa (notwithstanding the few missing independent variables in each of those cases, which are discussed in the analysis). The variables are entered stage by stage. Stage 0 includes basic social and demographic controls (age, gender, income, ethnicity, religiosity, and state politics). To account for electoral ergonomics, we run separate models for those voting in person on Election Day, in advance at polling stations, and using absentee ballots (proxy in France).

In this first instance, we look at the contribution of personality variables, including personality traits, morality hierarchization, and sociotropism. We use, our eight personality traits measured as factor scores from factor analyses (sensitivity, anxiety, freedom, extraversion, risk aversion, care/empathy, alienation, and confrontation) and likewise our eight components of moral hierarchization based on the Seven Deadly Sins and Ten Commandments (deprivation commandments, family commandments, truth commandments, aggression sins, narcissism sins, laziness sins, self-indulgence sins, and sexual sins). Moral hierarchy questions are missing for the UK. For sociotropism, for the US and UK we use implicit indices of its economic and social dimensions. For elsewhere, we use a self-declared measure, as those implicit indices are missing.

PERSONALITY TRAITS, MORALITY, SOCIOTROPISM, AND ELECTORAL BEHAVIOUR

We first look at the impact of the personality variables on electoral behaviour, beginning with electoral choice. Figure 4.2 shows that these predictors

Behaviour models improvement—stage 1

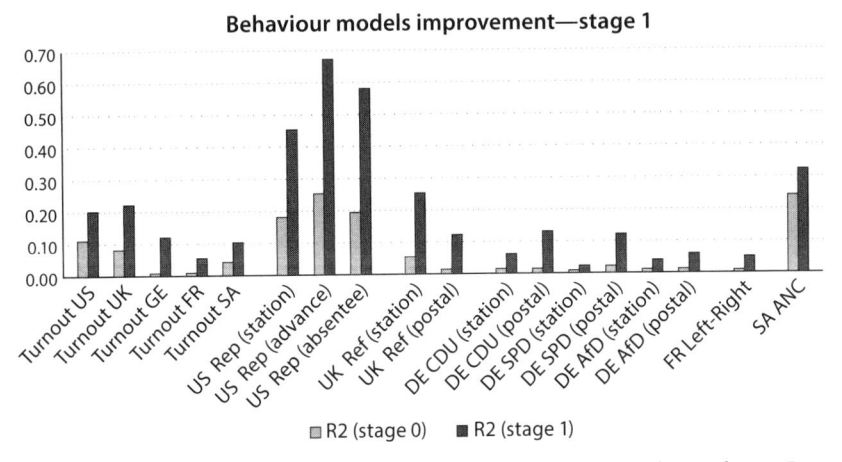

[Bar chart showing R² (stage 0) and R² (stage 1) for: Turnout US, Turnout UK, Turnout GE, Turnout FR, Turnout SA, US Rep (station), US Rep (advance), US Rep (absentee), UK Ref (station), UK Ref (postal), DE CDU (station), DE CDU (postal), DE SPD (station), DE SPD (postal), DE AfD (station), DE AfD (postal), FR Left-Right, SA ANC]

FIGURE 4.2: Stage 1: Improvement to electoral behaviour models—personality predictors. Bars represent R^2

vastly improve the models' R^2 or Nagelkerke pseudo-R^2 compared to the baseline control model. The greatest improvement to the pseudo-R^2 comes from the US (+0.27 to +0.42), where the model performs particularly well, but model improvement is also substantial in the UK, despite the absence of moral hierarchization variables, in South Africa, and for postal voters in Germany, whilst other models show more modest improvements. In France, the vote variable is based on a continuous left/right coding, and the model test thus uses a linear regression instead of a binary logistic regression, so the results are based on a change of R^2 rather than of Nagelkerke pseudo-R^2. We then turn to individual variable effects (in full models), in tables 4.1 and 4.2.

In the US, different personality traits have varying effects, depending on the voting mode. Risk aversion and alienation matter most for polling station voters, but care and confrontation impact absentee voters most. Extraversion is also significant. Outside the US, extraversion, risk aversion, alienation, and confrontation have the most common effects, but anxiety is significant in German and South African models. Directions of causality are consistent: a higher sense of alienation makes citizens more prone to vote for the right, whilst conversely, a more caring personality results in a higher likelihood of voting for the left. In Germany, people with caring personalities are also less likely to support the extreme right. By contrast, in the same country, those who favour the protection of individual freedom over public order are more likely to vote for it. Moral hierarchization is equally telling. Those who particularly resent aggressiveness, laziness, and sexual treachery

TABLE 4.1. Model of Electoral Choice in the US (Parsimonious version)

	Polling station voter			Advance voter			Absentee voter		
	b (se)	Wald χ^2	Exp (b)	b (se)	Wald χ^2	Exp (b)	b (se)	Wald χ^2	Exp (b)
Age	—	—	—	—	—	—	—	—	—
Gender	—	—	—	—	—	—	—	—	—
Income	—	—	—	—	—	—	—	—	—
Religiosity	−0.58 (0.15)	15.15***	0.56	−0.92 (0.41)	5.03**	0.40	−0.75 (0.27)	7.48***	0.48
State control (D/R)	−0.06 (0.03)	4.43**	0.94	−0.11 (0.08)	1.62	0.90	−0.03 (0.04)	0.41	0.97
Hispanic ethnic	—	—	—	—	—	—	—	—	—
African American ethnic	—	—	—	—	—	—	—	—	—
Sensitivity	—	—	—	—	—	—	—	—	—
Anxiety	—	—	—	—	—	—	—	—	—
Freedom	—	—	—	—	—	—	—	—	—
Extraversion	0.37 (0.23)	2.51	1.45	−0.98 (0.70)	1.98	0.38	−0.72 (0.43)	2.86*	0.49
Risk aversion	−0.63 (0.24)	6.82***	0.53	−1.24 (0.84)	2.17	0.29	0.06 (0.46)	0.02	1.07
Care	−0.38 (0.23)	2.81*	0.68	−0.54 (0.62)	0.74	0.59	−1.06 (0.51)	4.39**	0.35
Alienation	0.26 (0.11)	5.31**	1.29	0.31 (0.29)	1.10	1.36	−0.44 (0.23)	3.64*	0.65
Confrontation	−0.01 (0.11)	0.01	0.99	0.29 (0.31)	0.85	1.33	0.49 (0.21)	5.51**	1.63

Deprivation moral	—	—	—	—	—	—
Family moral	—	—	—	—	—	—
Truth moral	—	—	—	—	—	—
Aggression moral	−0.66 (0.32)	4.28**	0.52	−0.45 (0.97)	0.21	0.64	−0.74 (0.53)	1.94	0.48
Narcissism moral	—	—	—	—	—	—
Laziness moral	−0.23 (0.19)	1.53	0.79	−0.52 (0.58)	0.80	0.59	−1.04 (0.37)	7.97***	0.36
Sexuality moral	−0.34 (0.16)	4.45**	0.71	−0.51 (0.47)	1.15	0.60	−0.29 (0.28)	1.03	0.75
Sociotropism (econ.)	−0.79 (0.43)	3.31*	0.45	−2.14 (1.31)	2.67*	0.12	−0.72 (0.74)	0.95	0.49
Sociotropism (social)	−1.45 (0.34)	18.32***	0.24	0.86 (0.84)	1.05	0.42	−2.76 (0.74)	13.72***	0.06
Childhood memory	−0.63 (0.22)	7.93***	0.53	−0.42 (0.59)	0.52	0.66	0.05 (0.45)	0.01	1.05
First-time memory	—	—	—	—	—	—
First-time voter	−1.00 (0.37)	7.28***	0.37	−0.61 (1.20)	0.26	0.55	0.32 (0.59)	0.30	1.38
Electoral identity	0.11 (0.23)	0.24	1.12	1.03 (0.59)	3.03*	2.80	−0.15 (0.35)	0.17	0.87
Longitud. projection	—	—	—	—	—	—
Generat. projection	—	—	—	—	—	—
Empathic displacement	—	—	—	—	—	—
Projected efficacy	—	—	—	—	—	—
Constant	−38.68 (5289)			−338.62 (2172)			−3.79 (9223)		

Note: * = sig<0.05; ** = sig<0.01; *** = sig<0.001.

TABLE 4.2. Comparative Models of Vote

	UK/Scot. Scot. ref.	Germany CDU	Germany SPD	Germany AfD	France Left/right vote	South Africa ANC
Age	–**	–	+***	–	–	–***
Gender	–	+**	–***	–**	–	–*
Income	–	+***	–	–*	–	–
Ethnicity (Zulu SA only)						+***
Sensitivity	+**	–	–	–	–	–
Anxiety	–	–	+**	–	–*	–**
Freedom	–	–*	–+***	+**	–	–
Extraversion	–	–***	+**	–*	–	–
Risk aversion	+***	–***	–	–*	–***	–
Care	+**	+***	–	–	–	–
Alienation	–	+**	–*	–**	–	+*
Confrontation	–***	–	–	–	–	–
Deprivation moral	.	–	–	–	–	–
Family moral	.	–	–	–	–	–
Truth moral	.	–	–	–	–	–
Aggression moral	.	–***	+***	–*	–	–
Narcissism moral	.	–**	+***	+**	–	–
Laziness moral	.	–***	–	–	–***	–
Self-indulgence moral	.	–	+***	–	–*	–
Sexuality moral	.	–**	–	–	–***	–**
Sociotropism (self-decl.)	+***	–	–	–	–	–
Childhood memory	–***	–*	+***	–	–	–**
First-time memory	–	–	–	–	–*	+***
First-time voter	–	–	–	–	–	–**
Electoral identity	.–	+**	+***	–	.	–
Longitud. projection	–	.	.	.	.	.
Generat. projection	+***	.	–	–	.	.
Empathic displacement	–	.	–	–	–	–
Projected efficacy	–*	–***	–	–	–	–

Note: * = sig<0.05; ** = sig<0.01; *** = sig<0.001; — = not significant; . = variable not measured.

are less likely to vote for the Republicans in the US and for right-wing parties in Germany and France, confirming the bivariate results. In the US, sociotropism also results in choices which are more left-wing, particularly when it comes to its social dimension.

Overall, personality variables also explain differences in turnout, adding +0.05 to explained variance in France (using differences in actual R^2 as we measured cumulative turnout in this two-round election) and +0.06 in

TABLE 4.3. Model of Turnout in the US (Parsimonious version)

	b (se)	Wald χ2	Exp (b)
Age	0.05 (0.02)	10.07***	1.05
Gender	—	—	—
Income	—	—	—
State control (D/R)	—	—	—
Religiosity	—	—	—
Afr. Am. ethnic	—	—	—
Hispanic ethnic	—	—	—
Sensitivity	—	—	—
Anxiety	—	—	—
Freedom	—	—	—
Extraversion	—	—	—
Risk aversion	—	—	—
Care	—	—	—
Alienation	—	—	—
Confrontation	—	—	—
Deprivation moral	—	—	—
Family moral	—	—	—
Truth moral	—	—	—
Aggression moral	—	—	—
Narcissism moral	—	—	—
Laziness moral	—	—	—
Sexuality moral	—	—	—
Sociotropism (econ.)	—	—	—
Sociotropism (social)	—	—	—
Childhood memory	.	.	.
First-time memory	0.52 (0.24)	4.85**	1.68
First-time voter	.	—	—
Electoral identity	1.15 (0.32)	13.12***	3.15
Longitudinal projection	—	—	—
Generational projection	—	—	—
Empathic displacement	—	—	—
Projected efficacy	0.45 (0.10)	20.94***	1.56
Constant	0.98 (8.30)		

Note: * = sig<0.05; ** = sig<0.01; *** = sig<0.001; — = not significant; . = variable not measured.

South Africa to +0.12 and +0.14 respectively in Germany and the UK. Specific variable effects are presented in tables 4.3 and 4.4. Personality variables do not work very well in the US, but in other countries, extraversion and a sense of alienation make citizens more likely to vote, and a confrontational personality less so. We also find that those who care about laziness and

TABLE 4.4. Models of Turnout—Comparative

	UK/Scot.	Germany	France	South Africa
Age	+***	+**	—	+***
Gender	—	–***	—	—
Income	–*	+***	—	—
Ethnicity (Zulu SA only)	.	.	.	—
Sensitivity	—	—		
Anxiety	—	–*	—	—
Freedom	—	—	—	—
Extraversion	+**	—	—	—
Risk aversion	—	—	—	—
Care	—	—	+**	—
Alienation	+*	—	—	—
Confrontation	–***	—	—	—
Deprivation moral	.	—	—	—
Family moral	.	—	—	—
Truth moral	.	—	—	—
Aggression moral	.	—	—	—
Narcissism moral	.	—	–**	—
Laziness moral	.	—	–**	—
Self-indulgence moral	.	—	—	—
Sexuality moral	.	—	–*	—
Sociotropism (self-decl.)	—	+***	+**	—
Childhood memory	—	—	—	—
First-time memory	—	+***	—	+***
First-time voter	—	—	—	—
Electoral identity	—	—	.	+***
Longitudinal projection	—	.	.	.
Generational projection	+*	.	.	.
Empathic displacement	—	+***	+**	+*
Projected efficacy	—	+***	+***	+***

Note: * = sig<0.05; ** = sig<0.01; *** = sig<0.001; — = not significant; . = variable not measured.

narcissism are less likely to participate, but confirm the bivariate intuition that having a sociotropic personality significantly increases likelihood of turnout.

PERSONALITY TRAITS, MORALITY, SOCIOTROPISM, AND ELECTORAL EXPERIENCE

We next turn to the second dependent variable, electoral experience, and notably the question of whether personality variables affect citizens' likeli-

Experience models improvement—stage 1

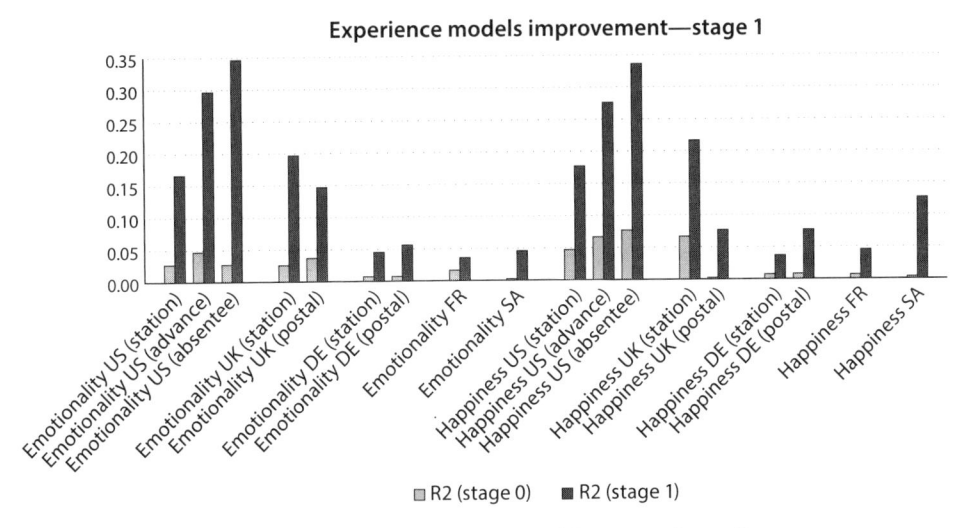

[Bar chart showing R² (stage 0) and R² (stage 1) values for Emotionality and Happiness across US (station), US (advance), US (absentee), UK (station), UK (postal), DE (station), DE (postal), FR, and SA, with values ranging from 0.00 to 0.35]

■ R2 (stage 0) ■ R2 (stage 1)

FIGURE 4.3: Stage 1: Improvement to electoral experience models—personality predictors

hood of feeling emotional and happy in elections. In contrast to the focus in the literature on turnout and electoral choice, little attention has been devoted to considering when elections might make an electoral experience more or less emotional and positive. The overall contribution of personality traits, moral hierarchization, and sociotropism to electoral experience is presented in figure 4.3. This contribution is again very substantial. Baseline social and demographic controls performed much worse at explaining experience than electoral behaviour in the first instance, but by contrast, the additional value of personality attributes is similar to that in models of electoral choice (measured by change in R^2 in OLS regressions, due to the continuous nature of the dependent variables). The explanatory power of personality variables is also much higher than in turnout models. The model works less well in France (+0.02 for emotionality and +0.04 for happiness) and Germany (+0.03 and +0.07) than in the UK (+0.08 and +0.17) and US (+0.13 and +0.32). In all cases except South Africa, personality traits, morality, and sociotropism are better at explaining electoral emotionality than happiness. The contribution of specific variables is shown in tables 4.5 and 4.6.

We start with models of emotionality. We first note that elections are more emotional for women than for men, across countries, and for members of ethnic minorities in the US, though it should be remembered that the first case used was the re-election of Barack Obama, which represented

TABLE 4.5. Models of Electoral Experience in the US (Parsimonious version)

	Emotionality model			Happiness model		
	Polling station voter	Advance voter	Absentee voter	Polling station voter	Advance voter	Absentee voter
Constant	1.95 (3.97)	−9.95 (9.78)	4.12	2.99 (4.37)	3.00 (11.94)	5.19 (4.62)
Age	—	—	—	—	—	—
Gender	0.49 (0.23)**	−0.52 (0.45)	−0.07 (0.33)	0.48 (0.26)*	0.09 (0.55)	−0.72 (0.37)*
Religiosity	—	—	—	—	—	—
Income	—	—	—	—	—	—
State control (D/R)	—	—	—	—	—	—
Hispanic ethnic	−0.90 (1.18)	0.88 (1.66)	3.45 (1.61)**	—	—	—
Afr. Am. ethnic	—	—	—	—	—	—
Sensitivity	—	—	—	—	2.44 (1.43)**	1.05 (1.33)
Anxiety	−0.13 (0.14)	−0.15 (0.22)	0.62 (0.16)***	—	—	—
Freedom	—	—	—	—	—	—
Extraversion	−0.21 (0.13)*	0.36 (0.20)*	−0.28 (0.16)*	—	—	—
Risk Aversion	—	—	—	−0.19 (0.15)	−0.15 (0.27)	−0.39 (0.21)*
Care	−0.04 (0.06)	−0.15 (0.10)	−0.19 (0.09)**	0.03 (0.14)	0.26 (0.25)	0.52 (0.22)**
Alienation	−0.00 (0.06)	0.16 (0.09)*	0.02 (0.07)	—	—	—
Confrontation	—	—	—	—	—	—

Deprivation moral	0.51 (0.25)**	0.76 (0.76)	−0.50 (0.32)	—	—
Truth moral	0.19 (0.14)	0.37 (0.44)	−0.42 (0.18)**	—	—
Aggression moral	−0.19 (0.15)	0.05 (0.19)	−0.30 (0.16)*	—	—
Laziness moral	−0.05 (0.07)	0.03 (0.10)	−0.30 (0.12)**	−0.09 (0.13)	−0.17 (0.14)
Self-indulgence moral	—	—	—	—	—
Family sin	0.68 (0.37)	1.57 (1.15)	−1.08 (0.46)**	—	—
Sexuality sin	−0.18 (0.08)**	0.15 (0.14)	−0.10 (0.11)	—	—
Sociotrop. (econ.)	—	—	—	—	—
Sociotrop. (social)	—	—	—	−0.38 (0.37)	0.16 (0.26)
Childhood election	—	—	—	—	—
First election	—	—	—	—	—
First-/second-time voter	—	—	—	1.54 (2.35)	1.66 (0.93)*
Electoral identity	−0.00 (0.19)	0.89 (0.40)***	−0.04 (0.25)	0.44 (0.48)	0.23 (0.28)
Longitudinal projection	—	—	—	—	—
Generational projection	—	—	—	—	—
Empathic displacement	0.14 (0.05)***	−0.01 (0.08)	−0.10 (0.06)	—	—
Projected efficacy	—	—	0.06 (0.07)	0.15 (0.11)	0.18 (0.08)**

Note: * = sig<0.05; ** = sig<0.01; *** = sig<0.001; — = not significant.

TABLE 4.6. Comparative Models of Electoral Experience

	UK/Scot. Emot. Poll	UK/Scot. Emot. Post	UK/Scot. Happy Poll	UK/Scot. Happy Post	Germany Emot. Poll	Germany Emot. Post	Germany Happy Poll	Germany Happy Post	France Emot. All	France Happy All	South Africa Emot. All	South Africa Happy All
Age	—	—	−***	−*	—	—	−**	—	—	—	—	—
Gender	—	+***	—	—	+***	+**	—	—	+**	—	—	+**
Income	—	—	—	—	—	—	—	—	—	—	—	—
Ethnicity (Zulu SA only)	.	.	.	.	.	.	.	.	.	.	—	—
Sensitivity	—	—	—	+*	—	—	—	—	—	—	—	—
Anxiety	+**	—	—	—	—	+**	−***	—	—	—	—	−***
Freedom	—	+**	+*	+**	—	−*	—	−**	—	—	—	—
Extraversion	—	−**	—	—	—	—	—	—	—	—	−**	−***
Risk aversion	—	—	—	—	—	—	—	—	—	—	—	—
Care	—	—	—	—	—	—	—	—	—	—	—	—
Alienation	+*	—	—	—	—	−***	—	—	—	—	—	+*
Confrontation	—	—	—	—	—	—	—	—	—	—	−***	—
Deprivation moral	.	.	.	.	—	—	—	—	—	—	—	+**
Family moral	.	.	.	.	—	—	—	—	—	—	—	—

	Truth moral	Aggression moral	Narcissism moral	Laziness moral	Self-indulgence moral	Sexuality moral	Sociotropism (self-decl.)	Childhood memory	First-time memory	First-time voter	Electoral identity	Longitud. projection	Generat. projection	Empathic displacement	Projected efficacy
Truth moral	.	.	.	.	.	.	.	.	—	—	—	—	—	—	—
Aggression moral	.	.	.	.	.	.	—	—	—	—	—	—	—	—	—
Narcissism moral	.	.	.	.	.	.	—	—	—	—	—	—	+**	—	—
Laziness moral	.	.	.	.	.	.	—	—	—	—	—	—	+***	—	—
Self-indulgence moral	.	.	.	.	.	—*	—	—	—	—	—	—	+**	—	+*
Sexuality moral	+***	+*	+**	+***	+***	.	+***	—	—	—	—	—	—	—	—
Sociotropism (self-decl.)	—	—***	—*	—*	—*	.	+**	—	—	—	+*	—	—**	+*
Childhood memory	—	—	—	+***	+***	—	+***	.	—	+**	+**	+**	+***	+***	+***
First-time memory	+*	—	—	+***	—	—	+***	—	.	+*	+***	+**	—	—***	—
First-time voter	—	—	—	—	—	—	+*	—	—	.	—	—	—	—	—
Electoral identity	—	—	—	—	—	—	—	—	.	.	.	.	.	.	.
Longitud. projection	—**	+*	—	+**	—	+*	—	.	.	.	.	.	.	+*	—
Generat. projection	—	—	—	—	—	+**	+***	—	+*	+*	+***	+**	.	+**	—***
Empathic displacement	—	+***	—	—	+***	+***	+***	+***	—	+***	+***	+***	—	.	+**
Projected efficacy	.	.	.	.	.	.	+***	+*	+**	+*	+***	—	+***	+*	.

Note: * = sig<0.05; ** = sig<0.01; *** = sig<0.001; — = not significant; . = variable not measured.

a hope for integration and normalization of representation for many minority citizens. Regarding personality traits, elections are far more emotional for anxious citizens (notably in the US, UK, or Germany) and less so for extraverts and alienated citizens, as well as for confrontational ones in South Africa only. Moral hierarchization is also a strong predictor of electoral emotionality, especially in the US. The electoral experience of those who feel strongly about deprivation of life or property is more emotional, whilst those particularly shocked by lies, family-related, and sexual sins are less likely to feel emotional as a result of an election. Finally, except in the US, sociotropic citizens also tend to have significantly more emotional electoral experiences.

Models of electoral happiness give slightly different results. This time, many variables perform best in France and South Africa and less well in the US and Germany. In terms of personality elements, the main finding for the US is that caring citizens have happier electoral experiences, whilst risk-averse ones are left less happy by elections. Looking elsewhere, it is mostly anxiety which drives electoral happiness in South Africa and Germany, and extraversion in South Africa only. By contrast, a freedom-focused personality increases electoral enjoyment. Regarding moral prioritization, outrage at laziness has contradictory effects. It is associated with less happy electoral experiences in the US, but happier ones in France, where a focus on narcissism and sexual sins also lead to happier elections, as does a focus on deprivation in South Africa. Again, sociotropism is influential: except in France, sociotropic citizens have happier electoral experiences.

PERSONALITY TRAITS, MORALITY, SOCIOTROPISM, AND ELECTORAL RESOLUTION

Finally, we look at the effect of personality on the capacity of election to bring a sense of closure and resolution to citizens. As discussed above, this is measured by a sense of feeling closer to fellow citizens in the aftermath of the election. Once again, we start with the impact of personality variables on overall variance in electoral resolution. The results are presented in figure 4.4, and yet again show a significant contribution in explaining electoral resolution. Comparative differences are lower than in some of the other models. Personality questions still contribute an improvement to the R^2 of +0.06 in France and +0.08 in South Africa, whilst the increase is by +0.26 and +0.34 in some of the UK and US models.

Resolution models improvement—stage 1

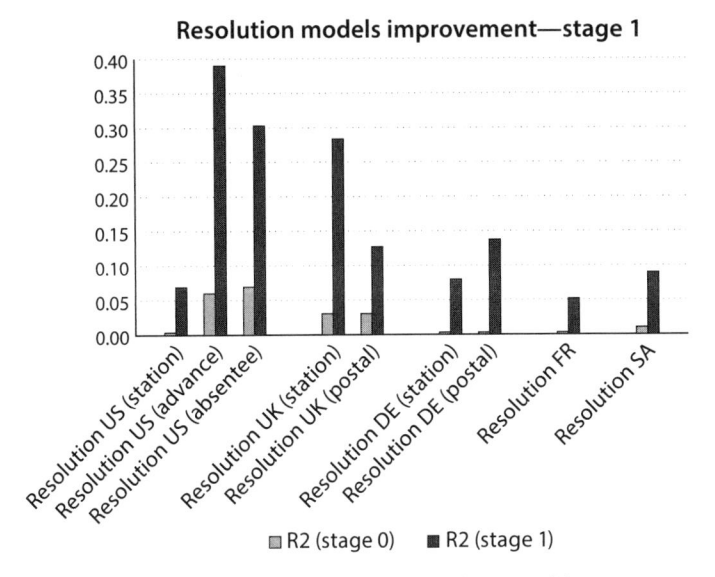

[Bar chart showing R2 (stage 0) and R2 (stage 1) values for: Resolution US (station), Resolution US (advance), Resolution US (absentee), Resolution UK (station), Resolution UK (postal), Resolution DE (station), Resolution DE (postal), Resolution FR, Resolution SA]

FIGURE 4.4: Stage 1: Improvement to electoral resolution models—personality predictors. Bars represent R

Individual variable contributions are reported in tables 4.7 and 4.8. Sensitivity, anxiety, and extraversion tend to make people much less likely to experience electoral resolution at the end of the electoral process, whilst a freedom-oriented personality, caringness (which we showed to lead to great emphasis on process), and alienation increase the likelihood of experiencing closure. In terms of moral prioritization, those who feel most outraged by narcissism, self-indulgence, and sexual immorality are more likely to experience electoral resolution as a result of the electoral process, whilst those who primarily condemn laziness are less likely to feel closure. Yet again, sociotropism has a strong effect, greatly increasing perceptions of electoral resolution, except in South Africa. In the US, this time, it is the economic dimension which has the more robust effect.

We have seen that, on the whole, personality traits, moral hierarchization, and sociotropism all have a significant impact on electoral choice, the nature of citizens' electoral experience, and their sense of electoral resolution, but not really upon turnout. The impact of personality also seems more straightforward amongst remote voters than for those who go to vote in their polling station on Election Day. Results tend to be largely consistent across our five countries.

TABLE 4.7. Full Model of Electoral Resolution (USA)

	Polling station voter	Advance voter	Absentee voter
Constant	0.97 (3.70)	−1.69 (9.55)	−5.72 (5.24)
Age	—	—	—
Gender	—	—	—
Income	—		
Religiosity	—	—	—
State control (D/R)	—	—	—
Afr. Am. ethnic	—	—	—
Hispanic ethnic	—	—	—
Sensitivity	−0.07 (0.14)	−0.46 (0.22)**	0.01 (0.22)
Anxiety	—	—	—
Freedom	0.05 (0.13)	0.34 (0.19)*	0.15 (0.20)
Extraversion	−0.03 (0.13)	−0.40 (0.19)**	−0.03 (0.20)
Risk aversion	—	—	—
Care	—	—	—
Alienation	—	—	—
Confrontation	0.10 (0.06)*	−0.03 (0.09)	0.04 (0.09)
Deprivation moral	—	—	—
Family moral	—	—	—
Truth moral	—	—	—
Aggression moral	—	—	—
Narcissism moral	—	—	0.54 (0.20)***
Laziness moral	—	—	0.38 (0.14)***
Self-indulgence moral	−0.04 (0.07)	−0.13 (0.12)	—
Sexuality moral	0.03 (0.08)	0.28 (0.13)**	0.18 (0.14)
Sociotropism (econ.)	−0.39 (0.23)*	0.66 (0.38)*	0.06 (0.39)
Sociotropism (social)	—	—	—
Childhood memory	−0.01 (0.13)	−0.66 (0.20)***	−0.07 (0.22)
First-time memory	0.21 (0.12)*	0.03 (0.20)	0.17 (0.23)
First-time voter	—	—	—
Electoral identity	—	—	—
Longitudinal projection	—		—
Generational projection	0.30 (0.13)**	0.20 (0.22)	−0.14 (0.17)
Empathic displacement	—	—	—
Projected efficacy	0.10 (0.06)	0.15 (0.09)*	0.16 (0.09)*

Note: * = sig<0.05; ** = sig<0.01; *** = sig<0.001; — = not significant.

TABLE 4.8. Comparative Models of Electoral Resolution

	UK/Scot. Polling station	UK/Scot. Postal	Germany Polling station	Germany Postal	France All	South Africa All
Age	−*	—	+*	—	—	—
Gender	—	—	—	—	—	—
Income	—	+**	—	—	—	—
Ethnicity (Zulu SA only)	.	.	.	.	.	—
Sensitivity	−**	—	—	−**	—	—
Anxiety	—	—	—	−**	—	−**
Freedom	—	**	—	—	—	—
Extraversion	−*	—	−*	−**	—	−***
Risk aversion	+**	—	−**	—	—	—
Care	—	—	+*	+***	—	—
Alienation	+**	+***	+**	—	+**	—
Confrontation	—	−***	—	+*	—	—
Deprivation moral	.	.	—	—	—	—
Family moral	.	.	—	—	—	—
Truth moral	.	.	—	—	—	—
Aggression moral	.	.	—	—	—	—
Narcissism moral	.	.	—	−*	+**	—
Laziness moral	.	.	.	−***	+*	—
Self-indulgence moral	.	.	+**	—	—	—
Sexuality moral	.	.	+***	−***	—	—
Sociotropism (self-decl.)	+***	+**	+***	+***	+**	—
Childhood memory	—	—	—	—	—	—
First-time memory	—	*	+***	—	+***	+***
First-time voter	—	—	—	—	—	—
Electoral identity	—	+**	—	+**	—	—
Longitud. projection	—	—	.	.	.	.
Generat. projection	—	—	.	.	.	.
Empathic displacement	—	—	+**	—	+**	—
Projected efficacy	—	+**	+*	—	+***	+***

Note: * = sig<0.05; ** = sig<0.01; *** = sig<0.001; — = not significant; . = variable not measured.

In the next chapter, we move from personality to the question of electoral memory, the cumulative content of which is itself likely to be shaped by the different outlooks associated with contrasting personality types and moral sensitivities, and citizens' sociotropic and projective orientations.

5

Electoral Memory

What Is Electoral Memory?

In chapter 2, we saw that much of the existing electoral behaviour literature has assumed that citizens have no reliable memory of past elections because they often fail to remember how they voted in recent elections and rationalize their past behaviour instead. We revisited psychological models of visual, auditory, and haptic memory to derive a new understanding of what citizens may remember from past elections, and how those memories may influence future behaviour. We showed that reliable recollection of past voting was always an unlikely aspect of electoral memory, yet voters may be fundamentally influenced by other internalized memories of their interaction with the system and with others. We now test how citizens internalize and accumulate electoral memory, from childhood elections and their first vote to discussions and arguments about elections. This chapter reframes electoral memory by posing questions pertaining to what type and which aspects of elections voters remember, and how that cumulated memory influences their future electoral behaviour, experience, and resolution.

If citizens did not recall previous electoral experiences, on each new Election Day they would face the daunting task of learning how the electoral process works again, from what parties and candidates stand for to what matters to themselves. With every new election, they would experience emotions ranging from excitement through to frustration. In short, classical models of electoral do in fact implicitly assume that citizens possess some electoral memory, which enables them to build up knowledge and experience of the vote over time and develop habituation. In chapter 2, we concluded that a range of internalized (personal), traumatic, and atmospheric haptic memories were far more likely to survive prominently and accumulate in citizens' minds than is typically expected by political scientists. We first tested these expectations by asking what citizens spontaneously remember from past elections, resulting in the word cloud in figure 5.1, which confirms a focus on family and emotions.

In the rest of this chapter, we continue to dissect voters' electoral memory, using evidence from our in-depth interviews, on-the-spot-interviews, election diaries, and survey to cast a wide net over what citizens remember from which past elections, and how it influences them. We first explore which elections citizens remember, and start by considering an inductive panorama of what citizens remember from past elections, before comparing the importance of elections that are egocentrically and sociotropically meaningful in their lives. We then focus on two specific elections that citizens may remember: childhood elections, and their own first vote, which we consider here to be very influential. After looking at both types of memory quantitatively, using our panel data, we move on to narratives citizens associate with electoral events in their childhood and the first time they voted. We then tackle the equally significant question of what citizens remember from past elections. We will systematically map electoral memories in terms of their egocentric and sociotropic components, and of their auditory, visual, and haptic nature, considering both narratives of electoral memory and quantitative elements from the panel survey. Finally, the chapter focuses on why electoral memory matters, and on its impact. We consider some of the retrieval patterns of electoral memory (how citizens mobilize past memories in the context of a new election), and assess the impact of some prominent (notably childhood and first-election) memories, first on turnout and the vote, then on electoral identity, empathic displacement, and efficacy and projected efficacy, and finally in multivariate models of electoral behaviour, experience, and resolution.

National Moment or Personal Story? Which Elections Do Voters Remember?

We asked voters how well they remember various past elections in order to compare the salience of elections which are potentially personally meaningful, such as their first vote or childhood elections, and those that are

FIGURE 5.1: Citizens' memories of past elections - word cloud

societally notable, such as key realignment elections, recent first-order elections, and recent second-order elections. The list of the elections asked about in the survey thus compared childhood elections, one's first vote, and typically four additional specific elections, including the most recent first-order election, the most recent second-order election (local, European, etc.), the most recent key realignment or high-profile election (1997 in the UK, 2000 in the US, 2002 in France, etc.) and one older major or realignment election. In appendix 3,[1] we show how citizens remember each of these. Unsurprisingly, in every case, the election most citizens remember best is the most recent first-order election. However, things become more interesting in terms of the types of election vying for second place in people's memory. In the US, the UK, France, and Georgia, second place goes to a major recent realignment election (US 2000 with its contested result and the Florida ballots controversy, UK 1997 with the rise of New Labour, France 2002 with the first extreme right candidate qualifying for the run-off). However, in Germany and South Africa, citizens remember their own first vote better than any realignment election. In the UK and France, those personal first times easily take third place in citizens' electoral memory hierarchy.

When it comes to arbitrating between time and importance, the only second-order election which is highly remembered in people's memory is the 2010 congressional election in the US. By contrast, second-order elections are poorly remembered elsewhere, apart from the highly fractious referendum on an EU constitution in France in 1995. Finally, childhood elections are further down the rankings (penultimate in the US, South Africa, and Georgia).

The qualitative evidence from in-depth interviews revealed important nuances regarding the memory of traumatic elections. For example, in France, respondents frequently referred to the presidential elections of 2002. These memories were framed in terms of surprise, trauma, or a feeling of lost freedom associated with a heavy burden of responsibility in the second round of the election. The 2002 election was often mentioned spontaneously as one which stands out in citizens' electoral memory, echoing the way in which the media and candidates themselves often invoke the events of 'le 21 avril', to this day. In the UK, frequent references to the 1997 elections proved that voters do not need the elites to remind them of important realignment elections, and many older citizens also referred to shocks such as

---

1. Appendices referred to in this chapter are to be found online at www.epob.org.

when Margaret Thatcher rose to and fell from power (though not always clearly or accurately):

> Well a shock result was when in the '79 election Margaret Thatcher got to power and maybe the Lib-Lab pact of the seventies, when Harold Wilson [sic] scraped in with a few votes. UK65M012

> I think the one that really sticks in my mind is when Mrs Thatcher got voted in in London. UK75F010

> I can remember when my partner and I were in Greece and it was the downfall of Thatcher. We were absolutely enthralled—there was dancing on the streets—even the Greeks—and we were disappointed not to be in Britain at the time as it was an really important event. The other one I remember was when Tony Blair got in. The change in atmosphere when Tony Blair got in. UK40F013

> I remember the landslide elections when, most recently Tony Blair had a landslide in 1997; and I have a strong recall of Maggie Thatcher's election wins and her close allies all peering out of a rather small cramped window above 10 Downing Street. UK46M014

In the US, interviews echo similar stories, with references to the assassination of President Kennedy, Reagan's victory, and the Nixon scandal referred to several times by older voters:

> Big events such as Kennedy being shot or the Nixon scandal stay in memory. US6ZM019

> The shooting of JFK was a key issue at the moment. Kennedy had been so popular that many were devastated. US6ZM020

> My first vote was in 1984. I voted for Reagan as he was so popular at the time having starred in movies beforehand. It was exciting to vote for the first time, it felt important. Living in the countryside I didn't realize how important voting and politics are in everyday life. I learned this by living in a bigger city where government provides more services that become obvious in everyday life, such as metro and bus services. US5ZM021.

Some respondents evoke key elections through the prism of personal experience, poignantly illustrating the internalization process and crystallization of happy memories in voters' minds, whilst others recall memorable moments that marked their electoral memory:

> Just happy memories—1997 was a crucial one for me. It was a real start and opportunity and led on to many businesses and opportunities for me. UK39M023

> I remember seeing footage of Neil Kinnock during one of his campaigns walking in the sea and falling backwards! It made me laugh then and it still does! UK67M008

> I remember that when Mrs Thatcher was voted in, it was really weird at home for a while as the older men in the family were devastated that a woman was going to be running the country. That made me smile on the inside. UK75F010

In sum, regarding the sociotropic memory of elections, respondents focus on a few major traumatic or realignment elections, of which they remember the overall result, but which they also frequently associate with internalized memories, as exemplified in the French case below:

> I was really disappointed by Jospin's campaign, I thought Jospin's campaign was really bad, almost right-wing stuff, only saying 'Vote for me, my government did so well' and not proposing anything new. I didn't want him to have an easy ride, I wanted him to push a more left-wing agenda, so I voted for Besancenot [a Trotskyist candidate]. When I turned the TV on in the evening, I was mostly bored and hoping that many people would, like me, have sent a 'left-wing message' [sic] to Jospin. When journalists first mentioned a 'big surprise' I first did not understand what they meant and thought it was one of their gimmicks. Then the results were announced and I suddenly remembered one of my friends who had told me a few weeks earlier that there was a real 'Le Pen danger' in these elections, and that his unusually low forecast in the polls was probably mistaken. He was the first person I called, and I was crying. FRP36F059

Here, the sociotropic electoral reference is really used as a setting, in which the egocentric memory of the election is enacted. Citizens who remember not taking part in the first ballot, or voting for a minor candidate, often remember the 2002 presidential election to describe how they felt about their own choice. They also often evoke the following (societally minor) elections which represent the start of a civic 'redemption' process, as for those two young voters:

> I could have voted in May but couldn't be arsed. The campaign was so boring, the candidates were so far away from what I cared about. Chirac was lying, Jospin was arrogant, Besancenot was provoking. Pointless. I didn't want my first election to be a choice between these idiots. Two weeks later, I obviously went to vote, but mostly, to me, it was a parenthesis. I consider that I first voted in June for the legislative elections and even though my candidate didn't win, I felt relieved when I left the polling station, for the first time with a big smile on my face. FRT24M091 I'm not sure if I would have voted in April if my birthday had been on 9 April instead of 9 May. Because I turned eighteen between the two elections, I immediately went to register. I remember seeing on TV that there were huge queues of people wanting to register in the city councils of the large cities. No such problem here obviously, I was the only one! [. . .] I remember that my friends at school were all gutted and those who had gloated about how they would not go to vote were suddenly considered very uncool. FRT23F097

These two examples are symptomatic of several patterns in the interviews: even though traumatic elections are well remembered, the memories are often internalized, focusing on remembering one's feelings and discussions or reaction from family and friends. This effect is even stronger when the election represents the first vote for the respondent. UK respondents make similar comments:

> My first elections were the 1997 ones. Everyone around me were so fed up with the Tories that they kept saying they hoped my generation would make the difference this time. [. . .] I really trusted Blair. I voted Labour and my constituency went to Labour despite being traditionally Conservative, I was so happy! Now I vote Lib-Dem! Funny how things change. UKY28F047

> I remember the first election when Labour won. [. . .] I preferred the Conservatives but I didn't dare to make it too public because my friends wouldn't understand. I remember feeling gutted with the result. Since then, I've not always voted for the same party but almost always for a losing party, and always with some rage! UKH29M089

Altogether, recent elections were rarely mentioned spontaneously, even though we saw that people did remember them, while certain sociotropically traumatic elections were vividly remembered and mentioned by voters. Even in these cases, however, the memory typically relates to the internalization (social or emotional) of the election, rather than its abstract societal importance. The memory may involve strong senses of guilt or failure, which then make it fundamental as an electoral point of reference.

Building Up Electoral Memory during Childhood

Memories of important events start shaping before the events even occur. Elements of anticipation, apprehension, excitement, and preparation of an experience become part of the experience itself and shape how the memory will be built and crystallized. To understand this phenomenon in terms of early electoral memories and first-time voting, we focus on the findings from our French panel survey of pre-voters and young voters in two consecutive elections.

We first consider their memories of childhood elections. Roughly 70% report having accompanied their parents to the polling station in at least one election (as mentioned in chapter 3, the practice of Sunday voting in France is conducive to family polling station visits). In most cases, parents even took the child inside the curtained polling booth with them at least once, an experience shared by 53% of respondents; 44% also remember accompanying people other than their parents (such as their grandparents or their friends) to the polling station. Our findings suggest that when it comes to passive electoral learning—such as being exposed to debates and discussions about elections, friends and the wider family are almost as important as parents themselves. Young people are indeed more likely to have experienced other family members and friends arguing about elections (42%) than their own parents (31%). By contrast, active electoral learning still primarily (though by no means exclusively) centres on parents and the direct family. About 75% of young people discussed elections with their parents, 60% with other family members, 63% with teachers, and 59% with their friends.

There are significant gender differences as regards the likelihood of parents taking their child with them to the polling station, which had happened to 75% of young women, but to only 66% of young men. Similarly, 58% of young women, but only 47% of young men, were taken inside the polling booth. As those experiences are recalled, one might wonder whether young women simply remember polling station visits better, but there is no gender difference in memories of electoral discussions and arguments, which suggests that the difference in reported polling station experience is unlikely to be explained by differences in interest or recollection.

Building Up Memories of That Special First Time

Using the same data, we now focus on the first electoral opportunity to participate of young French voters. Strikingly, becoming a voter for the first time immediately makes young people's emotional relationship to elections far stronger. Only 29.7% of young people who had not yet voted remembered experiencing any positive emotion in relation to an election, but amongst first-time voters, this proportion sharply increases, to 45.4%. The same goes for negative electoral emotions, which are shared by 36.2% of young people who had never voted, and 54.2% of those who had voted for the first time. Symmetric valence controls for self-selection effects (if answers were rationalized based on enthusiasm about politics, the difference between pre-voters and first time voters would only pertain to positive emotions). Specifically, 43.7% of first-time voters associate their time in the polling station with positive emotions (47.3% neutral, and 8.9% negative), and 39.1% associate positive emotions with their time in the polling booth itself (51.7% neutral, 9.1% negative). The positivity also includes electoral discussions with family (39.2% positive, 38.9% neutral, 21.9% negative), friends (38.6% positive, 42.7% neutral, 18.7% negative), and at school (37.3% positive, 45.2% neutral, 17.5% negative). However, most first-time voters feel negatively towards candidates' debates (36%, vs 33.6% neutral and 27.5% positive), and campaign ads (35.9% negative, 43.4% neutral, and 20.7% positive),

The emotions first-time voters report are detailed in figure 5.2. They consider their participation in the election to be important for their country (81.3%) and, crucially, for themselves personally (77.2%), seeing it as a rite of passage and key life experience. They also feel proud (70.8%), excited (64.4%), closer to fellow citizens (64.1%), emotional (59.7%), happy (53.3%), and closer to their own family (48.8%) as a result of voting for the first time. By contrast, very few first-time voters feel out of place, disgust, or anger.

Beyond the positive valence of those emotions, the first vote appears as an eminently personal experience, which takes its significance from what it represents for the young person him/herself, its importance as an element of growing up, eliciting pride, excitement, emotionality, and even happiness. It changes young people's status and sense of belonging within society, making them closer and more equal to other citizens and even to the rest of their family. A first vote is an identity-shifting experience, one which transforms people's perception of themselves and of where they fit within their

Emotions felt by first-time voters

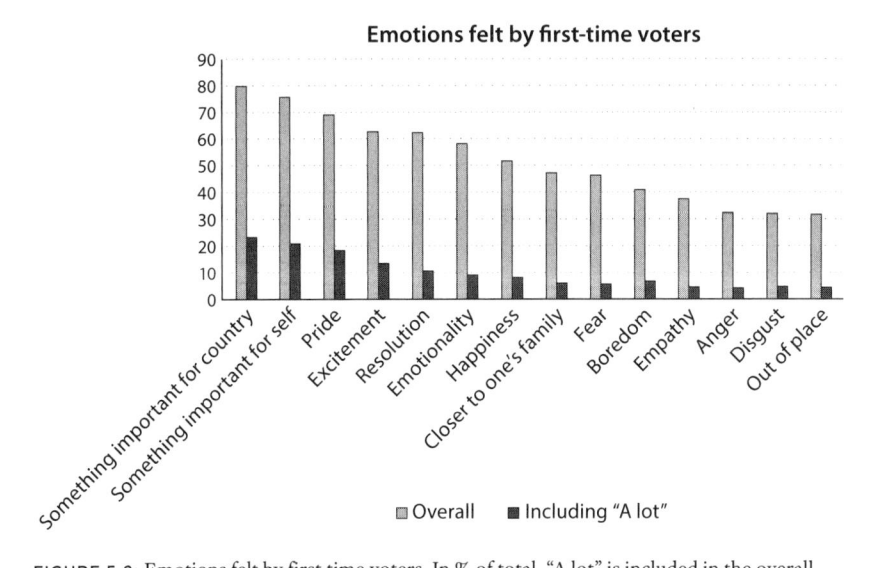

[Bar chart showing percentages for Overall and Including "A lot" across categories: Something important for country, Something important for self, Pride, Excitement, Resolution, Emotionality, Happiness, Closer to one's family, Fear, Boredom, Empathy, Anger, Disgust, Out of place]

FIGURE 5.2: Emotions felt by first time voters. In % of total. "A lot" is included in the overall total.

community. Beyond the emotion, it is this life-defining nature of the first vote that young people stress, despite their frequent reservations vis-à-vis much regarding politics and the institutional side of the electoral process.

Stories of Childhood Elections and That Special First Time

The unique place of childhood elections and first-vote elections may actually exceed the level of their conscious recollection in terms of importance and influence, and their role as the first stones on which a citizen's electoral memory is built up. It is actually quite remarkable that proportions ranging from 51.3% in Germany to 75% in France remember elections from their childhood (figure 5.3), as childhood memories tend to highlight important experiences and few hold many memories from before the age of six. Yet, for most citizens, those first encounters with electoral democracy before one is even an actor within it, are remembered durably and vividly. Furthermore, in our in-depth interviews, childhood memories often prove detailed and striking:

> The first election I remember was that of presidential candidate Eisenhower with Vice President candidate Nixon in 1956. I remember in particular going to a local speech to see them. US58F018

Percent remembering childhood election

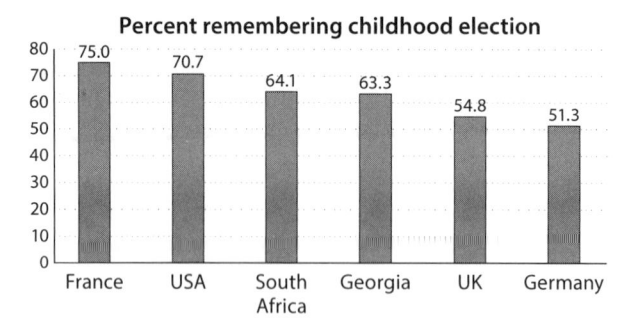

France	USA	South Africa	Georgia	UK	Germany
75.0	70.7	64.1	63.3	54.8	51.3

FIGURE 5.3: Proportion of citizens remembering a childhood election

I can remember a fair amount about all the elections going back to 1979 [. . .] I was really delighted when Thatcher got in because the country was on its knees from the Winter of Discontent. The 70s was a terrible decade of weak 'ping-pong' government [. . .] and the country was falling apart morale-wise. UK44F015

The first election I remember was the 2000 election. I went to a youth group at my church the day before the election. Young people were putting in prayer requests about who they wanted to win. The parents present said that wasn't a prayer, which was really interesting. I don't think I wrote anything. US29M023

Memories of accompanying parents to the polling station, the curiosity surrounding the secrecy of the process, and the shared excitement of the atmosphere between parents and children are frequently mentioned. Across interviews, these polling station visits are almost always remembered as positive and enjoyable socialization into the world of electoral democracy, the memory of which remains strong throughout the adult lives of many:

I have strong memories of going to vote with my parents. I remember closing the curtains, and all these levers. There was a big handle to pull down, which I got to do. I grew up in a rural area, so going to the polls was fun because we saw people we knew. Going to the polls was always exciting. US28F046

I have lots of memories of elections growing up. For a lot of my growing up, I was home-schooled. A big part of my civic education was shaking candidates' hands and asking them a question. US28M038

I remember going to vote with my mom, and her talking about it, and getting excited about the sticker. Dad talked about it too—he said you don't have a right to complain if you don't weigh in. They drilled in the importance of voting. US28F046

I remember when I was a child, I remember voting with my mom, and pressing the button. US28F059

We always went to the elections with them—had to wait outside for them in the car while they voted—five kids all waiting. Mostly we were bored outside waiting. My parents took me to vote at eighteen. I just threw away the paper. Blank voter. I would lie and not go. I would say that I was going with my sister or something and not vote. US47F026

I remember going to the polling place with my mom and being fascinated with the machines when I was little. US3ZM060

I remember my parents taking me down to the polling station and then waiting outside while they voted. UK18F002

I remember going to the polling station with my mum because our school was being used as a polling station. And I remember looking around the school she was voting in and comparing it to my own school. I remember she let us into the booth with her. But it wasn't a curtain, it was more like a phone booth with wood panelling between her and the voter next to her for privacy. And I remember her showing us what she was doing and explaining it all to us and about the person she had voted for. And I couldn't get my head around it that she hadn't voted for John Major or Tony Blair but some woman who lived in our area! UK20F001

I remember going with my mum, we'd go on the way to shopping and we'd pop in and we'd just stand there and watch everybody queue up, get a piece of paper, put a funny mark in the box. She wouldn't let us go behind the curtain with her. Then she would come out and put this piece of paper into a box. I remember saying 'Oooh I can't wait to do that,' [*laughs*] 'Go and see what's behind the curtain' [*laughing*], and 'Use that pencil!'. My daughter is twenty-four and if she totally disagreed with my views she would tell me in no uncertain words and she would vote in the way that she chose. It's her right to go and vote. If she knew that I put a sign on the fridge to say 'Don't forget to vote' she would say, 'Have you been yet?' to remind me. UK57F019

One thing that may make memories of childhood elections quite emotional to many is that they are, by nature, nostalgic memories of childhood, and of parents, которые frequently happy. As a result, when recollecting childhood elections, citizens often highlight the importance of their parental influence, which they can see positive, but also sometimes as negative or divisive:

> My dad used to vote Liberal and my mum voted Labour. There would be a big discussion. I remember thinking if everyone got together and voted Liberal and Labour then the Tories wouldn't get in. UK40M016

> I remember being very upset with my father in 1984 or '88 when he admitted that he voted for Reagan because of his position on handguns. My father inherited guns from his family. I asked him how he did not see the harm in his vote. US38F024

> We weren't citizens until I was seven or eight (my parents were Canadian and British). The first election they got to vote in was 1988. I think my mom and dad are on different sides. My mom was a school teacher—and was always Democrat. My dad leaned Republican. I think I spent more time with my mom so picked up her views. She would always explain why women's choice and rights were important. My dad would only talk about economics and social views. US36F013

> I discussed elections with my parents growing up in Japan. I have no idea what my parents' political leanings are. We didn't really talk about politics. I remember asking my mom who she voted for when I was a kid, and she wouldn't tell me. She said that was a thing you don't discuss with other people. So I thought, 'Whoa, this is serious'. My parents were not citizens until 1993 or '94, but we didn't talk about it. It was a secret thing to vote. US28F025

> My first political memory was in 1978 when I was four. I was in the car with my mom and an ad for prop 13 came on the radio. I asked her to explain what it was about, and she explained why it was bad. US38F024

Most adults also remember their first vote, in proportions ranging from 72.9% in the UK to 90.3% in South Africa (figure 5.4). In other words, between seven and nine out of ten adults carry those striking memories of their first vote for a considerable time after the event, as they would other significant (and perhaps more obvious) life-shaping 'first times'.

Percent remembering their first vote

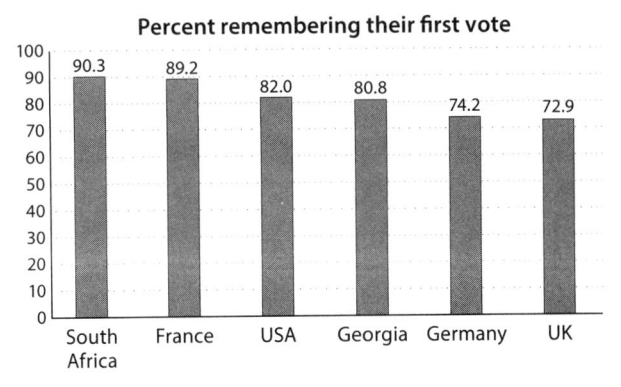

Country	%
South Africa	90.3
France	89.2
USA	82.0
Georgia	80.8
Germany	74.2
UK	72.9

FIGURE 5.4: Proportion of citizens remembering their first vote

Again, qualitative narratives often emphasize this status of one's first election as a substantive, meaningful, and foundational experience and rite of passage of adulthood:

> I had just turned eighteen, and I got a sticker at the voting centre which I showed to my classmates. My teacher of US History gave all Seniors that could vote and brought the sticker as proof a few bonus points, which I thought was great motivation and a special way to recognize the event. US46F036

> I just really remember the first time that I voted and how proud I was that I had the privilege to vote, and have a say as to who was going to run the country. UK72M007

> I can remember when I first voted, I was happy. I was working in London, commuted back and rushed into the polls. It was an important moment because I enjoyed being able to have my say and contribute to the country. UK39M023

> It was a special one, just the right time, I will always remember my first vote. UK18M024

> I remember the first time I voted it felt important. [...] I actually felt quite privileged because I actually felt 'I'm old enough to drink, I'm old enough to do this and now I'm old enough to vote.' Which is even sort of better. You gotta love it. UK24M025

> I remember going along with my parents when I voted for the first time. I went to my old school actually. I remember getting the polling card through the post and feeling very excited because I felt like a citizen of

> the country and I felt like I had my say. [. . .] It was a very exciting feeling walking into my old school and possibly making a difference and having a small effect on how the community that I live in and the country that I live in would be run and affected in the future. It was very exciting and a very worthwhile thing to do. I remember talking to friends and asking them who they were voting for. UK25F026

> I remember my first vote when I was eighteen. It was my right. I'd earned that right. I'd got to eighteen. And it was something legal. My vote became part of the count that made that person win or lose. UK57F019

> I remember being excited about going to put the cross in that box. Because I remember when I was a little girl I used to go to the polling station with my mum. And I remember saying to her once, 'Mum, can I put the little cross in the box,' and she said, 'No that's voting', so it was quite exciting when I could put the cross in the box. UK30F020

The first electoral experience shapes citizens' long-term electoral memory. Many respondents describe the sense of importance, responsibility, excitement, and inclusion in the community of that first electoral experience. Most associated memories are also overwhelmingly positive and imply a sense of efficacy which is sometimes lost as citizens' electoral experiences progress over time, and first votes are often remembered as particularly happy ones.

Despite many respondents recalling their first vote quite vividly, very few accurately remember specific details of when or what their first election was (though many would 'calculate' it in retrospect). By contrast, most respondents remembered and could describe what they said or were told, and how it made them feel, in great detail. This contrast is symptomatic of the phenomenon of electoral internalization that we discussed in chapter 1. National memories are weak, but personal ones are strong; details fade, but feelings remain. This contradiction is clearly illustrated by the first respondent below, who first explained that she did not remember when she first voted. She then proceeded to calculate it, thinking of the year she turned twenty-one, then when she turned eighteen, contrasted with further interviewees talking about their first election feelings in great detail:

> Oh yes, now I remember, I was the first generation allowed to vote at eighteen! FR25F005

> I remember very well that they were European elections. Now which ones? [. . .] Yes, it must have been 1994. I remember very well that they

were European elections because to me, that was the best, that's what I really wanted my first vote to be. UKL31M017

10 May 1981 and the election of Mitterrand! You can't really forget it because people wouldn't let you. I'm not even sure whether I voted for him or not but people kept saying it was a new generation in politics, so I think that even though I may not have even voted for him—I don't think I did, I was moved when the result was announced on TV. FRP45F054

I couldn't say what elections they were, but I remember the feeling very well. My parents talked to me to tell me it would be a big responsibility and did I know who I would vote for and that it was very personal but we could talk about it if I wanted because it would be a very important moment in my life. I felt really proud, I got really interested in politics before and even though it was only the local election I really got into reading the leaflets people left in our mailbox and I really knew who I wanted to win. My little sister was very jealous, kept asking me who I'd vote for and kept telling me who she would do. I pretended to be really secretive and wouldn't tell her but I thought it was funny we preferred the same guy while I knew my parents would vote for someone else. I think in a way it made me feel closer to her and we still talk about elections quite a lot with her and discuss our impressions of the candidates. UKY27F066

The third quote above illustrates how one's own vote can remain elusive to memory, even when prominent. By contrast, many refer to the excitement of having the right to vote, discussions, and emotions as they voted for the first time:

I'll remember all my life. I don't know when it was or who I voted for but we were supposed to go to the Ardennes with my parents for the weekend and I had a big fight with them. I said, 'We can't go, there is the election!', they said that we would be fine, that nobody would fine us, and I said it was beside the point, it was an election, it was my first election, maybe it didn't mean anything for them but for me it did and I would stay and vote. We had a big row. I won, and I have never missed an election in my entire life. FRW68M089

All I remember is that for my first vote, I just knew I wanted to vote against what my parents always told me about politics. In a way, it was my first opportunity to stand up for what I believed in. UK47F101

Memories of one's first voting experience are often closely linked to the socialization context and notably, parental influence on the voting decision. As exemplified by the quotes above and below, there is a clear trend of young citizens in particular remembering the influence of their parents on their first vote, be it positively or negatively, through parental transmission (below) or indeed confrontation and rebellion against family tradition (above).

> My parents voted for Republican Bush and I also voted for Bush. I was excited about being able to vote for the first time and there were rallies and information stands organized at the university to get the youth interested and remind them to vote. US3ZF028

> The first election I could vote was a family event, I went together with my parents and then we went out for lunch afterwards. We all voted Republican. Politics is like a nice family connection. US36M029

In summary, citizens seldom remember when they first voted, who won the election, or what happened in 'real life' unless prompted. However, they are overwhelmingly able to provide an immediate and detailed recollection of the feeling of becoming a 'full citizen', a voting citizen. They hardly ever remember whom they voted for themselves, but they remember the discussions that they had, how their new condition affected them and (in their eyes) the perception others had of them. It is through internalization that first elections are memorable.

Memories of early elections are important. They are rarely technically or societally precise, but they are emotionally clear and powerful. Crucially, childhood elections and first-vote elections are markers of our own lives, and emphasize the very essence of what it means to say that elections are first and foremost something that citizens experience, something which is meaningful because of the way it permeates and relates to their existence. Memories of childhood elections and first votes are very salient in the US, France, South Africa, and to an extent in Georgia, though rather less so in both the UK and Germany. Our findings illustrate that elections that are personally important to voters, because of where they fit in their lives (as opposed to because of the characteristics of the elections themselves), remain particularly strongly and durably vivid in the voters' minds. They are comparatively better remembered by respondents than are elections that are nationally or historically important, or simply recent. Electoral memory thus emerges as a continuous and durable recollection that starts building up very early in individuals' lives, typically around six or seven years old, and further crystallizes at the beginning of their actual voting life. We now turn to the question of which aspects of elections, *beyond* their own feelings (as amply confirmed above), citizens remember best.

Electoral Memory and the Interface between Individual and Society

Looking at components of electoral memory, we want in particular to validate the distinction between sociotropic and egocentric aspects that seemed to emerge from spontaneous recollections of early elections, and see how this informs us with regard to the interaction between individual and societal dimensions during the election period. We also want to confirm our first findings regarding those early elections, to the effect that voters tend to internalize elections and electoral memory. There are many elements voters might remember from past elections: personal memories include their voting experience, the atmosphere of the polling station, their emotions in the polling booth, hesitating about whether to vote, or indeed whom they voted for. In terms of interaction, they might remember discussions, arguments, or disputes with a family member, a friend or a colleague. Sociotropically, voters could recollect who won or lost the election, campaign promises, posters, or slogans. Of course, memories might also be timed diversely to encompass the pre-electoral period, Election Day itself, or Election Night and its aftermath.

Our results pertaining to which aspects of elections citizens remember are reported in appendix 3. In most cases, the list is topped by who citizens actually voted for, though we know these beliefs often to be inaccurate. The only exception is Georgia, where the top component of electoral memory is the election winner. It is worth remembering that such memories could be either 'direct' or internalized: when saying that they remember whom they voted for or who won, citizens may of course be referring to remembering feeling happy that their candidate won, or guilty that they wasted their vote. Germany is the only country where citizens better remember whether they hesitated to vote or not than who the losers of recent elections were.

Electoral memory varies according to some key attitudes and behaviours. With results shown in table 5.1, we first explore whether the form and strength of electoral memory is related to the egocentric and sociotropic personalities of voters, by analyzing correlations between the overall and

TABLE 5.1. Sociotropism and Memory

	UK					USA			
	Overall	Economic	Social	Safety	Misery	Overall	Economic	Social	Safety	Misery
WHICH ELECTION?										
Childhood	0.08*	—	—	—	0.13**	0.11*	0.09*	—	—	—
First vote	0.07*	—	—	—	0.11**	—	—	—	—	—
Realignment	0.11**	0.11**	—	—	0.10**	0.09*	0.12**	—	—	—
Last 1st-order	0.08	0.09**	—	—	0.10**	0.11**	0.12**	—	—	—
WHAT IS REMEMBERED?										
Discussions	0.09**	—	0.08*	—	0.09**	—	—	—	—	—
Arguments	0.08*	—	0.07*	—	0.09**	-0.09*	—	-0.10*	—	—
Haptic	0.08*	0.08*	—	—	0.08*	—	—	—	—	—
Hesit. choice	0.14**	0.11**	0.11**	0.08*	0.08*	—	—	—	0.11**	—
Hesit. turnout	0.08*	0.07*	—	—	—	—	—	—	—	—
Who voted for	—	—	—	—	0.07*	0.14**	0.15**	0.09*	—	—
Who won	—	0.08**	—	—	0.07*	0.10*	0.13**	0.08*	—	—

Note: * = sig<0.05; ** = sig<0.01; — = not significant.

four dimensional indices of sociotropism and the nature and contents of electoral memory.

The results are striking. First, typically, sociotropic voters have stronger electoral memories. In Britain, beyond the overall index, the misery dimension of sociotropism is most highly correlated with electoral memory, whilst in the US, it is the economic dimension. In the UK, sociotropism is mostly related to memories of early elections, though sociotropic voters also have stronger memories of key realignment elections. By contrast, in the US, sociotropism correlates with memories of most types of election, but not really of one's first vote.

The question of what people actually remember from past elections is also important. In Britain, the misery and overall dimensions of sociotropism are related to most components of electoral memory, but the economic and social dimensions strongly predict the strength of interactive memories (discussions, arguments) and the social dimension that of memories of electoral hesitation. Misery sociotropism is strongly related to memories of electoral interaction and haptic memories of the vote. For the US, sociotropism is mostly correlated with memories of one's vote and of election winners, though the safety dimension is a good predictor of memories of electoral hesitation. Interestingly, unlike for the UK, memories of hostile interaction with friends and families in the form of arguments and disputes over elections is higher among egocentric voters, and haptic memories are largely unrelated to sociotropism in the US case.

Overall, sociotropic voters have stronger electoral memories and, in the UK, particularly of early elections and of internalized aspects of the electoral experience (discussion, haptic memories of electoral experience, situations of electoral hesitation). On self-reported scales, people believe that they best remember whom they voted for and who won, but their detailed narrative memories contradict those self-beliefs: what the election meant to them, and how they experienced it personally, are overwhelmingly dominant in open-ended narratives, and as we will see, have more substantial effects on future behaviour and experience.

Haptic, Auditory and Sensorial Components of Electoral Memory

Let us now tease out more specific details regarding the components of electoral memory likely to make a lasting impression on voters—that is, those voters refer to as their 'main' electoral memories. In France and the

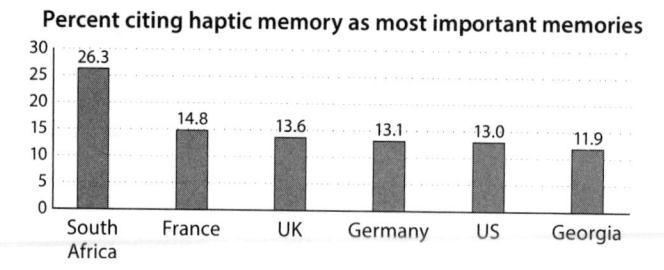

Percent citing haptic memory as most important memories

South Africa	France	UK	Germany	US	Georgia
26.3	14.8	13.6	13.1	13.0	11.9

FIGURE 5.5: Proportions of citizens citing a haptic memory of the polling station or election atmosphere as one of their top memories of past elections

US, large proportions of citizens still remember images of past Election Nights. This may be related to the ceremonial importance of Election Nights in these two countries, and the dramatic nature of personalized presidential elections. In the UK, South Africa, and Georgia, meanwhile, many citizens retain haptic memories of elections, notably the atmosphere of the polling station. Across countries, the interactive nature of elections also leaves a lasting trace, as many citizens remember discussions with friends, families, or colleagues during elections. In South Africa, Georgia, France, and the US, memories also encompass more dramatic arguments or tensions with fellow voters. By contrast, memories of campaigns and debates are only secondary, with a few exceptions (such as some campaign memories in Georgia, South Africa, and the US, and campaign posters in South Africa).

Haptic memories, however, often remain among the most vivid. Many citizens cite a haptic memory of the polling station, its atmosphere, or their personal experience of the moment of voting as among their most salient electoral memories, as shown in figure 5.5. Across countries, between 11.9% (Georgia) and 26.3% (South Africa) of citizens cite a haptic memory as one of the most vivid that they recall from past elections.

In figure 5.6, we focus similarly on interactive memories (discussions or arguments with family or friends). Memories of discussions represent the top memory of 6.6% of British citizens and 20.3% of South Africans. By contrast, arguments are cited as the leading memory by from 4.2% of citizens in the UK to 14.6% in South Africa. Overall, citizens reporting an interactive memory of the election as their most salient one thus vary from 10.8% in the UK to 34.9% in South Africa.

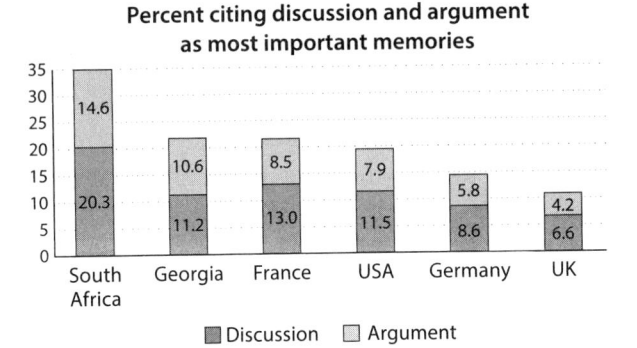

Percent citing discussion and argument as most important memories

Country	Discussion	Argument
South Africa	20.3	14.6
Georgia	11.2	10.6
France	13.0	8.5
USA	11.5	7.9
Germany	8.6	5.8
UK	6.6	4.2

FIGURE 5.6: Proportion of citizens who cite a discussion with family or friends and an argument with family or friends as one of their top memories of past elections

While the largest proportion of citizens claim that they remember whom they voted for and who won elections, internalized (both haptic and interactive) memories are often in fact the most meaningful that citizens recall from past elections, though with some comparative variations. British and German citizens are less likely to discuss elections widely with friends and family, compared to those of most other countries, notably South Africa, Georgia, France, and to a lesser extent the US, where interactive memories are most meaningful for from one in five to one in three citizens. Haptic and atmospheric impressions also represent the most vivid memories for over one in four South African citizens, and one in seven French or British. The actual nature of the polling station experience—from the length of queues to polling station parties (both of which are very frequent in South Africa)—may explain differences in the importance of haptic memories. Qualitative narratives amply confirm how internalized memories—be they haptic or interactive—remain prominent in people's minds years after a vote. Polling stations themselves are the object much memorialization, often but not always positive:

> I remember, basically, going to a school to vote, and I didn't like that, it didn't feel right, the school had shut for the polling day which I thought was wrong, to disrupt children. UK45F027

> I found it quite a funny experience. All these strangers gathering in my local community hall putting a cross on a slip of paper and putting it in a box. It was quite an odd experience. UK51M021

> I'm usually sad where I have to go to vote. My mother died a hundred yards away from where I stood. UK66M029

> Where I used to live, I remember that we would go to vote in the local tennis club. It always felt strange to go there to vote as it meant that I had to be serious but all I wanted to do there was play tennis with my friends. UK23F109

> For the past few years, we have voted in the school where our daughter goes. It is really nice as we often see her drawings on the wall as we are waiting to collect our ballots. US37F111

> I think the polling station's somewhere where you go to vote and you might see friends and neighbours and family and be wondering who they're going to vote for. So it's quite a suspicious time [*laughs*] where you're trying to guess what other people in your community . . . who they would vote for. UK25F026

From Past to Present: The Influence of Electoral Memory

Regardless of what electoral memory comprises, this book also aims to understand its effects on voters' future experiences and behaviour. Memories entrench the cumulative meaning of elections as an intimate and emotional moment likely to impact a citizen's future turnout, experiences, and the emotions triggered as they vote. To consider this variegated impact, we show in appendix 3 the contrasted electoral memories of voters and nonvoters. First, there is a very systematic relationship between remembering elections from one's childhood and one's first vote and electoral participation (though only partly in France and South Africa). The link between electoral memory and turnout later becomes a self-fulfilling prophecy, with voters more likely to remember other elections.

Particularly noteworthy are voters who remember switching their vote for the first time, such as a young woman from London switching to the Liberal Democrats in 2005 having always voted Labour. Her insight touches upon the importance of family projection (here, a younger brother) and a desire to protect his interests and protest against the perceived injustice of tuition fees:

> I turned eighteen just a few months before the start of the 1997 campaign. There was an incredible atmosphere among people of my generation and I was preparing to study politics for my degree which I did. I

voted Labour with both hands and hoped they would solve all the problems and inequalities that Thatcher had created in England. I voted even more enthusiastically in 2001, but voted Lib-Dem in 2005. There were two reasons. The first one is that my youngest brother didn't go to Uni because of tuition fees and I thought it was so unfair and so against what the values of the left should be. I don't mind Iraq that much, but the tuition fees felt like a betrayal. The other reason is that I had moved to a new part of London with my boyfriend, and it was a Tory constituency and it seemed that the Lib Dems were the only ones who could replace the Conservatives in that place. I was pleasantly surprised and I think I'll vote for them again this time. UKL29F015

A middle-aged man from Paris similarly remembers the first time he switched to the Front National. Again family projection is highlighted, the voter seeing his vote as an act of paternal defence of his daughter. This interviewee also remembers divisive family discussions which lead to fractures that cannot be not easily repaired even years after the election:

It was in 1986. I had voted Socialist all my life but I wanted to give Mitterrand and this pretentious Fabius a good kicking. I had really seen my district deteriorate under them even more than under the right, and a few months before the election, my daughter had been assaulted and some Arabs told her next time they saw her, they would f*** her in every hole. What I remember were the huge arguments I had with my wife at that time. We had never talked about politics much and we always agreed, but I said I would vote Le Pen and she was really annoyed and thought I was just trying to be a big mouth and provoke her. When she saw I was serious about it she became even more furious. It was the first and last time we ever talked about politics at home, and it is the election I remember best by a long shot. I still vote FN now and will this time again, but I think my wife still votes PS and I know she really likes Ségolène. FRP52M059

We also note that differences in strengths of electoral memory between voters and non-voters apply to virtually all aspects of electoral memory, not only regarding the vote itself (haptic memories, who won, or how one voted), but also to its broader context (discussions, arguments, or one's own hesitations and thought process—except for hesitations regarding participation in France and South Africa). The impact of childhood and first-election memories on electoral choice is also tested in our general model. In short,

TABLE 5.2A. Empathic Displacement and Electoral Memory

	USA Empathic Displacement	UK Empathic Displacement	France Empathic Displacement	Germany Empathic Displacement	South Africa Empathic Displacement	Georgia Empathic Displacement
WHICH ELECTION?						
Childhood	0.12**	0.16**	0.12**	0.19**	0.10**	0.11**
First vote	0.07**	0.14**	0.10**	0.20**	0.19**	0.12**
Realignment	—	0.09**	0.06*	0.16**	—	0.15**
Last 1st-order	0.07**	0.10**	0.06**	0.17**	0.12**	0.09**
WHAT IS REMEMBERED?						
Discussions	0.15**	0.24**	0.11**	0.25**	0.16**	0.05*
Arguments	0.15**	0.19**	0.19**	0.25**	0.14**	—
Haptic	0.15**	0.19**	0.13**	0.21**	0.24**	0.07**
Hesit. choice	0.08**	0.19**	0.15**	0.13**	0.11**	—
Hesit. turnout	0.07**	0.15**	0.08**	0.05**	0.12**	—
Who voted for	0.05*	0.09**	—	0.11**	0.12**	0.12**
Who won	0.10**	0.13**	—	0.13**	0.10**	0.08**

Note: * = sig<0.05; ** = sig<0.01; *** = sig<0.001; — = not significant.

it is not only the case that behaviour in the first two elections of a citizen's life largely shapes his/her future behaviour as a voter, but also that electoral memories get remobilized in electoral contexts, creating memorial path dependency and a thread of electoral experience memories that may help us to understand the logic of electoral habituation (see chapter 2).

Beyond attitudes and behaviour, however, electoral memory shapes the whole way in which citizens approach elections, their outlook and attitude. It defines their electoral experience, the way they relate to others and enact the interface between themselves, others, and society. Electoral memory can thus predispose citizens towards experiencing a sense of inclusion or, conversely, alienation and marginalization, as a result of an election. We further explore these effects in the next section, which addresses the impact of electoral memory on efficacy, projected efficacy, and empathic displacement.

Electoral Memory, Empathic Displacement, and Efficacy

We now turn to the relationship between what people remember from past elections—and in particular from childhood and their first vote—and their levels of empathic displacement, efficacy, and projected efficacy. Results of these analyses are presented in tables 5.2.a and 5.2.b.

TABLE 5.2B. Efficacy, Projected Efficacy, and Electoral Memory

	USA Effic.	USA Proj. Effic.	UK Effic.	UK Proj. Effic.	France Effic.	France Proj. Effic.	Germany Effic.	Germany Proj. Effic.	South Africa Effic.	South Africa Proj. Effic.	Georgia Effic.	Georgia Proj. Effic.
WHICH ELECTION?												
Childhood	0.08**	0.11**	0.09**	0.13**	0.07**	0.06*	0.15**	0.08**	—	−0.08*	0.11**	0.12**
First vote	0.16**	0.15**	0.22**	0.20**	0.15**	0.14**	0.21**	0.16**	0.22**	0.16**	0.16**	0.19**
Realignment	0.25**	0.27**	0.25**	0.26**	0.21**	0.21**	0.24**	0.18**	0.12**	0.10**	0.21**	0.24**
Last 1st-order	0.28**	0.33**	0.33**	0.31**	0.25**	0.24**	0.28**	0.21**	0.20**	0.21**	0.16**	0.23**
WHAT IS REMEMBERED?												
Discussions	0.22**	0.20**	0.25**	0.27**	0.18**	0.21**	0.22**	0.22**	0.17**	0.13**	0.11**	0.16**
Arguments	0.12**	0.14**	0.16**	0.15**	0.10**	0.11**	0.20**	0.15**	0.07*	—	0.10**	0.12**
Haptic	0.19**	0.17**	0.24**	0.27**	0.14**	0.12**	0.26**	0.25**	0.21**	0.22**	0.15**	0.20**
Hesit. choice	—	0.05*	0.11**	0.16**	0.12**	0.10**	0.17**	0.23**	0.08**	0.12**	—	0.05*
Hesit. turnout	—	—	0.08**	0.12**	0.06*	0.05*	0.13**	0.18**	0.07**	0.12**	—	—
Who voted for	0.23**	0.27**	0.30**	0.34**	0.22**	0.22**	0.27**	0.28**	0.28**	0.26**	0.14**	0.18**
Who won	0.20**	0.23**	0.26**	0.28**	0.15**	0.17**	0.26**	0.26**	0.15**	0.21**	0.12**	0.15**

Note: * = sig<0.05; ** = sig<0.01; *** = sig<0.001; — = not significant.

Electoral memory tends to correlate with higher efficacy (both individual and projected) and empathic displacement. However, there is an important distinction between the types of correlation that involve efficacy on the one hand, and empathic displacement on the other. When it comes to efficacy, the strong positive correlation primarily reflects aspects of electoral memory that could easily be related to the interest and attention that individual citizens devote to elections (memory of recent and realignment elections, of one's vote and election winners, etc.), suggesting a possibly spurious relationship between the two. All those variables—perhaps unsurprisingly—strongly and positively correlated with efficacy and projected efficacy, in both the UK and the US. For instance, the correlation between memory of the last first-order election and efficacy is 0.33** in the UK and 0.28** in the US, with an equivalent for projected efficacy of 0.31** in the UK and 0.33** in the US, while remembering who won the last election is correlated with efficacy at a level of 0.26** in the UK and 0.20** in the US, and with projected efficacy at 0.28** in the UK and 0.23** in the US.

By contrast, general memory of elections matters little with regard to citizens' empathic displacement, but lasting impressions left by childhood memories and one's first vote make a significant difference, as do internalized memories relating to interaction with fellow voters, haptic memories of the electoral experience, and memories related to one's electoral thinking process. Thus, empathic displacement correlates with memories of childhood elections (0.16** in the UK and 0.12** in the US), and of one's first vote (0.14** in the UK and 0.07** in the US). Turning to memory components, empathic displacement tends to be significantly higher for those who remember discussions with families or friends (0.24** in the UK and 0.15** in the US), arguments (0.19** in the UK and 0.15** in the US), and the atmosphere of the polling station (0.19** in the UK and 0.15** in the US). It is similarly higher for those who remember hesitating about their vote (0.19** and 0.08**) or about whether to vote at all (0.15** and 0.07**), suggesting that those with a more thoughtful introspective approach to the vote are also more likely to think of how their vote relates to that of the rest of the population.

In summary, memory of past elections is goes hand in hand with efficacy and projected efficacy, but we cannot exclude the possibility that this may be a spurious by-product of interest in (and awareness of) elections in the first place. By contrast, salient personal memories of early elections and internalization of electoral experience are strongly associated with higher empathic displacement. In other words, those who embrace and question their own electoral experience, particularly from an early age, later relate to elections' interpersonal and collective nature. We now turn to the broader implications of electoral memory in our model.

Second Model Stage: Does Electoral Memory Matter?

Our investigation into the electoral memory of voters shows that voters have strong memories, which keep accumulating and morphing throughout their electoral history. While recent elections are fresh in people's minds and thus remembered quite clearly, older memories—notably memories of childhood and of one's electoral 'initiation' are often the most vividly and richly remembered, and are those that most respondents spontaneously allude to in qualitative interviews. Even when referring to historically important elections, and despite most respondents claiming that they remember their own vote or who won the elections, it is the internalized components of the election—discussions, debates, memories of the atmosphere of the polling station or of how the person felt as they voted or discovered the result of the election—that are the most vibrant in memory, and the ones that people of all ages can recollect with precision and depth. The spontaneous qualitative evidence consistently reinforces the perception that electoral memory becomes most meaningful when citizens appropriate elections and electoral experience to relate it to their own stories, lives, and personal development, emphasizing individual relevance and connecting electoral memory to loved ones.

At this stage, we should remember that elections are but very short moments, every few years, in the life of an individual. As purely institutional events, and given most citizens' distrust of politics, they should really be irrelevant—and unmemorable—occasions. It is only because they are 'personal moments', internalized and invested by voters with deep personal meanings and connections, that they become vividly relevant to individuals. It is not so much that the voter is part of his/her country's electoral history, but rather that elections become part of a voter's life.

The litmus test for the value of our model of electoral memory—including the importance of one's first vote and of childhood elections—will again be its contribution to the explanation of electoral behaviour, experience, and resolution. In our full model, we use a more limited battery of items than in the case of personality, and on the basis of the findings presented in this chapter, we consider memories of childhood elections, first electoral experience, and whether a voter is a first time voter (in some countries, first- or second-time voters, on account of election cycles). The first two measures are self-reported, and the third is observed and deduced from age.

ELECTORAL MEMORY AND ELECTORAL BEHAVIOUR

Once again, we start with models of electoral behaviour and consider in particular whether electoral memory improves our understanding of electoral choice. The results in terms of change in R^2 or pseudo-R^2 are presented in figure 5.7. Adding electoral memory to the model significantly improves its explanatory power, across countries. On the face of it, improvements in R^2 are modest compared to stage 1—between 0.01 in most German models, for France, and among polling station voters in the British case, and 0.04 in the South African model, 0.05 in explaining the choice of postal voters in the British case, and even 0.07 among US polling station voters. Two things should be noted, however. First, as mentioned in chapter 2, our decision to assess model improvements in stages creates an inherent inequality between the three sets of explanatory variables. We give maximal credit to the control variables, and it remains much 'easier' for personality variables to claim the largely unexplained variance than it is for subsequent terms, which thus have far less 'mystery' left to explain. In other words, had we entered memory before personality, the contribution of the former would have looked significantly higher. Firstly, however, analytical logic has it that personality precedes and affects memory, just as identity stems from personality and accumulated memories. Secondly, unlike for personality, we only include for memory three individual markers, two of which are correlated internally (memories of childhood elections and of one's first vote), while the other is partly observationally dependent on the age control already in the model. This is because much of the reality of what matters in regard to electoral memory is qualitative in nature and hard to capture in quantified variables. Overall, then, we are content to note that electoral memory contributes to the models, rather than worrying about its scope.

At least one of the three individual electoral memory items significantly contributes to each electoral choice model in the US (table 4.1) and other countries (table 4.2) except when it comes to explaining the vote for the AfD in Germany. The most important factor is memory of childhood elections, which is globally associated with left-wing voting, though in France it is instead memories of one's first vote which have a similar effect; while in South Africa, childhood electoral memories are associated with a lower propensity to vote for the ANC, and memories of one's first vote with a

Behaviour models improvement—stage 2

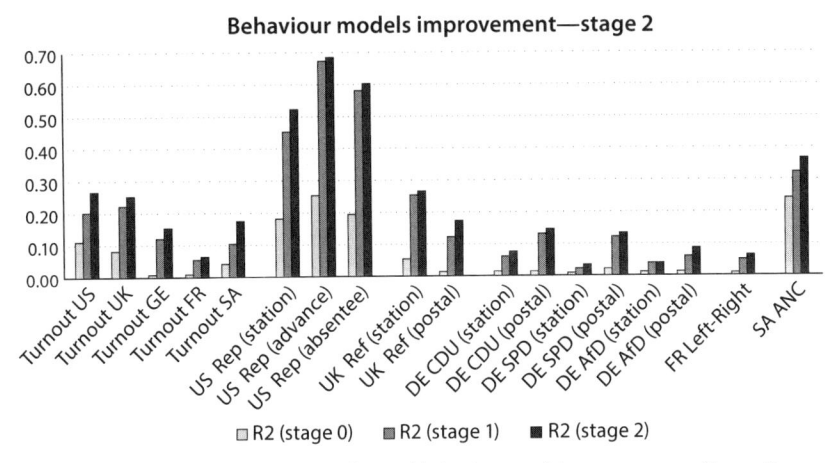

FIGURE 5.7: Stage 2: Improvement to electoral behaviour models—memory predictors. Bars represent R^2

greater propensity to do so. To confirm that this result is meaningful, we test for multicollinearity, but whilst there is a statistically significant correlation between childhood and first-time vote memories, it is only 0.14, which confirms that the two variables are distinct. Finally, in South Africa, being a first-time voter significantly lowers one's likelihood of voting for the ANC, notwithstanding age controls.

The positive contribution of electoral memory to turnout models is actually more substantial than for electoral choice. It is limited in France (+0.01), but important in the UK and Germany (+0.03), the US (+0.06), and South Africa (+0.07). However, the only variable consistently to have very significant effects (see tables 4.3 and 4.4, in chapter 4) is memory of one's first vote, which has a positive impact on turnout in the US, Germany, and South Africa.

ELECTORAL MEMORY AND ELECTORAL EXPERIENCE

We next turn to the effects of electoral memory on electoral experience. This impact is reported in figure 5.8. Once again, electoral memory improves the overall explanatory power of all the models of emotionality (+0.01 to +0.07) and happiness (+0.01 to +0.10), often but not always modestly. The effects are strongest amongst postal/absentee voters in the US and UK. (The impact of specific variables was reported in tables 4.5 and 4.6.) This time, in the US, only first-/second-time voting memories make the electoral experience of absentee voters a happier one. In other countries, however, the

Experience models improvement—stage 2

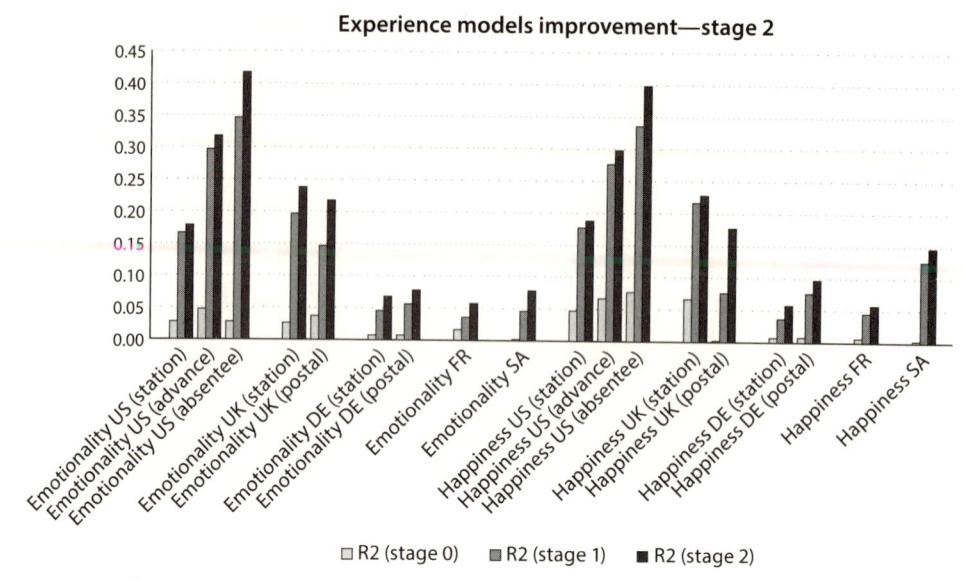

[Bar chart showing R2 (stage 0), R2 (stage 1), and R2 (stage 2) values for emotionality and happiness variables across US (station, advance, absentee), UK (station, postal), DE (station, postal), FR, and SA.]

FIGURE 5.8: Stage 2: Improvement to electoral experience models—memory predictors

effects are substantive. Typically, remembering childhood elections appears to make future electoral experiences less emotional, but remembering one's first vote makes them happier. Remembering being a first-time voter typically correlates with more emotional electoral experiences, except in South Africa, and, in Germany, with happier experiences.

ELECTORAL MEMORY AND ELECTORAL RESOLUTION

Finally, we consider the effects of electoral memory on electoral resolution. The contribution of memory variables to the overall model is presented in figure 5.9. Electoral memory makes a relatively modest contribution to the overall explanatory power of the models. This time, in the US, the model works best for advance (early) voters (+0.11). In other countries, however, the contribution of memory ranges from +0.01 to +0.03. Specific variable contributions were reported in table 4.7 for the US and table 4.8 for elsewhere. The memory variables are included in all country models, and suggest that stronger memories of one's first vote makes experience of resolution more likely. Being a first-time voter has no significant effect.

Overall, electoral memory makes a modest but important contribution to models of electoral choice, turnout, electoral experience, and electoral resolution. Citizens' memories of their first elections is particularly impor-

Resolution models improvement—stage 2

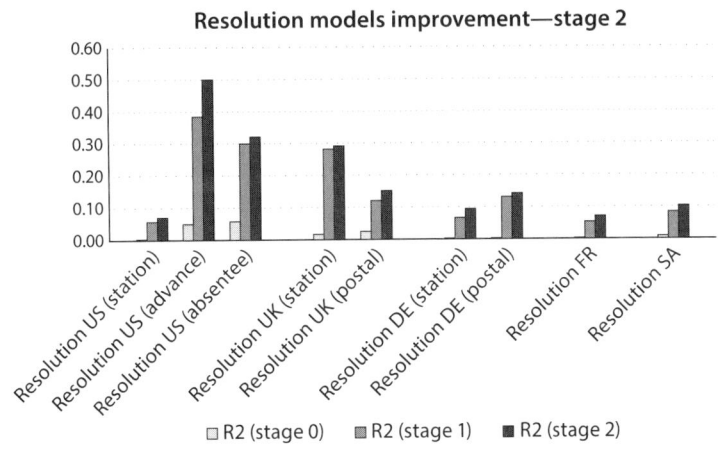

[Bar chart showing R² values for Resolution US (station), Resolution US (advance), Resolution US (absentee), Resolution UK (station), Resolution UK (postal), Resolution DE (station), Resolution DE (postal), Resolution FR, Resolution SA, with three bars each for R2 (stage 0), R2 (stage 1), and R2 (stage 2).]

FIGURE 5.9: Stage 2: Improvement to electoral resolution models—memory predictors. Bars represent R^2

tant in making their subsequent electoral experience happier, and in making it more likely that they will feel a sense of closure and democratic resolution from an election, as well as increasing propensity to participate. Remembering childhood elections, meanwhile, is associated with more left-wing tendencies. Finally, the unique nature of a first vote is meaningful, in that it makes the electoral experience more emotional and happier for first-time voters.

Whilst the explanatory power of electoral memory in our model is perhaps less comprehensive than in the case of personality, it is significant and coherent. The qualitative evidence also suggests that it permeates citizens' outlook, as often emotional electoral memories get remobilized election after election, particularly at the time when citizens go to vote. Thus, as explained in chapter 2, beyond models' performance, the impact of electoral memory is likely to be cumulative and indirect, and to be particularly influential through what we described as 'implicit retrieval', which we cannot test in a survey. In other words, it is not so much recalling a specific memory which will, in itself, affect us; more influential, rather, will be the way in which this may put us in a specific frame of mind, a specific mood, acutely attuning to given signals, emotions, and stimuli. Thus, by affecting citizens' natures and also the personae and roles that they inhabit with every new election, electoral memory is also likely to influence their electoral identities and their understanding of the relationship between individual and society in the context of an election. This is what we will consider in chapter 6.

6

Electoral Identity and Individual-Societal Dynamics

The Concept of Electoral Identity

In this chapter, we develop the new model of electoral identity we introduced in chapter 1. We suggest that notwithstanding the virtually unanimous assumption of the existing literature, the vote is not a straightforward measure of spontaneous preference. Instead, citizens go to the polling booth consciously or subconsciously inhabiting a role which determines their outlook, decision-process, experience, and ultimate choice. The behaviour of citizens is thus shaped by how they define their role as voters. We consider this role, or *electoral identity*, to be determined by any given individual's assimilation of the articulation between that individual and others in elections. In other words, individual citizens are profoundly aware that an election is an interface between our own actions and those of others, and electoral identity is constrained by what we believe is our relationship to, as well as responsibility towards, others. This leads to the concept of *empathic displacement*, which corresponds to how an individual factors in the experience and behaviour of the rest of society when experiencing the election and casting their own vote. Electoral identity also affects how we will react to election results and Election Night, and the extent to which electoral situations make us feel integrated or alienated.

Using the analogy of sports events, whereby parties and candidates are seen as the competing teams, we identify two alternative perceptions of the role of voters, with citizens split between those who see themselves predominantly as 'supporters', and those who think of their role as being 'referees' to varying degrees. We find that this distinction and scale (which does not follow known measures such as partisan identification, either conceptually or empirically) shapes voters' perceptions of the campaign and the types of election that they prefer, affects the stability of their preferences and the timing of when they may change their minds, and results in different emotions being experienced during and after the vote. We here test our electoral identity model, comparing distributions across systems and between elections and referenda. We then assess the relationship between electoral identity and egocentric and sociotropic voting, empathic displacement and the articulation between individual and society, polarization, and hostility towards other voters.

Virtually all electoral behaviour models implicitly or explicitly assume that a citizen's vote is the translation of his or her preference (this is especially explicit in utility functions, as per Downs, 1957). This assumption is so universal that it may seem obvious. What if things were not so simple, however? Equating the vote to the expression of a preference corresponds to the foundational logic of representative democracy, but in some ways is a rather unlikely assumption, given what we know of human psychology. Most of our actions are not the simple product of desires or pure preferences, but also result from perceptions of what we should and should not do, and ultimately of the role we embrace in the context of a decision, as asserted by Freud (1991) in terms of 'ego' and 'superego'. Thus, as suggested in chapter 2, people may not go to vote simply as 'people' (let alone self-centred and oblivious people), but more precisely as people assuming a certain role, embracing what they see as a voter's function, that is, expressing an electoral identity.

The intuition that voting is a matter of identity has in fact long been implied in some electoral models, most notably in the guise of 'partisan identification' in the Michigan model of the vote (Campbell et al., 1960; Butler and Stokes, 1969), but with an expectation that such identity would mirror partisan alignments (Lipset and Rokkan, 1967). As discussed in chapter 2, this model has been questioned at length, as regards both its theoretical logic and its practical value, and with both dismissive and sympathetic undertones (Key, 1966; Lewis-Beck et al., 2008). In this book, however, we assert that excluding the equation of partisanship with identity (because it is neither the way in which most people define themselves, nor a criterion which consistently shapes their human perceptions, attitudes, and behaviour) does not mean that voting is not at all shaped by an electoral identity. We do not propose to throw the identity baby out with the partisan bathwater. Rather, we consider a different basis for the nature of electoral identity, which we relate to the intimate, largely subconscious understanding of the role of a voter that we believe the citizen inhabits election after election, shaping to a large extent his/her electoral experience and behaviour.

In chapter 2, we gave the analogy—probably familiar to many readers—of an academic grading an exam. Whether consciously or subconsciously, he/she will do so in accordance with the 'cap' worn as a grader, with the outlook, constraints, and responsibilities that this entails, rather than expressing a spontaneous or personal preference, liking, or dislike for a student. The same will be true of a judge trying a case, a ground agent dealing with disrupted passengers, and, indeed, a parent educating a child, whose instinctive preference might be just to grant everything the child asks. We argue that the same is true of voters. In short, voting is more like a job or a responsibility than like opening the freezer to reach for that irresistible ice-cream.

The consequences of introducing electoral identity into our understanding of voters' experience, behaviour, and sense of electoral resolution are potentially immense. For example, if a vote does not express a preference or interest but rather the conclusive assessment performed under a certain role, this may question the whole logic underlying rational-choice electoral experiments based on incentives; and if identity only kicks in subconsciously as the electoral atmosphere builds up, as we suggest, this may explain the significant variation between individuals' expressed preferences in polls and their decisions in the polling booth, as they may be answering two different questions ('Who do I like best?' vs 'Who do I think I should vote for?') in the two settings.

This chapter is dedicated to our model of those 'roles' voters assume in elections, and raises key questions. How do voters consciously perceive their role and the function of elections? What do they believe that they are there to do? How will this affect their outlook as regards electoral reality, campaigns, debates, issues, and so on? How stable is electoral identity over time, at both individual and aggregate levels? When does it really 'kick in'? Does it explain some of the late and changing electoral decisions that many voters report in every election? How is electoral identity symptomatic of how we conceive the articulation between our vote and that of others, and thus affected by empathic displacement?

As explained above, our model of electoral identity is based on a sports analogy, which contrasts 'referees' with 'supporters'. We suggest that elections are akin to major sports games—like the final of the Super Bowl in the US, or of the football (soccer) World Cup—and that parties or candidates vying for citizens' votes are the players. We propose that on that basis, citizens are left with two possible roles to inhabit in the context of that event: supporters, embracing a side and cheering for its victory (or, indeed, booing its opponents), or referees, neutral and objective assessors of which teams deserves to win.

Function as Cognitive Disturbance

Throughout our lives, we experience a dichotomy between preference and function. As mentioned previously, this may often be the case in the professional arena. We look at situations and decisions differently, depending on our role as observers or as judges, onlookers or teachers, watchers or doctors. Function affects the grounds of our perceptions and behaviour as parents, friends, partners, or neighbours. Frequently, we are put in a position where we feel that we ought to behave in a way, which, frankly, would not be our easiest, most comfortable, or preferred option. How many parents have found themselves having to tell off their child not because they actually wanted to, but because they thought that it was their duty to speak up, and that following their preference of just 'letting things go' would undoubtedly do a disservice to the person they love and feel a responsibility to educate? The moment we inhabit our role and wear the corresponding 'hat', we change our approach, our criteria, often subconsciously and automatically, as we may do when we vote. Furthermore, over time, we may have learned to reflect on the roles that we enact daily (in work or family), but we may not have such or habits of reflection with regard to roles that we only inhabit infrequently, such as that of voter, embraced only every few years.

When acting in our individual, self-interested capacity, we may not need to project. For instance, when choosing whether to eat pizza or steak tonight, there is nothing gained by trying to understand what our neighbours may be cooking. By contrast, inhabiting a role makes information and projection necessary. Academics, for example, constantly seek information on how colleagues work, on new tools and approaches that improve the way they deliver the functions that their work demands, and reflect on conditions that may impair their ability to fulfil their role. Similarly, millions of parents have read books on what the role entails and how best to perform it. Thus, as regards voting, if it were purely intuitive, projection would be redundant; but if voting is a role, empathic displacement may become an indispensable part of performing it. Often, citizens express the notion that they are embracing and inhabiting a role when they vote, by referring to their own responsibility in the election:

> I feel voting is the utmost responsibility. It's something we have that so many people around the world don't have. It is a responsibility. People have fought and died. I have no patience for people that don't vote. US35M047

> At the ballot box I think about my responsibility I think about what can one person do. I think about how real that is. I am proud to vote. US63M052

> I feel attached to the process. I think it's a very emotional process. This is one way to feel you're a citizen of this country. Especially as an immigrant that hasn't grown up in this country and still gets to vote. US30M006

> I feel like a citizen mainly through elections. US44F042

> Solemn responsibility. I think of having the right to vote. How important that is. US4ZF054

This is where capturing how people see their role as voters is crucial, especially as elections can perform different institutional, political, and social functions, as we noted in chapter 2.

Existing Typologies and Their Limits

Political scientists have long tried to characterize types of voter. In fact, existing models of electoral behaviour have been based on understanding how different voters behave by creating categories: 'sincere and strategic' (Downs, 1957); 'materialist and post-materialist' (Inglehart, 1971); 'party identifiers and non-identifiers' (Campbell et al., 1960); 'aligned and de-aligned' (Franklin et al., 1992); 'informed and uninformed' (Bartels, 1996). Our model is no different in this respect, in that it too relies on typological approaches to differentiate between voter types; its originality, however, may be that it seeks to differentiate on the basis not of voting behaviour, but of a more fundamental difference in outlook and conception of democratic citizenship. We aim to categorize systematically what elections represent to individuals, and how they define the very nature of their role within the electoral process. The metaphorical referee/supporter model that we propose echoes other sporting analogies. Lakoff (e.g., Lakoff, 1993; Lakoff and Johnson, 2008) has pioneered analyses of major metaphors in political contestation in advanced democracies, highlighting in particular the use of family and health metaphors in political discourse. Similarly, Scheithauer (2007) studied how metaphors are used during Election Night television coverage in Britain, the United States, and Germany; whilst Musolff (2004) and Charteris-Black (2009) highlight the use of metaphors in European political discourse, and Semino and Masci (1996) analyze Silvio Berlusconi's political use of football analogies in Italy. While all are primarily interested in the use of metaphors in political discourse, we adapt the metaphorical approach to explore role self-perception within electoral politics. The perception of elections as 'contests' is long-standing, and the subconscious nature of established metaphors means that they work well in bottom-up models.

The Basic Model of Electoral Identity: 'Referees' and 'Supporters'

Looking back at the work of Lakoff and Johnson (2008) on political metaphors, we explore some of the metaphorical proxies used historically by citizens and leaders alike to distance the perception of politics from its elementary nature as a power relationship. Politics 'translates' into lexical fields which may come across as more concrete and closer to the everyday life of citizens. From a top-down perspective, a preferred 'translation' highlighted by Lakoff is the 'family' metaphor. However, the fact that politicians wish to portray themselves as 'family heads' in charge of citizens does not mean that voters themselves subscribe to the metaphor, or see themselves as the 'children' of political systems. The family metaphor is inclusive, but highly patriarchal, reducing to passive roles citizens who rarely, in fact, feel included by political systems, or assume there to be top-down empathy. Few would trust any politician as a second mother or father.

We feel that the alternative sports metaphor that we use in our model, already present in some electoral lexicons, is a more realistic one than that of the family, more frequently referred to in the academic literature (Lakoff, 1993). Elections have 'winners' and 'losers'. Parties have 'campaign teams', and candidates even have 'coaches', responsible for their communication and public relations. Candidates 'compete' for citizens' vote. Some elections are 'tight races' or even end with a 'photo finish' because there seems to be a 'tie' between the candidates, while others are 'open contests'. Almost every time, there is someone 'in the lead', or even candidates 'in pole position', while others may 'trail behind'. Indeed, some elections even have 'runners-up' or candidates who get 'disqualified'. Some campaigns are regularly described as 'marathons', and often elections feature a 'final sprint'. In multi-party systems, some of the 'contenders' may indeed face a 'duel', and in 'two-round' systems, those who qualify for the second ballot are often described as the 'finalists'.

In short, there is a very broad trend of describing elections as sports events, parties as teams, and candidates as players; the entire elections universe is filled with such metaphors. We claim here that these metaphors are also more consistent than others with most voters' perceptions of politics as external to them, sometimes separate to the point of being unreal, and occasionally fascinating. If, for the sake of argument, we accept that voters themselves subscribe to such metaphors, which need not imply excessive familiarity with politicians and parties, we need to understand how voters 'fit' in this sporting contest, and as outlined previously, our model allows for two roles which voters could assume: that of supporters, siding with one team and wanting it to win, or that of referees, who feel they have to arbitrate between the players and essentially decide who deserves to win. The referee/supporter model is actually spontaneously evoked by some:

> It's similar to watching sports. . . . So that is the team I'm rooting for. I'm following because it's an interesting game to watch. US23F050

> It was like the Super Bowl. My father couldn't vote, but he was really involved. US35M047

The 'Supporter' Electoral Identity

Almost all classic models of voting behaviour suggest that voters effectively 'belong' to a political camp. This is true of models of voters' alignments, most famously conceptualized by Lipset and Rokkan (1967), and models of partisan identification, first developed by Campbell et al. (1960). In fact, even rational-choice models (Downs, 1957) predict that voters effectively 'choose their camp' in elections according to whichever party maximizes their utility and offers policies best suiting their purposes. While these three models start from entirely different premises, all rely on the notion that voters are effectively supporters with a vested interest (be it pragmatic or identitarian) in a given party winning the election. Some of these models assume lifelong supporters who have, in effect, been to the stadium to cheer Liverpool ever since they were little children, while others depict more 'distant' supporters, who never really had an interest in bobsleigh, say, before, but whose heart is suddenly beating for that unknown champion. Nonetheless, in both cases, elections are about camps mobilizing their supporters, and the camp with the most supporters winning the election.

In this sense, a 'supporter' model of electoral identity is probably seemingly familiar and based on a 'preference' conceived as relatively straightforward. In this model, voters choose a camp, and to an extent, care about whether that camp wins or not. This is a 'final of the Super Bowl' where the voters, regardless of whether or not their home team will play have chosen a side in their hearts and will (quietly or cheeringly) support it. In electoral terms, 'supporters' will approach the election with hearts engaged, potentially polarized, and experience intense emotions that reach their height when they discover—on Election Night—whether their 'team' won.

The 'Referee' Electoral Identity

The alternative electoral identity is that of 'referee'. Many early thinkers believed electoral choice should be based on competence. Modern franchise models in the eighteenth and nineteenth centuries were based on the same assumption, with wealth and (as still nowadays) age deemed necessary for citizens to be able to evaluate candidates for their vote. Beyond that meritocratic model, we have ample evidence that many voters are cynical towards the politicians and political parties competing for their vote, and most unlikely truly to 'support' any of them. In survey after survey, many voters express a belief that parties are remote, 'all the same', and certainly not fighting 'for' them. Much political science has accepted these attitudes as a fact of life (be it called cynicism, disaffection, or by any other label), regarding it possibly as a reason for abstention or a radical vote, but not as fitting in with an electoral role and outlook.

It is also worth noting that, increasingly, citizens are given the opportunity to be self-appointed 'judges' of multiple contests in everyday life, from *The X Factor* to the Eurovision song contest, numerous audience awards, TripAdvisor reviews, or one of the thousands of websites and blogs asking for similar users' assessment, in addition to the more traditional duty of jury service. This phenomenon should not be underestimated in its likely effects on internal efficacy. Arguably, someone who feels competent to judge the quality of a film, a restaurant, or a figure skater as legitimately as does a Cannes Festival jury member, a Michelin guide critique, or an Olympic judge is likely also to feel legitimated to decide which party offers the most convincing and appropriate proposals in an election. The model suggests that when this happens, it will strengthen the habituation of voters to become 'judges' in multiple contests, alongside an increasing sense of distance from parties and politicians, thus making them election 'referees'.

We expect these referees to be voting with their heads rather than with their hearts, and likely to experience in particular emotions such as excitement and pride, along with a feeling of responsibility on their shoulders, as they vote. Unlike for supporters, the climax of their emotional response to elections may be at the moment when they actually cast their vote.

We measure electoral identity using both direct and indirect measures. Direct measures compare elections to highly salient sports competitions (the final of the Super Bowl in the US, of the football (soccer) World Cup, etc.), and ask voters to describe their own roles within that context. Indirectly, we measure a number of attitudes that are characteristic of a referee's or a supporter's view of the election. We also use mixed quantitative and qualitative measures to capture electoral identity across countries and contexts, recoding open questions relating to how voters see their role, in addition to a range of closed-question survey items.

We asked these questions across multiple elections and countries, to assess whether the supporter/referee distinction makes intuitive sense to citizens in the first place, and to see how consistent responses are, how citizens are distributed on the electoral identity scale across countries and elections, and how stable electoral identity is at both individual and aggregate levels within and across cycles.

The Role of Voters in Citizens' Own Words

One of the survey's open questions asked respondents how they would explain the role of a voter both to a child of seven and to an eighteen-year-old

ELECTORAL IDENTITY   193

Defining the role of a voter (open-ended in %)

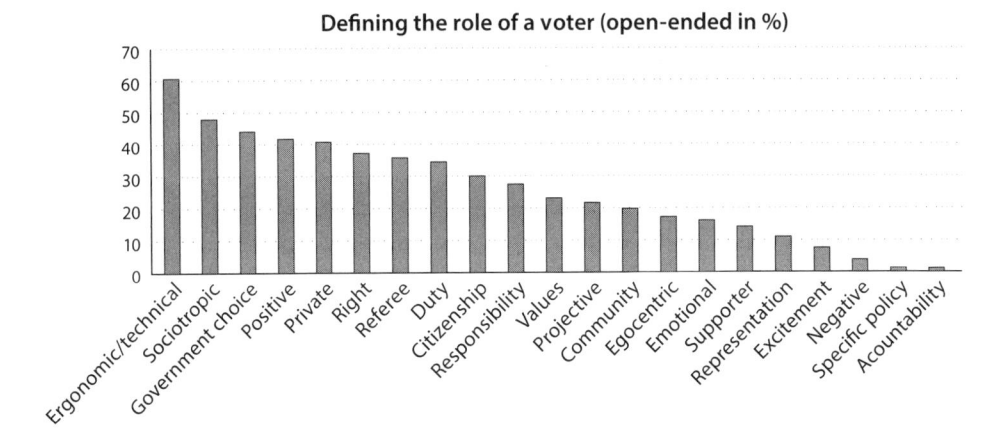

[Bar chart showing percentages for categories, from highest to lowest: Ergonomic/technical (~61), Sociotropic (~49), Government choice (~45), Positive (~43), Private (~42), Right (~38), Referee (~37), Duty (~35), Citizenship (~31), Responsibility (~28), Values (~25), Projective (~23), Community (~21), Egocentric (~18), Emotional (~17), Supporter (~15), Representation (~9), Excitement (~5), Negative (~4), Specific policy (~2), Accountability (~2)]

FIGURE 6.1: Main characteristics of the role of a voter as explained to a child (recoded open ended)

about to vote for the first time. This was because it is often easier for people to articulate deeply held perceptions and beliefs when referring to people other than themselves, so a description of the role of a voter addressed to someone else can help us to capture the functions citizens associate with voters. The results are summarized in figure 6.1. The main motifs citizens use to describe the role of voters are ergonomic and technical. Critically, however, a vast majority of citizens also make a resolute choice to describe the role of the voter to others as that of a referee rather than a supporter. Referee references (36.4%) are nearly 2.5 times more frequent than supporter equivalents (14.9%). This is further echoed by the predominance of description of the role of the voter in sociotropic (the second highest type of reference: 48.5% of cases) rather than egocentric terms (17.7%). Descriptions of the role of voters are also overwhelmingly positive (44.7%) rather than negative (4.2%). References to voting as a right (37.5%) only slightly exceed those to voting as a duty (35%), a responsibility (27.9%), or an act of citizenship (30.4%). Finally, one in six voters (16.5%) emphasizes the emotional dimension of the vote.

Spontaneously Confirming the Referee/Supporter Model

Beyond the generic reflections on the role of voters reported above, many respondents spontaneously echo our referee/supporter model by positioning themselves with references to elections as game-like. This was notably the case in the US, with unprompted Super Bowl evocations:

> I think that we're fed this story that the presidential election is like the Super Bowl. I'm angry that we're being manipulated by the media, which requires us to be glued to the TV. US29M049

> I live in CA and this state is going to vote for Obama. So that is the team I'm rooting for. I'm following because it's an interesting game to watch. US23F050

> It was like the Super Bowl. My father couldn't vote, but he was really involved. US35M047

Interestingly, in France, the referee position is emphasized by multiple respondents:

> I mean, it's like the final of the Coupe de France, if I was a supporter of one of the teams, I'd have to recuse myself as referee right? So you need to really be fair to all of them when you listen to what they say as fully and impartially as you can. FR44M077

> Honestly, what's the point of listening to a friend who behaves like a cheerleader? Referees have to be impartial or else you can't trust them to make the right decision. FR19F066

We now look systematically at voters' distributions on the identity scale, based on both explicit and implicit questions about voters' roles in our panel studies.

Referees and Supporters across Countries

When discussing the possible function of elections, we mentioned that different national and institutional contexts may favour different potential functions. Whilst the referee and supporter analogy can work anywhere, electoral 'games' differ nationally, such that either of the two roles may be more intuitive in different contexts. Referee/supporter distributions are shown in figure 6.2. We first verify how intuitive the model is to respondents by looking at those who answered 'Neither' to the referee/supporter self-placement question (see appendix 1).[1] This proportion is low, ranging from 2.9% in the Georgian presidential election and 11.5% in the South African general election to 31.3% in a German federal election. In terms of referee/supporter distribution, there are generally more supporters than

---

1. Appendices referred to in this chapter are to be found online at www.epob.org.

Distribution of referees and supporters by country/election

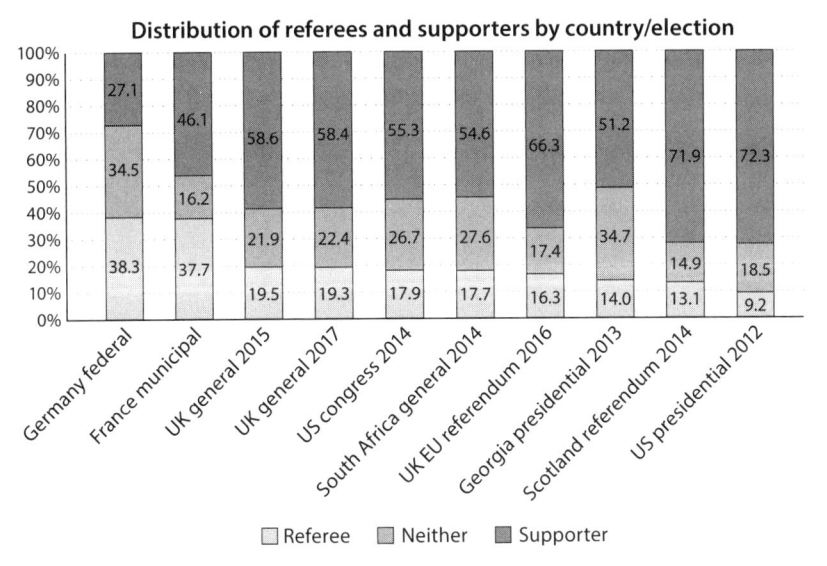

Election	Referee	Neither	Supporter
Germany federal	38.3	34.5	27.1
France municipal	37.7	16.2	46.1
UK general 2015	19.5	21.9	58.6
UK general 2017	19.3	22.4	58.4
US congress 2014	17.9	26.7	55.3
South Africa general 2014	17.7	27.6	54.6
UK EU referendum 2016	16.3	17.4	66.3
Georgia presidential 2013	14.0	34.7	51.2
Scotland referendum 2014	13.1	14.9	71.9
US presidential 2012	9.2	18.5	72.3

FIGURE 6.2: Referees and supporters across countries and elections

referees, but with important comparative differences. In Germany, referees outnumber supporters (38.3% vs 27.1%), whilst in France, supporters represent a relatively small majority (46.1% vs 37.7%). By contrast, a comfortable majority of respondents self-define as supporters in the UK (58.4% vs 19.3% in the 2017 general election), in South Africa (54.6 vs 17.7%), Georgia (51.2% vs 14%), and the US presidential election (72.3% vs 9.2%). Excepting the US, older democracies typically have larger proportions of referees than newer ones do, and more normally distributed referee/supporter scales.

Beyond comparative differences, we note that proportions of referees and supporters vary across election types. This is striking in the US and the UK. In the US, voter distribution is far more skewed towards supporters in presidential than in mid-term elections. In the UK, referenda also produce supporter-heavy electoral identity distributions, compared to elections.

Those two findings would be counter-intuitive if one expected the referee/supporter distribution to mimic the logic of partisan identification. In practice, the less party-centric the election, the more voters act as supporters. Indeed, the proportion of supporters is eight percentage points higher for the 2016 UK EU-membership referendum than for either the preceding or following general elections (66.3% as opposed to 58.6% and 58.4% respectively), even though that referendum blurred all existing partisan lines. Similarly, in the US, the very personalized presidential election of 2012 has a proportion of supporters seventeen percentage points higher than the party-centric mid-terms that followed two years later (72.3% vs 55.3%, this result being based on the same respondents). Had our model mirrored partisanship, we would expect party-centric elections to have had the greatest proportions of supporters and referenda to be most referee-centric, rather than the other way round.

A True Identity? Stability of Referee/Supporter Identification over Time

One of the essential foundations of identities in psychology theory is their stability (Herrmann et al., 2004; Bruter, 2005). We thus assess whether electoral identity behaves coherently over time, and test its stability at both aggregate and individual levels. The aggregate-level evaluation uses time series data, whilst the individual-level tests use panel study results, both within a given campaign cycle and across elections.

A limitation of the aggregate-level analysis is that, as already noted, the referee/supporter balance varies across election types, even within countries. However, this does not equate to instability in and of itself, as we argued that the function of elections varies according to their nature and setting, their arrangements, and their predominantly representative, accountable, or executive ethos. If the function of an election may legitimately vary, so can the roles that voters will embrace within them, with electoral identity being a genuine reflection of the different roles that voters may inhabit. We test this claim using dynamic election cycles in the UK, where two general elections took place, in 2015 and 2017, with a major referendum between them, in 2016. Figure 6.2 shows that the electoral identity of British voters was actually extremely similar in the 2017 and 2015 general elections. Over that period, the proportions of referees and supporters each decreased by only 0.2% (19.5 to 19.3% for referees, and 58.6 to 58.4% for supporters), whilst the number of people in the intermediate category increased by 0.5%, to 22.4% (from 21.9%). By contrast, the referendum between these two general elections was far more skewed towards supporters.

Moreover, in 2014, Scotland held its highly salient independence referendum. The two referenda obviously had different voting populations, but we note that the distribution of referees and supporters in the 2016 EU-membership referendum is much closer to that of the 2014 Scottish independence referendum than to those of the 2015 or 2017 general elections. For the EU referendum, there was no statistically significant difference be-

TABLE 6.1. Individual Stability across a Campaign Cycle: The UK 2016 referendum

		May–April (%)	July–April (%)
Full 5-point scale	No change	52.2	49.3
	+/− 1	27.1	26.1
	+/− 2	15.9	18.1
	Change > 2	4.7	6.6
Referee/Supporter identity	Unchanged identity	63.5	58.8
	Identity switch	8.4	9.8

TABLE 6.2. Individual Stability across Elections: USA 2012–2014

		2012–2014 (%)
Full 5-point scale	No change	45.3
	+/− 1	30.5
	+/− 2	19.0
	Change > 2	5.2
Referee/Supporter identity	Unchanged identity	56.6
	Identity switch	7.2

tween the mean electoral identity in Scotland and in other nations of the UK, which enables us to control for population differences. Thus, comparing like for like over a four-year period, the aggregate-level electoral identity of the British public differs across election types, but is extremely stable over time within a given election category.

Such similarities could nonetheless hide variations across individuals, and electoral identity stability must really be assessed at the individual level, using our panel study data. We do so twice: first within a given election cycle, by reassessing the electoral identity of voters in the 2016 UK referendum at three points during a three-month panel, and second, despite the caveat already noted with regard to electoral variations, by looking at the electoral identity of US respondents in the 2012 presidential and 2014 congressional elections. The results are shown in tables 6.1 and 6.2, respectively. The example of the 2016 UK referendum enables us to assess how referee and supporter identities get triggered through an election cycle, and for the US example across cycles, exploring how both component identities are mobilized in electoral situations.

Between April and July 2016, a proportion of the British electorate slowly but surely switched from a predominantly referee to a predominantly supporter role. Supporters were always a majority throughout the campaign, but overtook referees even more significantly by Referendum Day. Whilst a number of respondents progressively migrated towards more strongly supportive electoral roles, table 6.1 depicts a general trend of great stability. On a full five-point scale, half of the respondents give the exact same answer in July as they did in April. Over three-quarters of respondents are also within one point of their original answer by Referendum Day. Moreover, less than 10% of respondents changed their dominant electoral identity from referee to supporter or vice versa between waves 1 and 3.

We then assess electoral identity stability over a much longer time period, spanning two consecutive US elections. Here again, despite the long panel gap and the different types of election being compared, electoral identity proves very stable in the long run. Only 7.2% of respondents switched from referee to supporter identity or vice versa during the two-year panel period. On the full five-point scale, nearly 50% of respondents gave the exact same result two years apart, and over three-quarters are within one point of their original answer two years later. Electoral identity proves as strong and stable across two different types of election two years apart in the US as it did within the framework of a three-month campaign cycle in the UK referendum of 2016. These results hold true regardless of the operationalization of the scale (including or excluding those who answer 'Neither' to the self-placement question).

Electoral identity therefore passes the crucial stability and coherence test of an identity. Not only is the scale meaningful to voters, but their placement is very stable over time, both within and across election cycles. This stability is true at both individual and aggregate levels (in the latter case, within election types). Individually, only between one in fifteen and one in ten voters change their electoral identity from referee to supporter or vice versa over a two-year period, a negligible proportion, by panel data standards, with such large samples and long lag between the waves.

Referees and Supporters: Social, Demographic, and Psychological Profiles

We now consider the comparative profiles of referees and supporters, looking at differences across key social and demographic variables. Results are presented in table 6.3. With the possible exception of age, none of the usual key demographic and social control variables explains much variance in

TABLE 6.3. Social and Demographic Predictors of Electoral Identity

	Age	Female	Education	Income	Right-wing-ideology	Religiosity
UK general election	+**	—	—	—	–**	NA
Scotland referendum	+**	—	—	–*	—	NA
US presidential election	+**	+**	—	+*	–**	+*
Germany federal election	—	—	—	—	—	NA
France municipal election	—	—	—	—	—	NA
South Africa general election	+**	—	+*	—	—	NA
Georgia presidential election	—	—	—	—	—	NA

Note: Entries represent the sign and level of statistical significance of correlation coefficients (* = <0.05; ** = <0.01).

electoral identity. Age-wise, older voters are more likely to be supporters in the UK (including Scotland), the US, and South Africa. By contrast, gender has no significant effect on electoral identity, except in the US, where women are more likely to be supporters than men. Education has little bearing on electoral identity except in South Africa, where more educated voters are more likely to be supporters. Income appears to be a contradictory factor, with wealthier citizens more likely to be supporters in the US, but referees in Scotland. There is no relationship between citizens' ideology and electoral identity except in the US and the UK, where left-wing attitudes are associated with supporter identity. Lastly, in the US, religiosity is also associated with supporters. Whilst social and demographic predictors of electoral identity are scarce, we turn to psychological profiles and the relationship between our eight personality traits and electoral identity, with the results presented in appendix 3.

No personality trait works universally across countries, but several have a coherent and significant effect. Thus, being sensitive (UK, Scotland, South Africa), risk-averse (UK, Scotland, Georgia), and attached to freedom (UK, Georgia) is predominantly associated with referees. By contrast, being anxious (US mid-term, UK, South Africa, Germany), confrontational (US presidential, South Africa, Georgia), an extravert (Scotland), and feeling alienated (in the US) are associated with supporters. The effects of caringness are unclear.

Finally, we enter all the demographic, social, and personality predictors of electoral identity in country-based regressions, to see which of those predictors remain significant in explaining electoral identity in a multivariate context. The results are presented in table 6.4. Again, social and

TABLE 6.4. Multivariate Model of Electoral Identity

	US 2012	US 2014	UK ref.	Scot. ref.	South Afr.	Germany	Georgia
Constant	1.95 (0.20)**	1.79 (0.40)**	2.33 (0.16)**	2.27 (0.35)**	0.97 (0.31)**	0.66 (0.10)**	1.30 (0.05)**
Gender	0.25 (0.06)**	—	—	—	—	—	—
Age	0.01 (0.00)**	0.01 (0.00)**	0.13 (0.02)**	0.02 (0.00)**	0.01 (0.00)**	—	—
Education	—	—	—	—	0.10 (0.03)**	—	—
Income	—	—	—	—	—	0.01 (0.00)*	—
Religiosity	—	—	.	—	.	.	—
Ideology	—	—	—	—	—	—	—
Sensitivity	—	−0.16 (0.07)**	−0.09 (0.03)**	−0.13 (0.06)*	−0.10 (0.05)*	—	—
Anxiety	—	0.17 (0.07)**	—	0.12 (0.06)*	—	0.04 (0.02)*	—
Freedom	−0.06 (0.03)*	—	−0.09 (0.03)**	—	—	—	—
Extraversion	—	—	—	—	—	—	—
Risk aversion	—	—	−0.09 (0.04)*	−A*#	—	—	−0.05 (0.02)**
Care	—	—	−0.06 (0.03)*	—	—	—	0.04 (0.02)*
Alienation	—	—	—	—	—	—	—
Confrontation	—	—	—	—	0.04 (0.02)*	—	0.03 (0.01)**
R^2	0.06	0.05	0.07	0.09	0.05	0.01	0.02

Notes: Entries are b-unstandardized regression coefficients and only indicated for variables with statistically significant effects. Religiosity question only asked in the US. * = sig≤0.05; ** = sig≤0.01. A#: Two models were run for the Scottish referendum based on electoral identity in referendum and in general elections. Risk aversion had a statistically significant negative effect in the context of general elections, but here we present the referendum results.

demographic predictors work poorly except for age, with older citizens becoming increasingly likely to identify as supporters other than in Germany and Georgia. Other social and demographic indicators only have an exceptional effect—women are more likely to be supporters in a US presidential election, as are wealthier people in Germany. By contrast, psychological traits retain their effect on electoral identity. Sensitive respondents are more likely to identify as referees in the US (congressional elections), UK, Scotland, and South Africa. Anxious people are more likely to be supporters in the US (congressional elections), Scotland, and Germany, and risk-averse people identify as referees in the UK, Scotland, and Georgia. Three more personality traits retain statistically significant effects in two countries each: attachment to freedom is associated with referees in the US (presidential election) and the UK, confrontational personalities with supporters in South Africa and Georgia, and caringness increases the propensity to identify as a referee in the UK, and as a supporter in Georgia.

The impact of risk aversion, sensitivity, confrontational attitudes, and attachment to freedom is noteworthy. It suggests that electoral identity is not an extension of partisan identification or interest in elections, but rather pertains to the articulation between the individual and the collective. This chapter defines electoral identity as an understanding of the role of voters and how elections are articulated around their relationship to others. The link between personality traits and electoral identity suggests that this goes to the heart of how elections are conceived as social instruments intended to constrain, manage, and resolve conflict. Personality traits which explain attitude towards conflict thus best explain voters identifying as referees or supporters.

The Consequences of Electoral Identity

We next consider electoral identity as an independent variable, and assess its effect on various electoral attitudes and behaviour. The results are shown in appendix 3. First, elections typically seem more enjoyable for supporters than for referees. In every country, supporters are more likely to enjoy the atmosphere of Election Night—regardless of the winner—and in Georgia, they are also more likely to enjoy the atmosphere of the polling station. Supporters also tend to feel more efficacious (US 2012, UK, Georgia) and more projectively efficacious (same countries). They are more likely to trust their preferred party in technical, moral, and ideological terms than are referees, but also, in the US (2014 elections) to trust Congress within its technical role. Behaviourally, supporters are more likely than referees to claim always to vote (US 2012, UK, and Georgia), but in terms of actual turnout, the situation is overall more contrasted, with supporters having higher turnout than referees in the US in 2012 and the UK only.

More importantly, supporters and referees use their vote differently. Supporters are more likely always to vote for the same party (US 2014, UK, and Germany) and sincerely (US, UK, and Georgia). They concomitantly feel more guilty if they do not vote (US 2012, UK, Georgia) and if they do not support a major party (UK, Germany), except in South Africa. By contrast, referees are more likely to cast a protest vote (US in both elections, UK, and Germany) or vote strategically (US in both elections and South Africa). Referees also consider campaigns and debates when they vote (UK and US), and discussions with their family and friends, with an open mind. They are thus more likely to change their minds on Election Day (UK, South Africa, Germany, and Georgia).

Three last findings on the consequences of electoral identity are noteworthy. First, elections can be emotional for both supporters and referees. For instance, supporters were more likely already to have cried because of an election in the US in 2012 and in Georgia, but referees were more likely to shed electoral tears in South Africa. Second, whilst supporters will self-declare as sociotropic (US 2012, UK, and Georgia), when using implicit measures, we find that it is actually referees who behave most sociotropically, both in the US and in the UK. Indeed, electoral identity is correlated at 0.11* with economic sociotropism in the US, and at 0.08* with the safety sociotropic dimension in the UK. Finally, US supporters are more likely to be projective (0.09*), though only in the 2012 presidential election.

This difference between self-perception and actual behaviour, from turnout to sociotropism, is critical. Supporters are more likely than referees to overestimate the extent to which they are 'model voters', and ultimately display a poorer understanding of their own motivations, which is likely to diverge from the actuality of their electoral behaviour.

Mirrors and Projections—Elections as an Articulation between Self and Society

Both referees and supporters conceive their role as voters (whether consciously or subconsciously) on the basis of a certain relationship to the rest of society. In the case of supporters, elections represent an opposition between two blocs, while in the case of referees, it they constitute a collective evaluation of the quality of the options offered to the polity. These differences also have implications for how different voters may feel a sense of responsibility, empathy, and/or shared destiny with others, and who those others are. In both cases, the vote is therefore also projective, and derives its meaning and effectiveness from the way it interacts with the decisions and behaviours of others. This leads us to introduce the question of how voters articulate the relationship between their individual selves and the societal collective in electoral contexts, and in particular the concepts of empathic displacement and projected efficacy.

Identities are not purely introspective. We do not think of our own natures as in a vacuum, disconnected from others, alternatives, and environments. The importance of others in the definition of our own being is best recognised in two different articulations: the notion of collective identity, whereby an individual defines who he/she is in in terms of inclusion within a predetermined group; and ingroup/outgroup theories, whereby individuals define their identity not vis-à-vis groups they belong to, but rather against groups from which they differentiate themselves. However, the individual–societal dialectic nature of identities is far broader, and valid as a reference point for individual just as much as collective identities. (Bruter, 2005)

Elections offer a unique context in which to articulate the detailed ways in which an individual interacts with his/her community. By its nature, liberal democracy asks citizens to express individual preference in the context of a collective decision, and conversely, individual behaviour is only ascribed its meaning by virtue of the choices made concurrently by others. In chapter 3, we showed that at the time they vote, a large proportion of citizens question the behaviour of others and potentially integrate it into their own electoral thinking, experience, and ultimately decision. We also found that citizens insist on taking electoral responsibility upon their shoulders, which engages them vis-à-vis both those who depend on them, or whose future they wish to protect, and the rest of their societal community. This combines with oft-repeated claims that in the context of the vote, citizens feel part of something bigger and more powerful than themselves.

Imagining the Future: Temporal and Generational Projection

In this framework, before turning to two electoral aspects of projection (empathic displacement and projected efficacy), we first revisit projection, as framed in chapter 4, to see how citizens displace the temporal and personal implications of their actions. Projection effectively involves intellectually displacing those effects, either in time or onto specific categories of populations. Both types of projection are potentially highly relevant to electoral considerations and are included in all models.

We first consider longitudinal projection. This corresponds to individuals' tendency to consider shorter- or longer-term consequences of decisions, preferring either an immediate reward, or, on the contrary, short-term sacrifices in order to deliver medium- or longer-term benefits. We use implicit scenarii to assess how short- or long-term minded a given individual tends to be. Electorally, this concerns the arbitration between immediate rewards, or short-term restrictions, and austerity in the name of longer-term benefits, such as sustainability and environmental protection.

Then comes generational projection. This refers to individuals' tendency to privilege the interest of either younger generations or—in rarer cases—older generations over the interest of their own. In electoral contexts, it is a crucial consideration in the context of policies such as pension reform, but also of our exploration of hope and hopelessness (see chapter 9). Indeed, not only do citizens frequently claim willingness to accept sacrifices for the ultimate benefit of their children, but it is when they lose the hope of their children (rather than themselves) living better that expressions of hopelessness become most frequent.

We now consider, finally, two key aspects of individual–societal articulation: empathic displacement and projected efficacy.

Reintegrating Identity: Empathic Displacement and Electoral Identity

Empathic displacement, first introduced in chapter 1, corresponds to a citizen's tendency to imagine and integrate the involvement and behaviour of others as part of his/her own electoral process, experience, and decisions. This concept captures and extends a number of phenomena widely observed in the existing literature, such as strategic voting, which implicitly requires voters to make assumptions about the electoral choice of others. In our model, we disassociate consideration of others from issues of sophistication, strategy, or effectiveness. A well-informed and sophisticated voter may not let that knowledge affect his/her own electoral behaviour, and conversely, an uninformed but sincere citizen may dedicate time and energy to wondering how others are voting, in a way that shapes his/her own electoral experience and sense of either integration or alienation. We thus ask citizens

Evolution of empathic displacement through election cycle

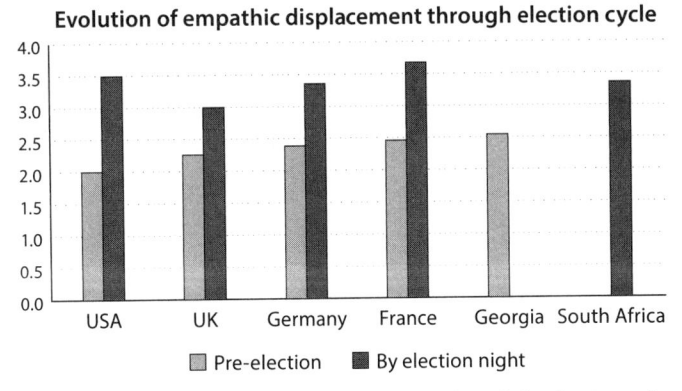

[Bar chart showing Pre-election and By election night values for USA, UK, Germany, France, Georgia, South Africa]

FIGURE 6.3: Evolution of empathic displacement through the election cycle

the extent to which they think of the way others are voting throughout the election cycle. The results are presented in figure 6.3.

When the electoral cycle starts, few respondents claim to consider how others vote. On a scale from 0–7, mean empathic displacement is as low as 2.20 in the US, 2.40 in the UK, and barely reaches a maximum of 2.66 in Georgia. Note that standard deviations are high, suggesting polarized approaches (from 2.25 in the US to 2.53 in Georgia). However, the situation changes dramatically when respondents are asked the same question on Election Night. Then, mean empathic displacement often increases spectacularly, from 2.51 to 3.48 in Germany, from 2.59 to 3.78 in France, and from 2.20 to 3.63 in the US.

The change is even more evocative in terms of distributions. Outside peak electoral periods, about a third of respondents claim to be usual empathic displacers in elections (from 30.7% in the US to 37.7% in Georgia). By contrast, when the exact same question is asked on Election Night in relation to the election that just took place, the proportion of empathic displacers exceeds 50% in all cases but one, from 45% in the UK to 52.3% in Germany, 53% in South Africa, 54.6% in the US, and 57% in France. Overall, citizens do not realize how focused they are on others' electoral behaviour until they are actually in the electoral context itself, and, in particular, about to cast their vote.

Projected Efficacy

Another aspect of the articulation of individual–societal connections in the electoral mind of a voter is captured by the concept of projected

Efficacy and projected efficacy pre- and post-election

[Bar chart showing efficacy pre-election, projected efficacy pre-election, efficacy by election night, and projected efficacy by election night for Germany, UK, France, USA, South Africa, and Georgia]

□ Efficacy pre-election   ▨ Efficacy by election night
■ Projected efficacy pre-election   ■ Projected efficacy by election night

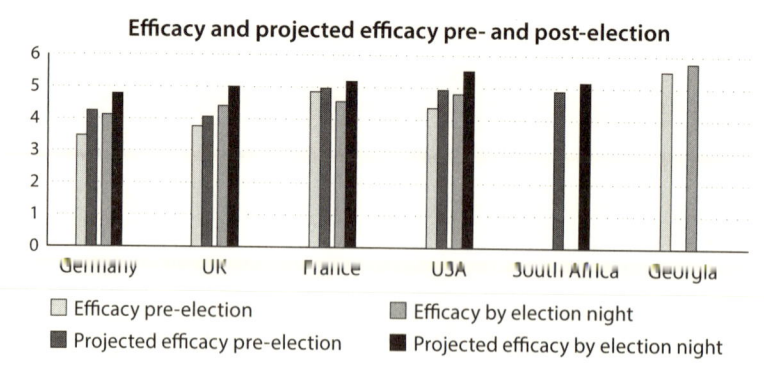

FIGURE 6.4: Evolution of efficacy and projected efficacy pre-election and by election night

efficacy, which we also introduced in chapter 1, showing that a large proportion of voters, even when they do not believe that their own vote can make a difference, have an intuitive capacity spontaneously to project their action—or lack thereof—onto a larger group of similar people. They feel that if those others behave like them (be it in a positive or a negative way), together they will have an impact. As previously observed, this is an electoral variation of the classic 'What if everyone did the same as you?' that parents frequently use to get children to behave civically. Note that projected efficacy differs from 'collective efficacy' (Bandura, 1993; Goddard, et al., 2004), which pertains to membership of collective identities of specific groups; projected efficacy is conceived more mechanically, as the 'multiplier effect' of an unspecified number and nature of others who will behave similarly to an individual and therefore amplify the effect of his/her actions.

That multiplier effect is an essential corollary of electoral identity. We examine its evolution through the electoral cycle and in comparison to standard external efficacy (figure 6.4). Crucially, projected efficacy is substantively higher than traditional efficacy, except in France, pre-election. Whatever effect most citizens feel their own electoral behaviour may achieve pales by comparison with their hopes that if people like them mobilize, they will achieve far more. On an eight-point scale, projected efficacy pre-election is higher than external efficacy by 0.2 points in Georgia, 0.3 points in the US, 0.65 in the UK, and 0.75 in Germany.

Ever more strikingly, except in Germany, projected efficacy increases far more with the electoral process than does standard efficacy. Whilst the latter increases over time (by 0.12 in France and by 0.8 in Germany), the increase in levels of projected efficacy by Election Night varies from 0.58 in Germany to 0.74 in the US. The 'projective bonus' thus increases from −0.12 (France) to +0.75 (Germany) pre-election, to become +0.17 (France), to +0.95 (UK) by Election Night.

Third Model Stage: Do Electoral Identity, Projection and Empathic Displacement Matter?

In the third stage of the test of our full model, we consider the contribution of electoral identity, including the referee/supporter dimension and measures of empathic displacement, projected efficacy, and temporal and generational projection on electoral behaviour, experience, and resolution. At the heart of our electoral identity model, the referee/supporter model dimension captures how citizens conceive and inhabit their role as voters. We have also discussed the importance of other conceptions of the individual–societal relationship, including empathic displacement, temporal and generational projection, and projected efficacy. The complete set of relevant measures was only deployed for the US and Scotland. The referee/supporter variable was not included in the French questionnaire, and implicit measures of generational and longitudinal projections were included for the US and Scotland alone. As already discussed, when it comes to overall contribution to the model, we sequentially enter variables in a manner which is very unfavourable to electoral identity predictors, by implicitly giving credit for any shared variance to control variables and the personality and memory variables entered in stages 1 and 2.

ELECTORAL IDENTITY AND ELECTORAL BEHAVIOUR

Once more, we start by considering the overall contribution, in this case of electoral identity to our understanding of electoral choice (both mainstream and extremist). These results are presented in figure 6.5. There is no change to the model R^2 in France (where only empathic displacement and projected efficacy are included), but elsewhere, pseudo-R^2 improvement ranges from +0.01, for South Africa, in-station CDU and SPD votes in Germany, and absentee voters in the US), to +0.08 and +0.10 for postal voters in Germany and Scotland. Note the strong model improvement for extremist votes in Germany.

Behaviour models improvement—stage 3

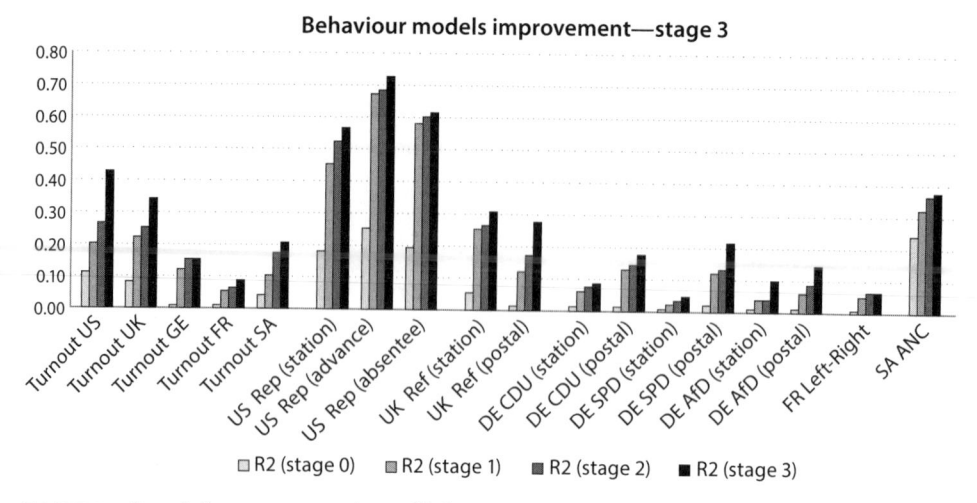

□ R2 (stage 0)   ▨ R2 (stage 1)   ▨ R2 (stage 2)   ■ R2 (stage 3)

FIGURE 6.5: Stage 3: Improvement to electoral behaviour models—identity predictors

Returning to tables 4.1 and 4.2, we consider electoral identity variables' effects in electoral choice models. The referee/supporter scale has a high impact on electoral choice in the US and Germany, where a supporter electoral identity makes it more likely for citizens to support the Republicans in the US and the CDU and SPD in Germany. Generational projection also makes citizens more likely to support Scottish independence, whilst projected efficacy results in lower support for the CDU and Scottish independence. No variable is statistically significant in electoral choice models for France and South Africa.

Overall, electoral identity makes a higher contribution to models of turnout than to models of electoral choice. The effect is particularly strong the UK (+0.09 change in pseudo-R^2) and the US (+0.16). However, electoral identity does not improve the turnout model in Germany. Looking at specific variable effects in tables 4.3 and 4.4, the referee/supporter scale has substantial significant effects on turnout in the US and South Africa, with supporters far more likely to vote than referees. Projected efficacy also has a strong positive effect on turnout in the US, Germany, France, and South Africa, suggesting that those who think of the potential effects of other similar-minded people mobilizing alongside them are more likely to vote. Likewise, empathic displacement has a strong, positive, and highly significant effect on turnout in Germany, France, and South Africa. Generational projection matters in the UK.

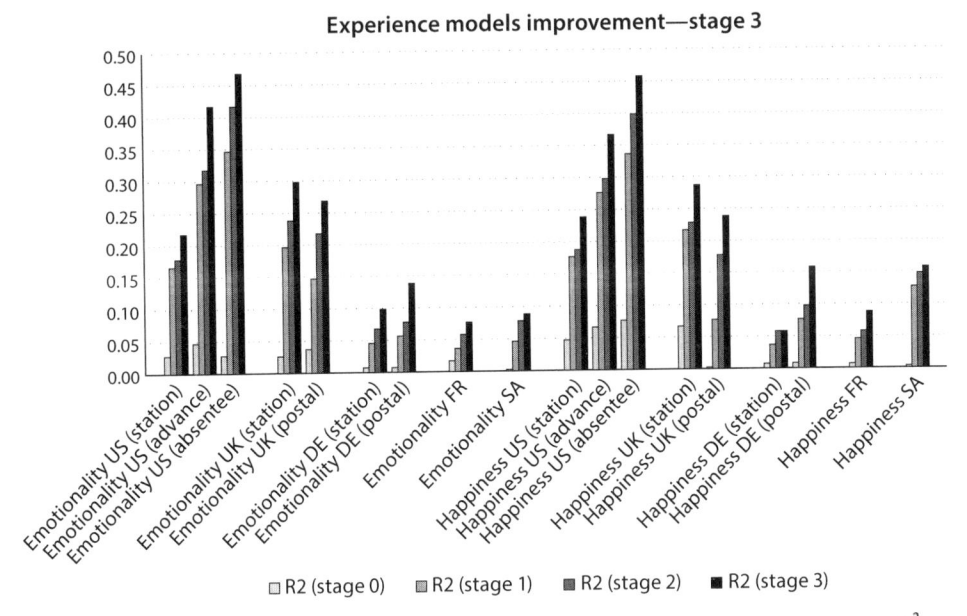

FIGURE 6.6: Stage 3: Improvement to electoral experience models—identity predictors. Bars represent R^2

ELECTORAL IDENTITY AND ELECTORAL EXPERIENCE

We turn now to the effect of electoral identity on electoral experience. Its contribution to overall models is reported in figure 6.6. The power of electoral identity variables is overall stronger in models of electoral experience than in models of behaviour, regarding both emotionality (+0.01 to +0.10) and happiness of electoral experience (0.00 to +0.07). The magnitude of the model improvement is lower in France and South Africa (where key identity variables are missing).

Tables 4.5 and 4.6 show which individual variables perform best in the full model. First, supporters prove more likely to have happy electoral experiences in the US and the UK, and emotional experiences in the US only. Empathic displacement also results in more emotional electoral experiences in the US, Germany, France, and South Africa, meaning that those who think of others tend to feel emotional during the election. In France, empathic displacement also leads to a happier experience. Similarly, projected efficacy has a strong positive impact on both the happiness and the emotionality of the electoral experience, particularly in the UK, Germany, and France, although in the US and South Africa the effect is only statistically significant when it comes to happiness. Finally, generational projection only

Resolution models improvement—stage 3

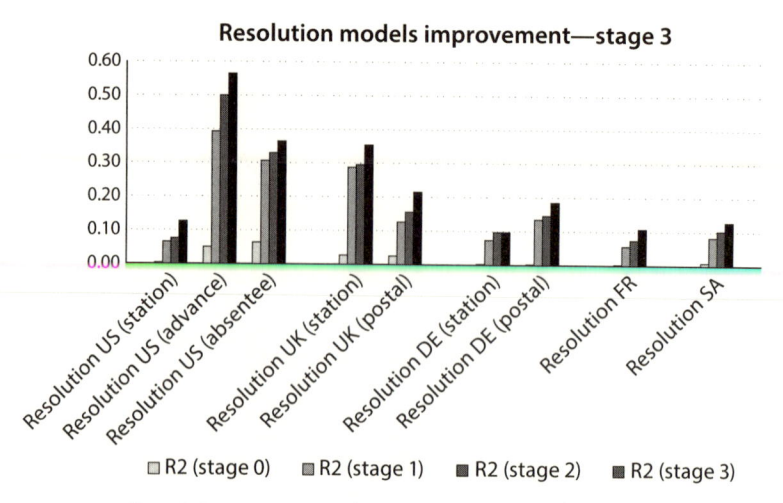

□ R2 (stage 0)   ■ R2 (stage 1)   ■ R2 (stage 2)   ■ R2 (stage 3)

FIGURE 6.7: Stage 3: Improvement to electoral resolution models—identity predictors. Bars represent R^2

has significant effects in the UK, where it makes citizens' electoral experience less emotional, but happier.

ELECTORAL IDENTITY AND ELECTORAL RESOLUTION

Finally in this chapter, we consider the impact of electoral identity and projection on perceptions of electoral resolution. Once again, as shown in figure 6.7, the third stage of the model improves explained variance in electoral resolution, notably in the US and UK (+0.04 to +0.06), where the full battery of predictors was included. The R^2 improves by 0.03 in France and 0.02 in South Africa.

The more interesting details, however, come from tables 4.7 and 4.8, which report the effects of individual electoral identity variables in the US and other countries. This time, whilst some variables have a significant effect everywhere, the picture seems to vary importantly across countries. Projected efficacy has a positive effect on electoral resolution in at least one of the voting mode models in all five countries included in the analysis. For the rest, results are often country-specific. For example, supporters are more likely than referees to experience electoral resolution in the UK and Germany. In the US, it is generational projection which increases the likelihood of electoral resolution. Finally, in Germany and France, empathic displacers are more likely to get a sense of closure from the election.

Electoral identity matters. The way citizens perceive and inhabit their own roles as voters, and the way in which they integrate others into their electoral outlook and experience by thinking of them as they vote—projecting the effect of the vote in time or onto other generations, or indeed considering the fact that if those similar to them act symbiotically on Election Day, they will be able collectively to influence their future—significantly impact electoral behaviour. The effect has notable magnitude as regards turnout, citizens' electoral experience, and the likelihood of getting a sense of closure and resolution from the election. This third stage of the model thus overwhelmingly reinforces a central claim of this book: that voters are not just individuals expressing a preference (notably not a 'spontaneous' preference), but people who believe that they have a role, a responsibility, which they embrace and enact the moment they don their voter 'hat'. This role, which only kicks in when voters become immersed in the atmosphere of the electoral process, matters, and affects their outlook and way of thinking, their experience, their behaviour, and the likelihood that the election will bring them a sense of closure and a relegitimized sense of inclusion within their society and community, or, on the contrary, a sense of alienation.

Of course, embracing and inhabiting a role also shapes the emotional experience of voters. It affects both what they feel and when they feel it, nuancing their sense of solemn responsibility, playing upon their feelings of happiness and anxiety, enhancing or diminishing anger or frustration at various points in the electoral process. In the next chapter, we return to the notion of electoral experience, and specifically to the question of the emotions that it entails and which citizens experience at various stages of the electoral process.

7

Elections and Emotions

One of the three interrelated dependent variables in our model is what we term 'electoral experience'. In the perspective of this work, the emotions that voters (and non-voters) feel during an electoral event, and in particular the emotionality and happiness associated with the vote, constitute direct operational measures of that experience.

Do elections make citizens feel happy, anxious, excited, emotional? Electoral emotions also matter because human beings only develop emotions if they care, and one of the core suggestions of this book is that many citizens care far more about elections—that elections are far more important in their lives, even when they are not actually interested in politics—than they would typically assume.

In this chapter, we decipher the emotions that citizens experience during elections, and particularly when they are in the polling booth. We do so by relying not only on their self-perceptions, but also on implicit measures whereby we consider the words that occur to them in electoral contexts, and even by directly observing the emotions that citizens physically display as they vote, by filming their shadows in the polling booth and interpreting the emotions that these display.

The chapter first shows that elections are indeed highly emotional experiences, to the point of potentially bringing many citizens to (happy or sad) tears. We also show that the emotions elicited by elections are on the whole overwhelmingly positive. In many ways, elections make people happy, even where politics makes them frustrated or annoyed.

The chapter also considers how electoral emotions vary across types of voter, and notably how elections are typically far more emotional for first time voters than for the rest of the population, thereby shedding further new light on the crucial nature of the first vote.

Of the Endogenous Nature of Emotions

When the electoral behaviour literature considers the emotionality of voters, which is perhaps not as often as it should, it is usually as an independent variable that may alter the way people vote. For instance, the 2016 UK EU-membership referendum was long presented as a likely clash between 'rational' Remainers and 'emotional' Leavers before it was finally understood that Remain voters were just as emotional, with views just as heartfelt, as their Leave counterparts. Conversely, emotionality has occasionally been considered as part and parcel of populist and extremist votes (Demertzis, 2006; Skonieczny, 2018). These models, however, all share the assumption that individual voters are either more or less emotional by nature, as though emotionality were largely an extension of personality. They also appear to assume an opposition between rationality and emotionality which has long been denounced as fallacious by psychologists. Indeed, reason and emotion are intimately intertwined: rationality is largely present in the genesis of our emotions (there is a very good reason why losing some loved one makes us sad, or getting our dream job or winning the lottery makes us happy), and conversely, emotions tightly constrain the lens through which we rationally consider the world around us.

In this book, we are interested primarily in how elections constitute an emotional occasion as such, and elicit specific emotions among voters, of which we wish to understand the nature and variation. We thus treat emotions as a dependent (rather than an independent) variable which encapsulates electoral experience, and do not presume any artificial tension between electoral emotions and reason. To the extent that the book is focused on the experience of voters, the emotions that citizens feel at different moments within an election cycle are a critical measure of the nature and evolution of that experience, and therefore critical facets of our dependent variable. Knowing whether elections make people happy or bring tears to their eyes is substantively as important as knowing why they vote for a left- or right-wing candidate. Arguably, the emotional aspect is more important to voters as well, and quite possibly for the state of democracy. Furthermore, in the context of our longitudinal investigations, surely, if an election makes someone happy, he/she will be more likely to vote again at the next opportunity? Thus the emotions associated with the electoral experience are as key a feature of an election process as any of the traditional mysteries of behavioural research.

At the same time, considering emotions as a dependent variable imposes increased methodological complexity, because unlike electoral choice or turnout, which have an objective nature (in theory), emotions are fluid and difficult to capture. Consequently, this chapter is also about methodological innovativeness beyond the shackles of self-reporting. What are the emotions that are elicited by elections? Do elections make people happy, and do they make them cry? How do those emotions evolve across the election cycle, and how do they shape it—through the debates, the discussions, the casting of the vote, the discovery of election results, and its aftermath? Under what circumstance do elections become more, less, or differently emotional? Can we capture citizens' electoral emotions beyond their own narratives and self-reports? These are some of the questions this chapter will address.

Emotions: Tension, Tears, and Happiness in Elections

This chapter systematically analyses the emotions that voters describe. At the heart of our model is the fact that elections mean more to citizens than is typically assumed. We believe that citizens feel far more emotional on account of elections than has been believed, and that their emotions are both important in their own right when it comes to their nature, timing, and triggers, and influential in terms of citizens' perceptions, attitudes, behaviour, and post-electoral sense of resolution. Our underlying expectation rejects assumptions that citizens are detached and impassive during the vote, and suggests, conversely, that voting is an emotional act in which voters invest their hearts and minds.

We measure these emotions using self-report questions at various moments during the election cycle, and directly observe them by means of a unique visual experiment that captures the emotions that people betray when they are in the polling booth. We expect the vote to elicit vibrant—and often positive—emotions, which are only mobilized at the height of the election (effectively, for most citizens, in and around the polling station and booth), and will differ according to electoral arrangements, the location of the vote, and the specific election citizens engage in. Observed emotions may vary from happiness and pride to anxiety, excitement, and frustration. This mixture of self-reported and externally observed emotions complements the dynamic design exploring when specifically they occur, from the campaign period to Election Day, the polling booth moment, and Election Night. This multifaceted approach enables us to provide exceptional insights into how emotional elections are for citizens, across countries and contexts. We then look at how emotions affect citizens' attitudes, and the way they change through the electoral period, including how they can affect the transformation of a pre-electoral voting intention into an actual voting decision. In this chapter, we study the nature and strength of those emotions, and establish the psychological and institutional conditions that trigger and highlight them. We combine three different methodologies:

- tension scales that ask voters about the types of emotion that they feel on Election Day, in the polling station, and in the polling booth or when they cast their vote remotely;
- implicit measures that target emotional responses to elections using items such as word completion or image-based questions;
- a direct observation of voters' physically displayed emotions as they vote, by means of a visual experiment and a coding of the emotions on display in the polling booth, using insights derived from the study of kinesics (Birdwhistell, 1970).

This triangulation enables us to tap into the subconscious aspects of emotions throughout the electoral process. The direct measures simply ask respondents to report the emotions that they feel when they vote. We use tension scales for both fundamental emotions (pride, happiness, worry, etc.) and emotional display (e.g., crying because of an election). These items were employed in every country investigated. The implicit measures use word-stem completion and image-based questions, and were used in the US, the UK, France, and South Africa. Finally, the visual experiment took place in Germany, and was then replicated in the UK. It consisted of a random assignment experiment whereby voters were invited to a mock election of the next president of the European Union, using three different types of paper and electronic ballot. The combination of methods was necessary to understand the range of the emotions that voters experience during the electoral process, when they occur (campaign period, Election Day, polling station, polling booth, Election Night), and how they vary between in-person and remote voters.

Electoral Tears

Before exploring self-reported and observed emotions, we consider one of the most iconic potential reflections of electoral emotionality: crying voters.

Few observers believe spontaneously that voters are moved by elections, and many will thus probably be surprised that in any given election, many voters may cry. One may also expect that, as an election result is announced, those who supported winners will be happy and those who supported losers will be sad. Yet our analysis suggests that things are far more complex than that. In the aftermath of some elections, the bulk of a society may experience relief and a sense of rejuvenated legitimization of the political system, even amongst supporters of losing camps. Conversely, elections may lead to social crispation (increasing tension) and antagonism, with both winners and losers displaying bitterness and anger towards the other camp, and tensions not receding as the election ends. In the most iconic of cases, this may lead citizens to cry.

The ample psychological research on the causes, meanings, and natures of crying as an emotional reaction (e.g., Izard, 1991; Oatley, 1992; Cornelius, 1996 and 2001; Vingerhoets et al., 2000) has shown that crying can stem from either positive or negative emotions, and reflect either deeper or 'lighter'—more nervous—reactions. It typically requires both a form of tension or intensity and the ability to recreate a symbolic context or experience that speaks to some deeply rooted conscious or subconscious emotion. Figure 7.1 reports the proportion of citizens who have already cried because of an election.

The significant overall proportion of citizens who report having already cried because of an election will likely surprise many readers. It varies between countries however—from 45% in France, where the memories of 'le 22 avril' 2002 are still vivid, to 15.2% in the UK up to the 2016 referendum (the proportion then increased massively, as we shall see). Between a quarter and a third of the population overall in most countries (and almost half in the case of France, and of the UK after 2016) have shed tears. This is typically many more than the proportion of people who claim really to care about politics and elections.

The dynamic nature of our panel and time series data, and the unique period this book studies, permit us to offer some exceptional insights on electoral tears, however. Whilst in 2010 the UK had, by far, the lowest proportion of people who had experienced electoral tears (15.2%), when we put the question to respondents in Scotland in 2014 on the evening of the independence referendum, the proportion confessing electoral tears had more than doubled, at 33.7%. We tested for local idiosyncrasies, but in 2010, the proportion of Scottish respondents who had cried because of an election in the course of their life was only 19.6%, just slightly above the national average, but well below the 2014 result. Even more remarkable, in the con-

Percent who have already cried because of an election

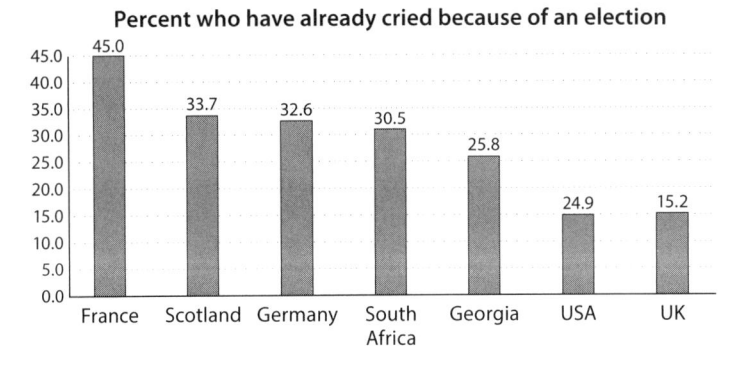

Country	Percent
France	45.0
Scotland	33.7
Germany	32.6
South Africa	30.5
Georgia	25.8
USA	24.9
UK	15.2

FIGURE 7.1: Proportion of citizens reporting having already cried because of an election

text of the 2016 referendum on the UK's membership of the European Union, the proportion of citizens reporting having tears in their eyes was significantly higher than normal. 28% of citizens reported crying as they discovered the result of the referendum, and 39% amongst young voters aged eighteen to twenty-four.

Conceivably, citizens may be more emotional in referenda than in candidate- or party-centric elections, a finding which would contradict models of partisan polarization. It could reflect citizens being more likely to see their role as that of 'supporters' rather than 'referees' (chapter 6) in referenda, as compared to elections. As a reminder: supporters made up 48% of our total sample in the 2016 UK referendum, but only 41.5% in the previous general election, whilst referee proportions were stable (14% and 13.8%, respectively). Still, that difference is far smaller than for electoral tears.

The reason for the higher emotionality of the 2016 referendum is thus to be found elsewhere. Firstly, the options were more polarized than in an election. The gap between staying in the European Union and leaving it is intuitively huge to many voters, far more so than most partisan alternatives. The referendum was thus high-stakes. Secondly, the alternatives were also far more definitive. An election is typically, at most, a 'five year sentence' for democracy, whereby voters know that they can reverse collective choices or fight the next battle after a relatively short period of time. By contrast, there was a sense of definitiveness to the Brexit question, with no obvious way back for those who disagreed with fellow voters' choice, or those who might regret their own. These combined differences caused the referendum vote to convey a more dramatic 'vibe' even than that of an archetypical first-order election. Alongside the UK, another important case study is Georgia, where over 40% of respondents claim already to have cried because of an election. We associate this finding with the extreme stakes of elections in democratizing contexts, though it is worth noting that in Georgia, vibrant emotionality produces low turnout in both presidential and parliamentary elections. The following quotes highlight the extreme emotionality that elections can stir within citizens.

> 2008 was awesome. I was in a bar. I cried when Obama got elected. It was inspirational. It was a historic moment. He was the first black president. I felt it was good vindication for a country that has a racist history. US30M006

One respondent explains that his recent electoral experiences started a rollercoaster of emotions, from tears of sadness in 2004 to tears of jubilation in 2008 with Obama's victory:

> In 2004, I cried all night and most of the next day. I thought what happened with Kerry was devastating. [. . .] In 2008, I cried when I voted and I biked down to the White House. A lot of crying. A Ghanaian taxi driver bear-hugged me and lifted me up. It was an amazing feeling. Part of it was relief that Bush was over, and part of it was that Obama was black, and what he was aiming to do. There was a lot of relief. US34M007

Predictably, overwhelming electoral emotions are particularly salient in the 2016 UK EU-membership referendum. In the words of those who were distressed by its result, the outcome of the vote was overwhelming and led to tears of sadness and distress:

> I just can't believe it, I cried. My daughter says she is in mourning. UK56F110

> The most upsetting thing for me personally was telling my kids yesterday morning, having been up all night, and then them bursting into tears as they started to realise the implications. UK48M142

> I am devastated. It was one of those things I didn't think would ever happen, I cried this morning and had a sinking feeling in my stomach. UK37F139

Equally, the result brought tears of happiness to citizens who supported leaving the EU:

> It is a great day for democracy! I had tears in my eyes this morning when I learned of the result and I couldn't wait to tell everyone. UK27M121

It has been so hard for me over the last few weeks, I didn't think we would win. I actually cried when I saw the result. It now all seems worth it. UK31F129

The tearfulness of citizens may come across as a gimmicky finding, but it is not. It reveals a level of emotional intensity and tension that the election is incapable of making subside and bringing to a healthy resolution. Whether positive or negative, it will make it more difficult for the political system to start a new chapter in a context of peaceful convergence of its underlying democratic forces. While electoral tears are not universal, when they do occur (the 2002 presidential election in France, the 2014 referendum in Scotland, and the 2016 referendum in the UK), they mark and shape citizens durably, and voters frequently refer to those tearful episodes in our narrative interviews. Moreover, as per our dynamic model of interrelated dependent variables, emotional tension is endogenous. It may thus notably translate into numerous political, societal, and psychological consequences, at both individual and societal levels. We will understand these better by analyzing the emotions citizens report feeling on Election Day in general, and in the polling booth in particular.

Positive Emotions in the Polling Booth

In chapter 3, we considered the thoughts voters reported from the polling booth, or as they cast their vote remotely. We observed the preponderance of highly emotional (and largely positive) thoughts in their answers. In this section, we look more directly at the emotions that citizens report on Election Day, at the polling station and in the polling booth. In our panel study survey, citizens chose from lists of emotions on tension scales from 'negative' to 'positive'. We asked them about those emotions in relation, firstly, to Election Day; secondly, to the moment they cast their ballot in the polling booth or remotely; and thirdly, to Election Night. The tension scales enable us to understand which emotions are relevant at each point in time, and their valence. We also compare their strength and occurrence throughout Election Day across traditional voters, remote voters, and non-voters, to feed our ongoing investigation of the impact of electoral ergonomics. We targeted ten emotional scales and two measures of emotional involvement (importance for the citizen and for the country). The results for traditional in-station voters, remote voters, and non-voters are presented in tables 7.1.a to 7.1.c.

TABLE 7.1. Emotions and the Vote for Polling Station Voters, Remote Voters, and Non-voters

Table 7.1a: Polling station voters

	US	UK	France	Germany	S. Africa	Georgia
Excited	5.58 (1.71)	4.81 (1.72)	4.36 (1.43)	4.48 (1.54)	5.67 (2.05)	5.93 (1.23)
Happy	5.23 (1.81)	4.71 (1.50)	4.49 (1.60)	4.40 (1.21)	5.65 (1.96)	3.79 (1.34)
Emotional	4.96 (1.67)	4.14 (1.69)	4.23 (1.66)	4.40 (1.62)	4.34 (2.13)	5.71 (1.71)
Intense	4.80 (1.64)	4.45 (1.50)	6.02 (1.68)	4.33 (1.50)	4.12 (2.16)	4.57 (1.70)
Resolution	5.01 (1.64)	4.50 (1.55)	4.71 (1.60)	4.63 (1.64)	5.53 (2.02)	6.44 (1.56)
Reassured	2.99 (1.90)	3.50 (1.59)	2.89 (1.86)	3.76 (1.61)	3.90 (2.26)	4.18 (1.57)
Relaxed	3.87 (2.20)	4.48 (2.07)	4.39 (1.83)	4.54 (1.85)	4.95 (2.45)	3.61 (1.48)
Optimistic	4.31 (2.08)	3.80 (2.04)	3.66 (2.12)	4.28 (1.80)	4.54 (2.42)	4.62 (1.52)
Important to me	6.56 (1.65)	5.86 (1.68)	5.95 (1.67)	5.45 (1.79)	6.40 (1.83)	6.55 (1.66)
Important to country	6.85 (1.52)	6.18 (1.62)	6.35 (1.65)	5.77 (1.74)	6.69 (1.71)	6.86 (1.57)
Proud	6.15 (1.76)	5.05 (1.59)	4.97 (1.64)	4.61 (1.40)	5.92 (2.01)	6.28 (1.37)

Table 7.1b: Remote voters

	US	UK	France	Germany
Excited	5.33 (1.68)	4.63 (1.62)	4.40 (1.31)	4.21 (1.47)
Happy	5.20 (1.74)	4.52 (1.38)	4.60 (1.59)	2.26 (1.20)
Emotional	4.92 (1.61)	3.93 (1.75)	4.47 (1.47)	4.27 (1.59)
Intense	4.96 (1.70)	4.44 (1.47)	5.59 (1.59)	4.15 (1.35)
Resolution	4.77 (1.79)	4.26 (1.58)	4.76 (1.65)	4.45 (1.60)

Reassured		2.59 (1.89)	3.25 (1.57)	3.34 (1.95)	3.62 (1.56)
Relaxed		3.36 (2.11)	4.31 (1.92)	4.07 (1.66)	4.72 (1.66)
Optimistic		4.20 (2.26)	3.83 (2.06)	4.06 (2.13)	4.13 (1.80)
Important to me		6.59 (1.62)	5.92 (1.59)	5.89 (1.59)	5.36 (1.73)
Important to country		6.95 (1.50)	6.22 (1.60)	6.21 (1.62)	5.64 (1.76)
Proud		5.96 (1.84)	4.73 (1.54)	5.09 (1.73)	4.49 (1.33)

Table 7.1.c: Abstentionists

	US	UK	France	Germany	S. Africa
Excited	3.82 (1.81)	3.34 (1.89)	3.89 (1.53)	3.35 (1.80)	3.68 (1.90)
Happy	3.80 (1.52)	3.89 (1.29)	3.87 (1.71)	3.98 (1.29)	3.73 (1.99)
Emotional	3.91 (1.89)	3.35 (1.89)	3.48 (1.93)	3.40 (1.86)	3.62 (2.12)
Intense	4.26 (1.37)	4.06 (1.24)	4.52 (1.39)	4.25 (1.02)	4.07 (1.73)
Resolution	3.96 (1.26)	3.66 (1.16)	3.62 (1.62)	3.66 (1.30)	3.68 (1.76)
Reassured	3.32 (1.68)	3.50 (1.24)	3.21 (1.81)	3.63 (1.43)	3.27 (1.95)
Relaxed	3.73 (1.64)	4.25 (1.61)	3.98 (1.96)	4.62 (1.63)	4.25 (2.20)
Optimistic	3.73 (1.74)	3.33 (1.68)	3.18 (1.82)	3.52 (1.59)	3.59 (2.15)
Important to me	4.32 (1.79)	3.73 (1.79)	4.26 (1.86)	3.52 (1.89)	4.59 (1.98)
Important to country	4.87 (1.89)	4.60 (1.61)	5.13 (1.86)	4.12 (1.67)	5.23 (2.10)
Proud	3.73 (1.50)	3.81 (1.00)	3.80 (1.33)	3.81 (1.23)	3.68 (2.02)

Notes: Regarding recoding for emotions scale, for each variable we recoded values, so high score always pertains to a positive score and low is negative, with 8 ascribed most positive through to 0 as most negative. No remote voters in the South African sample. No distinction between vote modes for the Georgian sample.

We first find that voting—both in person and, to a slightly lesser extent, remotely—is primarily an emotionally positive experience for voters, something which is worth emphasizing at a time when citizens repeatedly assert their critical feelings towards politics, parties, and institutions. Two of the main emotions reported by citizens when they vote are excitement and happiness, which are the two main reported vote-casting emotions in the US, the UK, and South Africa. In France and Germany, the top emotion reported by voters is electoral resolution and togetherness, followed by happiness. In Georgia, resolution is similarly followed by excitement. In general, across countries, the act of voting is an emotional and positive experience. It is also perceived as intense but worrying by many, suggesting that citizens do not take their responsibility to vote lightly, and are far from indifferent to the electoral process.

This striking finding also uncovers predictable but important gaps between the emotional experiences of voters and of non-voters. On the whole, the experience of abstentionists is far less either emotional or positive than it is for voters. Qualitative evidence echoes those findings:

> It's just in the last two elections where I've gotten more emotional. US50F003

> I do get emotional. Sometimes I get so frustrated with people. I typically talk about politics with people I know feel the same as I do. US53F005

> I like to be surrounded by other liberals. I have a fundamental belief that Republicans are destructive, selfish, and greedy. I have a really hard time associating with Republicans. US36F013.

> It is so divisive. There was an art walk and Jerome Stalks picture with it saying 'This man . . .' So many political divides and it can sometimes tear the community and sometimes it brings it together. US43F014

Voting traditionally, in a polling station, also elicits more positive emotions than does voting remotely, with the partial exception of proxy voting in France:

> I was so happy to vote. Pure happiness and excitement. I stayed to help in the polling station and I was smiling from ear to ear. US6ZM011

> I feel happiness when I go to the polling station to vote. US58M009

> I would describe it as . . . strange. Something out of the norm. It was quite an exciting day and interesting to look around at all the people who felt that it was important to take time out of their day to come to the polling

station to vote. We discussed the strangeness of the situation and how it goes so quick and putting your cross in the box is such a small thing to do yet all of them together make such a big experience. UK20F006

It's the first time I've ever voted in person. I've always done it by mail-in, so it was kind of fun. And it was a nice community feeling and it was very helpful. US3ZF066

Despite the fact that elections are normally a source of positive emotions, some voters experience dramatic and sometimes negative emotions. Election campaigns can be tense and divisive at times, and this atmosphere can spill over to leave citizens feeling ill at ease and resentful of the societal divisions they thereby associate with elections, as in these examples:

The country is so divided that people won't talk to each other. [. . .] That's happening to our population. It's never been this bad in my lifetime. [. . .] I'm very worried about that. I'm one of the few people that goes over and talks to tea party people as a liberal. But I see it getting worse, and I don't see it getting any better. US50F003

I have a strict rule not to discuss politics with my parents. But in the last election, I threw the first punch and then my dad started sending all these anti-Obama emails. It gets too emotional speaking in person. They hate Obama. I told a friend not to make out with someone because he was an undecided voter. US28F004

Elections . . . I feel hopelessness, embarrassment for America. US26F008

Voting is stressful. US60F010

Frustration. US5ZF012

Finally, in emerging democracies, the emotions associated with electoral democracy are mostly pride and optimism. In Georgia, 67% of respondents felt proud when they voted, and 79.6% felt optimistic whilst, by contrast, 'only' 57.8% claim to feel happy. We now consider how electoral emotions vary across gender, age, and first-time voters specifically.

How Do Electoral Emotions Differ between Male and Female Voters?

We have so far found relatively little impact of gender on electoral psychology. The issue of emotionality is slightly different, and a number of patterns seem to emerge, though in some cases, only in some of the countries studied. We illustrate the different emotional reactions of men and women in appendix 3.[1] First, voting is typically a more emotional (and more intense) experience for women than for men. 56% of US women reported feeling emotional when they voted, but only 44% of American men. Those proportions are respectively 37% and 26% for British women and men. However, we also note that the relationship is not statistically significant in South Africa, and is generally weak in France, Germany, and Georgia.

In many but not all countries, women also find voting a more positive experience than men do, with women reporting more excitement and happiness. In the US, 71.2% of women, but only 56.1% of men, felt excited as they cast their ballot. In the UK, those figures are 52.8% and 42.7% respectively, and in Germany, 38.2% and 30.3%. There is no statistically significant difference in South Africa, or Georgia, and in France, a reverse situation nears statistical significance. Overall, however, voting is explicitly happier for women than for men in the US (63.8% vs 50.8%) and South Africa (65.7% vs 61.9%), but, conversely, a happier experience for men than for women in France (36.6% vs 33.4%), Germany (30.9% vs 26.3%), and Georgia (29.8% vs 25.4%). When looking at granular distributions, however, the difference is only statistically significant in the US (with happier women) and France (with happier men), making for contrasting findings.

Finally, the strongest gender difference is that at the time they are casting their vote, women tend to feel significantly more worried and more nervous than men, with the gender gap in proportions of worried voters going from 4.6% in Georgia to 9.8% in France, and only not statistically significant in the US, and gaps in nervousness even reaching 20.1% in the US and 11.8% in the UK, though not statistically significant in South Africa and Georgia. Altogether, the emotional nature of voting seems to vary by gender, but not always consistently across countries. On the whole, the experience seems to be more emotionally intense for women than for men, but also more worrying and nerve-racking. There is a more confusing trend of emotional valence with happier US women than men, but happier French men than women.

How Do Electoral Emotions Change with Age?

We also consider, referring still to appendix 3, the impact of age on electoral emotions. On the face of it, the relationship between age and electoral emo-

---

1. Appendices referred to in this chapter are to be found online at www.epob.org.

tions is stronger and less complicated than that between electoral emotions and gender. First, voting is mostly an exciting as a well as a nerve-racking experience for young people, with both excitement and worry declining with age. The correlations between excitement and age are significant everywhere except in Georgia, ranging from −0.08** in South Africa to −0.16** in the UK and Germany. Correlations between age and nervousness are also statistically significant in all countries except Georgia, and typically even stronger, ranging from 0.12** in France and 0.13** in the US to 0.17** in South Africa, 0.22** in the UK, and 0.24** in Germany. The link between other emotional scales and age is less clear. Thus, younger citizens feel happier and more emotional when they cast their vote in the UK and in Germany, but not elsewhere. Regarding emotionality, the relationship is even reversed in France. Other emotions—including worry—are typically uncorrelated with age.

Crucially, generational emotional differences are meaningful and significant when it comes to voters, but inexistent amongst absentionists. The gaps are also less salient amongst remote voters as compared to polling station voters. Age differences are thus conditional on the actual experience of electoral participation being embraced and 'revealed'.

Correlations can be a crude and problematic measure for age, especially for tension-scale variables that are not only interested in valence but also in polarity (i.e., the strength of emotionality, whether positive or negative, as opposed to indifference). Age may not have continuous effects on emotions. In particular, the fact that some differences are specific to young people voting in polling stations suggests that greater emotionality may be related to the specific experience of voting for the first time, with its unique emotional connotation. Moreover, when it comes to the specific issue of tension scales, bivariate correlations could easily hide significant differences where some groups are in fact more prone to indifference than others. We thus explore electoral emotionality across a voter's life cycle and notably between first-time voters, second-time voters, and the rest of the population.

That Emotional First Time . . .

We have already had frequent occasion, on our journey into the minds of voters, to refer to the unique nature of a first election, and the combined importance for future behaviour of the first two elections when one is eligible to vote. The findings reported in chapter 5 regarding electoral memory clearly suggest that people are likely to remember their first electoral experience in detail, and overwhelmingly positively. There is good reason to suppose that such a memorial imprint is the result of an emotionally rich experience, and that the positivity of the memory may correspond to positive emotions during the original experience. In this section, we compare the emotions reported by first- and second-time voters to those of the rest of the electorate, in order to understand the emotional specificity of electoral first times. The operationalization of first- and second-time voters is based on age. The findings are presented in figures 7.2.a–7.2.f

Whilst correlation analysis treated age as a continuous variable, the targeted analysis of first- and second-time voters reveals far more striking and systematic specificities. First, whilst voting is an exciting experience for most, it is immensely more so for first-time voters, with 45% of these in France, over 75% in South Africa, and more than 95% in Georgia describing their electoral experience as exciting. The differential between first-time voters and the general population is substantial. In Germany, the proportion of first-time voters describing the moment of the vote as exciting is more than twice that of the rest of the population (64.3% vs 31.7%). In France, that differential is 19.2%, in the UK, 16.5%, in South Africa, 16.1%, and in the US (where first- and second-time voters are merged in the same sub-sample), 8.7%.

This intense emotionality reminds us of how a first vote is above all else a 'first time', with the correspondingly dramatic potential for excitement. Many young citizens eagerly anticipate their first active participation in an election, and in turn feel overwhelmed (positively) when they at last actually get to cast their vote. It does not seem to matter how disillusioned many young people feel towards political elites and institutions, how intimidated, or even how cynical they might be. Ultimately, their first vote is a moment of immense and intense excitement (and it is likely that worries about youth turnout would be more effectively addressed by harnessing that positive anticipation and excitement of the first time than by playing the 'duty to vote' card chosen by many current communication campaigns). This particular electoral rite of passage is perceived as extremely important by young citizens, and is arguably overlooked and misunderstood within their electoral and political systems. Moreover, the excitement tends to persist from the first to the second vote. In the UK, levels of excitement are even higher for second-time than for first-time voters (66.7% vs 61.5%).

Beyond being exciting, electoral first times also tend to be very happy experiences. Apart from in Georgia, between a half and two-thirds of first-time voters (43.6% in France and 70.7% in South Africa) report feeling happy as they cast a vote, distinctly more than for experienced voters. Levels of happiness are significantly higher for first-time voters than for the rest of the population in all countries except Georgia and the US, with differentials ranging from 7.9% in South Africa and 9.8% in France to 14.4% in the UK and 19.5% in Germany. The electoral experience of second-time voters is also, typically, significantly happier than for the rest of the population, with 39.4% in France to 61.7% in South Africa describing their experience as happy. Once again, in the UK, 'things only seem to get better' for voters between their first and their second electoral experience, before declining thereafter. In other countries, a unique first time is followed by a still very (but slightly less) positive second vote.

In many ways, the logical consequence of happy and exciting first times is that the first vote is an exceptionally emotional experience. This is notably the case in the US, where 61.6% of first- and second-time voters feel emotional as they vote (+10.8% compared to experienced voters), as well as in Germany, where 50% of first time voters reported the same (+10.3%), and 46.9% in the UK (+20%). However, differences in emotionality between first-time voters and the rest of the population are not statistically significant in France, South Africa, or Georgia.

The flip side of electoral first times eliciting excitement, happiness, and emotionality is that this inaugural voting experience may also be worrying and nerve-racking. Here, we should stress that virtually no country offers ad hoc support specifically for first-time voters, who are treated just as any other category of voter, despite not having any prior experience of how the voting process works. Inexperience and the unfamiliarity of electoral procedures undoubtedly increase the potential for worry and nervousness. In all countries investigated, first-time voters feel significantly more nervous than experienced voters, and in all countries but Germany, they are also significantly more likely to feel worried. Nervousness is higher for first-time voters than for the rest of the population in every country studied, with differentials ranging from 5.3% in Georgia (54.3% vs 49%) to 25.5% in the UK (46.9% vs 21.4%), and even 33.7% in the US (61.5% vs 37.8%) and 34.7% in Germany (51.2% vs 16.5%). The picture is considerably more contrastive concerning citizens who feel worried when they cast their vote. Voting is more worrying for first-time voters than for more experienced citizens everywhere, but differentials are less substantial, ranging from 1.8% in Germany (33.1% vs 31.5%), 4.2% in France (58.6% vs 54.4%), and 4.8% in South Africa (35.3% vs 30.5%) to 7.2% in Georgia (37.7% vs 30.5%) and 8.7% in

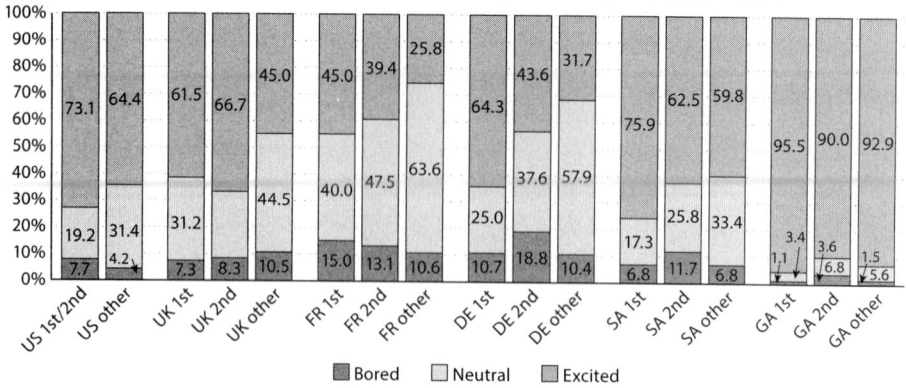

a.

Electoral excitement for 1st time, 2nd time, and other voters

	US 1st/2nd	US other	UK 1st	UK 2nd	UK other	FR 1st	FR 2nd	FR other	DE 1st	DE 2nd	DE other	SA 1st	SA 2nd	SA other	GA 1st	GA 2nd	GA other
Excited	73.1	64.4	61.5	66.7	45.0	45.0	39.4	25.8	64.3	43.6	31.7	75.9	62.5	59.8	95.5	90.0	92.9
Neutral	19.2	31.4	31.2	25.0	44.5	40.0	47.5	63.6	25.0	37.6	57.9	17.3	25.8	33.4	3.4	3.6	1.5
Bored	7.7	4.2	7.3	8.3	10.5	15.0	13.1	10.6	10.7	18.8	10.4	6.8	11.7	6.8	1.1	6.8	5.6

b.

Electoral happiness for 1st time, 2nd time, and other voters

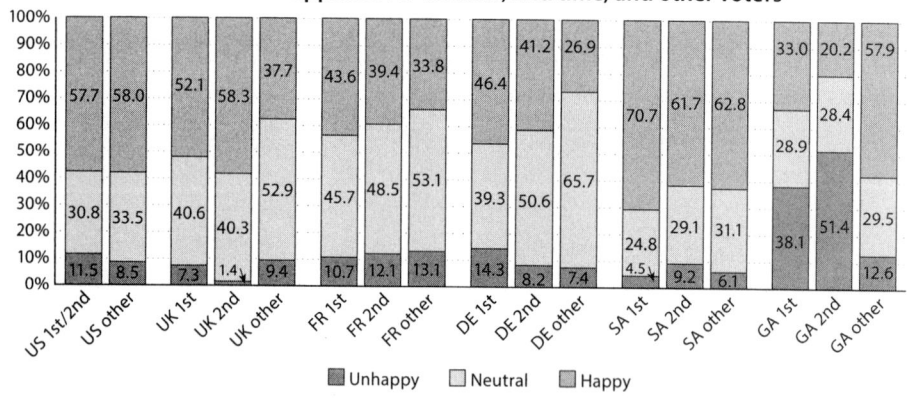

	US 1st/2nd	US other	UK 1st	UK 2nd	UK other	FR 1st	FR 2nd	FR other	DE 1st	DE 2nd	DE other	SA 1st	SA 2nd	SA other	GA 1st	GA 2nd	GA other
Happy	57.7	58.0	52.1	58.3	37.7	43.6	39.4	33.8	46.4	41.2	26.9	70.7	61.7	62.8	33.0	20.2	57.9
Neutral	30.8	33.5	40.6	40.3	52.9	45.7	48.5	53.1	39.3	50.6	65.7	24.8	29.1	31.1	28.9	28.4	29.5
Unhappy	11.5	8.5	7.3	1.4	9.4	10.7	12.1	13.1	14.3	8.2	7.4	4.5	9.2	6.1	38.1	51.4	12.6

c.

Electoral emotionality for 1st time, 2nd time, and other voters

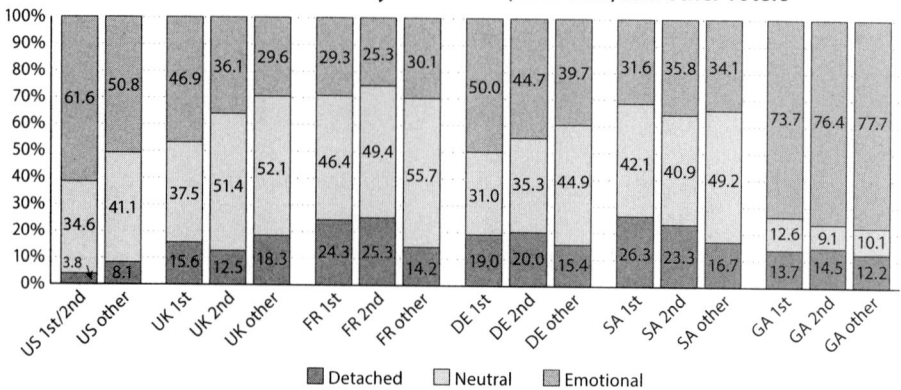

	US 1st/2nd	US other	UK 1st	UK 2nd	UK other	FR 1st	FR 2nd	FR other	DE 1st	DE 2nd	DE other	SA 1st	SA 2nd	SA other	GA 1st	GA 2nd	GA other
Emotional	61.6	50.8	46.9	36.1	29.6	29.3	25.3	30.1	50.0	44.7	39.7	31.6	35.8	34.1	73.7	76.4	77.7
Neutral	34.6	41.1	37.5	51.4	52.1	46.4	49.4	55.7	31.0	35.3	44.9	42.1	40.9	49.2	12.6	9.1	10.1
Detached	3.8	8.1	15.6	12.5	18.3	24.3	25.3	14.2	19.0	20.0	15.4	26.3	23.3	16.7	13.7	14.5	12.2

FIGURES 7.2.A TO 7.2.F: Electoral emotions of first and second time voters

d. **Sense of electoral resolution for 1st time, 2nd time, and other voters**

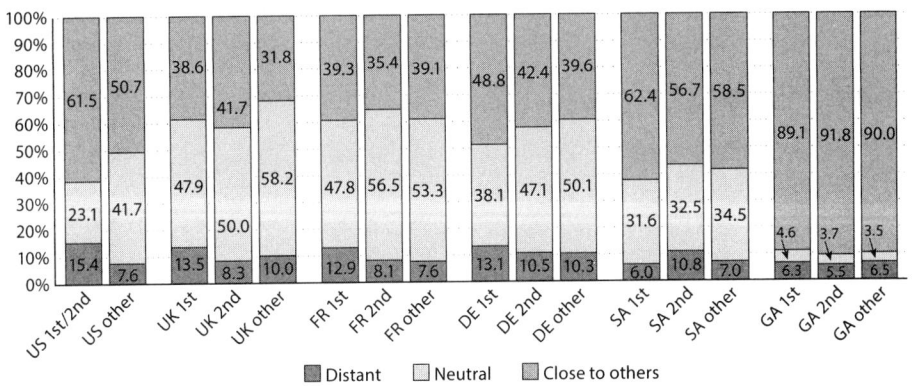

e. **Electoral worry for 1st time, 2nd time, and other voters**

f. **Electoral nervousness for 1st time, 2nd time, and other voters**

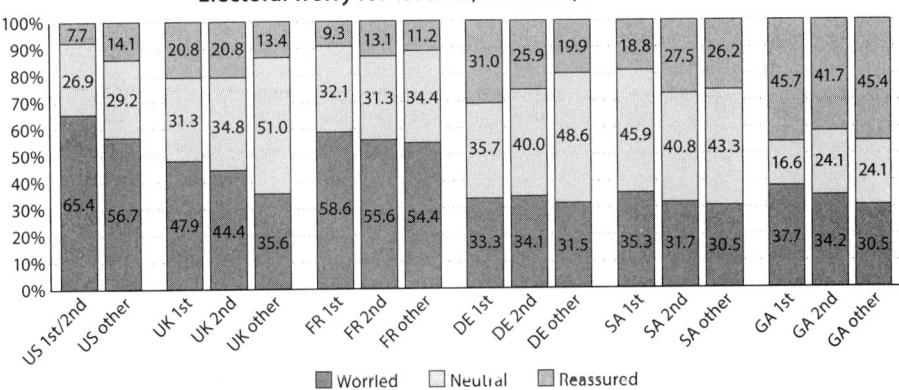

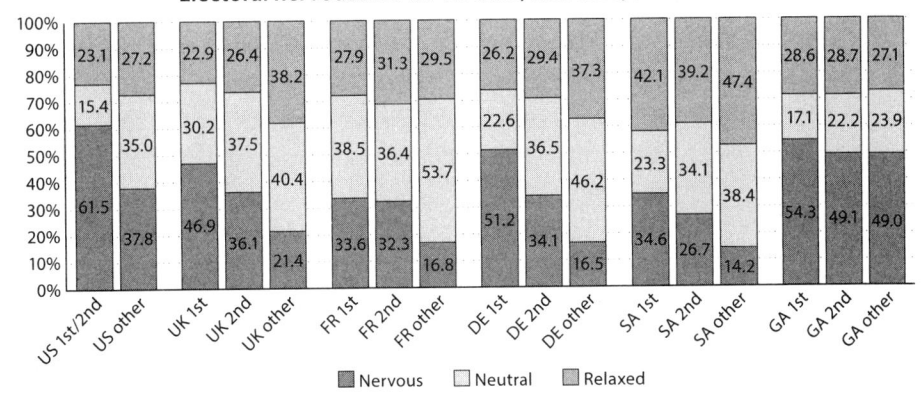

FIGURES 7.2.A TO 7.2.F: *(continued)*

the US (65.4% vs 56.7%). Thus, whilst first-time voters worry more than average, this seems to be more in line with a proportional consequence of age than a strong ad hoc specificity associated with the first vote. Finally, in most countries, voting is more likely to bring electoral resolution for first-time voters than for the rest of the population. This is particularly true in the US (61.5% vs 50.7%, a differential of 10.8%) and, in Germany (48.8% vs 39.6%, a differential of 9.2%), and in the UK (38.6% vs 31.8%, a differential of 6.8%), but is not verified for France or Georgia.

Qualitative narratives reinforce the sense of positive emotions associated with a first vote. First-time voters emphasize their excitement and happiness about their new experience:

> Everyone was really active in the whole voting process and everyone was getting excited talking about parties and policies and things, so I think that was what got me excited, the whole hype and so on. UK18F002

> I felt excited and wished that the process could last a bit longer so tried to drag it out a bit. Even though I knew who I was going to vote for I still studied the names and took in all my surroundings because I was a little bit over-excited [*laughs*] UK20F001

First-time voters also stress how voting makes them feel part of their community and represents an important rite of passage and a responsibility they feel proud to engage with:

> When I entered I felt excited because it was my first ever general election and I had always imagined it as I've gotten older. And also because it's quite a historic election I felt that I was a big part of it. US19M201

> There has been a lot about what an important election it is. Everyone will be voting and I think you could see that from the turnout. It was important to me too as it was my first election. Excitement as I'm actually allowed to vote. It's like learning to drive—crossing that barrier that everyone does. US18F056

> When I walked in there I was actually really excited. I never thought when I went to vote I would feel like that at the age of eighteen, that one vote could make a difference. When I got there I felt it was quite empowering having the chance to vote. FR20M043

> I wouldn't say it was an anti-climax, I think that's what a lot of people say. You think, oh it's going to be great to vote and then you go into this

> shabby booth with a pen, and then you put a cross in a box and put the paper in an old beaten-up box, but I thought it was quite exciting. UK18F002
>
> I was quite excited actually as it was my first time voting. Yes, it was a cool experience going down to the polling station. I've been looking things up over the past few weeks about what party I was going to vote for so it was an exciting experience really. UK18M003
>
> This was the first time I voted which was really cool—it gave me a sense of pride. My mom was proud. US36F00
>
> I got some chocolate afterwards—I wasn't expecting that so that was a nice surprise! UK18M005

Similarly, some of the responses to our on-the-spot interviews revealed the excitement and happiness of first-time voters in the US during the 2014 mid-term elections:

> I just kept thinking it was pretty awesome to be voting. I hope it counts. US2ZF042
>
> I was just happy to vote for the first time. US2ZF049
>
> GO-BAMA! That's what I'm talking about. And now I have to make sure I am not late for class! US2ZM044
>
> It was the first time I could vote, so I was very happy. US3ZF067

First-time voters interviewed on the spot also refer to the solemnity of their inaugural elections, sometimes combined with anxiety and nervousness:

> I wish I could know right now the outcome. It's killing me. US2ZF045
>
> I was so nervous that they wouldn't have me registered since it is my first time but I was just happy to get to vote. US2ZF046
>
> It's my first time voting so I just was focusing on getting the marks right. US2ZF041
>
> I just kept making sure and rechecking that I filled in the right bubbles. US2ZF043

By contrast, few young voters report feeling apathetic or bored, though some express how the weight of their responsibility makes them feel anxious and hesitant about their vote:

The main thing was working out which party I was going to vote for. I was quite conflicted a lot of the time so it took me a while to work out who I would vote for. FR19F033

Quantitatively and qualitatively, all this emphasizes the importance of the 'special first time'. Young people may first vote out of curiosity, but they likely keep voting because they find the experience cathartic, pleasant, and exciting. Conversely and crucially, young non-voters are excluded from these positive experiences and shared moments. The impact of enjoyment on long-term voting makes this critical. A first vote is by all accounts a uniquely emotional experience for most. First-time voters are more excited, but also more nervous, than experienced voters; voting makes them happier, and is more likely to result in a sense of electoral resolution. Early experiences of electoral democracy perform their role as a genuine introduction and welcome to democratic citizenship. First-time voters are largely immune to the risk of emotional indifference that can start affecting some (though not most) of those who have been invited to take part in elections many times before. Their positive emotionality also separates them from those who do not vote at those early opportunities. We noted how those who vote in the first two elections of their adult lives are likely to remain chronic participants, and those who do not, chronic abstentionists. This habituation is likely to be mediated by the strong emotional valence of those first two elections, which can make young voters and young abstentionists quickly drift further apart in terms of their respective happiness and indifference.

These intense positive emotions represent a unique potential, a very direct opportunity to attract young people who will be eager to experience, in the manner in which they anticipate the powerful and positive emotions of all first times, their electoral inauguration. Unfortunately, those responsible for the operation of political systems have proved chronically uninterested in (or incapable of) seizing this opportunity to fulfil the potential of youth participation by optimizing measures that address and emphasize the excitement and emotional intensity awaiting young voters who go to the polling station for the first time.

Implicit Measures of Emotion

To capture emotions beyond voters' conscious self-perceptions, we used implicit measures based on word completion and image association. In the

US, UK, and South African surveys, we employed a series of word-stem completion questions. Three examples of word-stem completion for all three countries are presented in figures 7.3.a–7.3.c, and all others in appendix 3. Respondents were asked to think about elections, then to complete word-stems of which the first one or two letters were provided. Most stems used were the same across countries, with additional single-letter stems in the UK. We aimed to capture subconscious emotions associated with the electoral experience. The word-stems are open enough to allow for a variety of common words to be proposed, with different connotations. We then counted the words most frequently chosen by respondents (only consolidating when of the same root and connotation: for instance, 'happy' consolidated with 'happiness', or 'horror' with 'horrible'—but not 'hope' with 'hopeless' or 'democracy' with 'Democrat' in the US context, as there connotations differ), and coded them along two dimensions: valence (negative to positive) and emotionality (non-emotional to emotional). Font size represents frequencies (multiplying frequencies by 0.2 in the UK and South Africa, and 0.4 in the US due to a lower total number of valid answers).

The findings overwhelmingly suggest that elections inspire positive and largely emotional thoughts. Across all three countries, 'happiness' is the word that comes most often to respondents' minds when offered the word-stem 'ha–'. It is evoked between 3.6 (South Africa) and 7.7 (USA) times more frequently than 'hate', the second most highly evoked word, which, whilst negative, is also highly emotional. Likewise, the stem 'ho–' overwhelmingly evokes the word 'hope', followed by 'home', 'honesty', and 'honour' across the three countries, except in the UK, where 'hopelessness' is also a frequent reference. Note that, in these results, variations across countries are a little more pronounced, with 'honesty' being a frequent point of reference in South Africa in the midst of the Zuma corruption scandals, whilst 'home' is a dominant reference in the UK and the US (almost as much as 'hope'), and 'honor' a significant reference in the US. In both the US and South Africa, 'pride' dominates the 'pr–' stem alongside 'president' (but also 'promise' in South Africa), and 'trust' the 'tr–' stem alongside 'truth' (but also 'try' in the US.)

'De–' proves the hardest stem to interpret. Whilst in South Africa it overwhelmingly evokes 'democracy' (followed by 'decision'), in the US, those two ideas are understandably overtaken by references to 'Democrats'. In the UK, 'democracy' is only evoked marginally by voters on Referendum Night, compared to a mixture of polarized 'depression', 'death', and 'delight'. This apparent contradiction underlines the violently emotional nature of

a.

UK—HO-

Positive ↑

Honest

Hope
Home

Holiday

Nonemotional ← — — — — — — — — — — — → Emotional

Horrible

Hopeless
Hostile

Negative ↓

b.

UK—HA-

Positive ↑

Happy

Have
Habit

Harmony

Nonemotional ← — — — — — — — — — — — → Emotional

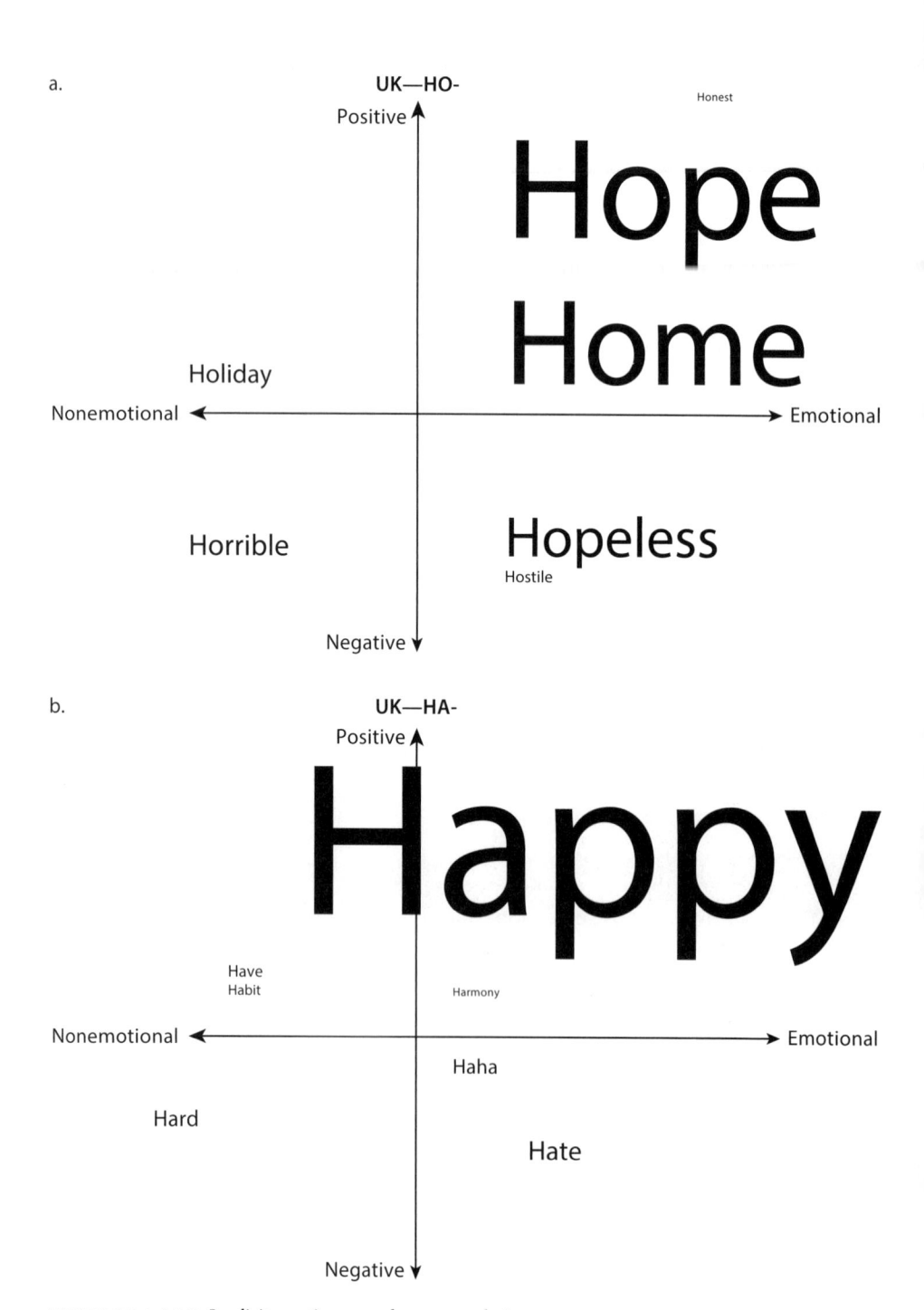

Haha

Hard

Hate

Negative ↓

FIGURE 7.3.A-7.3.N: Implicit emotions: word stem completions

ELECTIONS AND EMOTIONS   235

C.

SA—TR-

Positive ↑

                                    Trust
                                    Truth

Travel

Train   Transparent
Trade   Transformation
Tradition   Triumph
Trend
Trace
Transport

Nonemotional ←――――――――――――――――→ Emotional

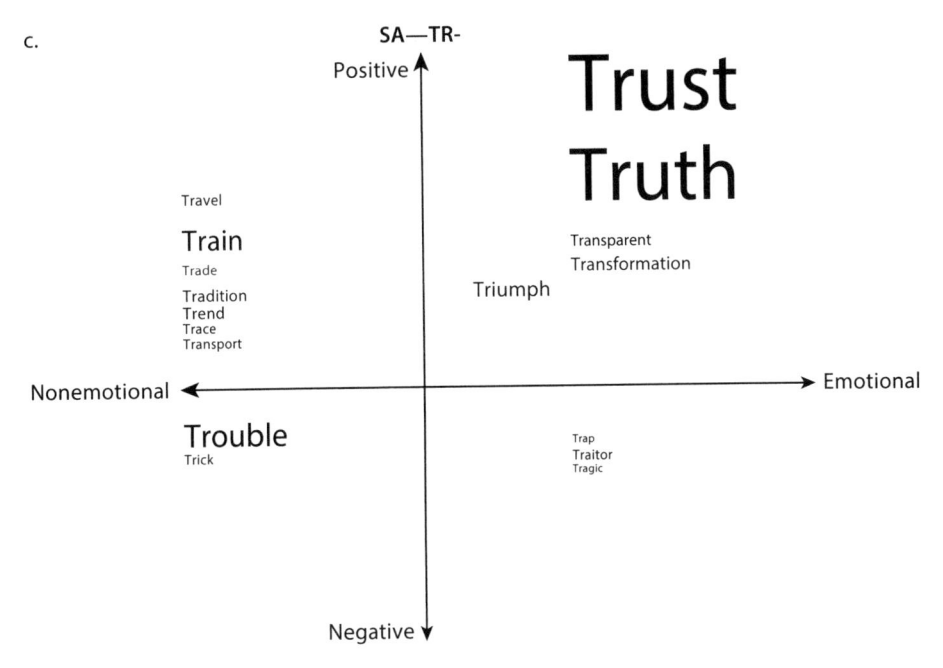

Trouble   Trap
Trick   Traitor
                             Tragic

Negative ↓

FIGURE 7.3.A-7.3.N: (*continued*)

the 2016 referendum (chapter 9) and its unique capacity to polarize voters and fuel feelings of mutual hostility.

Overall, word-stems show how elections elicit highly emotional reactions from citizens. In most cases, the response is also highly positive, except in the UK in the EU-membership referendum, which abundantly triggers both positive and negative emotional reactions, depending on the stem. The only case where a non-emotional word apparently prevails is in the US when the 'de–' stem evokes one of the two main parties in the minds of respondents, but even then, the word is still associated with positive or negative connotations by an important minority of respondents. The word-stems analysis gives unique insights into citizens' spontaneous associations; but as a logical next step, we used a visual experiment to infer directly the emotions of voters in the polling booth from their body language.

Visually Displayed Emotions in the Polling Booth and Kinesics Analysis

This unique (indeed, unprecedented in electoral analysis) third fieldwork component was conducted in Germany using a mock election for the next president of the European Union' (using credible candidates), which took place in a realistic polling station. This visual experiment was organized as part of the Falling Walls conference in Berlin (November 2012). We partnered with a camera crew to organize the lighting of the experimental polling station such as to enable them to record the shadows of volunteers whilst they were in the polling booth. This unique arrangement permitted us to capture the non-verbal behaviour and emotions that voters display during the highly secretive moment they spend in the polling booth, whilst preserving the secrecy of the ballot. We then double blind coded the recordings, using insights from kinesics (see chapter 2), to try and decipher the specific emotions displayed by the participants, using the following six scales: happiness–unhappiness; excitement–boredom; solemnity–casualness; reassurance–worry; relaxation–nervousness; and certainty–hesitation. The experiment was then replicated in the UK in 2019. Kinesics (Birdwhistell, 1970) is a body of research that spans disciplines from anthropology to psychiatry, involving the analysis of non-verbal communication. It was first used to understand the emotions experienced by autistic children and other patients who find it difficult to express themselves verbally, and later by anthropologists engaging in participant observation in communities whose languages they had not mastered. Here, we use the approach to interpret something that social scientists normally never see: the expressions that are displayed by voters' faces and bodies when they are casting their vote in the secretive intimacy of the polling booth, whilst respecting their anonymity (we only see their shadows through the curtain) and the secrecy of their votes.

We first assess the average valence of the emotions displayed on our six scales by all the experiment participants whilst in the polling booth. Results are shown in appendix 3. The first key result of the experiment is that voting is confirmed to be a very emotional act. Very few of the participants appeared to display little or no emotion, while the vast majority betrayed complex emotional reactions during the brief time they spent inside the polling booth. This confirms earlier, self-reported findings. The main emotions displayed by participants include a sense of solemnity (76.4%), excitement (also 76.4%), nervousness (72.2%), and happiness (63.9%). This is followed by hesitation (56.9%) and a sense of worry (38.9%).

We next focus on the average intensity of three of the main emotional scales: happiness, excitement, and solemnity. Once again, the results are telling. With theoretical scales ranging from zero (emotionally neutral) to ±2, average intensity extends from 1.11 on the happiness scale to 1.32 on the solemnity scale, suggesting that for a majority of participants, the emotions

a. Emotional valence by types of ballot paper

- French ballot paper
- UK ballot paper
- DRE electronic ballot

Categories: Happy vs. unhappy; Excited vs. bored; Solemn vs. casual

b. Anxiety-related emotions by type of ballot

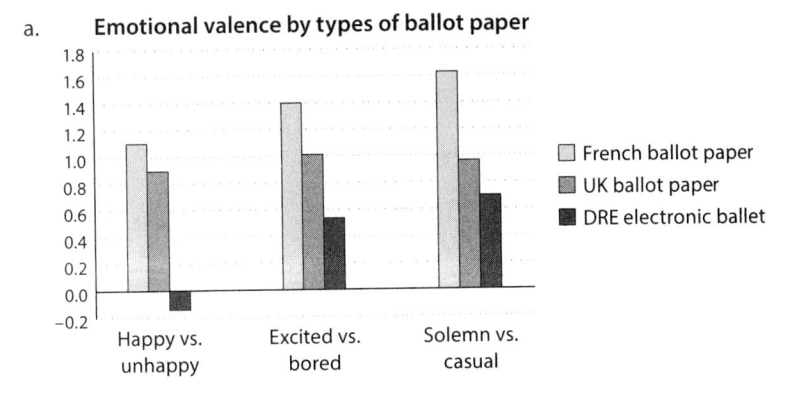

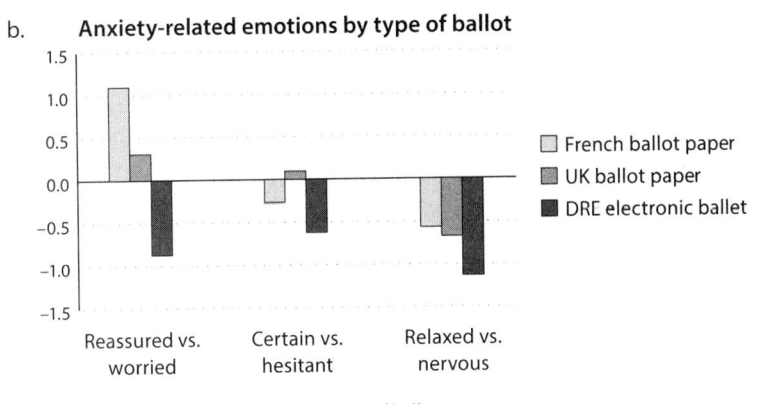

- French ballot paper
- UK ballot paper
- DRE electronic ballot

Categories: Reassured vs. worried; Certain vs. hesitant; Relaxed vs. nervous

FIGURE 7.4.A: Emotional valence by type of ballot paper
Note: All items coded on a -2 to 2 scale.
FIGURE 7.4.B: Anxiety-related emotions by type of ballot

that they subconsciously display in the polling booth are, in fact, much more intense than they self-report, a result all the more striking in so far as the self-reported scores stem from real elections and the visual experiment from a mock one.

We then start to consider the impact of electoral ergonomics (approached more thoroughly in chapter 8), as emotions experienced by voters in the polling booth are affected by the type of ballot paper used. The experiment participants used three different ballot papers (see chapter 8), and figures 7.4.a and 7.4.b show how these affect the emotions displayed by voters in the booth. The results are noteworthy, because despite the relatively small sample, which imposes a need for caution, they seem to highlight some fairly stark contrasts. On the whole, the emotions felt by those using the polypaper (French-type) ballot seem more positive than those who use a monopaper (UK-type) alternative, and those who vote using actual paper ballots display substantially more positive spontaneous emotional reactions than those who use electronic voting, even in the polling station. In fact, on the happiness scale, those using electronic voting appear to have a slightly unhappy mean, even though, once again, the sample size and nature of the coding (notwithstanding double blind coding) require that our interpretation be cautious.

The visual experiment shows, then, that the moment voters spend in the polling booth casting their vote is a very emotional one—in fact, probably more emotional than most people report. This may be because their remembered self-perception of the electoral experience merges the highly emotional time spent in the intimacy of the polling booth itself with more emotionally neutral moments on the same day. It also confirms that for voters, even in the less realistic context of a lab experiment, an election entails an element of solemnity, which underlines our suggestion that voters do not just 'cast a preference' in an election, but rather assume a role and a responsibility which inject greater complexity into models of electoral behaviour than is usually the case. Third, the experimental findings show that the emotions citizens experience in the polling booth tend overwhelmingly to be positive, though elements such as worry and nervousness are prominent, and the solemnity noted above could interact with either positive (excitement, happiness) or negative (worry, nervousness) emotions. Finally, the findings confirm—along the lines of the panel study analysis reported earlier in this chapter—that electoral emotions do not occur in a vacuum, but rather, that apparently innocent choices by electoral organizers, such as ballot paper design, will trigger different emotions and affect their intensity, valence, and, more broadly, citizens' experience of the vote. In this case in particular, there is a clear suggestion that voters display more positive and more intense emotions when voting using paper rather than electronic ballots.

Addictive Emotionality

In this book, we conceptualize the emotions felt by voters during elections as a symptom and an operationalization of electoral experience. We thus consider that how citizens feel during the election, notably on Election Day and as they cast their vote–*is* their electoral experience, with emotionality and happiness being the categories that encapsulate most emotional variations in the vote. This is why we use these as our two dependent variable measures of electoral experience.

In this chapter, we found that elections represent a highly emotional period for many citizens, and voting a highly emotional act. We showed that citizens amply report these emotions, but that when we measure them independently using a visual experiment, they appear even stronger—not least in the polling booth—and even more positive than citizens themselves realize. We suggest this may be because conscious perceptions do not distinguish between individual moments of varying emotional intensity that succeed each other within a very short time period. We also noted that emotionality peaks for first-time, and to an extent second-time, voters. First votes are uniquely emotional, exceptionally happy, and somewhat anxiety generating. Emotionally, they are quite simply a true 'first time', eliciting the types of emotional reaction one would expect from teenagers experiencing their first kiss, drink, job, or sexual experience.

Crucially, emotionality can be addictive. Human beings live to feel, and we subconsciously wish to relive what has produced emotions. In and of itself, this can illustrate the concept of habituation and what it may really hide: the interrelationship between electoral experience, behaviour, and resolution. The findings presented here interact with the narratives of Election Day and Election Night analyzed in chapter 3, and the sequencing of electoral atmosphere we explore in chapter 9. As seen in our visual experiment, emotions also stem from the interface between voters psychology and electoral organization which we label *electoral ergonomics*. As we will see in the next chapter, electoral ergonomics is intimately linked to the emotions that voters experience in the course of the electoral process.

8

Electoral Ergonomics

The Concept of Electoral Ergonomics

One of the most important concepts defined in this book is that of electoral ergonomics, introduced in chapter 1. We conceptualize it as the interface between every aspect of electoral organization and the psychology of the voters. In short, our claim is that every small detail in the organization of the vote matters, because it will trigger different aspects of our electoral personality, memory, emotions, and identity. It may affect the way citizens experience the vote (what they think about and for how long, the emotions that may be mobilized at the time they cast their vote), their attitudes (sense of efficacy, democratic satisfaction, trust, etc.), their likelihood of participating, and their electoral choice. This encompasses every aspect of the electoral experience, not just the elements traditionally studied in political science (such as the electoral system), but also all the smaller and often overlooked decisions that are made when organizing elections—usually under an assumption of neutrality—such as the choice of polling stations, design of the ballot paper, remote voting options, technicalities of identification checks (or lack thereof), the dematerialization of ballots, and so on.

The claim is ambitious and potentially ground-breaking. Routinely, election designers make decisions on how to organize the vote that are based on parties' preferences, financial constraints, or simply habits, as though those decisions might affect who votes, but not a given voter's experience or behaviour. For example, as discussed in chapter 2, the literature reflects a belief that allowing remote voting may make more people vote, but not that the same person would vote or experience elections differently if they avail themselves of that remote voting option, as opposed to voting traditionally in a polling station. We reject this neutrality assumption, and claim that organizational details will 'switch on and off' different aspects of citizens' personalities, memories, and identities, and in turn may shape how people vote, on what basis, and their perception of the election and of their place in the electoral process as a voter. Moreover, while many aspects of electoral organization (registration processes, internet voting, and the location of polling stations) have been considered to different extents in the literature, we reframe these elements under the concept of electoral ergonomics, which in itself is to make two important analytical claims. The first is that, as discussed previously, ergonomics is to be conceived as an interface (or interaction) between organizational design and voters' psychology, as opposed to focusing on direct effects of the design elements alone. Secondly, a key factor which must be included in our analysis, already discussed in chapter 6, is the 'function of elections'.

Indeed, while ergonomics pertains to 'the interactions among human and other elements of a system' with an aim 'to optimize human well-being and overall system performance' (International Ergonomics Association Executive Council, 2000), this deceptively simple definition can lead to a major misunderstanding. Ergonomics is seen by many as seeking to adapt systemic elements to the human body or mind. Yet, if an ergonomically designed pen were to be defined as 'a pen that is ideally grasped by the human hand', it would have the shape of a small water bottle, much easier to grasp than any existing writing device. This pen would fit the human hand perfectly, but would obviously be extremely uncomfortable to write with, and this indicates why ergonomics must instead be understood as the interface between system, humans, and function. If that function is misunderstood, ergonomics will become, literally, dysfunctional. We thus conceive the challenge of electoral ergonomics as being about optimally adapting an 'object'—elections—to humans, *given its function*. This aspect is critical, because in our vision of electoral ergonomics as an interface between design and psychology, we expect electoral function inherently to vary across individuals and groups of voters. Thus in this chapter we illustrate in particular the way in which certain components of electoral ergonomics, such as remote voting, affect specific types of voter, such as young people.

In order to unfold the concept of electoral ergonomics, in light of our discussion in chapters 2 and 6 of the function of elections and how it may vary, we focus on examples of electoral ergonomics effects in regard to two design components: remote voting (notably the implications of vote location and timing), and the haptic impact of ballot paper materialization. We use a mixture of experimental methods (including both traditional survey-based experiments and the visual experiment already referred to in chapter 7), and survey data in a context constitutive of a natural quasi-experiment in a true electoral context. Whilst experiments allow us to isolate causality very clearly, optimizing internal validity, the use of a natural quasi-experiment, whilst more exposed to the influence of parasitic independent variables, benefits from higher credibility when it comes to external validity.

The Puzzle of Remote Voting

Our first case studies of electoral ergonomics pertain to remote voting and its variations. The debates surrounding remote voting, with regard both to convenience and safety, as discussed in chapter 2, have been plentiful. 'Remote voting' refers to all forms of access to the vote that allow a citizen to vote without needing to be present in person in his/her registered polling station during polling hours. The remoteness can apply to any of the three main aspects of default electoral access. In other words, as a citizen is normally expected to vote in an election by being present in person, in polling station x, on day y, the remoteness may pertain to the voter's presence (personal remoteness), the place where he/she can vote (geographical remoteness), or the time when his/her vote can be cast (temporal remoteness), or a combination of these. Thus, personal remoteness may be exemplified by proxy voting, geographical remoteness by same-day remote e-voting, and temporal remoteness by advance voting, while postal voting or early-remote e-voting are both geographically *and* temporally remote (table 8.1).

Understanding remote voting thus involves multiple considerations. Does it make a difference whether citizens vote in person or entrust others to cast their votes for them? Does it make a difference whether they vote on the same day as the rest of the nation or earlier, and therefore with different (and potentially less complete) information than Election Day voters? Finally, what is the impact of voting from home as opposed to in a polling station?

An increasing number of Election Management Bodies are keen to explore new ways to delocalize and dematerialize voting procedures and make

TABLE 8.1: Main Forms of Remote Voting

GEOGRAPHICAL
Right to vote in any national polling station (e.g., Sweden)
Same-day remote e-voting (e.g., several US counties)

TEMPORAL
Advance voting (e.g., Australia, New Zealand)
Two stage early/advance voting (e.g., Georgia)
Limited advance voting for specific locations only (e.g., Ireland)

PERSONAL
Proxy voting (e.g., France, Poland)

GEOGRAPHICAL + TEMPORAL
Postal voting (e.g., UK, Austria, Germany)
Early remote e-voting (e.g., Estonia, Switzerland, several US counties)
Advance voting in any national polling station (e.g., Sweden, Finland)

Notes: France allows proxy voting without requiring proof of incapacity to attend. It also allows voters to cancel their postal vote by going to the polling station in person on the day. Postal voting is automatically remote both geographically and temporally, as voters need to mail their ballot before Election Day. Countries such as the UK allow postal voters implicitly to cancel their postal vote by going to the polling station on the day, in which case their postal vote is automatically superseded by their in-person vote.

it easy for voters to participate in elections without needing to go to a polling station on Election Day. Purportedly, election organizers are primarily aiming to make it easier for citizens to vote, by reducing the individual cost of voting along traditional rational-choice lines. Maybe, it is felt, if voters can vote from home, they will have no reason to abstain (which, of course, entirely ignores the fact that most of those who abstain do so not because voting is a psychologically or physically onerous action, but because, they claim, they resent the choice on offer). In particular, it is hoped to lower abstention among a crucial target group: young people, overwhelmingly perceived as highly 'digital' in their daily behaviour, and used to dematerialized, home-based 'low level democracy', from *X Factor* voting to social media opinion-voicing (Cohen and Kahne, 2011; Xenos et al., 2014; Jenkins et al., 2018). There is an expectation that if electoral democracy is transported into their domain, the young will embrace it more systematically and enthusiastically.

A less open but equally important argument for postal voting, and even for more remote e-voting (but not for advance voting), is that elections are expensive to organize and complex to securitize. The costs involved in opening, preparing, and staffing polling stations are substantial, and the physicality of polling stations comes with ample fraud risks (opening irregularities, voter intimidation, transfer of ballots or data between polling stations and counting centres). Those are undoubtedly excellent reasons why some countries with frequent votes, such as Switzerland, are at the forefront of the generalization of internet voting. Of course, both remote voting and e-voting systems must be secure, to instil confidence in the political process, user-friendly, so voters feel comfortable with the operation, and fit in with underlying cultural and institutional practices (Oostveen and van den Besselaar, 2009). Whilst only a handful of countries (such as Estonia) have decided to test new technologies facilitating remote e-voting, others, such as France, piloted it (in this case for citizens living abroad), but decided to suspend the process in 2017. Ireland cancelled its use of (non-remote) e-voting in two phases in 2009 and 2010, amidst major technology issues. There was also a noted fiasco with the release of the election results from voting machines in Belgium in the 2014 federal elections, and ample evidence of voters' increased distrust in the US where voting machines or remote e-voting are used.

One of the main arguments put forward by proponents of e-voting is that it has the potential to increase immediate turnout (Barrat Esteve, 2006). However, there is evidence that sometimes, remote e-voting can actually have significant negative consequences. Cammaerts et al. (2016) conducted an experiment with young pre-voters (fifteen- to seventeen-year-olds), testing the impact of remote e-voting. They found that those casting their ballot over the internet expressed less satisfaction, less happiness, and less excitement about the election than those going to a polling station. They also reported lower levels of efficacy. Crucially, remote e-voting actually led to lower turnout than voting in polling stations (17.4% vs 36.9%). Even more worrying, those who voted on the internet are less likely to vote at the next opportunity, because of low efficacy and satisfaction, which can trap young voters into a spiral of abstention, unlike in-station voting habituation. Similarly, there has been significant research on other forms of remote voting, including advance voting, postal voting, and to a lesser extent proxy voting, and problems with security (Stewart III, 2011), and the fiasco of the 2016 Austrian presidential election, underline the risks associated with their implementation. Despite some evidence that postal voting can increase turnout (Luechinger et al., 2007; Rallings et al., 2010), questions have been raised regarding the substantive effects of postal voting on citizens' perceptions, motivations, and electoral choice.

Logically, temporal remoteness and geographical remoteness have different practical effects. A corollary of temporally remote voting is that different citizens vote under different informational conditions, with some voting before crucial national debates take place. The possibility of geographically remote voting, meanwhile, impacts whether a citizen votes in an institutionally designed communal environment or in an uncontrolled and individual setting. Finally, little attention has been devoted to personal remoteness and proxy voting, the dominant remote voting option in countries like France and Poland, and many other systems, designed for blind or disabled voters. Proxy voting is often frowned upon because it implies that voters either need to discuss their vote with another person (thereby breaching its secrecy), or surrender their own right to vote, effectively giving a second vote to someone else through a 'trustee' transfer, and thus raising concerns about possible abuse by political parties, which may target non-voters to give trusted party members an extra vote.

All this draws a complex and intriguing picture. Remote voting solutions are seen as crucial tools to tackle decreasing turnout among key voter categories, but, as we will see with the following case studies, some versions lead potentially to counter-productive results, such as lower satisfaction, lower trust, less engaged citizens, and even lower long-term turnout and lower perceived legitimacy of the system. Many election designers hope that bringing elections to voters' homes (or smartphones) will ultimately significantly reduce the cost of electoral organization, and in due course afford electoral processes that are more secure; they tend simply to assume that voting remotely will affect positively both repeated turnout and voter satisfaction. Unfortunately, our findings suggest that both assumptions are fundamentally erroneous.

Electoral Ergonomics Case Study No. 1: The Importance of the Polling Station.

REMOTE VOTING AND ELECTORAL ATTITUDES: ADVANCE VS POSTAL VOTING IN THE US

In this first case study, we focus on the importance of the polling station visit itself, by comparing the attitudes of US citizens who use advance voting and postal (absentee) voting, drawing upon our panel study. In the US, the choice between remote voting options is largely devolved to individual states, or even counties, thereby creating a natural experiment. In 2016, thirty-seven states and the District of Columbia offered a form of advance

TABLE 8.2. Remote Voting and Electoral Attitudes in the US

Table 8.2.a: The impact of the polling station experience	2012		2014	
	Advance	Postal	Advance	Postal
Efficacy	6.36 (2.07)	6.10 (2.12)	6.28 (2.03)	5.59 (1.98)
Projected efficacy	6.90 (1.72)	6.60 (1.82)	6.76 (1.71)	6.48 (1.52)
Perception of importance	7.38 (1.24)	7.15 (1.53)	7.32 (1.19)	6.89 (1.47)
Sense of responsibility	6.21 (1.95)	6.05 (2.05)	6.10 (1.85)	5.99 (1.76)
Empathic displacement	4.54 (2.56)	4.26 (2.56)	4.09 (2.34)	4.01 (2.08)
Sociotropism	6.84 (1.68)	6.54 (1.86)	6.46 (1.63)	6.15 (1.67)

Table 8.2.b: Temporal remote voting and the societal dimension of the individual vote	2012		2014	
	Temporal remote	Election Day	Temporal remote	Election Day
Efficacy	6.21 (2.10)	5.92 (2.10)	5.83 (2.02)	5.52 (2.06)
Projected efficacy	6.73 (1.78)	6.52 (1.75)	6.58 (1.59)	6.27 (1.74)
Empathic displacement	4.38 (2.56)	4.82 (2.36)	4.03 (2.17)	4.55 (2.18)
Sociotropism	6.67 (1.79)	6.39 (1.86)	6.25 (1.66)	6.16 (1.60)

voting, starting between forty-five and four days before Election Day, and forty-seven states had an absentee voting option. Of those, twenty-seven plus the District of Columbia required no excuse on the part of the voter. Three states (Washington, Oregon, and Colorado) automatically mail ballots to all registered voters (National Conference of State Legislatures, 2018). The trend is therefore to prioritize the absentee ballot across the US, even though an increasing number of states and counties also make advance voting possible. As noted previously, absentee ballots are significantly cheaper and easier to organize than advance (including weekend) voting, and do not require the opening, staffing, and securitizing of polling stations for up to forty-five days and in numerous locations. Remote voting has become increasingly used by US voters. In presidential elections, the proportion of voters using advance or absentee voting increased from 7% in 1992, to 31.6% in 2012, to 36.6% in 2016.

However, the data show that these two options lead to significantly divergent attitudes towards electoral democracy. Table 8.2.a highlights that advance voters consistently feel more efficacious than absentee voters, in terms of both external and projected efficacy. Moreover, they perceive the election as markedly more important than do absentee voters.

We also evaluated the impact of temporal remoteness, as both advance and absentee ballots ensure that voters will vote earlier than the majority of the population, which votes on Election Day (table 8.2.b). Crucially, the findings show that people who vote before Election Day are far less likely to be empathic displacers. This affects elections in terms of their being the shared experience or 'civic communion' which we referred to earlier. It appears that this particular dimension reduces significantly when voters are not part of Election Day but instead vote beforehand. Furthermore, Election Day voters are significantly more likely to make up their minds in the week before they cast their vote (see appendix 3[1]), and particularly on the actual day they vote. By contrast, temporally remote voters largely escape the crucial atmospheric build-up of the last week (see chapter 9), during which up to 27% of Americans claim to make up or change their minds (in line with the 20–30% we find elsewhere, though in the present case, we consider only the voter's actual electoral choice, whilst late decision may also apply to the decision whether to vote at all). This finding thus sheds light on late deciders and converters in elections, showing their behaviour to be due not merely to purely internal electoral psychological processes (in which case the proportion of late deciders would be the same regardless of the timing of their final vote), but to the interaction between voter psychology and the campaign cycle and its atmospheric consequences, which lead citizens to consider their electoral choice under a different light in the final sprint.

Our findings thus suggest that both the polling station experience and participation in a common Election Day matter, but in different ways. Visiting a polling station to vote (as opposed to doing so from home) makes voters significantly more sociotropic, efficacious, and projectively efficacious. Voting on Election Day, meanwhile (as opposed to earlier in the campaign), reinforces their empathic displacement, sense of inclusion, and likelihood of considering or reconsidering their vote in the last week of the campaign or indeed on Election Day itself, in ways which are not mirrored by those who vote in anticipation. In sum, enabling people to vote from home (geographically remote voting) has a cost in terms of efficacy and selfishness in political decision-making which can be avoided when remote voting solutions retain the polling station visit, whilst allowing them to vote early has a cost in terms of their projection and sense of inclusion, and means that citizens vote on the basis of information different from that of other voters, and miss out on the most influential time of the campaign.

1. Appendices referred to in this chapter are to be found online at www.epob.org.

GEOGRAPHICALLY VS TEMPORALLY REMOTE VOTING, ELECTORAL EMOTIONS, AND ELECTORAL RESOLUTION

After electoral attitudes, and still based on the same data, we consider the effect of the two remote voting options on electoral experience, in particular the emotions that voting elicits, and electoral resolution. We thus investigate whether voting in a polling station makes voters more, or less, excited, worried, emotional, or happy than voting from home using an absentee ballot. Again, the US quasi-experimental setting enables us to address this by comparing the emotions reported by US citizens who voted using advance and absentee ballots, drawing upon the emotional tension scales in our panel survey. To reiterate, the underlying belief of electoral organizers is that remote voting should not affect voters' electoral experience and satisfaction, an assumption that should at any rate be tested. Figures 8.1.a–8.1.e show a generally more positive valence of emotions for people who vote traditionally in polling stations on Election Day, as compared to those who avail themselves of one or other form of remote voting, except to an extent in France, where proxy voting is associated with emotions that are typically as positive as for in-person voters. Differences in means are limited, but distributions across each side of the tension scales reveal striking differences. The analysis pertains to five scales: happiness, excitement, emotionality, and worry, as well as electoral resolution. Confirming differences in standard deviations, we find emotional polarization to be far higher for traditional than for remote voters. That is, people who vote remotely are far less likely to engage emotionally—be it positively or negatively—with the vote than those who vote in a polling station on Election Day. They are also far less likely to experience electoral resolution.

In the UK, 40.1% of those who voted in a polling station reported feeling happy, but only 34% of those who voted by post said the same. Likewise in Germany, 28.7% of those who went to a polling station felt happy when they cast their vote, but only 21.1% of those who voted by mail. Similar differences are found when it comes to excitement: in the UK, 64.6% of in-station voters felt excitement at the time they cast their vote, but that proportion went down to 55.9% among those who completed an absentee ballot; while in Germany, those proportions were 34.1% and 23.6% respectively. In Germany, the proportion of voters reporting emotionality as they cast their ballot was also six percentage points higher for in-person than for postal voters.

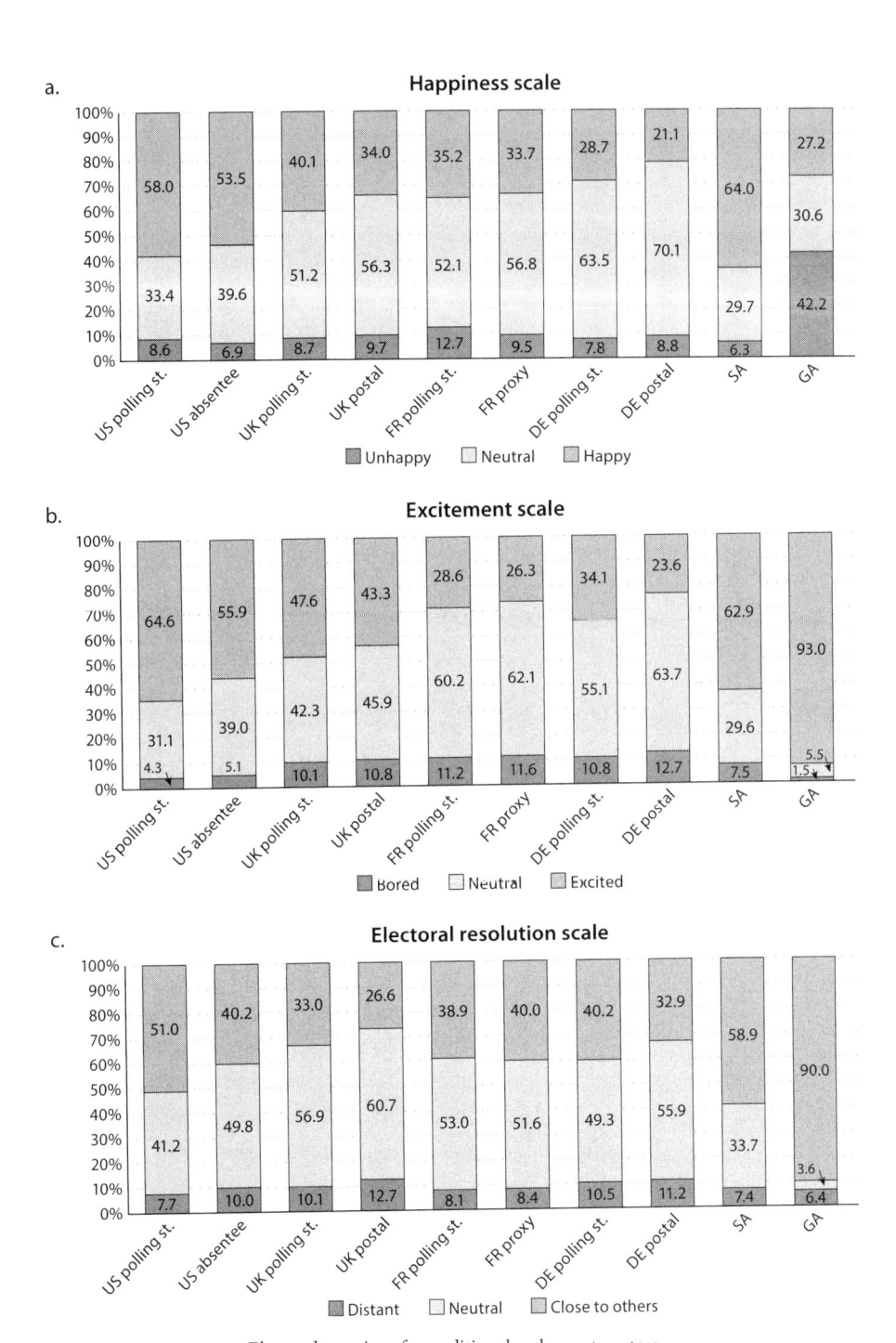

FIGURES 8.1.A TO 8.1.E: Electoral emotions for traditional and remote voters

250 CHAPTER 8

d.

Emotionality scale

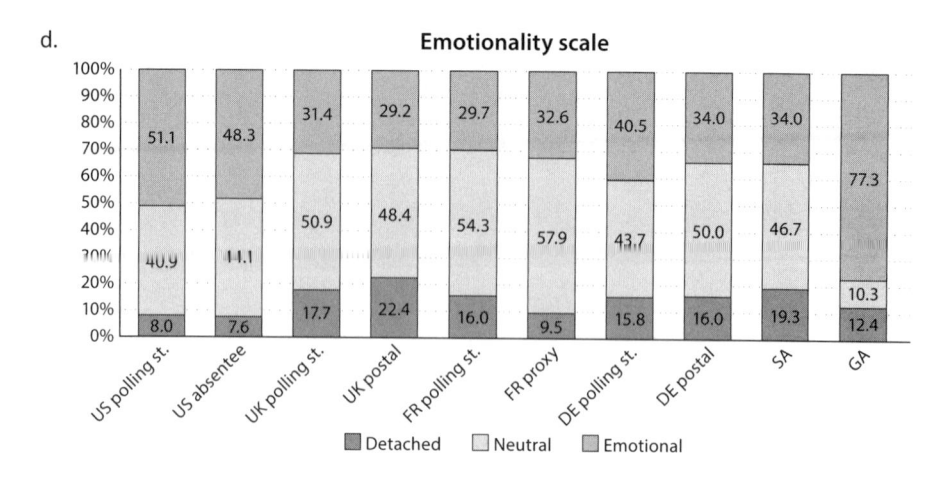

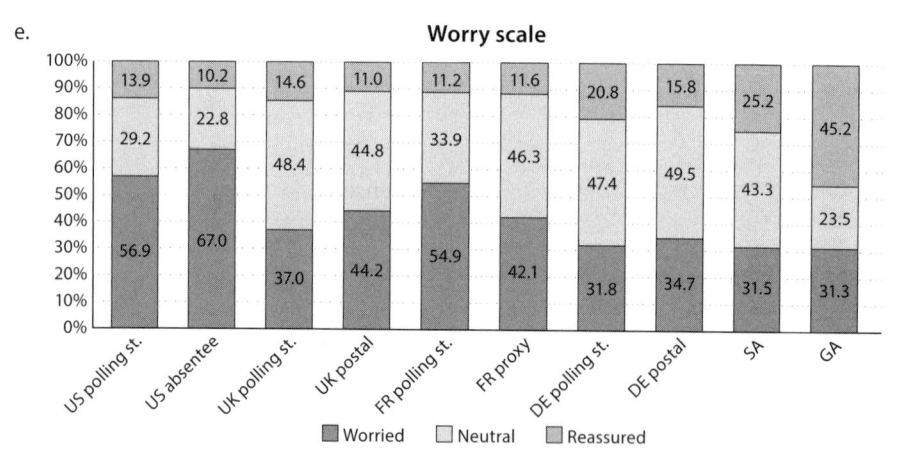

	US polling st.	US absentee	UK polling st.	UK postal	FR polling st.	FR proxy	DE polling st.	DE postal	SA	GA
Emotional	51.1	48.3	31.4	29.2	29.7	32.6	40.5	34.0	34.0	77.3
Neutral	40.9	44.1	50.9	48.4	54.3	57.9	43.7	50.0	46.7	10.3
Detached	8.0	7.6	17.7	22.4	16.0	9.5	15.8	16.0	19.3	12.4

■ Detached ☐ Neutral ■ Emotional

e.

Worry scale

	US polling st.	US absentee	UK polling st.	UK postal	FR polling st.	FR proxy	DE polling st.	DE postal	SA	GA
Reassured	13.9	10.2	14.6	11.0	11.2	11.6	20.8	15.8	25.2	45.2
Neutral	29.2	22.8	48.4	44.8	33.9	46.3	47.4	49.5	43.3	23.5
Worried	56.9	67.0	37.0	44.2	54.9	42.1	31.8	34.7	31.5	31.3

■ Worried ☐ Neutral ■ Reassured

FIGURES 8.1.A TO 8.1.E: *(continued)*

The same gaps are to be found when it comes to voters' negative emotions, such as worry. In the UK, 37% of polling station voters felt worried as they voted, but that proportion increased to 42.2% among postal voters. Likewise, in the US, 56.9% of in-station voters felt worried, but 67% of absentee voters. Engaging with fellow citizens through a polling station visit thus fosters not only positive emotionality, but also reassurance, compared to the solitary experience of remote voters. Only France's proxy voting goes against this trend. There, 54.9% of polling station voters felt some worry, but only 42.1% of proxy voters shared similar apprehensions. Thus it appears that, notwithstanding the other problems proxy voting raises, conditioning remote voting on a necessary interaction with another citizen results in voters feeling less rather than more worried.

ELECTORAL ERGONOMICS   251

Comparing the emotions of advance and absentee voters in the US

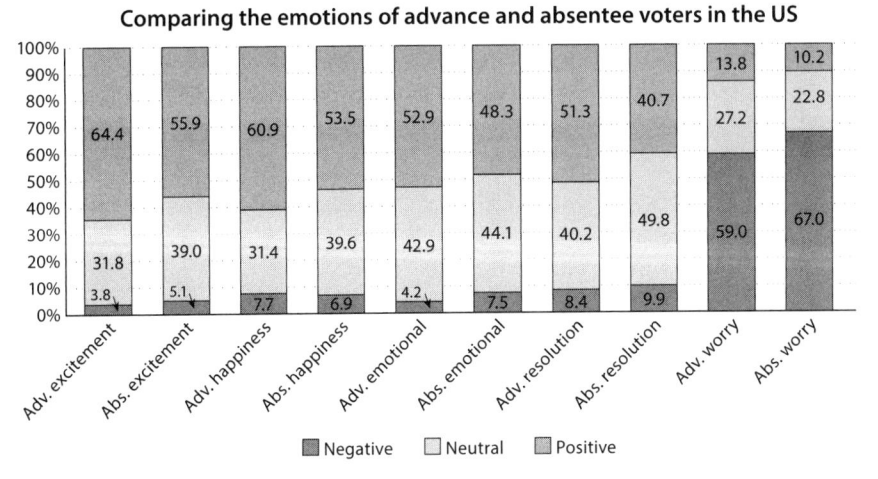

Category	Negative	Neutral	Positive
Adv. excitement	31.8	64.4	3.8
Abs. excitement	39.0	55.9	5.1
Adv. happiness	31.4	60.9	7.7
Abs. happiness	39.6	53.5	6.9
Adv. emotional	42.9	52.9	4.2
Abs. emotional	44.1	48.3	7.5
Adv. resolution	40.2	51.3	8.4
Abs. resolution	49.8	40.7	9.9
Adv. worry	59.0	27.2	13.8
Abs. worry	67.0	22.8	10.2

FIGURE 8.2: The emotional consequences of Advance vs Absentee voting

Even more strikingly than emotions, however, visiting a polling station strongly increases perceptions of electoral resolution. Of those US voters who went to a polling station, 51% feel a sense of resolution, compared to only 40.2% of those who cast an absentee ballot. In Germany, the gap is almost as spectacular: 40.2% of polling station voters feel resolution from the vote, but only 32.9% of those who cast their ballot postally. This confirms the unique symbolic societal value that participating in a vote among other citizens represents, as opposed to doing so without engaging in a collective physical process through the polling station experience. Yet again, French proxy voters are the only exception, being slightly more likely to experience resolution than traditional voters—highlighting once again the reconciliatory value of an interpersonal transaction.

We control for self-selection risks using the US case, where individual states and counties decide on the remote voting options to be offered (or not) to those unable or unwilling to attend the polling station on Election Day, with advance and absentee ballots being the two most common provisions. Whether an individual is offered an advance or an absentee ballot therefore solely depends on where they live, with no obvious bias in counties' choices of remote voting solution. This quasi-experiment showcases differences between the two remote voting options as regards emotionality and resolution (as opposed to comparing them to non-random traditional voting). The results are presented in figure 8.2, and confirm striking differences between the emotions and resolution experienced by advance and by absentee voters, on almost every dimension.

Advance voters were 11.1 percentage points more likely to experience resolution than were absentee voters (51.3% vs 40.2%). They were also 8.5% more likely to feel excited (64.4% vs 55.9%), 7.4% happier (60.9% vs 53.5%), and 4.6% more emotional (52.9% vs 48.3%). By the same token, they were 8% less likely to feel worried as they voted (59% vs 67%). These differences are large and systematic. Testing them in a quasi-experimental context confirms that the choice of remote voting solution has a major impact on the emotional value of the voting experience, as well as on resolution. In particular, geographical remoteness—that is, voting without going to a polling station—reduces the likelihood of experiencing positive emotions (excitement, happiness, emotionality) as one votes, and of resolution, and increases the likelihood of negative emotion (worry).

Controlling for voting intentions three weeks before the election, we find, finally, that advance voters are also more likely to change their minds when they finally cast their vote than are absentee voters, suggesting that the visit to a polling station retains an emotionally and atmospherically cathartic influence even when it is not made on Election Day.

In short, the experience of a postal or internet voter is less emotionally fulfilling than that of a polling station goer, ideally on Election Day, but even on an earlier date. The postal or internet voter's experience is also be far less likely to induce a sense of societal inclusion and, and, critically, partly fails to achieve electoral resolution. It deprives voters of one of the key social benefits of elections: to make citizens feel (usually) part of their national community. We also note that whilst proxy voting raises a whole range of issues with regard to electoral equality, secrecy, and integrity, it has a lower emotional 'cost' than postal or internet voting, due to requiring interpersonal transaction with another voter as part as the electoral process, and thereby avoiding the 'condition of solitude', or a 'human disconnection', which is inherent to most remote voting solutions, notably postal and internet voting.

Electoral Ergonomics Case Study No. 2: A Tale of Two Generations?

IN-STATION VS POSTAL VOTING, AND SUPPORT FOR EXTREME RIGHT PARTIES

The next case study still focuses on the impact of geographically and temporally remote voting, but turns to a different dependent variable—electoral choice—and the additional puzzle that electoral ergonomics may have asymmetric effects on different types of voter, such that given design elements may work better for some voters than for others. In this second case study, we look at the specific impact of remote voting solutions on the vote of young voters as opposed to older, more experienced ones. We consider two sources. First, voting patterns in an actual general election in the UK, which offers postal voting as a default solution to any voters and typically has the highest take-up of all the countries in our study for that particular (geographical and temporal) remote voting option. Additionally, we consider the results of an experiment that we ran on the use of home internet voting, in countries including the UK and France, on participants aged fifteen to seventeen who had never had a chance to vote in an election before.

Postal voting is available as an alternative to polling station voting for all citizens in the UK without a need to provide any reason or justification. It has a differential generational impact, however, for two reasons. Firstly, empirically, older voters are far more likely to make use of this option, despite young voters being the primary target of the policy. Secondly, whilst elderly voters are more likely to use it for health and mobility reasons, young people often have difficulties predicting where they will be on the day of an election at the time they need to register to vote, if they study or their work situation is fluid. In principle, British electoral law allows citizens to register in multiple locations (such as both the place of study and where parents live) concurrently, as long as they are both genuine residences and citizens only exercise their right to vote once. However, multiple registration requires both commitment and visibility, and postal voting still requires an ability to receive mail at the address of registration, which is unhelpful where young people's residential uncertainty is due to possible moves. Consequently, young voters are more likely than average to be unable not just to attend their polling stations on Election Day, but also to vote postally, especially when the vote occurs during university holidays, as it did for the 2016 EU-membership referendum. Moreover, whilst the argument behind the facilitation of postal voting—to reduce the cost of voting—assumes the development of remote voting options to be aimed primarily at the younger generation, those young people are less likely than other generations to opt for it, because they also see this as decreasing the benefits of voting, making it less exciting and sacrificing the quality of an experience the importance of which for them we noted earlier. Lastly, and more surprisingly, geographically remote voting would appear to affect the electoral choices of different generations, and notably their likelihood of voting for the extreme right.

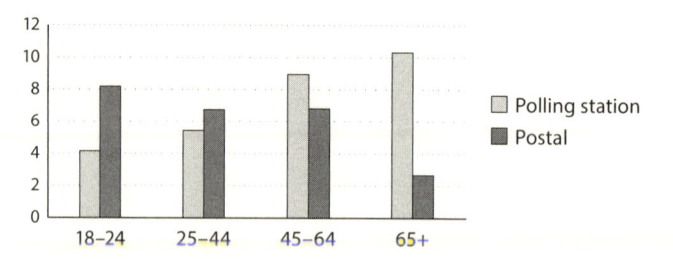

FIGURE 8.3: Vote for far right parties amongst polling station and postal voters by age group in the 2010 UK General elections

The results are shown in figure 8.3. Strikingly, among young voters, postal voting increased the likelihood to vote for the extreme right very significantly (+93% amongst eighteen- to twenty-four-year-olds, almost a doubling of the extreme right vote, and +25.5% amongst twenty-five- to forty-four-year-olds). The pattern does not hold true, however—and is in fact even reversed—for older generations. While this book has no normative message to deliver as to whether it is a good or a bad thing that some parties do better when remote voting is allowed, the difference it makes is analytically significant, particularly with regard to unhabituated voters. Moving elections away from polling stations, and from Election Day, is not 'electoral-choice neutral'.

Our findings also echo those of Cammaerts et al., (2014; 2016), who, using an experiment on young people aged fifteen to seventeen in six countries, found that those invited to vote over the internet have a lower turnout than those asked to visit a polling station. Participants were randomly divided into two groups for a mock election, with one group invited to vote in polling stations, and the second group to vote online. Convenience voting theory, highlighting the cost of voting as a key determinant of turnout, would lead us to expect more positive attitudes and higher turnout for the online voting group than for the traditional polling station group. The research found instead that online voting led to significantly more negative emotions and attitudes associated with the voting experience, and significantly lower turnout. On a happiness scale of zero to 2, happiness associated with the vote was 1.2 for polling stations voters and only 0.8 for online voters. Similarly, reported excitement was 0.2 points higher for polling station voters, and worry 0.2 points lower. In short, the experience of those young people whom the experiment required to vote on the internet was significantly more negative than that of those who went into a polling station.

Internet voting is regarded with enthusiasm by many Election Management Bodies worldwide. Not only does it drastically reduce electoral organization costs, but the argument is often put forward that it would likely resolve the crisis of youth participation, because internet and smartphone voting would fit in with young people's habits and intuitive modes of expression. Data suggest, however, that young people derive significantly more excitement and pleasure from participating in a traditional polling station electoral experience than from voting online. Thus, any reduction in the cost of voting achieved by internet voting is more than cancelled out by decreasing positive emotion associated with the vote. Combined as this is with notably lower turnout, the result is likely to be long-term turnout decline amongst the young people invited to vote online. While there are limits to the external validity of lab experiments, when the results of these are taken together with the UK election example discussed above, we find that Election Day and polling station experience are critical in making elections a formative and enjoyable social experience for young people, and fostering sense of inclusion and efficacy.

As many Election Management Bodies are considering ways to generalize station-less voting, our first two ergonomics case studies suggest that it is utterly untenable to assume that geographically remote voting is neutral with regard to electoral experience, and even behaviour. Instead, both temporal and geographical remoteness have significant negative effects on the positive emotions and attitudes associated with the vote. Moreover, we show that this impact is particularly negative for first-time voters, often seen as the prime target of efforts to lower the cost of voting, but who prove more than proportionally affected by the perceived worsening of the electoral experience. These findings are critical in understanding the real—and arguably potentially negative—consequences of some forms of remote voting for the long-term evolution of electoral satisfaction and turnout, as well as party fortunes.

Electoral Ergonomics Case Study No. 3: A Consequential Piece of Paper

We now move to a related technological advancement that many Election Management Bodies have already adopted and many more considered, and which we also mentioned at the start of this chapter: the dematerialization of ballot papers. For a long time, technology companies have proposed Election Management Bodies use various forms of electronic voting as opposed to paper ballots, for both in-station and remote voting. This is in addition to paper ballot designs themselves varying significantly across systems. This leads us to study the impacts of using a paper-based or electronic-based ballot in elections, as well as that of different paper designs. We focus on a very simple consequence: how long citizens think before casting their vote, our data deriving from the same visual experiment as was reported in chapter 7.

Ballot 'papers' can vary in a number of ways. First, as observed previously, they can actually be made of paper, or be electronic. Paper ballots themselves can vary significantly in design. In the US or in the Philippines, ballot papers will typically include votes for multiple elections on one single paper. In Germany too, two votes appear on the same ballot paper. By contrast, in the UK or in France, there is one ballot per vote, and therefore as many ballot papers as there are votes to be cast on a given Election Day. In France, sub-polling stations are organized for each of these separate votes, and citizens queue again and repeat full identification formalities for every one of them. In the US, ballot papers vary enormously across counties. In Palm Beach County, the ballot paper used for the controversial presidential election of 2000 was printed on both sides and punched in its centre, which resulted in multiple complaints and it being nicknamed a 'maze' by many voters and commentators. In countries with open list systems, it is not unusual to have the right to both 'tick' and 'cross' names on a same ballot paper, and in elections where the electoral system is either Single Transferable Vote or Alternative Voting (e.g., Ireland, Australia, London mayoral elections), numbers are generally used to rank candidates. In India, parties are represented using different colours, so that colour codes become a primary way for voters to signify their choice, regardless of literacy levels. In Japan, voters have to write the names of the parties or candidates whom they are voting for directly on the ballot paper. In the UK, crossing is the norm, but in parts of the former Soviet Union, it was more usual to circle one's choice, whilst many US counties will use either punch cards or optical-scan-ready ballot papers (whereby one blackens the little circle corresponding to one's choice). By contrast, in France, as in Israel, nothing should ever be written on a ballot paper, or it will invalidate it. Instead, ballot papers are individually pre-printed with the name of each party or candidate. The chosen one is to be enclosed in the envelope provided, without any alteration. In France, the pre-printed papers appear on a table, in randomly drawn order, and polling station officials regularly replenish the piles to ensure even stacks. Voters must take at least two ballot papers inside the fully curtained polling booth, to ensure the secrecy their vote, before disposing of unused ballot papers in large opaque rubbish bins. In Israel, the pre-printed ballots are instead placed on the polling booth wall in alphabetical order, and voters detach their choice. Parties are assigned a code (one, two, or three letters) which voters are expected to know, and parties, to maximize recognition, often fight for intuitively recognisable single letters (such as a party's or leader's initial), or series of two or three letters which spell out a memorable word (for instance, Netanyahu's Likud's letters spell 'forgiveness', while opposition Labour's three letters read 'truth'; Israel Beitenu's single letter is the initial of its leader, Liebermann; and religious party Shas and left-wing Meretz manage to spell their full names).

Electronic ballots also reach various levels of sophistication. In many US counties, voters use old-fashioned punched card voting machines, whereby they punch holes in their polling card which will then be fed into a computer system that will read and collate the results. Many developing countries, and others like Belgium, have chosen Direct Recording Voting machines, whereby the vote is recorded directly on a computer within the polling booth, without any physical ballot paper at all. However, Belgium is an unusual example, because whilst this is true of polling stations in large cities, smaller rural polling stations use traditional paper ballots instead. On the face of it, as many will think, all these are merely charming and colourful cultural differences that make no difference to the vote; but we experimentally test this assumption, and the effects of single or multiple, and paper or dematerialized ballots, on thinking time.

We tested these effects through the use of the visual experiment described in chapters 2 and 7, using three different ballot types: two paper-based ones (monopaper and polypaper) and one electronic one. There are good theoretical reasons to expect that thinking time will vary according to ballot design, and good scientific reasons to expect that this will matter. The former claim is based on two complementary sets of expectations arising from existing non-electoral literature. The first uses insights from the ample research that compares cognitive attention and response reaction time in the face of paper versus virtual information. Authors such as Kiesler and Sproull (1986), Boyer et al. (2002), and Shannon and Bradshaw (2002) and all highlight findings that illustrate that paper-based information elicits more thorough and more deliberate attention than electronically presented information. We expected that paper ballots would similarly lead to more careful deliberation than do electronic ballots, which would in turn translate into slower and longer decision times for the two paper-based ballots, as opposed to the electronic one. Additionally, we considered insights from priming theory, and particularly research on selective attention failure models (James, 1890; Neisser and Becklen, 1975; Miller, 1987) to assess the likely impact of monopaper and polypaper ballots. This literature suggests that materials design can not only result in positive object priming, but also that a consequent and corollary impact of this is attention failure when it comes to the objects that are not being primed. Eriksen and James (1986) note that priming can work as a 'zoom', and the implication of this is that while a primed object 'grows' in its visibility, other aspects of the picture are conversely excluded from the field of vision and decrease in importance, visibility, and consideration. Because voters typically come to the polling booth with a pre-existing (if not always conscious) voting intention, they will be primed to notice that choice and to omit its alternatives on a single paper. Selective attention failure will then be strong. However, the effect will evaporate with the use of multiple ballots, because unfocused vision disrupts the automaticity of priming effects—and thus of selective attention failure. In effect, voters are forced to consider each ballot paper, rather than be automatically drawn to their primed choice. On a synthetic and singular ballot, however, selective attention failure is facilitated, and omitted attention becomes automatic, thereby leading to a faster thinking process.

On the basis of these expectations, we hypothesized, firstly, that people voting using paper ballots will need more time to think of their vote than those who use electronic ('US') ballots; and, secondly, that the same will be true of voters needing to choose between multiple separate ballots ('French' system), as compared to those who are given a synthetic ('UK' or 'US' system) ballot. Indeed, the experimental results uncover very significant differences between the three procedures used in the experiment, based on the two conditions. The results are presented in figure 8.4, and show average thinking times of 21.6 seconds when using an electronic vote (standard deviation 14.6), 32.3 seconds when using a UK-style paper ballot (standard deviation 12.6), and 59.1 seconds with French-type ballots (standard deviation 19.0). Thus, voters spend roughly one and a half times longer thinking about their electoral choice with a paper as compared to an electronic ballot, and nearly three times longer when the alternative is a polypaper rather than monopaper ballot. We further ran a basic OLS regression to model thinking time in relation to the electronic or paper and single paper or polypaper nature of the ballot, controlling for gender and age. The results, in appendix 3, confirm that both paper support (b of 10.69, s.e. 1.95) and poly-

Thinking time by ballot type

- Electronic: 21.59
- UK: 32.30
- France: 59.14

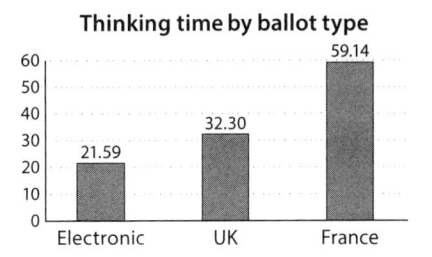

FIGURE 8.4: Decision time and type of ballot

paper ballots (b of 26.77, s.e. 1.69) have statistically significant and substantively meaningful impacts on thinking time, particularly the latter. Neither control variable has a statistically significant effect in our regression.

Neither paper materiality nor multiplicity has a statistically significant effect on electoral choice in our sample (though the sample size is limited). Even in the absence of a voting choice, however, the entire literature on deliberation (both in political science and in psychology) suggests that modifying the time citizens spend thinking over a critical choice may have a significant impact on their decision-making process and, in the present case, alter perceptions such as efficacy and satisfaction with democracy. In line with our theoretical model of selective attention failure, and our findings on vote change, it is also conceivable that the use of polypaper ballots may increase the likelihood of voters reconsidering their original voting intention whilst casting their final vote. This would further echo similar findings discussed earlier in this chapter, in relation to polling station voting (including advance voting) as compared to absentee voting.

Understanding the Full Effect of Electoral Ergonomics

Using three consecutive examples, we have shown that electoral ergonomics matters; that is, that small details of the organization of an election, from the design of the ballot paper to the choice of alternative modes of participation offered to those who are unable to visit a polling station on Election Day in the traditional manner, affect electoral attitudes, behaviour, experience, and resolution, either for the population in general or differently for specific groups. Crucially, no citizens would be consciously aware of these influences on their electoral experience and vote—so we have to move beyond citizens' declarations of how they make up their electoral minds, what they want, and ultimately their response, however sophisticated it may be, to perceived attempts by political institutions to shape, transform, or manipulate the organization of elections, if we want to understand the full impact of electoral ergonomics. Whilst we noted that young citizens' experiences tend to be more negative when voting online, which negatively affects their turnout, efficacy, and satisfaction, a large majority of people of that same age would say that they do want the option of being allowed to vote on the internet, and many would even suggest that it would increase the chance of them voting. Similarly, nobody would be consciously aware that whether they vote postally or in a polling station will effectively condition their likelihood of voting for particular parties. Election Management Bodies thus tend to react positively to populations explicitly asking to be given more ways to participate in elections remotely and informally, without needing to be constrained either geographically or temporally; whilst our experiments demonstrate that this can have important negative implications, not least in terms of harming voters' efficacy or even affecting their electoral choice, satisfaction, and long-term participation.

Throughout this book, we have insisted on the crucial need to ensure that our study of the psychology of voters does not rely solely on respondents' self-reporting either their decisions or the motivations and processes which shape them. The issue of ergonomics vibrantly demonstrates this need. Yet, many electoral behaviour experiments are survey based, and thus rely on self-reporting to measure changes in the dependent variable (usually electoral choice). It is quite likely that our visual experiment and quasi-experiments using variations in electoral organization would have reported different results if they had relied instead on self-reporting.

Interestingly, results seem coherent across the methods we used, including the visual experiment, which could serve as a useful alternative approach for research into electoral behaviour, whereby much of the electoral process and choice could in fact be observed, as long as strong and consistent measures were taken to ensure ethical protection of participants' privacy and anonymity. Because of the taboo surrounding the polling booth, such ethical safeguards were crucial to our experiment, and implied some sacrifice in terms of data nature, handling, and analysis. At the same time, using direct observation enabled us to capture a number of 'facts' about the act of voting, such as how long people think before casting their vote, both directly and accurately, without resorting to any form of self-reporting, relying instead on a method which is neither invasive nor unduly artificial, nor disturbing to participants and the polling station environment.

Visual experiments also have obvious limits. They are complex to organize under conditions that maintain a semblance of realism, are noninvasive and unobtrusive, and yet protective of the privacy and anonymity of the participants both during the experimental capture and in the later use, handling, and analysis of the data. Finally, there is an obvious element of interpretation of the visual evidence, which makes multiple coding critical, at least for emotions analysis. However, this no different from ample existing research conducted by zoologists, biologists, medical specialists, anthropologists, psychologists, or marketing scholars, and which consistently sheds new light on multiple facets of behaviour, particularly in highly secretive and taboo contexts like that of voters' conduct inside the polling booth. This is also why we paired our visual experiment with traditional survey-based experiments and quasi-experiments to confirm the impact of procedures usually deemed neutral by electoral organizers upon electoral attitudes, behaviour, experience, and sense of resolution. None of these effects would have been obvious from simple explicit survey measures.

It is crucial to note that the changes to voting procedures discussed here may have significant cumulative effects in the long run. If the use of internet and postal voting has negative effects on perceptions of external efficacy and satisfaction with electoral democracy, there is a risk that this will indirectly affect long-term turnout: we saw in chapter 6 that efficacy and projected efficacy are significant drivers of participation. Thus, electoral ergonomics may be a long-term modifier of electoral democracy. This is all the more important in that, as we have explained, our model of ergonomics as an interface between psychology and organization is not one of simple mechanics, but one rather of organizational variables which will trigger different personality traits, memories, and emotions, all of which would be subconscious. This also means that we cannot assume that voters would avoid choices of electoral arrangement that would in fact harm their own sense of democratic representation, efficacy, and satisfaction, since they would not necessarily be aware that they were doing so. In fact, measures aimed at improving voting opportunities and conditions may instead prove to be self-defeating options in the long run. In that regard, we should remember our findings concerning the differentiated effects of postal voting by age group. The differences noted may suggest that habituation (Dinas, 2012; Górecki, 2013, among others) may be relevant not only to turnout or electoral choice, but also to the more diffuse translation of the act of voting into senses of efficacy and representation. Older voters, used to traditional arrangements, may be more immune to the psycho-mechanical effects of electoral ergonomics than younger voters who may never have experienced another format of electoral arrangement.

Finally, our findings emphasize that the effects of electoral ergonomics, whilst very strong, are not idiosyncratic, one-off, or cancellable, but rather 'paths', the impact of which is cumulative over the course of one's voting life, because of its insidious 'triggering' effects, and the diffuse and lasting impact changed electoral experience may have on electoral identity and the emotions associated with the vote. Ergonomics is thus not about experimenting, but about shaping the representative link and voters' electoral identity in the long term. This leads us to return to the fundamental question of electoral resolution, and to some of the key concepts—such as electoral atmosphere and electoral hostility—that we associate with it in our model. In many ways, electoral resolution is the ultimate 'democratic goal' of elections at the societal level, and the acid test of their success. It is also, however, the main symptom of an apparently unprecedented transformation of electoral democracy, which we aim to reframe analytically.

9

Electoral Resolution and Atmosphere

FROM HOPE TO HOSTILITY

Electoral Resolution: Closing the Cycle

What is the point of elections, if not to resolve conflict and divisions within society? While this may be obvious to many political theorists, this fundamental end of electoral democracy is rarely acknowledged by behavioural studies, except in a few cases such as the 'Introduction' to Franklin et al. (1992). Arguably, elections are the grand shareholders' meetings of democracy, a regular event when those who often feel that their only power is to delegate their supposed sovereignty to a pre-set and exclusive group of candidates for power get a chance to test whether they can indeed be part of a majority able to, at least nominally, to inflect the political direction of their society. Franklin et al. follow the logical line of electoral choice studies, however, in wondering whether substantively resolving group rifts could end cleavages. By contrast, our book, focusing more on the voter's experience than on parties' fortunes, is interested in resolution per se—the capacity of elections to make citizens feel that democracy works, to give them a sense of temporary closure which will end an election cycle and start a new episode of democratic disagreement and mapped alternatives.

Earlier in this book, we raised the question of election cycles and noted that their behavioural logic—in terms of when an election cycle starts and ends—may differ from the institutional cycles logic which would have it that cycles should always start when a campaign does, and end when a result is announced. We explained that, intuitively, this does not always seem to be the case: that some results are contested by some voters without a cycle being allowed to end, while others may start well before an election is called, or encompass an incumbent's attempt at re-election. However, we have not fully spelt out the consequences of what may happen when an election fails to bring resolution and closure to citizens.

The consequence is an open conflict between behavioural and institutional cycles; a hiatus between an elected majority intending to exercise power and a part of the population disputing its legitimacy to do so. Such an extraordinary conflict between institutional and behavioural legitimacies has, in many ways, been so rare historically that behavioural scientists have hardly bothered even to consider the conditions for, consequences of, or solutions to such potentially dramatic democratic dissonance. Yet, in the period studied in this book, such dissonance has almost become the norm rather than the exception. In the US, a president is pursuing a policy programme which a significant part of the population is denouncing as undemocratic, amidst impeachment calls. In the UK, in 2019, , a prime minister intending to deliver a 'do or die' Brexit that does not include what he describes as an undemocratic 'backstop' was accused of himself being undemocratic by opponents who did not see him as having a mandate to take the country out of the European Union without a referendum on the final exit conditions that he agreed to. Neither this prime minister, nor his predecessor, nor their opponents seem to be in a position to gather majority popular support for any form of resolution to the thorny Brexit question, be it no deal, any deal, a new vote, or no Brexit. In France, the policies put forward by a president elected by two-thirds of the vote mere months previously are not accepted as democratic or legitimate by those who lost the election. In Italy and Belgium, supporters of irreconcilable ideologies keep hesitating between forming coalitions that they resent or provoking crises that they cannot handle, whilst in Spain and Israel, successive failures of voters to appoint clear winners, let alone of the opponents of these to accept anyone's legitimacy to govern, lead to repeated institutional impasse, followed by new elections, which revalidate more or less exactly the same unmanageable situations.

Electoral resolution—and its dual individual- and societal-level reality—is one of the three key interrelated dependent variables studied in this book, and this chapter is thus interested in the meaning, conditions, genesis, and implications of both electoral resolution and its alternative. In the next few pages, we interrogate the nature and condition of electoral atmosphere, the logic of election cycles, and the evolutions of citizens' feelings throughout the campaign, election, and aftermath period. We also explore what we believe to be the key ingredient of electoral resolution for both winners and losers: hope, and its alternative, hopelessness, and the sense that things at any rate 'can't get worse'. We unfold and analyze one key institutional consequence of electoral resolution: electoral honeymoons; and the deteriorative consequences of its alternative and of the failure of elections to bring closure: democratic hostility; primarily focusing on the US, the UK, and France. We also consider how change in the capacity of elections to generate electoral resolution has affected our period of study.

An Unprecedented Period?

Historical insight is like stepping away from a painting in a museum. Distance and an ability to look at the 'big picture' reveal a very different reality from what we saw when we stood so near a great master's work of art. What looked rather exceptional from up close suddenly becomes an almost negligible detail, whilst greater trends that were unnoticeable from a small distance suddenly make very different sense. Likewise, there is always a danger that what we believe to amount to change or uniqueness in a period that we are directly experiencing may prove to be mere 'noise' when we reconsider it years or decades later. The notion of electoral change (Inglehart, 1971; Franklin et al., 1992; Dalton, 1996, among others) has puzzled behaviour specialists for years, and they still cannot entirely agree on how deeply things changed over the 1980s and 1990s. Similarly, in coming years or decades, political scientists may well dismiss the seemingly profound changes that occurred in electoral democratic politics throughout the 2010s as a mere blip, and accuse us of over-dramatizing their importance. Whilst, lacking historical distance, we can use a pinch—or even a vat—of salt in estimating the scope of electoral change that occurred in the period, at first sight it might nevertheless appear rather exceptional, and the electoral landscape of 2019 seem profoundly different from that of 2010.

Longitudinal studies always start blind to the historical dynamics that will affect a project. Yet, anecdotally, in terms of contextual, historical, and electoral change in the six countries which we study in this book, a number of iconic evolutions can be immediately evoked. As regards the US, our project started at the height of Obama's first term, to end after the election (with the support of a majority of electoral college delegates, but not of the popular vote) of Donald Trump as president of a highly fractured United States. For the UK, our fieldwork started in the last months of the most durable period of Labour government in history to continue through three general elections, two of which produced (extremely rare) hung parliaments, and two major referenda (on Scottish independence and EU membership) that split their regions and countries, not to mention three successive Conservative prime ministers all equally unable to unite the nation—or even their own party—with regard to its relationship to the European Union. In South Africa, the end of the Mandela era transformed politics into a legitimacy crisis that embroiled Jacob Zuma and the ANC, with the historic party of post-apartheid South Africa losing control of most large cities in 2016 in the first truly competitive elections of South Africa's contemporary electoral history, before Zuma was forced to resign and be replaced by Cyril Ramaphosa. In France, an unpopular Nicolas Sarkozy was replaced by a soon even more unpopular François Hollande. Yet, at the time when most predicted that France would thus be the ideal victim of the continent's populist surge, the two historical left and right blocs were jointly defeated not by the extremes, but by an unprecedented promise of non-populist change, embodied in the victory of Emmanuel Macron and his civil society-grounded team, in a development watched with close attention by much of the world. Georgia mourned another attack on its territorial integrity by Russian troops, but also saw the replacement of its historical democratization forces by another billionaire-led team, before both parties started losing ground in elections. Comparatively, Germany looked like a prime example of electoral stability until almost the very end, persistently reconfirming Angela Merkel in power from 2005. Yet, in 2017, the country's status quo was also shaken, by traumatic terror attacks and further by divisions over the appropriate response to the influx of refugees from the Middle East, as the AfD (Alternative für Deutschland: 'Alternative for Germany') made a dramatic entrance into the Bundestag, and the two main government parties achieved their worst results in democratic history, to be forced into yet another grand coalition that both deeply resent, amidst respective leadership crises.

Elections without Government?

Such developments are not unique to the six countries covered in this book. Like France in 2017, Greece, Canada, and Israel have seen the emergence of new political forces forcing complete shifts in alliances or precipitating the collapse of historically dominant parties. Even more strikingly, however, the inability of elections to produce straightforward majorities, in states unused to such instability, reaches well beyond the British case. We have mentioned the two hung parliaments produced by three UK general elections between 2010 and 2017; similarly, in Australia, the 2010 elections gave seventy-two seats each to the Labor and Liberal-National blocs, with a single Green MP holding the balance of power between them; a most unusual situation for the country. Sweden, New Zealand, and Spain also experienced ungovernable or hung parliaments. In Spain and Israel, the scenario even repeated itself immediately, when the failure of elections to produce clear majorities led governments to call early new elections—only for the same majority-less situation to be reconfirmed. The Austrian 2016 presidential election led to a result so contested (with ergonomics implications) that the election was invalidated and re-run.

These situations involving impossible or unworkable majorities raise questions as to whether elections can still function as democratic resolution mechanisms. In some cases, the election winners might find it hard to enact any policy change for lack of a clear majority, thereby frustrating their voters. In other cases, those who voted for the losing party or candidates may find it hard to consider the winners legitimate, in view of the lack of a sufficiently obvious democratic mandate. In cases like Italy, Belgium, or the UK in 2010, majorities could only be found via coalitions so counter-intuitive that they would go on to produce policies wholly unexpected by individual coalition parties' voters. In all such cases, voters may feel frustrated, angry, or even start resenting other voters whose frustrations and wishes they find to be at odds with their own, as all sides require modes of political resolution that may go beyond what institutional logic can automatically produce. This, in turn can feed a trend that we label in this chapter *electoral hostility* (whereby citizens' long-held negative feelings towards political elites degenerate into negative feelings and emotions towards voters who do not share their preferences). We distinguish this from the partisan polarization and affective polarization models (see later in this chapter) by suggesting that it does not necessarily follow partisan divisions, nor principally affect citizens who strongly identify with parties or even care about politics. This phenomenon seems increasingly widespread by the end of the period under study, in Britain, the US, France, and beyond.

This chapter analyzes whether elections still function as resolution mechanisms in the six countries studied, throughout the period—focusing specifically on the US or the UK to test central concepts such as electoral atmosphere, honeymoons, and hostility—and what the outcome actually means. It also deals with concepts such as closure, hope, and hopelessness, and unwraps the notion of 'election cycle', suggesting that changes in the ability of elections to provide closure and resolution creates a fundamental diachrony with regard to institutional and behavioural conceptions of election cycles. The chapter mostly focuses on individual case studies to decipher some of the key transformations, new fracture lines, and in some cases threats, and assesses whether something may have changed for good in electoral politics, reanalyzing some of the historical transformations that affected electoral democracies during the 2010s.

Deciphering the Atmosphere of Elections: Two British Case Studies

As noted in chapter 3, an odd, impressionistic concept gets mentioned repeatedly in our interviews (and by politicians and the media): 'electoral atmosphere'. While many may be tempted to dismiss the concept as too fluid for science, historical trends highlighted in the previous section suggest that the notion of national mood cannot be entirely dismissed, and that somehow, positive and negative electoral 'vibes' and ambiences are created at the societal level that can apparently exceed the sum of individual perceptions. At the aggregate level, one can of course think of many objective factors that may influence this national electoral mood. Some have been widely studied as part of our endeavour to understand context (chapter 2): the economic situation, protest movements, candidates' personality, negative campaigning, and various aspects of incumbency. Beyond these supposedly objective factors, however, some more diffuse and impressionistic elements are frequently present in the minds of voters when it comes to characterizing a nebulous 'atmosphere' of elections which makes spontaneous intuitive sense to many people. Elections are decidedly described as 'atmospheric'. Some are perceived as tense, exciting, refreshing, gloomy, hopeful, or simply rotten. Their atmosphere may change through the electoral period—during the campaign, on Election Day, during Election Night, or even in its aftermath—raising the question of when an election cycle really ends. Many citizens pick up intangible signals that make up that atmosphere and shape their perceptions, behaviour, and reactions during the election, along with their views of candidates and of each other, and of the congruence or difference between their own electoral preference and the outcome of the vote.

Rather than dismissing the concept of electoral atmosphere as excessively fluid and impressionistic, we thus take it at face value, because it shapes citizens' electoral experience and behaviour, according to their own words. It also affects citizens' reading of the election and its outcomes, both at the time and retrospectively, in memory. It may be that somehow, collectively, they pick that electoral atmosphere, the mood of the period, in ways which are both coherent and meaningful, varying across and within elections. In chapter 2, we noted that 'atmosphere' is a concept taken seriously in disciplines such as architecture, arts, and marketing, related to such elements of organization and fittings as lighting and staging, but transforming and amplifying the reality of these, and their legacy. Similarly, humans perceive and are affected by the atmosphere of a place, a view, a play, a shop, or a family meal. They will often describe it in surprisingly similar terms, making up atmospheric scales which can also be applied to elections.

To illustrate the nature and variation of the perceived atmosphere of elections, we focus on the case study of the UK, and a comparison between two recent votes: the 2016 referendum on EU membership, and the 2017 general election. In both cases, we used a mixture of open and closed survey questions, first asking respondents to give us the first three words that came to their minds to describe the atmosphere of the election, then asking them to characterize it based on a closed list of potential adjectives. The first measure enables us to capture the spontaneous perception of the atmosphere of two elections that were experienced by the same public within a relatively short period of time (less than a year), and the second enables us to compare systematically how a number of potential atmospheric descriptions corresponded to each of these elections in the voters' minds.

The results of the spontaneous characterization of electoral atmospheres are shown in table 9.1. After merging very similar words (e.g., 'fearmongering' and 'scaremongering', 'great' and 'amazing', 'split' and 'divisive', etc.), we report, in order of frequency, all the words that represent at least 1% of total mentions (in bold), and other unique references made by over twenty respondents (i.e., words spontaneously used by at least twenty respondents to describe one of the votes but not the other). We code three main connotations: positive, negative-accusatory (hostility, belligerence, stupidity, etc.), and negative-regretful (boredom, predictability, stress, etc.). Atmospheric references are overwhelmingly negative. Fourteen and eleven words respectively account for at least 2% of total descriptions of the atmosphere of the EU-membership referendum and general election. In both cases, only one such word is positive ('exciting' for the referendum, and 'hopeful' for the general election). All others are negative. Moreover, the words used to

TABLE 9.1. Spontaneous Electoral Atmosphere References: 2016 UK Referendum & 2017 UK General Election

2016 EU membership referendum (%)		2017 general election (%)	
Divisive	**5.57**	*Boring/Tiring*	*5.29*
Lying	**4.75**	*Apathetic/Blasé*	*3.99*
Tensed	*4.48*	Hopeful	3.58
Confusing	*3.64*	*Wasteful/Futile*	*3.34*
Unpredictable/Unsettled	*3.62*	*Hopeless/Resigned*	*3.00*
Hostile/Hateful	**3.13**	*Predictable/Obvious*	*2.80*
Exciting	3.11	*Unpredictable/Unsettled*	*2.78*
Belligerent	**2.80**	**Lying**	**2.75**
Deceptive/Cheating	**2.73**	*Frustrating*	*2.56*
Racist/Xenophobic	**2.37**	*Worrisome*	*2.45*
Fearful	*2.26*	*Confusing*	*2.41*
Angry	**2.26**	Exciting	1.95
Ignorant	**2.13**	*Depressing/Devastating*	*1.85*
Emotional	2.04	**Deceptive/Cheating**	**1.76**
Stressful/Suffocating	*1.97*	*Fearful*	*1.71*
Happy/Fun	1.97	**Divisive**	**1.65**
Toxic/Poisonous	**1.80**	*Conservative*	*1.58*
Worrisome	*1.80*	*Stressful/Suffocating*	*1.39*
Adversarial/Aggressive	**1.77**	Positive/Optimistic	1.37
Frustrating	*1.73*	Historic/Important	1.28
Bigoted/Fanatical	**1.58**	*Tensed*	*1.24*
Bitchy/Bitter	**1.42**	Changing/Different	1.24
Manipulative	**1.40**	**Bigoted/Fanatical**	**1.19**
Awful/Evil	**1.33**	Happy/Fun	1.17
Good/Great/Amazing	1.22	**Forceful/Dominant**	**1.17**
Uncomfortable	*1.20*	Brexit	1.17
Hysterical/Hyperbolic	**1.09**	**Belligerent**	**1.15**
Shameful/Shocking	**1.09**	**Angry**	**1.11**
Boring/tiring	*1.04*	**Awful/Evil**	**1.04**
Nasty	**1.02**	**Arrogant/Patronizing**	**1.04**
Stupid/Daft	**1.02**	**Obnoxious**	**1.02**
...	...	...	...
Scaremongering	0.69	Labour	0.85
Relieving	0.55	*Hasty/Rushed*	*0.80*
Honest/Factual	0.49	*Repetitive*	*0.78*
Solidary	0.47	**Distrusting**	**0.74**
Backstabbing/Betraying	**0.44**	**Unfair**	**0.70**
Misguided	**0.44**	Relaxed	0.67
		Comical/Circus	**0.61**
		Necessary	0.61
		Costly	**0.52**
		Lackluster	*0.50*
		Expectant	0.50
		Tragic	*0.50*
		Uninspiring	*0.48*
		Criminal	**0.46**

Note: Boldface: negative mobilizing; italic: negative demobilizing; normal font: positive.

TABLE 9.2. Descriptors of Recent Electoral Atmosphere in the UK (Closed-question response)

Best atmosphere descriptors	Mean (0–10) + standard deviation
Tense	*6.59 (2.68)*
Fractious	**6.23 (2.76)**
Apprehensive	*6.04 (2.72)*
Democratic	5.87 (2.99)
Aggressive	**5.67 (2.88)**
Exciting	4.76 (3.04)
Stimulating	4.65 (2.81)
Constructive	4.04 (2.84)
Vulgar	**4.00 (3.15)**
Solemn	3.84 (2.72)
Respectful	3.51 (2.59)
Mysterious	3.29 (2.90)
Solidary	3.25 (2.66)

Note: Boldface: negative mobilizing; italic: negative demobilizing; normal font: positive.

describe the atmosphere of the two elections vary significantly. Of those top fourteen and eleven words, only three are shared (all negative): 'lying', 'unpredictable/unsettled', and 'confusing'.

The negative atmosphere associated with the EU-membership referendum largely focuses on accusatory concepts relating to divisions, aggressiveness, and disrespect: for instance, 'hostile', 'belligerent', 'deceptive', and 'racist/xenophobic'. By contrast, the main equally negative descriptions of the atmosphere of the 2017 general election are (in the psychological sense) demobilizing: 'boring', 'apathetic/blasé', 'futile', 'hopeless', 'predictable', 'frustrating', and 'worrisome'. Beyond references to the lies and confusion, most voters also see both electoral atmospheres as stressful, deceptive, frustrating, and fanatical. On a more positive note, references to excitement and happiness are frequent in both cases, partly balancing otherwise negative atmospheric perceptions.

The closed question findings shown in table 9.2 are similar. Despite equal numbers of proposed positive and negative descriptors, negative qualifications—both accusatory and demobilizing—overwhelmingly dominate voters' characterization of the atmosphere of both elections, with an emphasis on them being tense, fractious, and characterized by apprehension and to a lesser extent aggressiveness (though also democratic). The biggest standard deviation concerns the exciting nature of the atmosphere, which polarizes respondents. Such a degree of negativity may well constrain elections' ability to provide resolution, and make it impossible truly to bring closure to an election cycle.

ON THE NATURE OF ELECTION CYCLES

Our findings on electoral atmosphere also raise important questions as to how and when electoral atmosphere settles and changes over time. We mentioned that 20–30% of voters typically make up or change their minds during the final week of the electoral period, half of them on Election Day; and in chapter 8, we also confirmed that temporally remote voting leads to differences in electoral perceptions and experience compared to Election Day voting. All this is revealing of the nature and dynamics of election cycles as experienced by citizens, and we have already ventured the suggestion that the behavioural perceptions of those cycles may depart from the more straightforward institutional logic often relied on by the literature.

We therefore use respondents' daily and weekly entries to their election diaries to assess election cycles as experienced by them, focusing on the case of France. In this case, we look at the occurrence of a number of themes and connotations in their entries, highlighting the turning points of the electoral mood throughout the voting period. Results are presented in figure 9.1, and show how the voters' moods change through the election period.

Initially, two to three weeks before Election Day, the election is an abstract notion, eliciting institution-centric references and considerations of choice (i.e., the democratic decision to be made). This declines later. Respondents often focus on electoral ergonomics, as though trying to recreate the voting scene that they will join. In this initial phase, positive and negative references are both limited, and emotional and projective references virtually absent. Voters overwhelmingly embrace a 'supporter' identity at that stage of the election, and resist internalizing the election or associating it with anything personal or experiential.

In the second stage, the week before the vote, the situation has already changed. Negative references have now multiplied fivefold, and emotional ones by 2.5, whilst institutional and choice references remain high. At the same time, however, ergonomic references and thinking of elections as a citizenship right have declined significantly to make room, instead, for a sense of responsibility. When it comes to electoral identity, the supporter point of view is stable and still dominant, but, 'referee' references, absent at stage 1, also increasingly emerge.

ELECTORAL RESOLUTION AND ATMOSPHERE 273

a.

Electoral references throughout the election cycle

- Positive
- Negative
- Emotional
- Sociotropic
- Projective
- Atmospheric
- Ergonomic
- Experience/personal
- Symbolic

b.

- Right/citizenship
- Responsibility/duty
- Choice/democracy
- Change
- Referee
- Supporter
- Institution centric
- Excitement

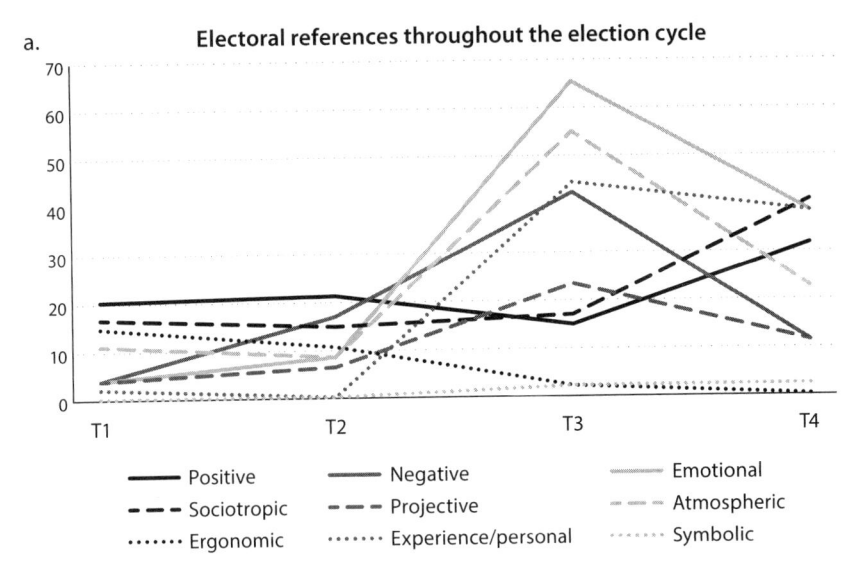

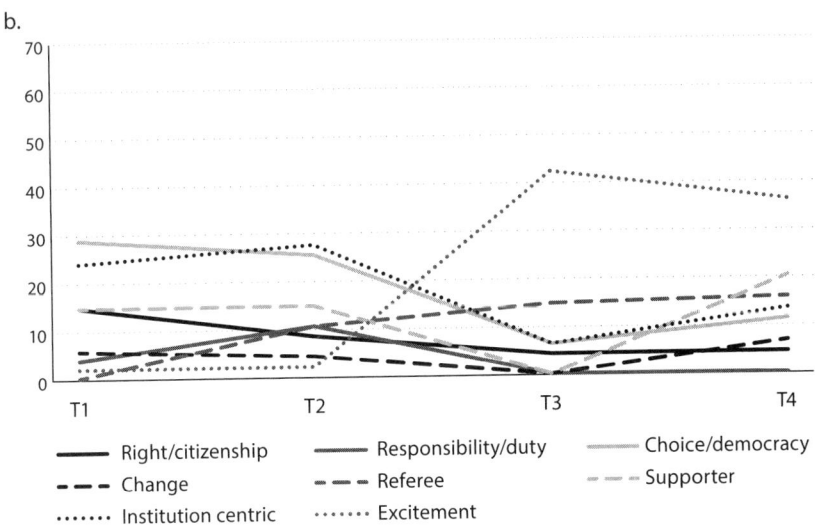

FIGURE 9.1 A AND B: Electoral references throughout the election cycle—French example

Stage 3 corresponds to Election Day for the first round of the presidential election, which in France, arguably, only marks the beginning of the voting sequence, almost like primary elections in the US. By then, implicit perceptions of elections have changed radically. There is notably a sharp increase in emotional, atmospheric, and internalized (personal) references. The election has ceased to be an external and institutional phenomenon, to become a very emotional and personal event which voters appropriate and experience directly, in line with our internalization model. The election has become atmospheric and societally projective, meaning that citizens have started to articulate their personal electoral experience and preference with those of the nation. Excitement increases spectacularly (references multiplied by twenty), to a peak. Synchronically, however, negative references also increase significantly. Abstract references to democracy, choice, citizenship, and rights have reduced considerably, as have institutional differences. Electoral identity has largely switched from supporter to referee, with referee references evening out in the final week and dominating by Election Day.

Stage 4, finally, corresponds to Election Night of the second election round. The election mood has become far more sociotropic, with such references multiplied by 2.5, to reach their peak. Positive references meanwhile double, to peak, whilst negative references are divided by four, to reach their second lowest level overall. Emotional, personal, experiential, and atmospheric references all decline slightly compared to the first round, but remain very high. By Election Night, both referee and supporter references are at their highest in the entire period, which may also explain both the potential for a honeymoon period of hope and reconciliation on the part of referees, and for the anchoring of hostility feelings on the part of supporters. References to elections in terms of duty and responsibility have completely disappeared, references to elections as a right of citizenship are minimal, and references to choice and democracy remain significantly lower than during the campaign.

By the end of the cycle, the election—once abstract and institutional—has become personal, internalized, experiential, atmospheric, exciting, and emotional. It has been absorbed into citizens' own lives—critically, beyond winning and losing issues. It is that personal and emotional take which has the potential powerfully to shape the electoral aftermath.

Glimmers of Hope and the Concept of the Electoral Honeymoon

This cycle of emotionality and Election Day climax mean that as the election process reaches its end, voters are normally at their most emotional and at their most connected with both system and community. Central to this positive reconnection is the notion of hope. In chapter 3, we saw that hope was one of the prime drivers of citizens' electoral experience and constant in their polling booth thoughts. However, reconsidering those findings in the light of electoral resolution and societal change, what does hope actually entail, and what are its conditions?

A recurrent spontaneous reference is that elections offer voters the ability to effect *change*. In fact, change is one of the prospects voters hold in highest esteem in their electoral thoughts. In qualitative evaluations, there is positivity associated with new beginnings and a specific value ascribed to parties and candidates seen as potentially different from the rest and from what voters have already experienced, which seemingly contradicts the logic of the phenomenon known as 'incumbency advantage'. This change can pertain to many of the electoral functions discussed in chapter 6, from policy direction to accountability (and getting rid of a disappointing incumbent). However, such initial conceptions of hope relate to electoral choice, and are thus putatively only relevant to those whose electoral preference is vindicated in the election.

By contrast, if we think of electoral hope rather in relation to electoral experience and resolution, that condition becomes irrelevant. In chapter 3, we saw that elections are largely seen as a democratic ritual and token of ownership of the political system by citizens. We suggested that through electoral resolution, this ritual boosts satisfaction with the democratic process in and of itself., We claim that, by 'contagion', it will benefit the way in which those who have won by means of such processes are perceived, even by voters who did not vote for them, but experienced the feeling of democratic ownership associated with the electoral process. Thus, as an institutional process and experience, an election will boost citizens' hope in the system, regardless of whether their preferred choice won or lost. We relate this phenomenon to the notion of 'electoral honeymoon', whereby the popularity of new election winners typically exceeds the proportion of voters who voted for them. We suggest that this is not caused by voters converting to the majority choice, but rather to the electoral experience itself, restoring citizens' faith in the process in a way that benefits the victors not as specific politicians or parties, but as the procedural output of the election.

We used panel data to test a very simple hypothesis: that the valence of the spontaneous visions of electoral democracy held by citizens differs before the start of and after the end of the electoral period. In other words, if we ask citizens a few weeks before an election what words they spontaneously associate with the concept 'elections' and compare their answers to what they say on Election Night, will those spontaneous associations have become more negative (hopelessness) or positive (hope)? We use the case

276 CHAPTER 9

a. **Electoral references—pre-election**

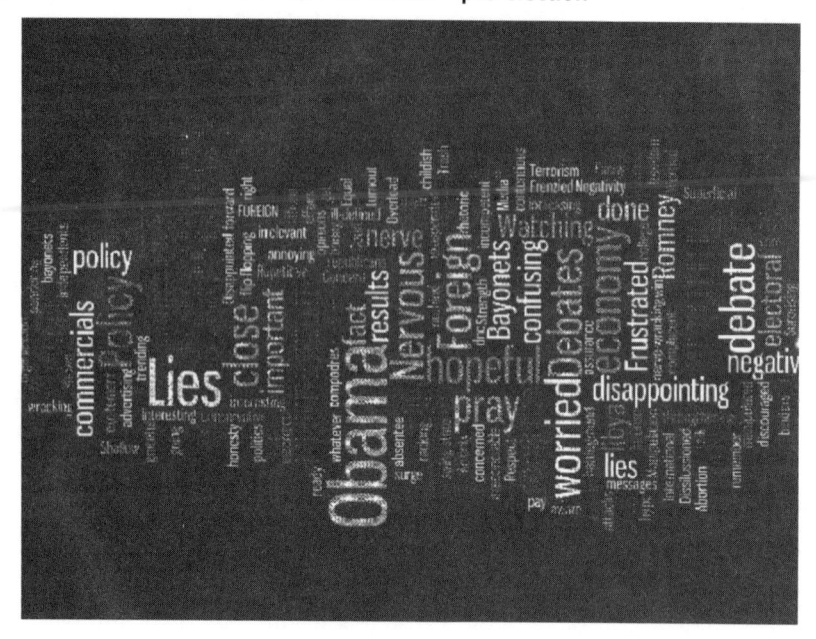

b. **Electoral references—election night**

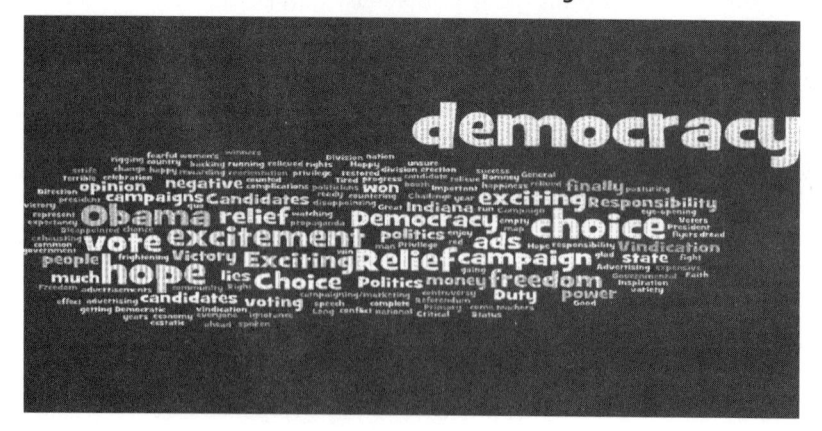

FIGURES 9.2.A-9.2.B: Word clouds: spontaneous election thoughts pre-election and during Election Night

study of the 2012 US presidential elections. The results are mapped in the word clouds in figures 9.2.a and 9.2.b.

Three weeks before the vote, the election evoked partly neutral and largely negative, but very rarely positive, associations. The most frequent reference is 'Obama', the incumbent, which illustrates our earlier suggestion that presidential incumbency can effectively prevent the start of the new election cycle and prolong, instead, the cycle introduced by the previous presidential election. The other main words brought to people's minds are overwhelmingly negative. They encompass references such as 'lies', 'worried', 'foreign', 'nervous', 'frustrating', and 'disappointing'. 'Debates' is the only frequent neutral reference. By contrast, by Election Night, connotations are distinctly more positive. By far the most frequently used word is 'democracy', followed by 'choice', 'hope', and 'relief'. The name of the election winner, Obama, is frequent, but less so than pre-election. Other words frequently chosen include 'excitement, and 'freedom', and none of the negative references of the pre-election wave appear frequently.

Crucially, the switch to greater positivity is true both of those who voted for Barack Obama, and, more importantly, of those who voted for Mitt Romney, who lost the election. This highlights a process of reconciliation and convergence constitutive of the honeymoon effect, which brings the winner support from quarters that did not vote for him/her. It may even shed new light on the process of rationalization of respondents when asked about their vote after an election (there are almost systematically higher proportions of citizens claiming to have voted for the winner than actually did), as a number of voters genuinely warm to the winners as a result of sheer procedural and democratic legitimacy.

'It Can't Possibly Get Worse, Anyway'

What of occasions when such legitimization does not occur, however? According to early post-election analyses, a symptomatic commonality between the 2016 UK referendum and the US presidential election of the same year is that many of those who voted for Brexit and for Trump seemed to be expressing some form of despair. Most experts had warned that the courses of action associated with Trump and Vote Leave proposals were based on unrealistic claims and doomed to produce economic, social, and/or political catastrophes. Many political scientists have wondered why so many voters apparently believed that such policies could prove successful; but what if, instead, the driver of their choice was a perception that 'things can't possibly get worse, anyway'?

Such feelings may not necessarily be identified by voters themselves as the explicit reason for their choice—in fact many may claim that their vote was indeed motivated by some genuine hope of change. Nevertheless, on the whole, despair and alienation can be uniquely disinhibiting, and perceptions

Hopelessness by country

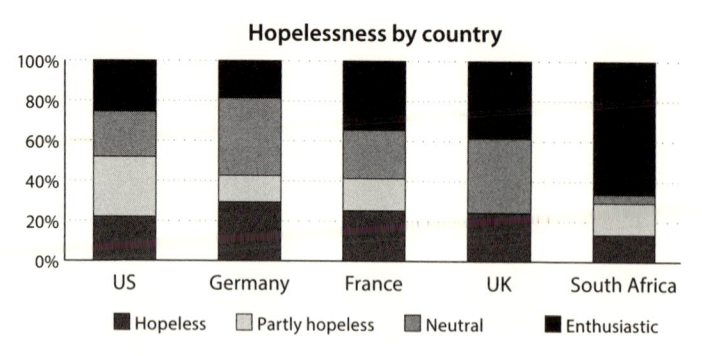

[Bar chart showing percentages for US, Germany, France, UK, South Africa across categories: Hopeless, Partly hopeless, Neutral, Enthusiastic]

FIGURE 9.3: Happiness with vote—Hopelessness by country

that things have become so bad that they could not possibly get worse were shared by many of our 2016 US and UK interviewees. In earlier surveys, one question particularly targeted the idea that voters may cast a ballot out of hopelessness: respondents were asked whether they voted out of enthusiasm for a party or candidate, or only as a choice of 'the lesser of evils'. The results are presented in figure 9.3.

Across countries, about a quarter of respondents admit to voting 'hopelessly' (i.e., for the 'lesser evil'), and in countries where multiple votes were held (either concurrently or across two ballots), an additional 15–30% voted 'partly hopelessly' (i.e., there was no candidate that they liked in at least one of the votes). By comparison, another quarter to one-third of voters voted either without enthusiasm or for a party/candidate that they truly supported. The only exception is South Africa, where 65% of voters cast a fully convinced vote. Complete or partial hopelessness affected in total 52.7% of voters in the US, 42.7% in Germany, and 42.4% in France (despite Germany and France having multi-party systems with many parties/candidates to choose from). In the UK, only one election was examined, in 2015, and hopelessness affected 25.3% of voters. This may have changed in 2017, but the question was not asked then.

Arguably, of course, things are never so bad that they could not get even worse. Moreover, most chaos and disaster warnings suggest that the very people who think that things could not get worse would typically be the hardest hit by the consequences of their own vote, such as inflation and a collapsing British pound due to Brexit, and the depletion of social protection mechanisms in the US. However, beyond the possible irrationality of the assessment itself, the feeling that things cannot get worse is powerfully disinhibiting for citizens who feel that they have exhausted other options and are willing to take the risk of 'blowing' the whole system to achieve change. Conversely, the absence of electoral hope and fearlessness of further deterioration are often implicitly the two sides of the very same coin, expressed sequentially, with voters first warning of their hopelessness before acting on their despair.

Generational Projection as an Antidote to Hopelessness

A noteworthy aspect of electoral hope—as opposed to hopelessness—is its reliance on long-term and generational projection. As hinted in chapter 3, a large proportion of citizens bases its entire electoral narrative on projection into the life conditions of future generations, and on long-term progress. We found important comparative and individual differences, with longitudinal and generational projection implicitly used as coping mechanisms by those who simultaneously express short-term negativity. We notably highlight the case of Georgia, where low turnout and high levels of dissatisfaction towards the main parties is nonetheless compatible with high levels of long-term optimism (79.6%) and high levels of generational projection (82.6%). Most Georgians have little hope for future improvements to their democracy and life, but many still maintain hope that in the longer term, their—or at any rate their children's—lives will improve significantly. This long-term perspective is also illustrated by the fact that 77.5% of Georgian respondents focused on a desire to see their country join the European Union, and an insistence on their European identity, whilst at the same expressing little to no interest in joining any other international or regional alliance.

In many ways, generational and longitudinal projections differentiate between pessimism and hopelessness, disappointment and frustration. Whilst large numbers of respondents, across the countries studied in this book, express dissatisfaction and disillusion with politics, it is fundamentally when citizens stop believing that their children will live better lives than themselves that this dissatisfaction turns into hopelessness. Disappointment and pessimism are not in and of themselves conditions sufficient to disinhibit political attitudes and behavior and open the road to support for radicalism and populism. The loss of the aptitude for longitudinal or generational positive projection is such a condition, however. At times, that hopelessness may also generate hostility.

Expressions of Hostility

A comparison the US and the UK at the beginning and at the end of the period covered by this book is striking. By the second part of the 2010s, it had become clear that the process of electoral honeymoon and reconciliation noted in both countries in 2010 and 2012 did not materialize any more. To make things worse, anecdotal evidence from our in-depth interviews suggested that perceptions of fellow voters are increasingly personal, and notably so when it comes to people who (are perceived to) vote differently. We thus started to explore systematically whether a form of electoral hostility had emerged. The analytical need to consider a model of hostility, rather than simply buy into models of affective partisan polarization, was driven by three anecdotal indications from the qualitative evidence. First, negativity towards fellow voters was not necessarily based on partisan identities. In the UK, Brexit fracture lines had largely trumped partisan ones. The notion that a referendum debate can generate its own identity more or less immediately, as has sometimes been claimed, seems frankly untenable, psychologically, and it seems rather that the Brexit rift became a proxy for deeper, older fractures that we had actually already uncovered in our earlier work on identity, as early as 2008–2012. Second, contrary to the affective polarization logic, hostile feelings did not seem to be primarily expressed by people who felt strongly in favour of Democrats, Republicans, Leave, or Remain. The affective polarization model implies that negative feelings are simply commensurate with strength of affiliation; but here, we had people expressing hostility who would not even vote in elections or referenda, and would sometimes even jointly equally hate the supporters of both camps. Third, there seemed to be an eminently psychological 'spiral of negativity', leading to ever-deteriorating hostile feelings, starting with a sense of inability to understand others but later degenerating into frustration, anger, contempt, disgust, and enmity.

We thus started by asking respondents open questions about the first three words that came to their minds when they were thinking of people who voted differently from them in the election. There was a certain ambiguity to the question. Most respondents took it as an invitation to characterize opposite voters, but a minority focused instead on their own feelings towards antagonistic voters. Rather clear patterns emerge with regard to prejudicial perceptions of those meaningful electoral others, and it is a picture of overwhelming negativity (nor does this go without saying: opposite

Spontaneous hostility references

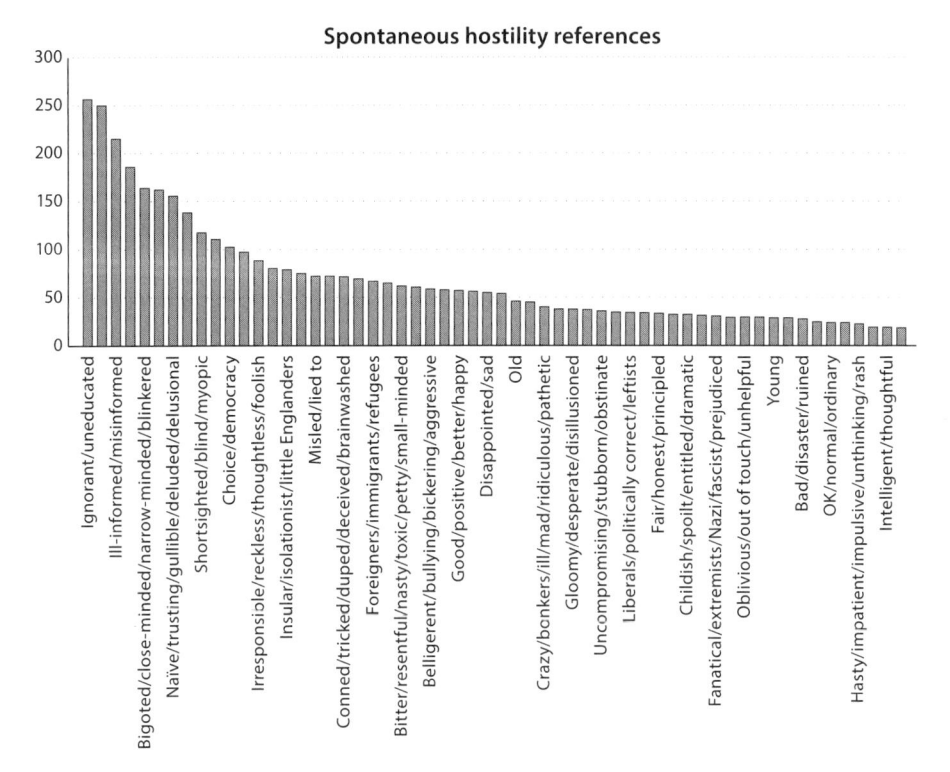

[Bar chart showing spontaneous hostility references in descending order: Ignorant/uneducated; Ill-informed/misinformed; Bigoted/close-minded/narrow-minded/blinkered; Naïve/trusting/gullible/deluded/delusional; Shortsighted/blind/myopic; Choice/democracy; Irresponsible/reckless/thoughtless/foolish; Insular/isolationist/little Englanders; Misled/lied to; Conned/tricked/duped/deceived/brainwashed; Foreigners/immigrants/refugees; Bitter/resentful/nasty/toxic/petty/small-minded; Belligerent/bullying/bickering/aggressive; Good/positive/better/happy; Disappointed/sad; Old; Crazy/bonkers/ill/mad/ridiculous/pathetic; Gloomy/desperate/disillusioned; Uncompromising/stubborn/obstinate; Liberals/politically correct/leftists; Fair/honest/principled; Childish/spoilt/entitled/dramatic; Fanatical/extremists/Nazi/fascist/prejudiced; Oblivious/out of touch/unhelpful; Young; Bad/disaster/ruined; OK/normal/ordinary; Hasty/impatient/impulsive/unthinking/rash; Intelligent/thoughtful]

FIGURE 9.4: Spontaneous hostility reference

voters could well be seen merely as having different opinions!) This was divided into two distinct categories: 'regretful' negativity, and aggressive or 'disparaging' negativity. The words that citizens spontaneously associate with people who voted differently from them in the 2017 UK general election are reported in figure 9.4.

In descending order of importance, the ten main references used by respondents are: 'ignorant'; 'idiotic'; 'ill-informed'; 'racist'; 'bigoted'; 'selfish'; 'naïve'; 'wrong'; 'short-sighted'; and 'hateful/hostile'; and only in eleventh place, 'exercising a democratic choice'. Other key references include 'irresponsible', 'insular', 'dishonest', 'conned', 'bitter', 'weak', 'toxic', or 'bullying', 'moaners', and 'sheep', along with characterizations of social status (e.g., 'middle class' or 'rich'), foreignness, political preferences (e.g., 'liberals', 'socialists', etc.) or age ('old' or 'young'). Extreme references to 'extremists/Nazis', 'traitors' or 'un-British' or 'morons', or the use of various insults, are all fairly recurrent, if thankfully rarer. In parallel, respondents also refer to their own attitudes towards those other voters employing terms such as 'scared', 'confused', 'angry', 'unpredictable', 'disappointing', 'frustrating', 'distrusting', or even 'disgusting'. References implying acceptance are, by contrast, marginal.

On the whole, the often violent negativity of references is terrifying. References to feeling good or positive about people who vote differently from the respondent only come in twenty-seventh position; thinking of them as fair or principled takes forty-first place, as idealists forty-second, as intelligent or thoughtful fifty-seventh; and references to being accepting of them and optimistic come in at sixty-third and sixty-eighth place respectively. The differentiation between regretful and aggressive vocabulary is important. Referring to opposite voters as ill-informed or wrong, naïve or conned is typically regretful, and whilst indeed disparaging, it seems to blame the system more than the people, and suggest that the respondent feels more sorry for than hostile towards alternative voters. Describing them as idiots, racist, selfish, bigots, traitors, or extremists takes the hostility to an entirely different level, whereby opposite voters are squarely blamed for their 'wrong' vote. Likewise, in terms of citizens' own reactions, feeling confused or disappointed is quite different from feeling angry or disgusted, with feelings like frustration being somewhere in between these two ends of the negativity spectrum. There is, really, a sliding scale of negative feelings that voters reserve for people who vote differently from them, its gradations differing quite dramatically in their logic, intensity, and implications for social cohesion and democratic legitimacy.

We next tested these variations, using closed questions to ask how citizens feel towards people who voted differently from them, offering a range of possible positive and negative feelings and emotions ranging from sympathy or a sense of reconciliation, to regretfully negative feelings such as distrust, frustration, and ever-growing distance, to aggressively negative feelings such as anger, contempt, and disgust. The results are presented in table 9.3.

Strikingly, even the most extreme forms of negativity–such as disgust and contempt—are used more frequently by respondents to describe their feelings towards those who vote differently from them than are the most frequent positive feelings such as sympathy. Frustration is the most frequent descriptor used by respondents to refer to opposite voters, followed by a desire to stick to one's guns and distrust, which seems symptomatic of combined annoyance, inability to understand, and a sense of powerlessness. Response distributions are even more striking. 51.1% of British voters claim to feel angry at people who voted differently from them, while 44.9% claim to feel contempt, and 44.7% disgust—two very powerful and violent emotions which are perhaps surprisingly widespread. Frustration is overwhelm-

TABLE 9.3. Feelings toward Opposite Voters: UK 2017 General Election

	Mean (S.D.)	% who feel
Frustration	1.88 (1.07)	68.4
Desire to stick to my guns	1.79 (1.00)	63.6
Distrust	1.60 (1.06)	56.1
Sense of ever-growing distance	1.60 (1.00)	56.2
Anger	**1.47 (1.08)**	51.1
Disgust	**1.34 (1.09)**	44.7
Contempt	**1.32 (1.04)**	44.9
Enmity	**1.09 (0.94)**	31.6
Desire to reconcile	1.02 (0.92)	29.5
Sense of reconciliation	1.00 (0.86)	26.3
Sympathy	0.92 (0.92)	26.9
Envy	*0.55 (0.82)*	*12.9*

Note: Means are on a 0–3 scale, where 3 is highest. Percentages are the sum of respondents claiming to feel each emotion "a lot" or "somewhat." Boldface: negative mobilizing; italic: negative demobilizing; normal font: positive.

ing—shared by 68.4% of respondents; and almost a third (31.4%) feel enmity. Nearly 60% of respondents also see electoral hostility as increasing over time, whilst only a quarter sense reconciliation. We retested those measures in 2019 with largely similar—in fact slightly worsened—results.

Hostility varies significantly by party. In the UK typically, hostility feelings are higher among Labour and Liberal Democrat voters and lower amongst Conservatives, perhaps because of their victory and the pre-eminence of Brexit divisions as a source of electoral hostility. However, people with a high propensity to vote for the BNP (British National Party) are more likely to feel enmity and contempt towards opposite voters, whilst at the same time, those with a high propensity to vote for the BNP and UKIP (UK Independence Party) alike are more likely to feel envy, which stresses the perception by many of these voters of a clear dividing line between 'elites' and 'the people'. SNP (Scottish National Party) and UKIP voters are most likely to want to stick to their guns against opposite voters.

We then asked respondents how they perceive electoral hostility and its evolution in society. Again, choices included both positive ('Each side seems to respect the other', 'The two sides seem to be coming together'), and negative phrasings ('Those who voted one way seem to dislike those who voted the other way', 'People now pick on other citizens who disagree with them where they used only to blame opposite politicians and media before', etc.), static and dynamic, and general and personal ('I have personally felt a sense of hostility from some other people after we have disagreed politically', 'I am worried about people around me becoming or aggressive when they realize that I disagree with them politically'). The results, presented in appendix 3,[1] are again heavily weighted to the negative. Firstly, there is absolutely no support for either of the two positive statements offered, about people respecting opposite voters or coming together after the rift of the referendum. The net agreement with those statements is −41.1 and −39.0 respectively. Secondly, there is an overwhelming sense that electoral hostility is real, and has significantly worsened in recent years. On people blaming not only opposite politicians but also opposite voters, the net agreement is +46.8, and +32.9 on voters disliking those who vote differently from them. There is a similarly clear belief that people are likely to fight (the strong phrasing was used on purpose) with family and close friends because of political disagreements (+7.3). A negative dynamic is clearly acknowledged: asked whether people pick on opposite voters more than before, the net agreement is +22.8. However, respondents are more nuanced when it comes to personal experience. 35.3% have personally been victims of electoral hostility, whilst 49.4% have not (though a third of the population personally experiencing hostility is perhaps already worrying). Whilst 31.3% are no more worried today about others' negativity than before, 49.1% are more worried.

Overall, respondents are overwhelmingly convinced that electoral hostility is high in the UK, even though this conviction derives from personal experiences for only a third of them. This gap between perceptions of others and personal experience could be interpreted in multiple ways. An optimistic interpretation would be that perceptions of (growing) hostility are merely a prejudice based on reports of fractiousness in the media. A far more pessimistic version would relate to self-selection (Zaller, 1992) and partisan polarization (Abramowitz and Saunders, 1998; Iyengar and Westwood, 2015), and suggest that people are increasingly likely to 'politically sift' their entourage and thus be unlikely to interact with those who disagree with them politically. They would therefore be unlikely to experience hostility at first hand, precisely because they pro-actively exclude dissonant others from their lives.

1. Appendices referred to in this chapter are to be found online at www.epob.org.

In the next section, we consider the ways in which electoral hostility affects citizens' behaviour, based, in particular, on 2019 UK data, and what proportions of citizens prefer to enact their hostility through silos and avoidance, rather than expose themselves to dissonant opinions. We also look at societal and civic implications, such as people resenting their taxes being spent on protecting those who precipitated electoral outcomes that they disagreed with in the first place.

'Hatred 2.0'? Irreconcilability, Silos, and the Populist Fracture

Whilst entirely distinct phenomena taken at face value, many will see the rise of electoral hostility as inseparable from the rise of populism which has shocked many in the late 2010s. Donald Trump's victory in the 2016 US presidential election not only gave free rein to negative feelings towards liberal and conservative voters themselves, but was often portrayed as a clash between two Americas, two incompatible sets of values, and two irreconcilable groups with contempt for one another. The UK 2016 referendum not only revealed durable and venomous opposition between Remainers and Leavers, but was similarly characterized as a rift between two Britains, caricatured as young vs old, cities vs country, well off vs left behind. Research highlighted the fracture between those who saw the value of EU membership from a purely 'consumerist' point of view and those who saw it as part of their identity (Bruter and Harrison, 2016), and the rivalry between competing conceptions not so much of Europe, as of Britain and British society itself. It was noted in chapter 2 that in order to understand the sources of this 'hatred 2.0' phenomenon, Huddy et al. (2015) and Iyengar and Westwood (2015) use the model of affective polarization, whilst we propose an alternative based on slightly diverging assumptions regarding the form of electoral hostility. Both models are compatible with Iyengar and Hahn's (2009) suggestion that negativity is strengthened by uncommunicating information flows—the so-called 'silo' phenomenon—which can entrench and worsen social, geographical, and generational fault lines. This silo phenomenon is further reinforced by social media which enable citizens to 'hand pick' the information—and informers—that they are willing to listen to. In the course of our exploration of electoral hostility, we found that in June 2019, 30% of British people were willing to unfriend people on social media if they disagreed with them on same sex marriage, whilst 27% would never want to speak again to someone with whom they strongly disagree on Brexit, and 30% would avoid going to dinner with someone with whom they disagreed on whether some religions are incompatible with British values.

That elections consequently are unable to bring resolution between incompatible conceptions of societies and nations, and irreconcilable visions of a desirable future, is similarly supported by the qualitative evidence that we gathered. Electoral hostility does not rely merely on ideological distance, but also on citizens' artificial perception of (their own and opposite) secluded, politically homogeneous groups. Large numbers of interviewees declared that they did not know any or many people supporting the other camp. This not only confirmed that they were largely surrounded by likeminded citizens sharing, repeating, and reinforcing their views, but even led them to doubt the reality of the strength of 'the other side' as characterized by opinion polls. The relative novelty of the current populist fracture (Taggart, 2000; Mudde and Kaltwasser, 2017) also makes discussion virtually impossible between those who believe that politics is to any extent about ideological or policy choices (be these left/right, or concerning climate, redistribution of wealth, or same-sex marriage), and those who denounce these as artificial debates within what they consider to be an underlying consensus of the powerful.

We earlier highlighted the tendency towards hopelessness that had grown by the end of the period covered. Political pessimism is not new, and many voters have expressed similar depressing worries for years. However, until the 2010s, a safety mechanism seemed to prevent many citizens experiencing hopelessness from enacting a populist vote, seen as economically, socially, and politically dangerous, and causing them to prefer to choose begrudgingly between mainstream parties, or instead abstain. We are reminded of the concept of 'diffuse support' (Easton, 1965; Gibson et al., 2005), the 'reservoir of good will' which makes citizens accept the legitimacy of a given institution, even as they disagree with its policy outcomes (specific support). Crucially, however, the underlying assumption of this model is that elections are accountability mechanisms. Thus, citizens alienated by government hope to have their preferred policies implemented a few years later, so that the reservoir of good will gets replenished and the legitimacy of the institutions is renewed. What happens if there is no hope of change? Or if the reservoir is never replenished, because citizens' faith in the system dissolves? Could the legitimacy reservoir reach a state of total drought?

We mentioned the difference between pessimism and hopelessness as often being contained in the perception that generational and longitudinal projections do not allow voters devoid of hope to imagine even a long-term positive future, for their children's or grandchildren's generations. The populist temptation emanates from parts of the population who often consider traditional political offerings as illegitimate, but conversely, populist politics is deemed illegitimate by many other voters, who consider it grounded in untruths and unrealistic or immoral solutions. Thus, in the 2010s, the 'area of acceptability' of politics of the Rabinowitz and Macdonald (1989) model has changed for some voters but not for others; or rather, both populist and non-populist voters are navigating in ideas that are outside one another's area of acceptability. Each camp thus explicitly or implicitly questions the very democratic legitimacy of the other. Furthermore, populist politics being able to win votes represents a test for both camps. Populist solutions are to be tested against reality, and if they are as unrealistic and counter-productive as their opponents claim, especially with regard to vulnerable categories, will mainstream voters accept continuing to contribute to protect the very categories they hostilely associate with a catastrophic choice in the first place? If Brexit leaves pensioners and farmers worse off due to inflation and the end of the CAP, will the anti-Brexit educated, middle-class, urban and cosmopolitan populations still willingly pay into the system in the name of solidarity with those they feel have endangered their hopes and the country's future?

Furthermore, if the predictions of doom are confirmed in practice, the feelings of previously integrated voters can switch to exclusion and hopelessness *without* those of the previously hopeless voters, who have finally been granted a rare victory, conversely switching to regained hope: which can have a doubly negative effect on the perceived legitimacy of the democratic process. When voters no longer feel that elections bring closure, and do not believe them to entrench the true majority will—might they cease to feel bound by the outcomes of the democratic process and social contract? Some interviewees went so far as to claim a 'constitutional duty' not to respect a democratic verdict they thought unacceptable and unfair. Is this a mere anecdotal bleep, or a broader trend of change shaking our world?

Electoral Resolution Revisited

Behind conceptual notions of electoral resolution, atmosphere, hostility, hope, and hopelessness, the question is indeed how fundamental the changes that have occurred over the past ten years across the democratic world will prove to be. Since some of the concepts we study are newly defined or operationalized in this book, there are limits to the historical comparison that we can develop: we have only glimpses of their long-term individual- and societal-level evolutions. They are mirror effects and consequences of elections as an articulation between individuals and their image of the collective, as discussed in chapter 6; but it is somehow particularly hard to determine whether individuals are dramatizing, or merely acknowledging, a profound change to the collective. Relating the analytical concepts listed above and what we have learned about them to key historical and contextual developments and transformations that have affected each of the six countries included in our analysis throughout the period of study is extremely difficult. We do this in appendix 4, relating historical developments in the past decades in each of the six countries studied to the analytical models tested throughout this book, in order also to ground a complex model in a no less complex historical reality spanning a whole decade, considering how elections' apparent capacity to provide closure, or on the contrary to entrench wounds, hostility, and division, has evolved.

Indeed, at the end of our period of study, all six countries covered by this book are facing significant political crises, with unprecedented numbers of citizens having joined forces to express anger and dissatisfaction at 'the system'. In all six cases, furthermore, they have frequently done so with high turnout, flatly contradicting traditional perceptions that extremes benefit from low participation and that high turnout favours moderate outcomes. Instead, many habitual abstentionists seem to have decided, for the first time in years, to rise and join forces with radical voters to punish decisively the people they perceive to be the power in place, opening an entirely unknown page in the history of electoral democracy in their respective countries.

This transformation of electoral resolution across the decade requires acceptance of a number of apparent contradictions. First, voters focus, towards the end of the period, on a highly negative yet highly emotional perception of electoral atmosphere; but that negativity has not prevented them from participating, frequently in higher numbers than previously in recent years, in some critical elections; nor does it contradict the fact that many people feel positive emotions as they vote. Second, hope and hopelessness do not necessarily represent the opposite ends of a continuum. Indeed, we found that high levels of pessimism may be compatible with hope where citizens can still believe that, ultimately, their children or grandchildren will benefit from better lives than theirs. Where this hope disappears, however, hopelessness does take over, and occasionally violent negative feelings may be expressed. 'It can't get worse, anyway' represents a powerful emotion which may prompt voters to explore populist offerings or 'torpedo' an existing system. When they do so, it can be in the almost naïve hope that solutions that many experts would deem grotesque may work after all. Third, electoral negativity changes targets. After years of dissatisfaction predominantly directed at political institutions and personnel, the emergence of the phenomenon of electoral hostility has seen increasing numbers of citizens seemingly harbouring negative feelings and emotions towards one another (as opposed to their leaders), because of the way that others vote or are perceived to vote. Fourth, the ability of elections to provide closure and resolution is contingent upon individual, societal, and historical variations. Electoral resolution is asymmetric, and not as simple as believing that winners will be appeased and losers furious. Indeed, in many cases towards the end of the period under study, those who voted for a winning cause, candidate, or party proved to feel just as democratically frustrated as those who supported losing camps, and perhaps even more unable to achieve democratic closure than their disappointed rivals. It is perhaps a uniquely symptomatic outcome of populist attitudes that many people who voted for populist outcomes, and won a corresponding election or referendum against all odds, still implicitly behave as and consider themselves election losers. In fact, they often react as though the camp that they were convinced represented the source of all problems in their country, and which they managed to defeat, was in fact still in power and preventing their champions from imposing their agenda.

These paradoxes are reinforced by the 'silo' phenomenon discussed above, evident in both real life and social media, with 20–30% of respondents being willing never to speak again with, avoid a dinner invitation with, or unfriend those people with whom they disagree on any given major moral or political issue. The silo phenomenon is also mediated by the complex cycles of electoral atmosphere and heightened emotions that progressively take voters from egocentric to sociotropic, direct to projective, and supporter to referee perspectives between the start of a campaign and Election Night.

These discrepancies between the various stages of the electoral period emphasize our finding regarding the behavioural nature of election cycles being highly complex and largely misunderstood. A behavioural election cycle does not match an electoral term, can span multiple ones (for instance, in the case of incumbent runs, or where first-order elections are downgraded to mere yardsticks as in the aftermath of the Brexit referendum), and can start or end before or after what institutional logics would expect. These are critical historical and analytical consequences of our model and our dependent variable displacement, and it is those implications which it is now time to explore.

10

Coda: Flipping the Electoral World Upside-Down

HOMO SUFFRAGATOR BEYOND THE AGE OF REASON

Switching the Lights

In analyses of political behaviour, we tend to think that the 'be-all and end-all' of questions is that of whom an individual will vote for, or, at the aggregate level, who will be victorious in an election. Everything else—the economic situation, social determinants, voters' personalities and socialization, context—constitutes likely causes of or routes towards that ultimate result.

What if this was actually the wrong question, and if we were looking at the world from the wrong side of the lens? What if who wins elections did not really matter in terms of democracy, as long as people feel happy and elections serve their purpose of making citizens comfortable regarding their role within their political system, and satisfied with their control of and interaction with society? What if, with regard to the relationship between how you vote and how you experience elections, the important question was not how your experience of the election affects your electoral behaviour, but rather whether your behaviour affects your experience of electoral democracy, the ability of elections to bring you a sense of peace, and how they contribute to and shape your life?

Throughout this book, we have shown that how citizens appropriate electoral cycles, events, and narratives, and integrate them into their lives, is largely different from what institutional logic would dictate. Democracy may be built on the myth of an osmosis between citizens and their institutions, but in this relationship, perspectives most definitely differ, hierarchies are rarely shared, and climaxes are more often than not diachronic. Consequently, to think of the electoral decision itself as the 'be-all and end-all' of electoral democracy might work under a system-centric assumption—what one could describe as an institutionalist vision of behaviour—but simply misses the point of a citizen-centric perspective: rather like a shop assistant insisting on understanding whether the customer prefers the blue t-shirt or the red one whilst all the customer is thinking about is whether he/she needs a t-shirt and can afford clothes at all after an expensive night out.

Throughout the book, we have learned about the nature, behaviour, and experience of *Homo Suffragator*. We have explored how elections shape his/her life, the circumstances under which they bring a sense of resolution, or, conversely, reinforce hostility, how *Homo Suffragator* perceives their atmosphere, uses elections to redefine his/her relationship with others and integrate them into his/her electoral thinking and experience, and how elections change our perspective on time, identity, responsibility, and self-importance. In this final chapter, we highlight some of the essential and sometimes counter-intuitive findings uncovered in the course the book, and consider their implications and the new mysteries that they elicit.

Some Consequential Findings on the Mystery of the Voter's Mind

In the process of considering the critical questions highlighted above and analyzing a diverse body of data spanning a decade and six countries, our book has revealed important and at times surprising findings, which have significant implications for the way in which we study and understand voters and their interaction with electoral democracy. Some of the most notable of these are as follows.

A vote is not the raw expression of an individual's personal preference. It is, instead, the outcome of a complex (conscious and subconscious) decision process by an individual who assumes a given role as a voter. This has radical implications for the validity of many of the models—and even methods—that we typically use to explain or predict the vote.

The role voters assume and inhabit varies across individuals, countries, and indeed elections. Citizens split into 'referees' and 'supporters', with radically different perceptions and experiences of, and reactions to, campaigns, debates, the vote, and the election aftermath.

Electoral identity also means that voters can be coherent in ways that differ from our party-centric visions. Someone voting for three different parties in three different elections may be entirely coherent because he/she behaved as a referee throughout, and simply reached different conclusions as to whose programme was best suited to the country each time. Between 20% and 30% of voters also make up or change their minds within a week of a typical election, half of them on Election Day; this is not fickleness, however, but part of the logic of the electoral atmosphere, which crystallizes as the election becomes more emotional.

The electoral identity of a voter builds up over time, assimilated from elements of the individual's personality, hierarchization of moral priorities, and way of integrating others into his/her considerations and actions, but also deriving from that individual's accumulated memory of past elections from childhood and his/her own (often very consequential) first vote onwards.

Electoral behaviour has its own nature in terms of election cycles. Those cycles do not follow the logic of institutionalized cycles based on electoral terms, or campaign dates, or electoral hierarchies, or media prompts. At times, a behavioural election cycle may encompass several institutional terms, upset the balance between first- and second-order elections, or even seemingly fail to close. These cycles result in the atmosphere of an election building up as Election Day approaches, triggering specific feelings, memories, emotions, and reactions, and leading voters to trade their 'raw preference' perspective for their electoral identity one.

Citizens' experience of elections intersects to a large extent with their personal and even intimate spheres. Citizens internalize elections, and this is why they become part of their lives. The most powerful memories of elections relate to personal relations and family, and one's history as a voter largely mirrors the memory of one's own history as an individual.

Elections are highly emotional. They are associated with emotional memories and reactions, and many citizens cry because of elections, even when they do not really care about politics. Approximately a third of our respondents claimed already to have shed tears because of an election. Nearly a third of British voters admitted to having tears in their eyes as a result of the 2016 EU-membership referendum alone.

Elections permanently redefine the conscious and subconscious relationship between citizens and others—those they are responsible for, those they come to see as enemies, past and future generations, and society as a whole. This interaction is multifaceted. The concept of sociotropism raises the question of whether we vote according to what is best for ourselves or for the nation. That of empathic displacement is about how we take others' vote into account in our own experience and behaviour. Projected efficacy pertains to seeing our vote as efficacious not on its own, but to the extent that people like us might behave as we do. Generational projection relates to our ability to sacrifice our own comfort and interests for the good of younger generations, notably our children or grandchildren, and is intimately related to longitudinal projection, which is about being willing to make short-term sacrifices for bigger longer-term positive outcomes. Finally, hostility is about developing negative feelings towards those we think vote differently from us. All of these elements intertwine with each other to shape our electoral identity.

The permanent dialectic between the individual and the societal redefines the very nature of electoral rationality. Empathic displacement means that voters constantly consider the behaviour of others in an election, based on polls, heuristics, personal networks, and discussions including on social media. It is claimed in this book that this explains many recent electoral 'surprises' in terms not of polls being mistaken, but rather of polls leading to a changing behaviour that contradicted their own predictions. Ultimately, voters' thinking during, and experience of, an election is largely projective, predominantly sociotropic, and leads them implicitly to question their own responsibility, power, and vulnerability. Elections leave citizens feeling more strongly part of society, or else excluded from and marginalized by it.

Elections bring out the best in people. Most voters feel the weight of electoral responsibility on their shoulders, and try to think and act accordingly.

Voters' psychology is in permanent interface with electoral organization, to create electoral ergonomics. Different aspects—such as visiting a polling station or not, voting using paper or a machine, voting on Election Day or before—will have an impact on how voters experience the election, which emotions and memories are elicited, the time they spend thinking about their vote and likelihood of changing it, and their electoral attitudes and behaviour.

For citizens, elections have an atmosphere, which builds up over time and which they can characterize with some specificity. This atmosphere changes over time, and its perception is affected by citizens' own experience (e.g., whether they are voters or not, and vote in person or remotely), outlook, electoral identity, and behaviour (whether they support winners or losers), creating an individualized dimension of context. That atmosphere is cumulative, and determines the capacity of elections to bring closure and resolution, hope or hopelessness, and a sense of integration with or, on the contrary, alienation from—even hostility towards—others.

The logic of electoral perceptions, behaviour, experience, and resolution is overwhelmingly subconscious. Research relying on self-characterization entails a risk of significant misperception. For example, voters underestimate (or under-report) their emotions as they vote, as well as the positive valence of those emotions (perhaps because their political emotions are in fact far more negative than their electoral ones). We also know that, on the basis of self-reports, the literature has assumed sociotropism to increase with age, whereas we found instead, using implicit measures, that sociotropism is related to vulnerabilities, and that whilst younger voters are more egocentric in economic terms (because they often feel more vulnerable on that front), they are in fact more sociotropic in terms of safety and misery sociotropism scales, according to which it is instead older citizens who feel more vulnerable, and thus become more egocentric. The mystery of elections is almost as dense for voters as it is for academics.

Let us now consider some of the implications of these important findings, and what they tell us regarding how we might need to reconsider our approach to thinking about elections and voters in established and emerging electoral democracies.

Have We Uncovered the Truth about Electoral Chickens and Eggs?

This book throws the whole causality that electoral research traditionally assumes into question. Our findings suggest that rather than electoral experience being a predictor of electoral behaviour, the relationship between the two amounts to an instance of the famous 'chicken-and-egg'—inextricable—scenario. For example, when it comes to turnout, while we generally rely on known predictors to explain participation, how enjoyable the experience of the previous election was is a major predictor of participation in the next. Particularly in the context of young people, voting in person in a polling station leads to a more emotionally positive electoral experience, and in turn a greater likelihood of turning out again at the next opportunity (see chapter 7). Thus, experience in cycle 1 influences behaviour in cycle 2, and arguably, experience—rather than behaviour—becomes the truly critical dependent variable at the end of cycle 1.

Similarly, in chapter 9, we found that the nature of a voter's behaviour can affect his/her likelihood of experiencing political closure and resolution. Thus, whilst many elections covered in this book resulted in 'electoral honeymoons', whereby newly elected governments benefited from significant support from people who had not voted for them in the first place, this did not happen in the UK referendum of 2016, or when Donald Trump was elected US president. In turn, a citizen's electoral behaviour leads to a number of experiential outcomes reversing the traditional causality of interest whereby we think of behaviour as the ultimate variable to explain. Indeed, when it comes to the dynamics of elections, the behaviour of voters is in fact an explanatory variable for the situations of hostility or hope described and analyzed in chapter 9. For instance, we found that abstentionists are much less likely than voters to obtain closure from elections.

Similarly, our findings regarding the impact of the polling station experience on empathic displacement and projected efficacy show that beyond the electoral experience of citizens, electoral organization also triggers different personality traits and emotions, and in turns, that the interface between psychology and design affects their understanding of how they fit in with fellow voters and society. Even the finding that voters are more likely to change their minds from their original voting intention when their remote voting option is temporal only (they vote early, but in a polling station) but not when it is geographical (they cast their vote from home), underlines the crucial implications of the electoral experience on a voter's permeability to societal influences within the voting process.

Do Personality, Electoral Memory, and Electoral Identity Matter? The Static Models

Our model makes important claims regarding the impact of electoral personality, memory, and identity on electoral behaviour, experience (including the emotions that it elicits), and resolution. We tested those claims in particular through chapters 4, 5, and 6. However, at the start of this book we also made two perhaps even more ambitious claims, restated here: that those three dependent variables are interrelated, and that they interact dynamically. In this section, we review some of the performances of our model, but also touch upon that additional claim of interaction.

CODA 297

Turnout (all)
0.12 + 0.09 + 0.06 + 0.16 = 0.43

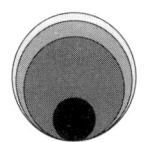

Electoral choice
(in person)
0.19 + 0.27 + 0.07 + 0.04 = 0.57

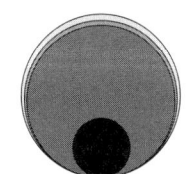

Electoral choice
(advance)
0.26 + 0.42 + 0.01 + 0.04 = 0.73

Electoral choice
(absentee)
0.20 + 0.39 + 0.02 + 0.01 = 0.62

Emotionality
(in person)
0.03 + 0.14 + 0.01 + 0.04 = 0.22

Emotionality
(advance)
0.05 + 0.25 + 0.02 + 0.10 = 0.42

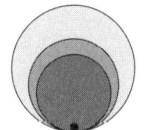

Emotionality
(absentee)
0.03 + 0.32 + 0.07 + 0.05 = 0.47

Happiness
(in person)
0.05 + 0.07 + 0.01 + 0.05 = 0.18

Happiness
(advance)
0.13 + 0.21 + 0.02 + 0.07 = 0.43

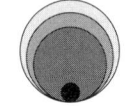

Happiness
(absentee)
0.08 + 0.26 + 0.06 + 0.06 = 0.46

Electoral resolution
(in person)
0.01 + 0.06 + 0.01 + 0.05 = 0.13

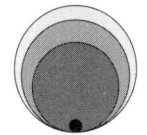

Electoral resolution
(advance)
0.06 + 0.34 + 0.11 + 0.06 = 0.57

Electoral resolution
(absentee)
0.07 + 0.24 + 0.02 + 0.04 = 0.37

FIGURE 10.1: Overall models performance and stage contributions—the US case

Let us first return to the overall performance of our main models of electoral behaviour, experience, and resolution, based on linear and binary logistic regressions, which we considered in detail in chapters 4, 5, and 6. Figures 10.1 (the US) and 10.2.a–10.2.e (all countries studied) remind us of the total contributive variance explained at each of the three model stages.

298 CHAPTER 10

a.
Models of electoral behaviour—choice

Bars (left to right): US (advance), US (absentee), US (station), SA, UK (station), UK (postal), GE (SPD, postal), GE (CDU, postal), GE (AfD, postal), GE (AfD, station), GE (CDU, station), FR, GE (SPD, station)

Legend: ☐ Stage 0 ■ Stage 1 ■ Stage 2 ■ Stage 3 ☐ Unexplained

b.
Models of electoral behaviour—turnout

Bars: US, UK, SA, GE, FR

Legend: ☐ Stage 0 ■ Stage 1 ■ Stage 2 ■ Stage 3 ☐ Unexplained

c.
Models of electoral experience—emotionality

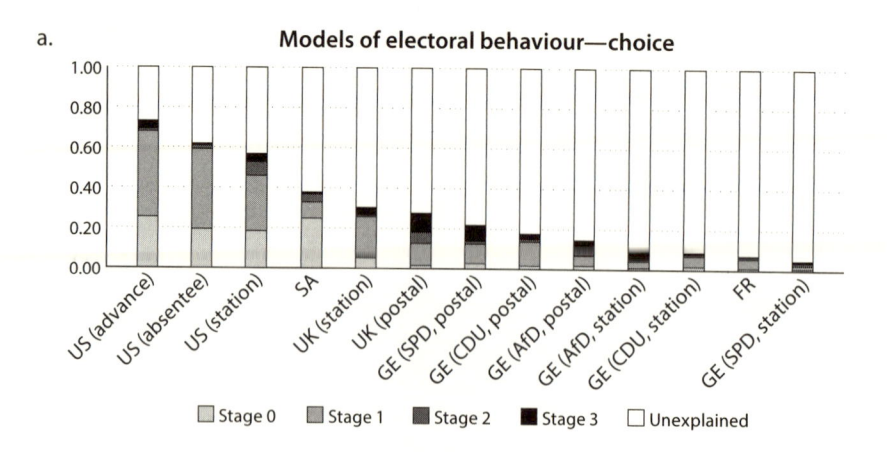

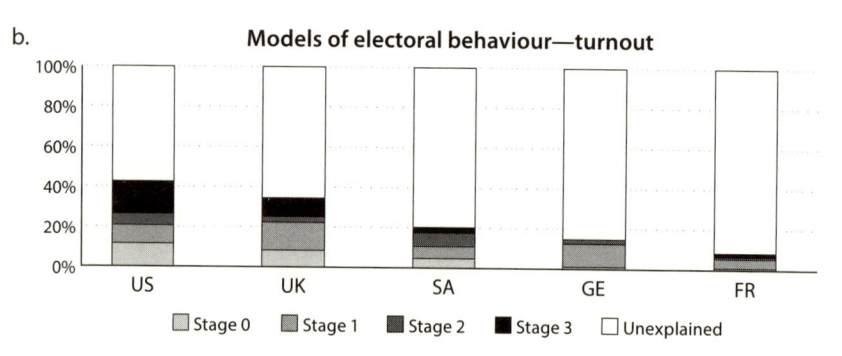

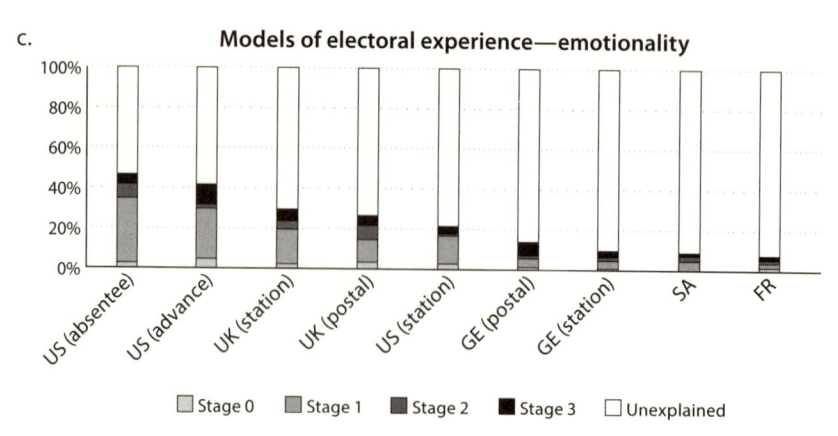

Bars (left to right): US (absentee), US (advance), UK (station), UK (postal), US (station), GE (postal), GE (station), SA, FR

Legend: ☐ Stage 0 ■ Stage 1 ■ Stage 2 ■ Stage 3 ☐ Unexplained

FIGURES 10.2.A TO 10.2.E: Overall models performance and stage contributions—all

Stage 0 was the baseline model that included major social, demographic, and political variables; stage 1 added personality variables including personality traits, moral hierarchization, and sociotropism; stage 2 also included electoral memory, notably childhood memories, first-time memories, and whether the respondent is a first-time voter—or, in the US, a first- or second-

d.

Models of electoral experience—happiness

[Bar chart showing Stage 0, Stage 1, Stage 2, Stage 3, and Unexplained proportions for: US (absentee), US (advance), UK (station), UK (postal), US (station), SA, GE (postal), FR, GE (station)]

e.

Models of electoral resolution

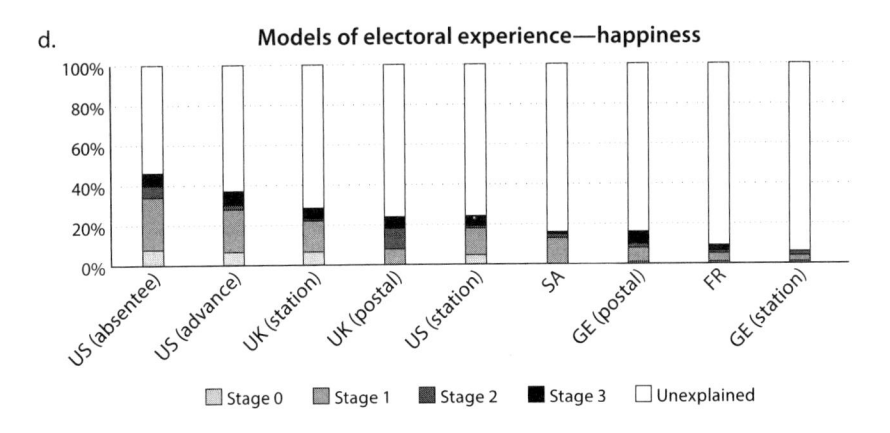

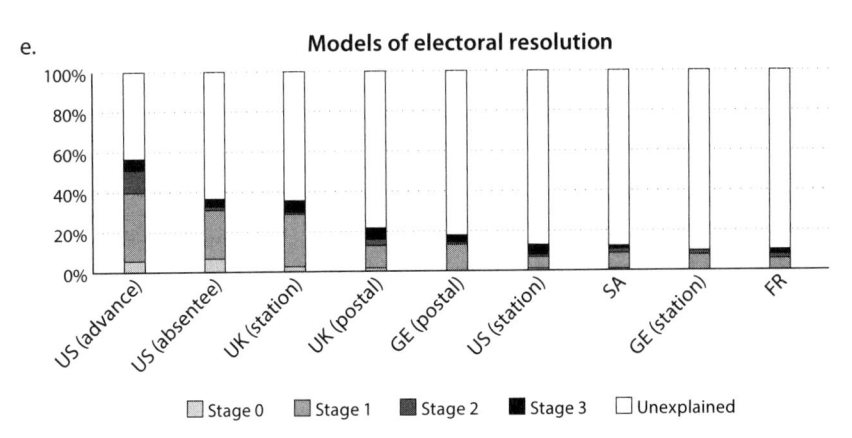

[Bar chart showing Stage 0, Stage 1, Stage 2, Stage 3, and Unexplained proportions for: US (advance), US (absentee), UK (station), UK (postal), GE (postal), US (station), SA, GE (station), FR]

FIGURES 10.2.A TO 10.2.E· *(continued)*

time voter); and stage 3 factored in electoral identity variables (including the perceived referee/supporter role of the voter, longitudinal and generational projection, empathic displacement, and projected efficacy). Once again, the US is the only country in which the static models are fully specified, with all the relevant variables, whilst other countries miss some of the independent variable models, such as morality questions in the UK, electoral identity in France, and so on. In the context of electoral models, where low explained variance is often the norm, our results are striking in at least four different ways.

First, in some cases, especially in the US, our models explain very significant proportions of the total variance. For all model series, the top regression explains between 43% (turnout in the US) to 73% (electoral choice of US advance voters) of total variance, with the best models for electoral resolution and experience in between these percentages. Each time, this result includes very substantial improvements in the three electoral psychology stages (personality, memory, and identity) of the model rather than being due to the default control stage. Indeed, the three meaningful stage model contributions for the best fitting case study add from +0.31 for US turnout to +0.51 for electoral resolution amongst US advance voters.

Second, to an extent conversely, some of the models work a lot better than others. Typically, models explaining turnout and whether an electoral experience is happy are slightly weaker than for electoral choice, emotionality of electoral experience, and electoral resolution.

Third, model performance also varies significantly across countries and election modes (in person, advance/early, or postal/absentee). Our models tend to perform more poorly in France and Germany, and generally very well in the US and the UK (which have, respectively, the only fully specified model, and the one closest to full specification). The South African situation is rather unusual, as the models perform relatively poorly on electoral experience and resolution, but strongly on electoral behaviour. At the same time, electoral ergonomics matters, to the extent that models perform differently depending whether it comes to explaining polling station or remote experience and behaviour, though these effects are not consistent. Typically, in the US and Germany, the models prove better for remote than for in-station voters, but in the UK the opposite is true.

Finally, a particularly interesting aspect of the full models presented in chapter 4 is that virtually all variables included in the multivariate model— the different personality traits, options of moral hierarchization, sociotropism, memories of a childhood or a first election, being a first time voter, the referee/supporter dimension, longitudinal and generational projection, empathic displacement, and projected efficacy—have meaningful and statistically significant effects in some of the parsimonious models. This suggests that each of these factors has a role to play in our understanding of citizens' electoral behaviour, experience, and resolution, if not necessarily in all countries and models. We summarize those complex flows in figure 10.3, which shows how well each set of independent variables works in each of the five dependent-variable models. The thickness of each arrow represents the proportion of models in which the independent variable set has some meaningful and statistically significant effects.

These results also help to relativize the apparent hierarchy between the stages of the model. On the face of it, including personality in the model seems to improve the models most, followed by the inclusion of electoral identity and projection, and finally electoral memory. However, as mentioned previously, this is undoubtedly artificially affected by the ordering of

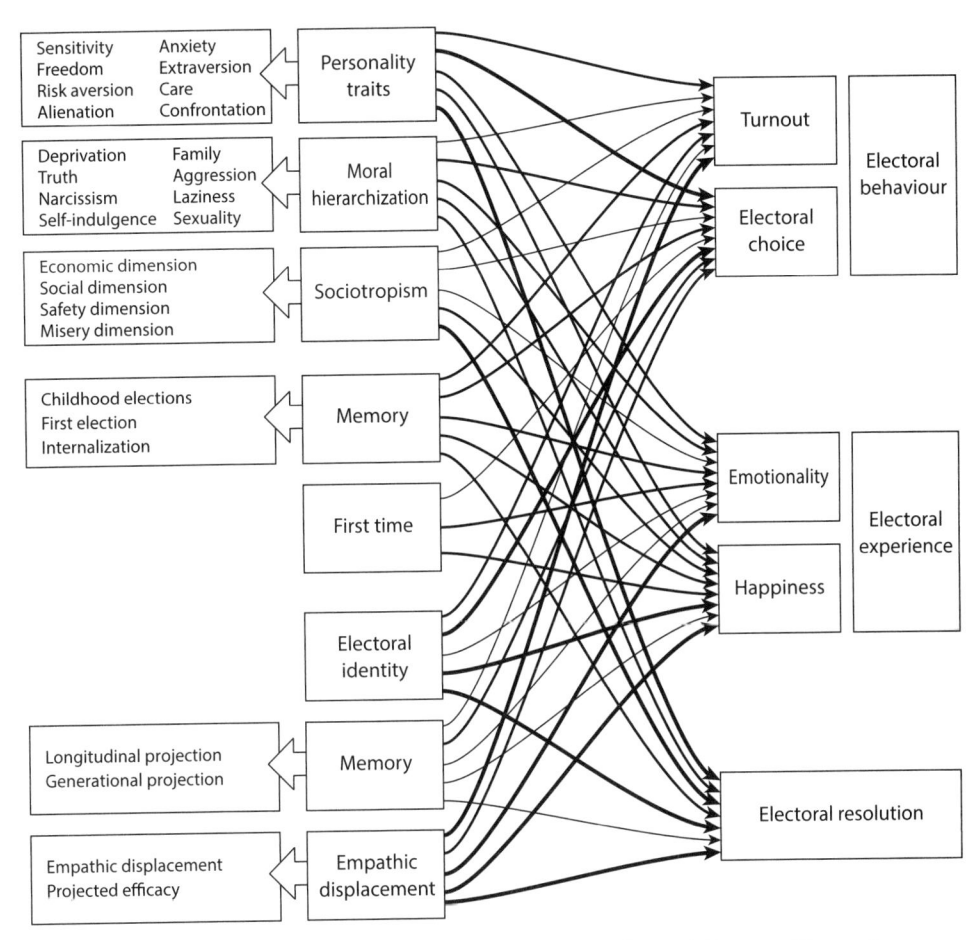

FIGURE 10.3: Full flow models—All dependent variables and independent variable sets—All countries

the stages, which makes it much 'easier' for personality to claim unexplained variance than it is for variable sets entered later. By contrast, looking at the final version of the models shows that even electoral memory—especially remembering one's childhood elections or one's first vote—has an important impact on electoral experience, behaviour, and dealing with the electoral aftermath.

Interactive Dynamic Models

As mentioned earlier, however, whilst those static models are ambitious and novel in both their dependent variables of interest and the causality that they explore, we make another, potentially even bolder claim: that our three sets of dependent variables of interest—'classic' electoral behaviour (turnout and electoral choice), but also electoral experience and the sense of electoral resolution one gets from the electoral process—are interactive in dynamic terms; in other words, that being happy when you vote in election 1 will make you more likely to vote in election 2, or that voting for the winner in election 1 will affect your experience of election 2, and so on. These claims can only really be tested dynamically, because behaviour, experience, and sense of resolution are largely concomitant in a given election. To complete the assessment of our models, we now add this interactive and dynamic element to the model. We use the case of the 2014 US mid-term election (the main model uses the presidential election instead), replicating the full specification of the static model, but also adding the levels of the dependent variables of interest in the previous election—the US 2012 presidential vote. Of course, each time, we omit similar sets of variables (so to assess interactive and dynamic effects on electoral choice in 2014, we include electoral experience and resolution in 2012, but neither the 2012 electoral choice nor turnout, and to model electoral happiness, we do not include either happiness or emotionality as independent predictors).

We assess these contributions both globally—for the whole sample—and including the electoral ergonomics interface model, by repeating the use of split samples as in the main models. The results are shown in figure 10.4.

The results are striking. First, looking at overall models, the only one where there are no interactive effects based on previous behaviour and sense of resolution is the emotionality model for the 2014 election. For everything else, dynamic interactive effects from other 2012 model dependent variables improve the R^2 or pseudo-R^2 in the overall models by from 0.03 (turnout) to 0.05 (electoral choice), 0.12 (electoral resolution), and even 0.14 (happiness). In other words, having voted in 2012 and experienced electoral resolution made a given citizen far more likely to have a happy electoral experience in 2014. The overall dynamic models have R^2 or pseudo-R^2 of from 0.16 (happiness) to 0.46 (Republican vote, i.e., electoral choice).

Disaggregation between in-person, advance, and absentee voters has to be carried out with much more caution than for the 2012 model, because losses in respondents over the two-year period means that the sample of absentee and advance voters was by then significantly smaller, which artificially increases variance explained. As a result, both the total variance explained and the contribution of dynamic interactive effects now look higher, with the models being particularly successful at explaining the experience

Turnout
0.33 + 0.03 = 0.36

Electoral choice
0.41 + 0.05 = 0.46

Happiness
0.19 + 0.14 = 0.33

Emotionality
0.16 + 0.00 = 0.16

Electoral resolution
0.15 + 0.12 − 0.27

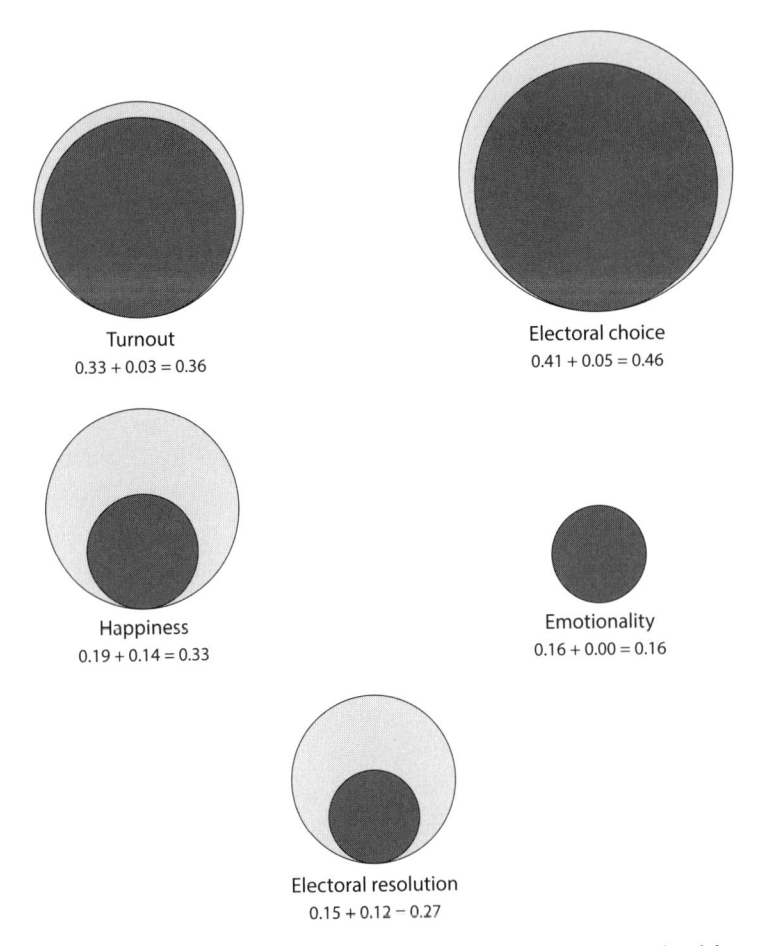

FIGURE 10.4: Dynamic models: contribution of initial model and inter-related dependent variables at t-1 to the overall R^2

and behaviour of absentee voters. The contribution of dynamic interactive effects to the R^2 or pseudo-R^2 for the disaggregated models now ranges from 0 (electoral choice of absentee voters, but starting from a near complete variance explained already) to +0.16 for the electoral resolution of in-person voters, and +0.20 for the happiness of their next electoral experience.

On the whole, not only do our electoral psychology models explain significant aspects of the variance in citizens' electoral behaviour, experience, and sense of resolution, but they also show that those three components are interrelated and act dynamically over time, such that your turnout and electoral choice affect your future electoral happiness, just as happy electoral experiences followed by a sense of resolution will affect your future turnout and electoral choice. In many ways, these were arguably the most complex claims of our model, and among those which could only be tested using a detailed panel study spanning two consecutive elections.

Internalizing Election Day

In an age of unprecedented political cynicism, many politicians, journalists, and political scientists alike would likely assume that Election Day is only important to them, and a day when most citizens would prefer to go to the beach or carry on with work as usual. There is of course no doubt that some do, but this book has shown that for the rest, our frequent assumptions regarding what elections mean to people grossly underestimate their real importance in their lives. That importance, however, largely operates through internalization.

In chapter 1, we suggested that elections remain the ultimate moment of civic communion between citizens and their political systems, and our model suggests they represent the moment when democracy is 'validated' (or relegitimized) in citizens' minds. When things work well, this leads to electoral resolution, democratic hope, and, through this process of relegitimization, what we usually call an 'electoral honeymoon', even among many who did not vote for the winners. Elections are citizens' opportunity to reclaim ownership of a political system purportedly organized to be 'of the people, by the people, and for the people', as per Lincoln's famous Gettysburg Address description, (Lincoln, 1994), but rarely feels like that to them.

However, in chapter 3, we also showed that beyond institutional legitimation, elections are experiences which citizens internalize. They become part of their private, intimate, and family lives, and relate to their own development as human beings. In the context of elections, the 'small' (or private) history thus regularly overlaps and merges with the 'big' (or national) one. As a result, the meaning of elections and the construction of a cumulative memory associated with them predominantly rests on that internalization. Citizens remember elections from their childhood and they remember their first time. They remember discussions and arguments, falling out with their friends, or breaking up with their lover or simply crying, laughing, or celebrating. They adopt elections into their lives, and this is how they remember them.

Throughout this book, we have aimed to elucidate what elections mean to citizens, both narratively and analytically, but also the complex interface between elections which revalidate the democratic credentials of political systems and restore citizens' sense of ownership of democracy, and elections that become historical and personal yardsticks within a citizen's life and personal development. That internalization also contributes to making elections so narratively powerful for citizens (chapter 3) and so emotionally intense (chapter 7).

An Intense Experience

Our visual experiment showed that voting leads to strong and largely positive emotions, irrespective of electoral choice. In fact, even in an experimental context, the emotions that citizens betray as they vote prove even more intense and even more positive than they themselves report. In an electoral context, this is again confirmed by our implicit measures and word associations for those who vote, regardless of whether it is for a winner or a loser. This suggests that it is the electoral experience itself (and not the victory of a preferred candidate) which produces primary emotions. Our findings on 'electoral tears', showing that very significant proportions of citizens with no major interest in politics can get very emotional in intense electoral experiences (be it in positively or negatively), confirm this emotionality of elections even more bluntly. The crucial condition, however, remains that of taking part, and indeed, those who abstain drift further apart from the majority of emotional voters, and perpetuate divergence in a way which may explain habituation phenomena.

We have also seen that the emotionality of elections is heightened when people vote for the first time, and to a lesser extent for the second time. They typically feel happier, more excited, and closer to the rest of society, though also more nervous, thereby entrenching one's first vote as a real 'first time'. Elections matter, not only as events, but also as occasions to test one's own place in society, one's own role, almost the ability to give the best of oneself in this collective rendezvous, especially the first time that one is invited to it. Furthermore, we have shown that the way young voters live their electoral experience remains uniquely influential and memorable, and will durably shape their future outlook on elections and state of mind in future electoral experiences. We also found that in cases such as the UK's 2016 EU-membership referendum, young voters were even more likely than others to be brought to tears during the electoral sequence.

Through our model of electoral identity (chapter 6), we have also seen that citizens tend very much to 'inhabit' their experience of elections by assuming functions and roles—typically those of referee or supporter—

which add a dramatic (in the theatrical sense of the term) dimension to their experience. The importance of electoral identity as giving weight to electoral experience should not be underestimated. As we have seen, it affects the way people absorb the campaign and relate to its atmosphere, the way they appropriate their decision-making process, and relate to others, the way they experience Election Day and Election Night.

In fact, our findings also show that this personal investment and functional take on one's electoral role results in different aspects being perceived and recalled by voters, both instantaneously, and cumulatively and durably over time. The high level of personalization in electoral memories (discussions, arguments, the atmosphere of the polling station, etc.) points, yet again, to the importance of the experiential nature of elections, their ability to penetrate the personal sphere and become part of a citizen's intimate world for days, rather than being the detached, external, and rather occasional events that one might assume them to be from research that shows that, consciously at least, citizens are honestly persuaded that they could not care less about politics and therefore, we hastily infer, about elections.

We started this book by highlighting the paradox whereby behavioural research often assumes that people do not care—and indeed care less and less—about elections, but our observation, by contrast, suggests that even people arguably not politically involved in fact experience elections intensely, often very personally. We suggested that our perception might be wrong and would need to be tested; but ultimately, all of our quantitative, qualitative, and experimental evidence points to the acute and cathartic emotional intensity of elections.

Endless Cycles

With this paradox in mind, it is clear that such emotionally intense electoral experience results in behavioural electoral cycles being much more heterogeneous and complex than political scientists typically assume on the basis of their alternative, but only marginally relevant, institutional logic.

Typically, we expect an election cycle to start with the launch of election campaigns, peak on Election Day, and end in a resolution once the result is known and confirmed and a government is formed. Instead, none of those three points—start, peak, and end of the election cycle—necessarily prove definitive from a citizen's perspective. The starting point of an election cycle can be volatile. It often arguably precedes the time an election is even announced, or on the contrary may start well after the official campaign has begun, according to our analysis of diaries. The peak of the electoral cycle may be Election Day for many, but it can equally be Election Night, or again, for an increasing proportion of citizens voting remotely, it could be their own voting time, well before an official Election Day that can then be reinvented as a democratic anticlimax. As for the capacity of the results to bring closure to the election cycle, we have seen that whilst this often happens, there are numerous recent cases—such as the 2016 UK referendum, the 2016 US presidential election, and the 2017 UK general election—when it did not, and the end of an official election period failed to close the cycle in citizens' perceptions and behaviour.

Similarly, the variability of electoral experiences and the intensity of electoral emotions come to disturb the predictability of the transition between successive election cycles. In chapter 8, we noted that there is often confusion as to when one election cycle ends and the next begins, or how much overlap there is between them, consequently confusing voters' psychology and references. Furthermore, not all elections are 'created equal', and this inequality proves far more complex and unpredictable than our knowledge assumes.

Thus, the second-order election model follows a strictly institutional logic to assert that there is one type of first-order election in every system (presidential in the US, France, or Georgia, general in the UK or South Africa, federal in Germany, etc.) and that all other votes (local, regional, European, referenda, etc.) only matter in relation to this first-order election cycle. Our findings reported in chapter 9 suggest that this electoral hierarchy was substantially shaken by the 2016 EU-membership referendum in the UK. Not only did this referendum act as a first-order vote in many ways, but it arguably relegated the 2017 general election that followed a year later to the rank of second-order election and tributary of the Brexit referendum cycle. There is no way that this could possibly make sense in the terms of traditional institutionalist models of electoral hierarchy, and it shows that, ultimately, it is what voters make of an election that creates the final hierarchy of ordered votes, the final arbitration between conflicting and overlapping election cycles. It is voters who invest elections with meaning, appropriate the dramatic value of electoral debates and fractures, and, through their experience of and investment in electoral processes, rewrite national electoral history, often against the expectations (and arguably, the will and intention) of institutional designers, the media, and political elites.

Getting the Best out of People

This narrative and emotional appropriation constitutes a strange form of historical and quasi-philosophical democratic ownership. The appropriation of the electoral experience by voters, and the function they assume in and inhabit in elections, have thoroughgoing and counter-intuitive consequences. In many ways, politics represents a context that can lead to flaring tensions, and which many citizens consider 'dirty', perhaps with good reason, as it can even lead to hostility (chapter 9). Nevertheless, elections themselves seem to have a way of 'getting the best out of' voters.

This is a multifaceted reality. First, both narratively and implicitly, we found that a large majority of voters are sociotropic throughout the electoral process. Crucially, we showed that when giving self-reported evidence, 'supporters', people highly interested in politics, and older voters are more likely to think of their own behaviour as sociotropic, but that, on the contrary, when using implicit measures of sociotropism, 'referees' and young people are in fact more sociotropic than the rest on some dimensions. This contradiction arises because the literature has focused purely on economics, whilst sociotropism is in fact multidimensional, and influenced by vulnerabilities—we act egocentrically when we feel fragile and worried, and different groups feel vulnerable on different political dimensions, including economics, but also safety or even diversity. This is a notable finding at a time when many accuse young people of being self-centred, materialistic, and uninterested in the life of their community, whilst they are in fact at the forefront of many idealistic battles in relation to the environment, tolerance, or equality. Even more importantly, we show that the very act of voting leads to greater sociotropism and empathic displacement than does abstention.

Indeed, empathic displacement is a critical motor of electoral perceptions and behaviour; unlike sociotropism, which involves citizens thinking about what is best for their country, it is about elections fostering empathy for and awareness of the rest of the population, their intentions, and the logic behind their fears, hopes, preferences, and behaviour. Indeed, we show that empathic displacement is not only associated with greater turnout, but also affects electoral choice, and, ultimately, sense of electoral resolution. Similarly, transgenerational and longitudinal projection, in particular a concern for the situation of future generations, also affects electoral behaviour, experiences, and resolution significantly. Elections get the best out of citizens, because they lead people to try to see the world from the point of view of others around them, and when they do so, they are more likely to feel that elections perform their function even if they result in outcomes that they themselves have not chosen.

Our findings on personality and morality and their impact on the vote, meanwhile, lead to interesting conclusions as to how elections 'improve' citizens. They also show the impact of the intimate intricacies of one's psychology, including one's personality and morality, which do not necessarily result in the patterns of behaviour many would predict. We demonstrated that a number of discrete personality traits—such as sensitivity, anxiety, risk aversion, alienation, caringness, and empathy are related to both turnout and electoral choice (left vs right, or moderate vs extreme), even for contexts where the 'Big Five' showed no strong effect in previous research.

Our findings on morality are perhaps even more telling. There is much research suggesting that right-wing voters consciously claim a stronger emphasis on moral value than their left-wing counterparts, but our findings tell a different story: one which suggests that the picture is not so much about who cares about morality and who does not, but instead about personal systems of hierarchization of often incompatible priorities. We are back to competing conceptions of what the world and life in society are and should be—competing visions of what we should agree is non-negotiable, good, and desirable for the future.

We suggest that our findings on moral hierarchization shed unprecedented light on the phenomenon of electoral hostility that we analyze in chapter 9. Given the nature of the negative emotions that constitute electoral hostility, we believe that voters implicitly blame opposite voters for being immoral, because they show no respect for moral values they themselves see as inalienable. In fact, the opposite voters may be aware of and may even ideally want to protect those moral values, but feel that they have to sacrifice them in order to protect what they see as an even bigger moral prerequisite. Thus, 'We may need to seize and close polluting industrial plants to protect the life of future generations', or denial of this claim, is interpreted as not caring about private property on the one hand, or not caring about the life of future generations on the other, by those with opposing hierarchies. In a way, this almost works as conflicting Mokken scale of the same moral variables. Those who believe that respect for the property of others is in fact the most fundamental of all moral values will naturally tend to assume that anyone who may fail at times to respect private property has 'moral compass' whatsoever. By contrast, that 'immoral villain' may simply be someone who feels that there is no greater sin than lying, and is therefore convinced that the person judging him/her, by tolerating lies to protect private property, is likewise demonstrating a complete lack of concern for the most fundamental of moral precepts.

Thus, elections bring the best out of people, but also show their naked senses of moral and political arbitration to others who do not share these and are consequently willing to judge—and perhaps sometimes misjudge—them in that regard. This portrays voters as to some extent Jekyll-and-Hyde characters, showing their very best side as they vote, often sociotropic and empathic, but sometimes hasty and judgmental as they react to others who do not reach the same political and moral conclusions as they do, and whom they cannot understand.

Dr Jekyll and Mr Hyde? Paradoxes of Hostility

Elections bringing out the best in people would indeed seem to be compatible, in practice, with growing populism, narratives of hatred, and as we saw in chapter 9, a mounting and arguably worrying sense of electoral hostility across many democracies. Could elections be on the one hand catalysts that engage many citizens in the exercise of positive functions and a sense of responsibility, sociotropism, and selfless idealism, and on the other hand events that increasingly serve to anchor negative feelings, not only towards political systems, but towards other citizens, both at the same time?

Whilst this may sound counter-intuitive, it is not particularly challenging to consider the two phenomena as taking place simultaneously, and it does not even require a suggestion that self-bettering and hostility would affect different people. A first reason for this surprising compatibility is time. In chapter 9, we showed that electoral honeymoons rest on citizens sublimating negative perceptions of electoral democracy into frequently enthusiastic responses to the election itself as a democratic process. There is thus a temporal duality between elections considered as periods, and elections considered as participatory events, with wildly diverging connotations. A second reason is that seeing one's role as a voter as a democratic function, an important responsibility, and an occasion that imposes the need for sociotropism and societal responsibility does not in itself mean that the responsible and sociotopic voter will necessarily be any more tolerant of others. In fact, such voters may be all the more upset by them, on account of their own noble perspective, precisely because they see those opposite voters as less responsible, more self-centred, corrupt, or generally unworthy, in their perceived thought processes, motivation, or behavior, of that important civic responsibility. As we have just observed, never is this more obvious than when moral hierarchies conflict due to essentially incompatible trade-offs.

In that perspective, we return to electoral identity and our distinction between referees and supporters. Whilst supporters might easily develop negative feelings towards opposite voters through polarization, referees will instead likely develop those negative emotions against the backdrop of a perceived betrayal on the part of those opposite voters of their civic responsibility. Critically, this means that one does not need to be highly engaged in politics to develop electoral hostility (indeed, it could arise in citizens who typically do not feel that they care). It similarly implies that hostility need not necessarily be based in partisanship, nor even target voters of very distant parties (it could, for instance, be directed at voters who only make a single different arbitration whilst agreeing with one on most major principles, or abstentionists). Referees and supporters thus develop different ways not only of following and engaging with campaigns and of voting, but even too of hating.

Nemeses and Victims

As a result of the increasingly complex relationship between betterment and hostility, the same voters may be in turn certain other voters' saviours, victims, and nemeses. Let us consider the logic of some of the populist victories occurring during the later part of the period covered by this book, and discussed in chapter 9. While a sense of victimization appears to be a key reason for people to vote in favour of populist candidates, parties, and rhetoric, there is no doubt that when this results in an overall populist victory, it creates a similar sense of victimization and democratic marginalization or vulnerability among those who had, thus far, generally enjoyed a perception of democratic inclusion. In fact, in the narratives of populist voters, there is occasionally an evocation of 'revenge'—or at any rate a visiting of just deserts—upon groups of voters whom they consider guilty of being naïve, selfish, and unpatriotic, but above all 'in power'.

What happens, however, when such a switch of electoral fortunes occurs? If perceptions of integration and alienation are related purely to being on the winning side, then the former majority would start to feel alienated, and, conversely, those who supported a winning populist outcome would revert to a sense of societal connection, instead of marginalization. If, on the contrary, individual–societal electoral connection is irrelevant, and feelings of inclusion or exclusion derive rather from enduring social and economic conditions, those who lost would continue in a sense of undisturbed societal connection, whilst those who felt marginalized would not see their situation as improving as a result of the electoral success of their preferred option.

However, as shown in chapter 9, electoral resolution and senses of inclusion and alienation seem asymmetric. In responses to our open questions collected after the UK EU-membership referendum and our interviews following the 2016 US election, we find *both* clear signs of systemic and societal alienation on the part of social categories rarely associated with marginalization, but who found themselves on the losing side of electoral battles they deem fundamental, *and* of resilient feelings of alienation and marginalization on the part of those who voted for Brexit and for Trump, despite their desired electoral outcome winning the day. In other words, populist victories do not seem to lead to a reversal of integration fortunes, but instead replace a plurality of perceptions of integration and alienation by a quasi-unanimous perception of alienation, albeit resting on conflicting bases.

This provides a possible explanation for the rising hostility that we noted following victories for electoral outcomes often deemed populist. That is, these outcomes may result in feelings of vulnerability, alienation, and marginalization actually being shared across the entire spectrum of voters, as opposed to afflicting the losing side only, as traditionally in the aftermath of elections. In turn, this raises questions regarding the potential (or lack thereof) for societal-level electoral resolution in contexts where no part of the electorate feels entirely reassured and integrated by a given electoral result, and, indeed, all components of the spectrum feel themselves to be to some degree victims of the system.

Ultimate Hopes, Ultimate Risks? The Psychology of Electoral Peace

What does all this tell us about how electoral behaviour, outcomes, and experiences interact with voters' psychology to legitimize or, on the contrary, to threaten a democratic system? One of the original features of this book is to bring together some long-established and far more recent democracies and analyze a number of phenomena across their diversity.

One of the questions that we asked across countries pertains to what citizens would be willing to do when they radically object to a democratic outcome and the policies that ensue. In Georgia, 23.5% explain that they would engage in another revolution if need be, and in South Africa, that proportion even increases to 31.5%. Even in Scotland, 19% say that if they were unhappy with the political situation in the country, they would take part in a revolution, whilst 19.7% would also consider leaving the country. In other consolidated democracies, the option of a revolution was not offered to respondents, but in the US, 11.9% said that they would consider voting for a radical or revolutionary party, and 8.1% that they would leave the country. In France, those proportions were 33% and 21.5% respectively. In short, across emerging and consolidated democracies, substantial minorities of citizens would consider radical—and even violent—responses when they feel that elections do not bring resolution.

Concurrently, we noted that an implication of increasingly hostile references in the British and American contexts is the apparent impossibility of convergence, reconciliation, and therefore resolution between those who supported the winning and losing camps in the 2016 UK referendum and US presidential election. We evoked a possible scenario whereby electoral hostility could result in the contesting of existing models of solidarity. In other words, we questioned what would happen if the formerly 'integrated' sections of society were to object to paying any longer into the system, as previously they had done out of solidarity with the formerly disconnected groups of the population who are often the first predicted victims of populist policies. This was offered not as a prediction, but rather as a hypothesis symptomatic of how deeply things have changed during the decade of electoral politics studied in this book. In other words, we consider solidarity the litmus test of the ability of electoral democracy to bring resolution, reconcile the polity in the aftermath of a fractious election, and close the election cycle. Thus, hostility may still be manageable by electoral democracies if, even under conditions of animosity, winners and losers still 'play ball', continuing to act civically towards each other as a result of recurrent electoral processes, and continuing to contribute willingly to the system in a spirit of solidarity with the very people they have just accused of betraying their own future. If, on the other hand, electoral hostility leads to the denunciation of those solidarity mechanisms, this could result in the terrifying end of the ability of the electoral system to regulate conflict and disagreement between opposing members of the *Homo Suffragator* community.

As we saw in chapter 9, at the time this book goes to print, not only would about one in five people never want to speak again to someone who disagrees with them on fundamental issues, and over one in ten be able to imagine having a physical fight with them, but over a third of voters now resent paying taxes to protect those who voted for electoral outcomes that they themselves denounced.

The book will close with this question mark. We have seen that the majority of citizens show the 'good will' required to embrace and inhabit roles as voters and consider their relationship to others in elections. In this sense, elections 'bring out the best' in people. The vast majority of voters try to do what they believe to be right, and do so in ways which are empathic, projective, and societally-minded. Yet, in an age of electoral hostility, animosity towards opposite voters seems to have less to do with personal disagreement, and often more to do with a sense of moral and projective outrage, as though those opposite voters were not simply favourable towards a different future, but espoused conceptions of society and a collective identity intrinsically contrary to the interest and values of the polity—a betrayal of its identity, even a selfish frustration of the hopes of its young. Just as the concept of electoral identity implies that people do not merely express a selfish preference, based on the role they personally inhabit, in the polling booth, so too it is that identity that they embrace when they judge and even hate others who reach different conclusions from their own; it is often on behalf of society and its future that they abhor them.

Homo Suffragator must decide whether he/she still believes in electoral democracy as an effective way of regulating disagreement and improving the collective future; a worthwhile path to keep alive the hope that one day, their young will live better and more happily than they do. The alternative—that *Homo Suffragator* has already given up—is nothing short of terrifying.

GLOSSARY OF CONCEPTS

ATMOSPHERE

This book introduces the concept of 'electoral atmosphere', defined as the largely implicit emotional perceptions citizens associate with the mood of the election, based on an infinite set of perceptions of the events, behaviour, and tone of election actors, commentators, and citizens themselves. That elections have an atmosphere is spontaneously and repeatedly evoked by respondents in the qualitative part of our research, and is indeed frequently mentioned by citizens and electoral commentators alike. In the social sciences, we are nevertheless often tempted to dismiss the concept as overly fluid and impressionistic. Yet, in chapter 2, we show that in other disciplines—from architecture and arts to business and museum design—the notion of atmosphere is taken very seriously and analyzed very systematically, in terms of both its dimensions and its determinants. In this book, we thus try to emulate those disciplines and see whether we can arrive at a systematic understanding of how voters perceive the atmosphere of elections and how that atmosphere can vary across them. In chapter 2, we model electoral atmosphere as being determined by electoral ergonomics and context, as well as the capacity of the previous election to bring about a sense of electoral resolution and closure (see entries for 'context' and 'electoral resolution' below). Chapter 9 shows how voters perceived the atmosphere of two consecutive elections, using both open- and closed-question measures.

CONTEXT

Over the past sixty years, many approaches have been popular in electoral research, including political sociology (the impact of social and demographic characteristics on the vote), political economy (the impact of calculations and economic conditions), and, more recently, studies of 'context'. This trend has emerged precisely due to the understanding that models expected to be universal often fail to take into account idiosyncratic elements such as campaign incidents, debates, scandals, media coverage, and financial or international events, or even simply the personalities and demeanours of candidates, which have the power to lead to electoral outcomes that the models may fail to predict. In that sense, 'context' often mirrors the 'short-term factors' that Campbell et al. (1960) identified in the Michigan model of the vote. Crucially, however, context is predominantly used to explain aggregate-level outcomes based on aggregate-level predictors. In this book, we question whether the psychology of voters might in some way determine an individual dimension of context, because it has the potential to explain different individual reactions to specific contextual prompts. We also claim that electoral ergonomics may constrain contextual effects in elections. The relationship between context, electoral psychology, and electoral ergonomics (see entry below) is developed in chapter 2.

ELECTION CYCLE

Most readers will consider that it is understood perfectly well what an election cycle is. Indeed, the electoral literature universally defines this as the time elapsed between two elections—or at least two 'first-order' elections. Yet, in this book, we question this definition, by pointing out that, whilst being used in *behavioural* models, it is, in fact, very *institution-centric*. In chapter 1, we point out that there is no obvious reason to assume that an election cycle as experienced by an individual voter or a collective electorate should necessarily follow an institution-centric logic. We question whether election cycles may not span multiple elections (for instance, in cases where an incumbent easily achieves re-election) or realignment elections, whether they might be disrupted by open terms and snap elections, and whether the logic of first- and second-order elections is necessarily fixed (taking the example of the 2017 UK general election, which almost appears as a sub-vote within the election cycle centred on the EU-membership referendum of 2016). In terms of theory, in chapters 9 and 10 we relate the concept of the election cycle to that of electoral resolution, and suggest that behaviourally, election cycles are determined not only by institutionalized rhythms, but also by the relative ability of a given election to bring closure (or 'resolution'—see entry below) and thereby end a cycle. We suggest that this also means that a given electoral cycle may continue well after Election Day and the announcement of the results, be it merely in an extended post-election period (see 'electoral honeymoon' below), or long enough to encompass the next election in the country.

ELECTION DAY

In our model, Election Day is a hypothesized to be a special day for many citizens, whether or not they are conscious of that specificity. For most citizens, this will be a day when the world around them speaks and thinks of the election, thereby creating a unique atmosphere (see entry above) and conditions of empathic displacement (see entry below). Election Day includes a number of phases, which will vary depending on whether a citizen is a voter (and in that case in-person or remotely) or an abstentionist, For a traditional in-station voter, Election Day will include a period of preparation and anticipation, the trip to the polling station, the polling station visit, the polling booth experience, the aftermath of the vote, the awaiting of the result, and Election Night (see entry below) and the electoral debriefing. Remote voters and abstentionists will escape some of those steps but still be exposed to flux of information and discussion of the election, as well as a sense of being excluded from phases which serve precisely to unite much of the rest of the country. Indeed, this participation in, or avoidance of, a societally shared, ritualized pattern has the potential to make citizens feel more integrated in or excluded from the rest of the community, and will generate a form of solemnity and potentially tension, enliven the roles that individual citizens inhabit as voters, trigger unique memories, and elicit specific sets of emotions that are characteristic of Election Day(s) alone and are constitutive of its perceived atmosphere. Election Day may include traditions both collective (e.g., election cakes, civic barbecues) or individualized (e.g., going to vote with given family members or neighbours, often at a given time, perhaps following a specific route), rituals, and iconographies, some shared and some idiosyncratic. The details of Election Day are discussed in chapter 3.

ELECTION NIGHT

Election Night is a specific component of Election Day. Its timing is usually ritualized on the basis of legal constraints and frameworks, when results will be estimated and revealed, and of course individual habits and practices. Just like Election Day, Election Night will have its own form of iconography and traditions both collectively (regular presenters or commentators, preference of TV channel or source of estimations or results, imagery, etc.) and individually (many voters will follow specific habits during Election Night, often inspired by early memories of elections, and often share them with the same people election after election). Examples of such traditions and rituals are described in chapter 3. There is almost no political behaviour research focusing on Election Night (indeed, at the time in question, most political scientists are more concerned with analyzing the results of the vote than with the concurrent behaviour of citizens discovering those results); but we find that for many, memories of Election Night are even stronger than of the earlier parts of Election Day, in part thanks to deeply rooted iconographies and highly ritualized habits. We suggest that, just like Election Day, Election Night triggers its own sense of solemnity and collective bonding, its own series of memories and emotions, and also potentially reinforces empathic displacement and sociotropism (see entries below), or, on the contrary, may increase a sense of alienation amongst citizens who did not take part in the vote, or, in a different manner, amongst those who voted for parties or candidates who lost the election. These discrepancies and potential senses of integration or alienation are theorized as affecting a given citizen's sense of electoral resolution (see entry below).

ELECTORAL BEHAVIOUR

Electoral behaviour is one of the most important traditional fields of political science research, in particular since the 1950s. It has also been at the heart of some research in neighbouring disciplines such as sociology, (social) psychology, anthropology, law, and communication, to constitute what we refer to in this book as 'electoral science'. Electoral behaviour research may be interested in either individual- or aggregate-level behaviour. At the individual level, it is predominantly concerned with two specific decisions made by citizens during an election: whether or not to vote (turnout), and which party or candidate to support, or what order of parties/candidates in preferential voting systems ('electoral choice': see entry below). Sometimes, the dependent variable may be formulated as a specification of variation of one of those factors (e.g., habitual voting as a longitudinal extension of turnout; see further examples below relating to sub-components of electoral choice). At the aggregate level, such research is typically interested in election outcomes (which parties or candidates win elections) or, again, overall turnout, with variations regarding specific aspects of these topics (e.g., electoral stability, or incumbency effects upon whether or not people in power get re-elected). Electoral behaviour has been the object of a number of key approaches such as those of political sociology (the impact of social and demographic differences on the vote), political economy (including both economic calculations in voting and the impact of economic situations on electoral outcomes), institutional approaches (for instance, partisanship and the study of the consequences of electoral systems), context studies (the impact of campaign effects, candidates' personalities, anecdotal events, and, more broadly, short-term factors bearing upon electoral outcomes), and electoral psychology, which is the perspective predominantly embraced by this book. Whilst they are not strictly 'behavioural', electoral research has also focused on attitudinal dependent variables (such as satisfaction, efficacy, perceptions of representation, etc.) and other related phenomena such as political socialization. Chapter 2 discusses where our electoral psychology approach in general and this book in particular fit within the field of electoral science.

ELECTORAL CHOICE

'Electoral choice' is one of the two main dependent variables studied by electoral behaviour (see entry above) research concerned with individual-level models. Electoral choice focuses on which parties or candidates a given voter chooses to give his/her vote(s) to, or how he/she ranks them in the context of preferential voting systems such as Single Transferable Vote or Alternative Vote. The concept of electoral choice may also pertain to specific aspects of that voting decision: for example, the decision to vote for an extremist party, split-ticket voting, or spoiled ballots. Electoral choice can be studied in the context of a specific election or over time (i.e., the consistency of electoral choice across one's lifetime or across different types of election). We situate our research vis-à-vis the current state of electoral choice research in chapter 2, but also explain in chapters 1 and 2 why we believe that electoral choice, including the decision to participate, is in fact the 'wrong' dependent variable for electoral science research, or at any rate, should not be the only such variable, as we propose associating electoral behavior with electoral experience and electoral resolution, neither of which is 'behavioural', strictly speaking, but both of which, in the perspective of this book, are considered to be complementary to and interrelated with electoral behaviour.

ELECTORAL ERGONOMICS (POLLING STATION, BALLOT, ETC.)

We conceptualize electoral ergonomics as the interface between electoral psychology (see entry below) and the organization and management of elections. Usually, electoral organization is studied on its own by electoral science, with a primary focus on its direct effects, not least its impact on who will vote. However, our take on electoral ergonomics, as an interface, makes it quite different. Indeed, it suggests that different elements of electoral management or organization will in fact trigger different personality traits, memories, identity components, or emotions from the very same voters as they vote. Consequently, whilst research on convenience voting, for example, focuses on whether different people end up voting when remote voting options are introduced, our electoral ergonomics approach asks rather whether the same people will have different electoral behaviour, experience, and likelihood of electoral resolution depending upon whether they vote in a polling station or from home, on Election Day or before. One essential point that we make in our conceptualization is that, whilst many understand ergonomics to be the matching of an object or process to human aptitudes, it is more precisely the matching of that object or process to human aptitudes *given its function*. We use the example of an ergonomically designed pen, which would look like a small water bottle were it not for the fact that one needs to be able to write with it. In the context of electoral ergonomics, this means that we need to understand the impact of electoral design in the light not only of electoral psychology, but also of the function ascribed to elections (see entry below: 'function of elections'). We devote chapter 8 specifically to electoral ergonomics, and refer to it throughout the book in relation to design elements such as polling station design, forms of ballot, vote dematerialization, and remote voting.

ELECTORAL EXPERIENCE

'Electoral experience' is one of three key, interrelated dependent variables in our model, alongside electoral behaviour and electoral resolution (see entries above and below, respectively). One of our important claims is that elections permeate the lives of individuals and that their individual 'small' histories intersect with 'big' national history through a process of internalization (see entry below); because, that is, voters end up assimilating electoral cycles, events, behaviour, and functions into their personal lives. The nature of the electoral experience is also shaped by the role of elections as a moment of 'civic communion' between voters and their political system (see Déloye and Ihl, 2008). In operational terms, we also theorize that the emotions people feel before, during, and after their vote in relation to the election, including tears (see entry below), emotionality, and happiness, are critical measures of the nature of the electoral experience. Electoral experience can vary across countries, elections, individuals, or indeed for a given individual across different elections. We suggest in particular that first-time voters will experience elections differently from—and far more emotionally than—the rest of the population. In terms of our interrelated dependent variables, we suggest that electoral behaviour (voting or not, and for whom) will affect citizens' electoral experience, and their electoral experience (notably its emotionality and happiness) will affect the likelihood that a citizen will experience electoral resolution, as well as their likely behaviour in future elections. Electoral experience is evoked throughout the book, but described specifically, with narrative detail in chapter 3.

ELECTORAL HONEYMOON

'Electoral honeymoon' is a popular term that has been used by electoral scientists and commentators alike to refer to the fact that a newly elected political leader will often experience a surge in popularity ratings directly after his/her election. In this book, we note that such honeymoon ratings reflect the phenomenon of elected politicians not merely continuing to enjoy the whole of their electoral support at the start of their mandate, but typically exceeding their electoral performance, sometimes to a significant extent. Within a given election cycle (see entry above), we suggest, such an apparent anomaly is in fact a positive side-effect of electoral resolution (see entry below). Thus, when an election fails to produce electoral resolution, the election winner will not, we believe, benefit from an electoral honeymoon. We discuss electoral honeymoons in chapter 9, in the contexts of electoral resolution and of hope (see entry below), and suggest that electoral honeymoons stem from elections relegitimizing electoral democracy in the eyes of voters. As a result, the honeymoon effect is not personal, or to be taken to imply the conversion of adverse voters, but is rather procedural, and pertains to the winner in so far as he/she represents the outcome of a successful process.

ELECTORAL HOSTILITY

'Electoral hostility' is one of the major concepts introduced by this book, and it pertains to the negative feelings that voters can hold towards others whom they perceive to vote differently from them. We claim that these negative feelings are hierarchized, starting with misunderstanding, then morphing into frustration and distrust, then anger, followed by contempt and disgust, and ultimately a sense of enmity. We also claim that electoral hostility can degrade over time, following that hierarchy. There is an important literature on affective polarization, which suggests that those who identify with opposing parties will grow further apart, and as they do so, will start to develop increasingly negative feelings towards one another. However, our electoral hostility model is different in a number of ways. First, it is not based on partisanship. Second, it is not necessarily grounded on actually divergent votes, but can focus instead on electoral prejudices (e.g., 'old people voted for Brexit' or 'Londoners are "Remoaners"'). Third, because electoral hostility is in our view not based on partisanship, it is not necessary for anyone strongly to support a party—or even to regularly vote for one, or to vote at all—to experience it. In fact, analytically, we conceive electoral hostility not as a stage in partisan identification, but instead as a degradation of political cynicism, whereby citizens who have come to distrust and dislike their politicians and institutions extend those negative feelings to those who vote for them. We note a number of important points with regard to electoral hostility, such as its relationship to moral hierarchization (see entry below), such that when a voter accepts the sacrifice of a moral principle A, which he/she believes is necessary in order to protect (more highly valued) moral principle B, voters with different hierarchies, for whom no moral principle is more sacred than principle A, will see him/her as immoral, because ready to compromise on the principle they see as most important of all. We also note that electoral hostility may take different shapes according to electoral identity (see entry below), 'supporters' being likely to see opposite voters as in an incompatible 'camp', whilst 'referees' are more likely to resent opposite voters for not having reached their electoral conclusion with the same degree of sociotropism (see entry below) and probity as themselves. As a result, electoral hostility is paradoxically compatible with elections 'getting the best out of people'. It is discussed specifically in chapter 9.

ELECTORAL IDENTITY

'Electoral identity' is a key concept introduced by our book. It captures the notion that when people go to vote, they do not merely express a 'pure' or spontaneous preference, but rather inhabit a role and cast their vote according to the particular function of the role that they assume. We use the analogies of a teacher grading a paper not according to whether they like a student or not, but rather according to how they believe that they should value it as a teacher, or of parents admonishing their child for misbehaviour not because it is their preference to do so, but because they feel that not intervening in such a case would be remiss in the context of their role, function, and identity as parents. Our definition of electoral identity is entirely unrelated to the partisan identity model of *The American Voter* (Campbell et al., 1960). Instead, it focuses on potential variations in the relationship between the individual and the collective in the vote; that is, how voters relate to others when subconsciously understanding their role in an election through such elements as sociotropism, projection, and emphatic displacement (see respective entries below). Our key model of electoral identity suggests that if we think of elections as a major game or sports event, and parties or candidates as the teams competing for citizens' votes, a voter can see his/her role as that of a 'supporter' of one of the teams, or that of a 'referee' responsible for fairly and objectively adjudicating between them. Note that we conceive of electoral identity as predominantly subconscious. It is the subject specifically of chapter 6.

ELECTORAL MEMORY

'Electoral memory' is the accumulation of all the implicit and explicit memories citizens carry on from past elections and electoral periods. Whilst much of the literature has focused on citizens' memories of their past vote, we make the case, based on existing research on memory, that those are neither the most likely nor the most powerful memories they are likely to hold about past elections. When discussing electoral memory, we refer to existing categories of visual, auditive, and haptic memories, to the way memories are stored and transformed and how they interact, to the importance of internalization (see entry below) and to how memories are retrieved, whether explicitly or implicitly, in future electoral contexts. Cumulative memories need not be 'objectively true' to be influential. They will certainly be rationalized and to an extent altered. Crucially, however, the fact that they may not be 'reachable' by citizens in non-electoral contexts does not mean that they will not be influential when a citizen is back in an environment in which those memories were created and meaningful, and their influence may also differ depending on whether a citizen votes in a polling station, where priming is likely to be more significant, or from home. In this book, we discuss electoral memory specifically in chapter 5, and show that childhood and first-vote elections make for some of the most influential electoral memories, as do memories of electoral internalization—

such as discussions, arguments, and haptic memories of electoral atmosphere on Election Day and Night.

ELECTORAL PSYCHOLOGY

Inside the Mind of a Voter could in a way be seen as a 'manifesto for electoral psychology', inviting readers and the disciplines to reconsider how voters' psychology could shape the sources, consequences, and methods that we consider and embrace when looking at citizens in connection with elections. In terms of sources, we focus on key psychological predictors such as personality, morality, memory, and identity. We also try to systematize our understanding of the concept of electoral atmosphere, and see how electoral psychology is in interface with electoral design and management to create electoral ergonomics (see entry above). In terms of consequences, we claim that electoral choice is in fact an unnatural dependent variable for electoral research, and unlikely to be the most important consequence of elections from voters' points of view, compared to the nature and emotions elicited by the electoral experience (Do elections make people happy? Emotional? Worried?), and the capacity of elections to bring citizens a sense of closure and resolution. We also look at other psychological consequences of elections, including hope, hopelessness, hostility, and more. Regarding methodology and analysis, we suggest that taking an electoral-psychological approach requires us to remember that most electoral thoughts, processes, and behaviours are likely to be subconscious, and that our methodologies need to be adapted to this fact. We therefore make extensive use of visual experiments, implicit questions, and external observation in combination with self-report-based quantitative and qualitative (usually narrative) methodologies.

ELECTORAL RESOLUTION

'Electoral resolution' is one of the three key, interrelated dependent variables covered in this book and perhaps, in terms of democratic theory, the most important of them. It refers to the capacity of elections to bring to individuals and societies a sense of closure, an impression that the election has successfully ended an election cycle, by democratically resolving the potential tension between opposed preferences, beliefs, and/or interests. At the start of the book, we state the claim that elections make the human being a *Homo Suffragator*, changing our collective condition by presenting us with a new and different mechanism to resolve conflict, divergence, and rivalry by polling the whole polity and asking it to determine how to conduct public affairs for the next few years in a way that translates social equilibria into political authority. This implies that the electoral process will be (explicitly or implicitly) perceived as successful and legitimate by citizens, in a way which will relegitimize democracy and the system for a period of time, generating good will, diffuse support, acceptance, and ultimately civic behaviour on the part of citizens, whether or not their personal preferences are vindicated by the election result. When this works and electoral resolution is delivered, this leads, we claim, to an electoral honeymoon (see entry above). When it does not work, some citizens will consider the outcome of the election illegitimate (regardless of whether they see it as fair or as fraudulent) and such a honeymoon will not occur. Electoral resolution (or lack thereof) and its train of consequences, including hope, hopelessness, and electoral hostility, is the main subject of chapter 9.

EMOTIONS

When electoral research has considered emotion, it has most frequently been as a potential motive of electoral choice, including suggestions that 'emotional' voters would somehow be opposed to 'rational' voters, and more likely to vote for extremist or populist parties. However, research in psychology has long moved away from the crude opposition between reason and emotions to consider the two as instead largely intertwined and shaping each other. Emotions are addressed in a variety of ways in the psychology literature. Some distinguish between their positive or negative valence, or mobilizing and demobilizing emotions; some simply focus on discrete emotions, and in the particular context of electoral behaviour, on affective intelligence in particular. In this book, however, what is radically different from much research in the field is that we consider that the emotions people experience as they vote (predominantly considered as discrete emotions, and to an extent based on their valence and mobilizing or demobilizing quality) should really be treated as a dependent variable in electoral models and operational measures of electoral experience. In short, we believe that knowing whether elections make people happy, emotional, or anxious is more important—for themselves, for science, and from the point of view of democratic theory—than whether they vote for a left- or right-wing candidate or party, or indeed vote at all. We also integrate emotions within our dynamic models, suggesting that positive emotions during a given election will make one more likely to experience a sense of electoral resolution or to turn out in the next election. We measure emotions using explicit and implicit questions, as well as a visual experiment.

EMPATHIC DISPLACEMENT

A significant aspect of our model of elections and of electoral identity regards how citizens relate their own individual behaviour to the rest of society. One particular aspect of this is 'empathic displacement', conceived as the process whereby individual voters consider the electoral experience and behaviour of others as they conduct their own. The idea of empathic displacement is arguably assumed in many models that implicitly suppose that voters alter their own vote in accordance with what they believe others will do at the same time (for example, believing that a party or candidate has no chance of winning is tantamount to imagining that few people will be voting for them). However, in our model, empathic displacement is thought of not as a mere utilitarian calculation to maximize the impact of one's vote, but rather as a state of mind, a permanent condition and dimension of conceptualizing an election as an interface between individual and societal experience and choice. Empathic displacement has a narrative value—that is, it can occupy and influence people's thoughts during the election and notably on Election Day; it can also contribute to citizens' sense of efficacy through projected efficacy (see entry below), and ultimately affect their sense of integration or exclusion within society, as well as their sense of electoral resolution (see entry above). We study empathic displacement predominantly in relation to electoral identity, in chapter 6, using explicit measures, and in terms of its qualitative narrative salience in chapter 3.

FIRST-TIME VOTER

In our model, we conceive of one's first electoral experience as a 'first time' just like one's first kiss, first job, first alcoholic drink, or first sexual experience. We suggest that this nature shapes the anticipation and emotionality of one's first vote and will affect, through internalization (see entry below), the influence of one's first electoral experience as part of electoral memory, and, through its implicit mobilization, habituation. We also claim that this first time is consequently unique in terms of emotionality and of sensitivity to electoral ergonomics (in particular, the effect of voting in a polling station or not), and that the experience of the first two elections of one's life largely determines whether one will be a chronic participant or chronic abstentionist. We define first votes primarily on the basis of primary (first-order) elections, and assess their nature and effect in our final model and specifically in chapters 5 on electoral memory and 7 on emotions (see respective entries above).

FUNCTION OF ELECTIONS

In chapters 2 and 6, we discuss the different possible functions of elections. We claim, on the basis of democratic theory and behavioural evidence, that elections can have competing institutional functions (such as choosing representatives, defining the policy of the country, or accountability: that is, getting rid of people voters are dissatisfied with), but can also serve functions centred on the voter rather than the institution—such as giving citizens a sense of control, making them feel part of society, and generating cyclical timelines which can in turn foster acceptance of the system by providing citizens with a sense of when they may be given another chance of questioning an electoral outcome that they do not approve of. Note that this implies a particular status for referenda, when citizens may not have any transparent perspective of cyclical rectification. The function of elections may vary by country (e.g., proportional systems are more likely to favour representative functions and majoritarian and plurality systems policy direction and accountability), by type of election, by citizens, or indeed for a given citizen across different elections. Function closely relates to electoral identity and to electoral ergonomics (see respective entries above).

HOMO SUFFRAGATOR

Before it became *Inside the Mind of a Voter*, the initial title of this book project was in fact *Homo Suffragator*. *Homo Suffragator* means 'man (in the species sense) who can vote', and the implication is that the process of democratic elections has changed the condition of humans and their way of thinking and interacting by offering them a new and different mode of difference resolution and adjudication of contradictory preferences and beliefs, using peaceful and cyclical polity-encompassing democratic decisional processes. The evolution of humankind has followed not only a physical and technological trajectory, but also encompasses the ability at each new stage to master new skills and habits, such as agriculture, burying the dead, and the mastering of language and script. We ask whether being

Homo Suffragator, and mastering the process of elections, is a radically new *modus operandi* of the social contract and the management of political divergence and conflict. May it, in turn, come to be seen as a fundamental new skill, a profound change in the nature of mankind and its psyche? Potential anthropological and psychological implications are discussed in chapter 1.

HOPE

In our model, 'hope' plays a critical part in the process of electoral resolution (see entry above). Hope is partly related to the nature of election cycles, and partly to other, more profound forms of projection (see entry below), notably generational and longitudinal projection. The cyclical element is fairly straightforward. Not having one's way in an election will have a different psychological meaning depending on whether or not one has the hope of getting another chance to change the course of the country's politics after a few years. This has implications in the contexts both of marginalized voters—those who feel that they support a line which will never win—and of referenda, which can be associated with a perception of definitive rather than cyclical outcomes, as for example in the case of the the UK's 2016 referendum on EU membership. The second element is more rarely considered, but in our analysis just as important. We find on the basis of narratives that, more than in the case of hope for one's own conditions and fortunes, there seems to be a radical divergence between those who believe that their children will live better than themselves and those who do not. Thus, many citizens seem willing to accept significant sacrifices if they believe that these will at least result in better conditions and situations for following generations, but if they fail to have that hope, they switch to a mood of hopelessness (see entry below), with potentially critical experiential, emotional, attitudinal, and behavioural consequences, discussed in chapter 9.

HOPELESSNESS

'Hopelessness' is a critically significant state of mind which develops when citizens cease to hold any (electoral) hope (see entry above), derived either from a lack of cyclical perspectives for improvement or from negative perceptions in relation to longitudinal and generational projection (see entry below). In chapter 9, we characterize hopelessness as the feeling that 'things can't get worse, anyway'. In our model, hopelessness stems partly from an inability of elections to bring a sense of electoral resolution (see entry above) to citizens. It has the potential to disinhibit behaviour such as populist and extremist voting, and can feed electoral hostility.

INTERNALIZATION

In our model, the process of 'internalization' is integral to the experiential nature of elections, and part of the reason why we challenge what we consider to be overly institution-centric conceptions of what matters in relation to them. Because our model is based on the centrality of the electoral experience (see entry above), we try to consider the ways in which elections permeate citizens' lives, and the way, in turn, that citizens appropriate elections and relate them to their own personal lives and development. The process of internalization encompasses those effects. Citizens will think of elections in terms of what they represent in their own personal lives: for instance, because their first vote corresponds to a certain stage of their growing up, or because a meaningful discussion or falling-out with a loved one on account of an election emphasizes how the election has impacted their life meaningfully. Internalization is about how the 'small history' of individual lives intersects and interacts with the 'big history' of nations, and thus how citizens reclaim elections and their meanings. We believe that internalization has a major impact on the salient and impactful aspects of electoral memory (see entry above), and shapes electoral emotions and identities in the long term. We discuss it throughout the book, but particularly in chapters 3 and 5.

MORAL HIERARCHIZATION

The role of morality in political behaviour has been studied by many, but predominantly to assess whether some voters care more about morals than others, or how they react to specific moral breaches or positions on the part of leaders, such as lies or apologies. In this book, we adopt a different perspective, suggesting that people generally do have moral values that matter to them, but that on the other hand, the hierarchy of such values may vary between them. We thus assess this hierarchization as a zero sum game based on the classic Ten Commandments and Seven Deadly Sins. Our model suggests that hierarchies of moral values that may be in tension with one another in everyday life can spawn potentially powerful electoral consequences. We also suggest that these conflicting hierarchies generate misunderstanding between citizens, as a person who cares about value A

even more than value *B* may accept sacrifice of the latter to protect the former, but someone who feels that value *B* is in fact the most important of all moral principles will assume that a person who is willing to betray value *B* may be willing to compromise on anything, and is thus immoral. We consider moral hierarchization to be a component of personality alongside personality traits and sociotropism (see respective entries below) and that it will shape the electoral personality of a citizen in the long run. We study moral hierarchization and its impact on elections principally in chapter 4.

PERSONALITY TRAITS

The impact of personality on electoral experience, behaviour, and resolution is a crucial part of our model, and the main subject of chapter 4. A number of political scientists are interested in the impact of personality on political behaviour. Much of their work relies on the use of the so-called 'Big Five' (or 'OCEAN' model); however, that model was never intended for political science models, but rather to diagnose certain specific psychiatric conditions. We therefore suggest that rather than relying on the Big Five, we should instead consider the role of eight discrete personality traits: sensitivity, anxiety, alienation, freedom aspiration, extraversion, risk aversion, caringness, and confrontation, with only minimal overlap with the Big Five model (mostly as regards extraversion). Personality traits allow us to look at the impact of more specific aspects of personality than do the broader dimensions of personality of the OCEAN model. We complement this approach by the study too of 'personality derivatives': preferences (such as preferred colour or the animal one would compare oneself to), which are affected by personality and emotions.

PROJECTED EFFICACY

'Efficacy' is a concept crucial to the study of political attitudes. It comprises an external dimension (the extent to which individuals feel that they can influence politics) and an internal one (the extent to which they feel competent and legitimate in doing so). However, efficacy is typically conceived as an individual perception, in apparent denial of the obvious reality that in practice, individuals are unlikely to be able genuinely to affect most political outcomes. Rather than dismissing efficacy as an unrealistic notion, however, we introduce a new concept of 'projected efficacy', which can be summarized as the feeling that 'if others like me mobilize, then together we can make a difference'. In that sense, projected efficacy is also intrinsically linked to the notion of empathic displacement (see entry above). We base our model of projected efficacy on a simple human projective capacity, and use the example of parents explaining to their children that if everyone threw their rubbish on the street, the city would soon become disgusting and uninhabitable. In other words, human beings are capable of projecting their own behaviour into a vision of the multiplying effects of others' acting similarly. We believe that this can resolve the apparent paradox of rationality regarding feelings of efficacy. Note that projected efficacy is different from the sociological concept of 'collective efficacy', which pertains to the efficacy of a constituted group; projected efficacy does not assume any form of group membership, but simply considers efficacy through multiplication and projection. We discuss projected efficacy in chapter 6, and find that it has more powerful electoral effects than does traditional efficacy.

PROJECTION (INCLUDING LONGITUDINAL AND GENERATIONAL PROJECTION)

'Projection' corresponds to the ability of voters abstractly to project the effects of potential electoral decisions or outcomes onto different people or times. Whilst citizens might be projective in a broad number of ways, in this book, we focus on two primary dimensions: time (longitudinal projection) and generations (generational projection). These two dimensions address the extent to which citizens are willing to make short-term sacrifices to ensure long-term benefits, or sacrifice the interest of their own generation to benefit younger ones. Both are highly topical in relation to debates such as those concerning the sustainability of pensions systems, climate change, and issues of equality. In the model, we claim that projection pertains to each citizen's conception of the individual–societal articulation in elections, and thus to his/her electoral identity. It is discussed specifically in chapter 6. We find that both longitudinal and generational projections play significant roles in shaping electoral behaviour, experience, and resolution.

REMOTE VOTING

Remote voting allows citizens to vote in a manner different from the default 'in person, on Election Day, in the polling station of registration' procedure. Remote voting takes one or more of three forms, depending on which of the traditional conditions are relaxed: personal (if the voter need not cast his/her vote in person); geographical (if the voter need not go to the polling station where he/she is registered in order to vote); and/or temporal (if the voter need not cast his/her vote during normal voting hours on Election Day). For example, proxy voting is normally a form of personal remote voting (in some countries, it may be paired with geographically remote voting), and postal voting is both temporal and geographical, because the voter can cast a postal ballot from home, as well as it being before Election Day. We see remote voting as one of the crucial components of electoral ergonomics (see entry above). That is because, whilst most of the literature has typically seen remote voting as a form of 'convenience voting', reducing cost and thereby potentially bringing additional voters to the polls, we also and primarily see it as an ergonomic issue, because we believe that voting remotely, be it geographically—involving not benefiting from the polling station experience—or temporally—involving voting before others—will affect a voters' experience, and beyond that, their electoral behaviour and likelihood of experiencing electoral resolution (see respective entries above). This is in fact what we show in chapter 8: remote voting does not so much bring new voters to the polls as affect the electoral behaviour, experience (including satisfaction, emotions, and sense of efficacy), and likelihood of experiencing resolution of given voters, in a manner different from what would have occurred had they voted traditionally, and also affects their longer-term behaviour and chances of electoral resolution.

SOCIOTROPISM (AND EGOCENTRISM)

Models of sociotropic and egocentric political behaviour suggest that some citizens will make political decisions based on their own self-interest ('pocketbook') and others on the basis of the collective good. Those differences are central to the work of Kinder and Kiewiet (1981). This model focuses solely on economic sociotropism, however, and in this book we suggest that sociotropism could in fact have a number of dimensions, and in particular the economic, the social, and with regard to safety and to misery. We also claim that using self-reported measures of sociotropism alone is likely to lead to biased results, due to the high contagion of social desirability in sociotropism variables. Finally, we argue that egocentric/sociotropic scales may not necessarily be linear. By diverging from traditional models in these ways, we come up with some critical new findings. These include the fact that egocentrism is linked to perceptions of vulnerability, and the suggestion in the literature that sociotropism increases with age thus simply reflects the traditional sole focus on economic sociotropism; in fact, younger people are *more* sociotropic on the safety and misery dimensions of sociotropism. We also show that the effects of sociotropic scales on electoral behaviour are not linear, with the egocentric end of the scale having greater impact than the sociotropic end. The nature and effects of sociotropism are discussed in chapter 6.

SUBCONSCIOUS (INCLUDING METHODOLOGY: IMPLICIT QUESTIONS, VISUAL EXPERIMENT, ETC.)

Existing research suggests that over 90% of everything a human being feels and does is due to subconscious rather than conscious mechanisms. Electoral attitudes and behaviour are no exception. This means that even if people were entirely truthful, they would still be unable to tell us why they think about elections or vote in the way that they do. For an electoral-psychological model, this is a particularly significant issue, because it affects not only the dependent variables that we are interested in, but also their independent predictors, such as personality, memory, and identity. We thus need to identify methods of capturing the sources, nature, and consequences of the electoral experience in ways that go beyond self-reporting. As explained in chapter 2, in this book, we do so by using such methodologies as a visual experiment, implicit questions, direct observation in partnership with election officials, and a quasi-experimental setting to investigate electoral ergonomics in the US. We combine these approaches with more traditional explicit questioning, interviews, on-the-spot interviews, and diaries, targeting the more conscious side of electoral behaviour, experience, and resolution.

TEARS

Tears are the ultimate symbol of emotionality, and we use the proportion of citizens who have already cried because of an election as a proxy for the emotional nature of the electoral experience, and to get a sense of which parts of the election cycle are most emotional. We find that across countries, over a quarter of people claim already to have cried because of an election, and that proportion was significantly higher during the French 2002 presidential election and in the UK 2016 referendum on EU membership, in which 28% of Britons (and 39% of those aged eighteen to twenty-five) claimed to have had tears in their eyes at the time they discovered the referendum result. These findings are discussed in chapter 7, and suggest that even people who claim not to care about politics can be very emotional in electoral contexts.

BIBLIOGRAPHY

Abramowitz, A. I. and Saunders, K. L., 1998. 'Ideological realignment in the US electorate'. *The Journal of Politics* 60(3): 634–52.

Acevedo, M. and Krueger, J. I., 2004. 'Two egocentric sources of the decision to vote: The voter's illusion and the belief in personal relevance'. *Political Psychology* 25(1):115–34.

Ajzen, I., 2005. *Attitudes, Personality and Behaviour*. Maidenhead: Open University Press, McGraw-Hill Education (UK).

Alvarez, R. and Nagler, J., 2000. 'A new approach for modelling strategic voting in multiparty elections'. *British Journal of Political Science* 30(1): 57–75.

Alvarez, R. M. and Schousen, M. M., 1993. 'Policy moderation or conflicting expectations? Testing the intentional models of split-ticket voting'. *American Politics Quarterly* 21(4): 410–38.

Anderson, C. J., 2000. 'Economic voting and political context: A comparative perspective'. *Electoral Studies* 19(2–3): 151–70.

Aral, S., 2012. 'Social science: Poked to vote'. *Nature* 489(7415): 212–14.

Arcuri, L., Castelli, L., Galdi, S., Zogmaister, C., and Amadori, A., 2008. 'Predicting the vote: Implicit attitudes as predictors of the future behavior of decided and undecided voters'. *Political Psychology* 29(3): 369–87.

Atkeson, L. and Saunders, K., 2007. 'The effect of election administration on voter confidence: A local matter?'. *PS: Political Science & Politics* 40(4): 655–60.

Atkinson, R. C. and Shiffrin, R. M., 1968. 'Human memory: A proposed system and its control processes', in K. W. Spence and J. T. Spence (eds), *Psychology of Learning and Motivation* (vol. 2). New York: Academic Press, pp. 89–195

Baddeley, A., 2013. *Essentials of Human Memory* (classic edn). Hove: Psychology Press.

Bakker, B. N., Hopmann, D. N., and Persson, M., 2015. 'Personality traits and party identification over time'. *European Journal of Political Research* 54(2), 197–215.

Baldassarri, D. and Gelman, A., 2008. 'Partisans without constraint: Political polarization and trends in American public opinion'. *American Journal of Sociology* 114(2): 408–46.

Bandura, A., 1993. 'Perceived self-efficacy in cognitive development and functioning'. *Educational Psychologist* 28(2):117–48.

Banerjee, M., 2017. *Why India Votes?* Delhi: Routledge India.

Barrat Esteve, J., 2006. 'A preliminary question: Is e-voting actually useful for our democratic institutions? What do we need it for?', in R. Krimmer (ed.), *Proceedings of the Second International Conference on Electronic Voting*. Bregenz, Austria: GI-Edition, pp. 51–60.

Barry, B., 1975. 'Political accommodation and consociational democracy'. *British Journal of Political Science* 5(4): 477–505.

This is a list of work cited in the book. Please note that the book also comprises a fuller online bibliography of electoral psychology research available on www.epob.org as part of the book's appendices.

Bartels, L. M., 1996. 'Uninformed votes: Information effects in presidential elections'. *American Journal of Political Science* 40(1):194–230.
Baumeister, R. and Exline, J. J., 1999. 'Virtue, personality, and social relations: Self-control as the moral muscle. *Journal of Personality* 67(6): 1165–94.
Baumeister, R. F. and Exline, J. J., 2000. 'Self-control, morality, and human strength'. *Journal of Social and Clinical Psychology* 19(1): 29–42.
Berelson, B. R., Lazarsfeld, P. F., and McPhee, W. N., (1954). *Voting: A Study of Opinion Formation in a Presidential Campaign*. Chicago: University of Chicago Press.
Berger, M, Meredith, M, and Wheeler, S. C., 2008. 'Contextual priming: Where people vote affects how they vote'. *Proceedings of the National Academy of Sciences* 105(26): 8846–9.
Berry, C. R. and Howell, W. G., 2007. 'Accountability and local elections: Rethinking retrospective voting'. *The Journal of Politics* 69(3): 844–58.
Bertsou, E., 2016. 'Analysing Attitudes of Political Distrust in Europe'. PhD thesis, London School of Economics and Political Science.
Birdwhistell, R., 1970. *Kinesics and Context*. Philadelphia: University of Pennsylvania Press
Birren, F., 1973. 'Color preference as a clue to personality'. *Art Psychotherapy* 1(1): 13–16.
Blais, A., 2000. *To vote or not to vote?: The merits and limits of rational choice theory*. Pittsburgh, PA: University of Pittsburgh Press.
Blais, A. and Nadeau, R., 1996. 'Measuring strategic voting: A two-step procedure'. *Electoral Studies* 15(1): 39–52.
Blais, A. and St-Vincent, S. L., 2011. 'Personality traits, political attitudes and the propensity to vote'. *European Journal of Political Research* 50(3): 395–417.
Boutyline, A. and Willer, R., 2017. 'The social structure of political echo chambers: Variation in ideological homophily in online networks'. *Political Psychology* 38(3) : 551–69.
Bowler, S. and Lanoue, D., 1992. 'Strategic and protest voting for third parties: The case of the Canadian NDP'. *The Western Political Quarterly* 45(2): 485–99.
Boyer, K. K., Olson, J. R., Calantone, R. J., and Jackson, E. C., 2002. 'Print versus electronic surveys: A comparison of two data collection methodologies'. *Journal of Operations Management* 20(4): 357–73.
Boyle, G. J., Stankov, L., and Cattell, R. B., 1995. 'Measurement and statistical models in the study of personality and intelligence', in D. H. Saklofske and M. Zeidner (eds), *International Handbook of Personality and Intelligence*. New York: Plenum, pp. 431–3).
Brader, T., 2006. *Campaigning for Hearts and Minds: How Emotional Appeals in Political Ads Work*. Chicago: University of Chicago Press.
Breakwell, G. M., 2004. 'Identity change in the context of the growing influence of European Union institutions', in Herrmann et al., *Transnational Identities: Becoming European in the EU*, pp. 25–39.
Britt, L., and Heise, D., 2000. 'From shame to pride in identity politics', in S. Stryker, T. Owens, and R. White (eds), *Self, Identity, and Social Movements*. Minneapolis: University of Minnesota Press, pp. 252–68.
Brugman, D., Heymans, P. G., Boom, J., Podolskij, A. I., Karabanova, O., and Idobaeva, O., 2003. 'Perception of moral atmosphere in school and norm transgressive behaviour in adolescents: An intervention study'. *International Journal of Behavioral Development* 27(4): 289–300.
Bruter, M. 2005. *Citizens of Europe?* Basingstoke: Palgrave Macmillan.
Bruter, M. and Clary, A.-J., 2015. *Les jeunes et le vote. Rapport d'enquête*. Paris: ANACEJ.
Bruter, M., Erikson, R., and Strauss, A., 2010. 'Uncertain candidates, valence, and the dynamics of candidate position-taking'. *Public Choice* 144(1): 153–68.
Bruter, M. and Harrison, S., 2009a. *The Future of Our Democracies?* Basingstoke: Palgrave Macmillan.
Bruter, M. and Harrison, S., 2009b. 'Tomorrow's leaders: Understanding the involvement of

young party members in six European democracies'. *Comparative Political Studies* 42(10): 1259–90.

Bruter, M. and Harrison, S., 2016. *The Impact of Brexit on Consumer Behaviour* (report). London: Opinium Research. http://opinium.co.uk/wpcontent/uploads/2016/08/the_impact_of _brexit_on_consumer_behaviour_0.pdf

Bruter, M. and Harrison, S., 2017. 'Understanding the emotional act of voting'. *Nature Human Behaviour* 1(1) art.0024: 1–3.

Butler, D. and Stokes, D., 1969. *Political Change in Britain: Forces Shaping Electoral Choice*. Basingstoke: Palgrave Macmillan.

Cammaerts, B., Bruter, M., Banaji, S., Harrison, S., and Anstead, N., 2014. 'The myth of youth apathy: Young Europeans' critical attitudes toward democratic life'. *American Behavioral Scientist* 58(5): 645–64.

Cammaerts, B., Bruter, M., Banaji, S., Harrison, S., and Anstead, N., 2016. *Youth Participation in Democratic Life*. Basingstoke: Palgrave Macmillan.

Campbell, A., Converse, P., Miller, W., and Stokes, D., 1960. *The American Voter*. Ann Arbor: University of Michigan Press.

Campbell, A. and Miller, W. E., 1957. 'The motivational basis of straight and split ticket voting'. *American Political Science Review*, 51(2): 293–312.

Cappella, J. N. and Jamieson, K. H., 1996. 'News frames, political cynicism, and media cynicism'. *The Annals of the American Academy of Political and Social Science*, 546(1): 71–84.

Caprara, G. V., Schwartz, S., Capanna, C., Vecchione, M., and Barbaranelli, C., 2006. 'Personality and politics: Values, traits, and political choice'. *Political Psychology* 27(1): 1–28.

Carrubba, C. and Timpone, R. J., 2005. 'Explaining vote switching across first- and second-order elections: Evidence from Europe'. *Comparative Political Studies* 38(3): 260–81.

Carter, J. and Guerette, S., 1992. 'An experimental study of expressive voting'. *Public Choice* 73(3): 251–60.

Charteris-Black, J., 2009. 'Metaphor and political communication', in Andreas Musolff and Jörg Zinken (eds), *Metaphor and Discourse*. Basingstoke: Palgrave Macmillan, pp. 97–115.

Cohen, C. J. and Kahne, J., 2011. *Participatory Politics. New Media and Youth Political Action*. Oakland, CA: YPP Research Network. https://ypp.dmlcentral.net/publications/107.html (accessed 5 December 2019).

Colleoni, E., Rozza, A., and Arvidsson, A., 2014. 'Echo chamber or public sphere? Predicting political orientation and measuring political homophily in Twitter using big data'. *Journal of Communication* 64(2): 317–32.

Cornelius, R. R., 1996. *The Science of Emotion: Research and Tradition in the Psychology of Emotions*. London: Prentice-Hall.

Cornelius, R. R., 2001. 'Crying and catharsis', in A.J.J.M. Vingerhoets and R. R. Cornelius (eds), *Adult Crying: A Biopsychosocial Approach*, Hove: Brunner-Routledge, pp. 199–212.

Cox, G. W., 1997. *Making Votes Count: Strategic Coordination in the World's Electoral Systems*. Cambridge: Cambridge University Press.

Dahl, R. A., 2013. *A Preface to Democratic Theory*. Chicago: University of Chicago Press.

Dalton, R. J., 1996. 'Political cleavages, issues, and electoral change', in L. LeDuc, R. G. Niemi, and P. Norris (eds), *Comparing Democracies: Elections and Voting in Global Perspective*. Thousand Oaks, CA: Sage, pp. 319–42.

Dalton, R. J. and Flanagan, S. E., 2017. *Electoral Change in Advanced Industrial Democracies: Realignment or Dealignment?*. Princeton, NJ: Princeton University Press.

de Vreese, C., 2004. 'The effects of strategic news on political cynicism, issue evaluations, and policy support: A two-wave experiment'. *Mass Communication & Society*, 7(2): 191–214.

Déloye, Y. and Bruter, M. (eds), 2007. *Encyclopaedia of European Elections*. Basingstoke: Palgrave Macmillan.

Déloye, Y. and Ihl, O., 2008. *L'acte de vote*. Paris: Presses de Sciences Po.

Demertzis, N., 2006. 'Emotions and populism', in S. Clarke, P. Hoggett, and S. Thompson (eds), *Emotion, Politics and Society*. Basingstoke: Palgrave Macmillan, pp. 103–22.

Dennis, J. 1970. 'Support for the institution of elections by the mass public'. *American Political Science Review* 64(3): 819–35.

Dewey, J., 2002. *Human Nature and Conduct*. North Chelmsford, MA: Courier Corporation.

Di Palma, G. and McClosky, H., 1970. 'Personality and conformity: The learning of political attitudes'. *American Political Science Review* 64(4): 1054–73.

Díez Medrano, J. and Gutiérrez, P., 2001. 'Nested identities: National and European identity in Spain'. *Ethnic and Racial Studies* 24(5): 753–78.

DiFranza, J., Savageau, J., Fletcher, K., Ockene, J., Rigotti, N., McNeill, A., Coleman, M., and Wood, C., 2004. 'Recollections and repercussions of the first inhaled cigarette'. *Addictive Behaviors* 29(2): 261–72.

Dinas, E., 2012. 'The formation of voting habits'. *Journal of Elections, Public Opinion and Parties* 22(4): 431–56.

Donovan, R., Rossiter, J., Marcoolyn, G., and Nesdale, A., 1994. 'Store atmosphere and purchasing behavior'. *Journal of Retailing* 70(3: 283–94.

Dowding, K. (2005) 'Is it rational to vote? Five types of answer and a suggestion'. *The British Journal of Politics and International Relations* 7(3): 442–59.

Downs, A., 1957. 'An economic theory of political action in a democracy. *Journal of Political Economy* 65(2): 135–50.

Duverger, M., 1954. *Political Parties: Their Organization and Activity in the Modern State*. New York: Wiley.

Easton, D., 1965. *A Systems Analysis of Political Life*. New York: John Wiley.

Emmanuel, O., 2007. 'Elections: An exploration of theoretical postulations'. *Journal of African Elections* 6(2): 4–13.

Eriksen, C. W. and James, J.D.S., 1986. 'Visual attention within and around the field of focal attention: A zoom lens model'. *Perception & Psychophysics* 40(4): 225–40.

Erikson, R. S., MacKuen, M. B., and Stimson, J. A., 2002. *The Macro Polity*. Cambridge: Cambridge University Press.

Eulau, H. and Karps, P., 1977. 'The puzzle of representation: Specifying components of responsiveness'. *Legislative Studies Quarterly*: 233–54.

Eysenck, H. J. (ed.), 2012. *A Model for Personality*. Berlin: Springer.

Fast, J., 1988. *Body Language*. New York: Simon and Schuster.

Fatke, M., 2017. 'Personality traits and political ideology: A first global assessment'. *Political Psychology* 38(5): 881–99.

Fiorina, M. P., Abrams, S. A., and Pope, J. C., 2008. 'Polarization in the American public: Misconceptions and misreadings'. *The Journal of Politics* 70(2): 556–60.

Forgas, J. and Jolliffe, C., 1994. 'How conservative are Greenies? Environmental attitudes, conservatism, and traditional morality among university students'. *Australian Journal of Psychology* 46(3): 123–30.

Fournier, P., Nadeau, R., Blais, A., Gidengil, E., and Nevitte, N., 2004. 'Time-of-voting decision and susceptibility to campaign effects'. *Electoral Studies* 23(4): 661–81.

Fowler, J. H., 2006. 'Altruism and turnout'. *The Journal of Politics* 68(3): 674–83.

Franklin, M. N., Mackie, T. T., and Valen, H., 1992. *Electoral Change: Responses to Evolving Social and Attitudinal Structures in Western Nations*. Cambridge: Cambridge University Press.

Freud, S., 1991. *On Metapsychology. Theory of Psychoanalysis*. London: Penguin.

Furnham, A., 1986. 'Response bias, social desirability and dissimulation'. *Personality and Individual Differences* 7(3): 385–400.

Gelineau, E., 1981. 'A psychometric approach to the measurement of color preference'. *Perceptual and Motor Skills* 53(1): 163–74.
Gibson, J. L., 1992. 'Alternative measures of political tolerance: Must tolerance be "least-liked"?'. *American Journal of Political Science* 36(2): 560–77.
Gibson, J. L., Caldeira, G. A., and Spence, L. K., 2005. 'Why do people accept public policies they oppose? Testing legitimacy theory with a survey-based experiment'. *Political Research Quarterly* 58(2): 187–201.
Gidengil, E., Blais, A., Nevitte, N., and Nadeau, R., 2002. 'Priming and campaign context: Evidence from recent Canadian elections', in D. M. Farrell and R. Schmitt-Beck (eds), *Do Political Campaigns Matter? London: Campaign Effects in Elections and Referendums*. London: Routledge, pp. 76–91.
Goddard, R. D., Hoy, W. K., and Hoy, A. W., 2004. 'Collective efficacy beliefs: Theoretical developments, empirical evidence, and future directions'. *Educational Researcher* 33(3): 3–13.
Gosling, S. D., Rentfrow, P. J., and Swann, Jr, W. B., 2003. 'A very brief measure of the Big-Five personality domains'. *Journal of Research in Personality* 37(6): 504–28.
Górecki, M., 2013. 'Electoral context, habit-formation and voter turnout: A new analysis'. *Electoral Studies* 32(1): 140–52.
Granberg, D. and Holmberg, S., 1986. 'Prior behavior, recalled behavior, and the prediction of subsequent voting behavior in Sweden and the US'. *Human Relations* 39(2): 135–48.
Greenstein, F., 1965. *Children and Politics*. New Haven, CT: Yale University Press.
Greenstein, F. I., 1967. 'The impact of personality on politics: An attempt to clear away underbrush'. *American Political Science Review* 61(3): 629–41.
Harrison, S., 2018. 'Young voters in the general election 2017'. *Parliamentary Affairs*, vol. 71, issue suppl_1, March 2018: 255–66. https://doi.org/10.1093/pa/gsx068 (accessed 5 December 2019).
Harrison, S., 2020. 'Democratic frustration: concept, dimensions, and behavioural consequences'. *Electoral Psychology* special issue vol 10.1: 19.
Harrison, S. and Bruter, M., 2011. *Mapping Extreme Right Ideology: An Empirical Geography of the European Extreme Right*. Basingstoke: Palgrave Macmillan.
Hayes, D., 2010. 'Trait voting in US senate elections'. *American Politics Research* 38(6): 1102–29.
Herrmann, R. K., Risse, T., and Brewer, M. B. (eds), 2004. *Transnational Identities: Becoming a European in the EU*. Oxford: Rowman & Littlefield.
Himmelweit, H. T., Biberian, M. J., and Stockdale, J., 1978. 'Memory for past vote: implications of a study of bias in recall'. *British Journal of Political Science* 8(3): 365–75.
Horowitz, D. L., 1990. 'Comparing democratic systems'. *Journal of Democracy* 1(4), 73–9.
Huckfeldt, R. and Sprague, J., 1987. 'Networks in context: The social flow of political information'. *American Political Science Review* 81(4): 1197–216.
Huddy, L., Mason, L., and Aarøe, L., 2015. 'Expressive partisanship: Campaign involvement, political emotion, and partisan identity'. *American Political Science Review*. 109(1): 1–17.
Inglehart, R., 1971. 'The silent revolution in Europe: Intergenerational change in post-industrial societies'. *American Political Science Review* 65(4): 991–1017.
International Ergonomics Association Executive Council, August (2000). http://www.iea.cc/whats/index.html (accessed 30 January 2017).
Iyengar, S. and Hahn, K. S., 2009. 'Red media, blue media: Evidence of ideological selectivity in media use'. *Journal of Communication* 59(1): 19–39.
Iyengar, S. and Westwood, S., 2015. 'Fear and loathing across partisan lines: New evidence on group polarization'. *American Journal of Political Science* 59(3): 690–707.
Izard, C. E., 1991. *The Psychology of Emotions*. New York: Springer.
James, W., 1890. 'Attention', in *The Principles of Psychology*, vol. 1. New York: Henry Holt & Co., pp. 402–58 (ch. 11).

Jenkins, H., Shresthova, S., Gamber-Thompson, L., Kligler-Vilenchik, N., and Zimmerman, A., 2018. *By Any Media Necessary: The New Youth Activism*. New York: NYU Press.

Jinadu, L., 1997. 'Matters arising: African elections and the problem of electoral administration'. *African Journal of Political Science/Revue Africaine de Science Politique* 2(1): 1–11.

Johnston, R., Dorling, D., Tunstall, H., Rossiter, D., MacAllister, I., and Pattie, C., 2000. 'Locating the altruistic voter: Context, egocentric voting, and support for the Conservative Party at the 1997 general election in England and Wales'. *Environment and Planning A* 32(4): 673–94.

Karp, J. A., Nai, A., and Norris, P., 2018. 'Dial "F" for fraud: Explaining citizens suspicions about elections. *Electoral Studies* 53(2): 11–19.

Katz, R. S., 1997. *Democracy and Elections*. Oxford: Oxford University Press.

Key, V. O., 1966. *The Responsible Electorate*. Cambridge, MA: Harvard University Press.

Kiesler, S. and Sproull, L. S., 1986. 'Response effects in the electronic survey'. *Public Opinion Quarterly* 50(3): 402–13.

Kinder, D. R., 1994. 'Reason and emotion in American political life', in R. C. Schank and E. Langer (eds), *Beliefs, Reasoning, and Decision Making: Psycho-Logic in Honor of Bob Abelson*. Hillsdale, NJ: Erlbaum, pp. 277–314.

Kinder, D. and Kiewiet, D., 1981. 'Sociotropic politics: The American case'. *British Journal of Political Science* 11(2): 129–61.

Kinder, D. R., Peters, M. D., Abelson, R. P., and Fiske, S. T., 1980. 'Presidential prototypes'. *Political Behavior* 2(4): 315–37.

King, M., 1967. 'Measuring the religious variable: Nine proposed dimensions'. *Journal for the Scientific Study of Religion* 6(2):173–90.

Kitschelt, H., 2003. 'Political-economic context and partisan strategies in the German federal elections, 1990–2002'. *West European Politics* 26(4): 125–52.

Knack, S., 1992. 'Civic norms, social sanctions, and voter turnout'. *Rationality and Society* 4(2): 133–56.

Kraft, P. W., 2018. 'Measuring morality in political attitude expression'. *The Journal of Politics*, 80(3): 1028–33.

Krueger, J. I. and Acevedo, M., 2005. 'Social projection and the psychology of choice', in M. D. Alicke, D. A. Dunning, and J. I. Krueger (eds), *The Self in Social Judgment*. New York: Psychology Press, pp. 17–41.

Kuklinski, J. H., Luskin, R. C., and Bolland, J., 1991. 'Where is the schema? Going beyond the "S" word in political psychology'. *American Political Science Review* 85(4): 1341–80.

Kushin, M. J. and Yamamoto, M., 2013. 'Did social media really matter? College students' use of online media and political decision making in the 2008 election', in T. J. Johnson and D. D. Perlmutter (eds), *New Media, Campaigning and the 2008 Facebook Election*. London: Routledge, pp. 63–86.

Lakoff, G., 1993. 'The contemporary theory of metaphor', in A. Ortony (ed.), *Metaphor and Thought*. Cambridge: Cambridge University Press, pp. 202–51.

Lakoff, G. and Johnson, M., 2008. *Metaphors We Live By*. Chicago: University of Chicago Press.

Lane, R. E., 1955. 'Political personality and electoral choice'. *American Political Science Review* 49(1): 173–90.

Lanyon, R. I. and Goodstein, L. D., 1997. *Personality Assessment*. Oxford: John Wiley.

Lazarsfeld, P. F., Berelson, B., and Gaudet, H., 1944. *The People's Choice. How the Voter Makes up his Mind in a Presidential Campaign*. New York: Columbia University Press.

Lazarus, R. S., 1991. *Emotion and Adaptation*. Oxford: Oxford University Press

Lewis-Beck, M. S. and Nadeau, R., 2004. 'Split-ticket voting: The effects of cognitive Madisonianism'. *The Journal of Politics* 66(1): 97–112.

Lewis-Beck, M. S., Norpoth, H., Jacoby, W. G., and Weisberg, H. F., 2008. *The American Voter Revisited*. University of Michigan Press.

Lincoln, A., 1994. *Gettysburg Address, 1863*. Chicago: Lakeside Press.

Lipset, S. M. and Rokkan, S. (eds), 1967. *Party Systems and Voter Alignments: Cross-National Perspectives*. New York: Free Press.

Loader, B. D., Vromen, A., and Xenos, M. A., 2014. 'The networked young citizen: Social media, political participation and civic engagement'. *Information, Communication & Society* 17(2): 143–50.

Lord Ashcroft Polls, 2016. *How the United Kingdom Voted and Why*. https://lordashcroftpolls.com/2016/06/how-the-united-kingdom-voted-and-why/ (accessed 5 December 2019).

Luechinger, S., Rosinger, M., and Stutzer, A., 2007. 'The impact of postal voting on participation: Evidence for Switzerland'. *Swiss Political Science Review* 13(2): 167–202.

Lutzer, E. W., 1989. *Measuring Morality: A Comparison of Ethical Systems*. Chicago: Probe Books.

Lyons, T., 2004. 'Post-conflict elections and the process of demilitarizing politics: The role of electoral administration'. *Democratization* 11(3): 36–62.

MacKuen, M., Erikson, R., and Stimson, J., 1992. 'Peasants or bankers? The American electorate and the US economy'. *American Political Science Review* 86(3): 597–611.

Marcus, G. E., 2010. *The Sentimental Citizen: Emotion in Democratic Politics*. University Park, PA: Pennsylvania State University Press.

Marcus, G. E. and MacKuen, M. B., 1993. 'Anxiety, enthusiasm, and the vote: The emotional underpinnings of learning and involvement during presidential campaigns'. *American Political Science Review* 87(3): 672–85.

Marcus, G. E., Neuman, W. R., and MacKuen, M., 2000. *Affective Intelligence and Political Judgment*. Chicago: University of Chicago Press.

Marsh, M., 1998. 'Testing the second-order election model after four European elections'. *British Journal of Political Science* 28(4): 591–607.

Maslow, A., 1943. 'A theory of human motivation'. *Psychological Review* 50(4): 370–96.

Mayo, H., 1960. *An Introduction to Democratic Theory*. Oxford: Oxford University Press.

McAdams, D. P., 1995. 'What do we know when we know a person?'. *Journal of Personality* 63(3): 365–96.

McClurg, S. D., 2006. 'The electoral relevance of political talk: Examining disagreement and expertise effects in social networks on political participation' *American Journal of Political Science* 50(3): 737–54.

McPherson, M., Smith-Lovin, L., and Cook, J. M., 2001. 'Birds of a feather: Homophily in social networks'. *Annual Review of Sociology* 27(1): 415–44.

Meehl, P., 1977. 'The selfish voter paradox and the thrown-away vote argument'. *American Political Science Review* 52(1): 11–30.

Meinhof, U., 2003. 'Migrating borders: An introduction to European identity construction in process'. *Journal of Ethnic and Migration Studies* 29(5): 781–96.

Miles, A. and Vaisey, S., 2015. Morality and politics: Comparing alternate theories. *Social Science Research* 53: 252–69.

Miller, B., Roberts, G., and Ommundsen, Y., 2005. 'Effect of perceived motivational climate on moral functioning, team moral atmosphere perceptions, and the legitimacy of intentionally injurious acts among competitive youth football players'. *Psychology of Sport and Exercise* 6(4): 461–77.

Miller, J., 1987. 'Priming is not necessary for selective-attention failures: Semantic effects of unattended, unprimed letters'. *Perception & Psychophysics* 41(5): 419–34.

Mishler, W. and Rose, R., 1997. 'Trust, distrust, and skepticism: Popular evaluations of civil and political institutions in post-communist societies. *The Journal of Politics* 59(2): 418–51.

Mudde, C. and Kaltwasser, C. R., 2017. *Populism: A Very Short Introduction*. Oxford: Oxford University Press.

Mueller, D. C., 2003. *Public choice III*. Cambridge: Cambridge University Press.

Musolff, A., 2004. *Metaphor and Political Discourse: Analogical Reasoning in Debates about Europe*. Basingstoke: Palgave Macmillan.

National Conference of State Legislatures 'Absentee and Early Voting', 2018. http://www.ncsl.org/research/elections-and-campaigns/absentee-and-early-voting.aspx (accessed 5 December 2019).

Neisser, U. and Becklen, R., 1975. 'Selective looking: Attending to visually specified events'. *Cognitive Psychology* 7(4): 480–94.

Neuman, W. R., Marcus, G. E., MacKuen, M., and Crigler, A. N., 2007. 'Theorizing affect's effects', in eidem (eds), *The Affect Effect: Dynamics of Emotion in Political Thinking and Behavior*. Chicago: University of Chicago Press, pp. 1–20.

Norris, P., 2003. 'Will new technology boost turnout? Evaluating experiments in e-voting v. all-postal voting facilities in UK local elections'. *KSG Working Papers Series No. RWP03–034*. https://papers.ssrn.com/sol3/papers.cfm?abstract_id=437140 (accessed 13 December 2019).

Norris, P., Wynter, T., and Cameron, S., 2018. *Electoral Integrity & Campaign Media*. http://www.electoralintegrityproject.com (accessed 13 December 2019).

Oatley, K., 1992. *Best Laid Schemes: The Psychology of the Emotions*. Cambridge: Cambridge University Press.

Olson, M., 2009. *The Logic of Collective Action*. Cambridge, MA: Harvard University Press.

Oostveen, A.-M. and van den Besselaar, P., 2009. 'Users' experiences with e-voting: A comparative case study'. *Journal of Electronic Governance* 2(4): 357–77.

Pallasmaa, J., 2014. 'Space, place, and atmosphere: Emotion and peripherical perception in existential experience', in C. Borch (ed.), *Architectural Atmospheres: On the Experience and Politics of Architecture*. Basel: De Gruyter, pp.18–41.

Pastor, R. 1999. 'The role of electoral administration in democratic transitions: Implications for policy and research'. *Democratization* 6(4): 1–27.

Pattie, C. and Johnston, R., 2001. 'Talk as a political context: Conversation and electoral change in British elections, 1992–1997'. *Electoral Studies* 20(1): 17–40.

Paunonen, S. V., 1998. 'Hierarchical organization of personality and prediction of behavior'. *Journal of Personality and Social Psychology* 74(2): 538–56.

Paunonen, S. V. and Ashton, M. S., 2001. 'Big Five factors and facets and the prediction of behavior'. *Journal of Personality and Social Psychology* 81(3): 524–39.

Paunonen, S. V. and Jackson, D. N., 2000. 'What is beyond the big five? Plenty!'. *Journal of Personality* 68(5): 821–35.

DeYoung, C. G., Quilty, L. C., and Peterson, J. B., 2007. 'Between facets and domains: 10 aspects of the Big Five'. *Journal of Personality and Social Psychology* 93(5): 880–96.

Peterson, C. and Park, N., 2009. 'Classifying and measuring strengths of character', in S. J. Lopez and C. R. Snyder (eds), *Oxford Handbook of Positive Psychology*. Oxford: Oxford University Press, pp. 25–33.

Powell, Jr, G. B. and Whitten, G. D., 1993. 'A cross-national analysis of economic voting: Taking account of the political context'. *American Journal of Political Science* 37(2): 391–414.

Price, V., Tewksbury, D., and Powers, E., 1997. 'Switching trains of thought: The impact of news frames on readers' cognitive responses'. *Communication Research* 24(5): 481–506.

Przeworski, A., Stokes, S., and Manin, B. (eds), 1999. *Democracy, Accountability, and Representation*. Cambridge: Cambridge University Press.

Puntscher-Riekmann, S. and Wessels, W. (eds), 2006. *The Making of a European Constitution:*

Dynamics and Limits of the Convention Experience. Wiesbaden: Verlag für Sozialwissenschaften.

Rabinowitz, G. and McDonald, S., 1989. 'A directional theory of issue voting'. *American Political Science Review* 83(1): 93–121.

Rallings, C., Thrasher, M., and Borisyuk, G., 2010. 'Much ado about not very much: The electoral consequences of postal voting at the 2005 British general election'. *The British Journal of Politics and International Relations* 12(2): 223–38.

Redlawsk, D. P., Civettini, A. J., and Lau, R. R., 2007. 'Affective intelligence and voting: Information processing and learning in a campaign', in Neumen et al. (eds), *The Affect Effect: Dynamics of Emotion in Political Thinking and Behavior*, pp. 152–79.

Reif, K. and Schmitt, H., 1980. 'Nine second-order national elections: A conceptual framework for the analysis of European election results'. *European Journal of Political Research* 8(1): 3–44.

Riesman, D., Glazer, N., and Denney, R., 2001. *The Lonely Crowd*. New Haven, CT: Yale University Press.

Rigby, A., Leach, C., and Greasley, P., 2001. 'Primary nursing: Staff perception of changes in ward atmosphere and role'. *Journal of Psychiatric and Mental Health Nursing* 8(6): 525–32.

Riker, W. H. and Ordeshook, P. C., 1973. *An Introduction to Positive Political Theory*. Englewood Cliffs, NJ: Prentice-Hall.

Robinson, J. P., Shaver, P. R., and Wrightsman, L. S. (eds), 2013. *Measures of Personality and Social Psychological Attitudes*. San Diego, CA: Academic Press.

Rosema, M., 2004. 'The Sincere Vote: A Psychological Study of Voting'. PhD thesis, University of Leiden.

Rousseau, J.-J., (1762). *Du contract social; ou, principes du droit politique*. Amsterdam.

Rutchick A. M., 2010. '*Deus ex Machina*: The influence of polling place on voting behavior'. *Political Psychology* 31(2): 209–25.

Sartori, G., 1965. *Democratic Theory*. New York: Praeger.

Schacter, D. L. and Tulving, E. (eds), 1994. *Memory Systems*. Cambridge, MA: Harvard University Press.

Schedler, A., Diamond, L., and Plattner, M. (eds), 1999. *The Self-Restraining State: Power and Accountability in New Democracies*. Boulder, CO: Lynne Rienner.

Scheithauer, R., 2007. 'Metaphors in election night television coverage in Britain, the United States and Germany', in A. Fetzer and G. E. Lauerbach (eds), *Political Discourse in the Media: Cross-Cultural Perspectives*. Amsterdam: John Benjamins, pp. 75–106.

Schoen, H., 2014. 'Voting behavior and public opinion', in M. Sasaki, J. Goldstone, E. Zimmermann, and S. K. Sanderson (eds), *Concise Encyclopedia of Comparative Sociology*. Leiden: Brill, pp. 360–9.

Schuck, A. R., Vliegenthart, R., Boomgaarden, H. G., Elenbaas, M., Azrout, R., van Spanje, J., and de Vreese, C. H., 2013. 'Explaining campaign news coverage: How medium, time, and context explain variation in the media framing of the 2009 European parliamentary elections'. *Journal of Political Marketing* 12(1): 8–28.

Semino, E. and Masci, M., 1996. 'Politics is football: Metaphor in the discourse of Silvio Berlusconi in Italy'. *Discourse & Society*: 7(2): 243–69.

Shachar, R. and Shamir, M., 1996. 'Estimating vote persistence sources without panel data'. *Political Analysis* 6(1): 107–24.

Shannon, D. M. and Bradshaw, C. C., 2002. 'A comparison of response rate, response time, and costs of mail and electronic surveys'. *The Journal of Experimental Education* 70(2): 179–92.

Skonieczny, A., 2018. 'Emotions and political narratives: Populism, Trump and trade'. *Politics and Governance* 6(4): 62–72.

Smith, M. B., Bruner, J. S., and White, R. W., 1956. *Opinions and Personality*. New York: John Wiley.

Sniderman, P. M., Forbes, H. D., and Melzer, I., 1974. 'Party loyalty and electoral volatility: A study of the Canadian party system'. *Canadian Journal of Political Science/Revue canadienne de science politique* 7(2): 268–88.

Squire, L. R., 1992. 'Declarative and nondeclarative memory: Multiple brain systems supporting learning and memory'. *Journal of Cognitive Neuroscience* 4(3): 232–43.

Stewart III, C., 2011. 'Voting technologies'. *Annual Review of Political Science* 14(1): 353–78.

Taggart, P., 2000. *Populism*. Buckingham: Open University Press.

Thomassen, J. (ed.), 2014. *Elections and Democracy: Representation and Accountability*. Oxford: Oxford University Press.

Tulving, E. and Schacter, D. L., 1990. 'Priming and human memory systems'. *Science* 247(4940): 301–6.

van der Brug W., Fennema, M., and Tillie, J., 2000. 'Anti-immigrant parties in Europe: Ideological or protest vote?'. *European Journal of Political Research* 37(1): 77–102.

van der Brug, W., van der Eijk, C., and Franklin, M., 2007. *The Economy and the Vote: Economic Conditions and Elections in Fifteen Countries*. Cambridge: Cambridge University Press.

van der Eijk, C. and Franklin, M. (eds), 1996. *Choosing Europe?*. Ann Arbor: University of Michigan Press.

Veselka, L., Giammarco, E. A., and Vernon, P. A., 2014. 'The Dark Triad and the seven deadly sins'. *Personality and Individual Differences* 67: 75–80.

Vingerhoets, A. J., Cornelius, R. R., van Heck, G. L., and Becht, M. C., 2000. 'Adult crying: A model and review of the literature'. *Review of General Psychology* 4(4): 354–77.

Vrabel, J. K., 2018. 'Seven deadly sins', in V. Zeigler-Hill and T. K. Shackelford (eds), *Encyclopedia of Personality and Individual Differences*. New York: Springer, pp. 1–5.

Waismel-Manor, I., Ifergane, G., and Cohen, H., 2011. 'When endocrinology and democracy collide: Emotions, cortisol and voting at national elections'. *European Neuropsychopharmacology* 21(11): 789–95.

Wall, A., Ellis, A., Ayoub, A., Dundas, C. W., Rukambe, J., and Staino, S., 2006. *Electoral Management Design: The International IDEA Handbook*. Stockholm: International IDEA.

Walters, J., Apter, M. J., and Svebak, S., 1982. 'Color preference, arousal, and the theory of psychological reversals'. *Motivation and Emotion* 6(3): 193–215.

Xenos, M., Vromen, A., and Loader, B. D., 2014. 'The great equalizer? Patterns of social media use and youth political engagement in three advanced democracies'. *Information, Communication & Society* 17(2): 151–67.

Zaleskiewicz, T., 2001. 'Beyond risk seeking and risk aversion: Personality and the dual nature of economic risk taking'. *European Journal of Personality* 15(1): 105–22.

Zaller, J., 1992. *The Nature and Origins of Mass Opinion*. Cambridge: Cambridge University Press.

Zettler, I., Hilbig, B. E., and Haubrich, J., 2011. 'Altruism at the ballots: Predicting political attitudes and behavior'. *Journal of Research in Personality* 45(1): 130–3.

Zillig, L.M.P., Hemenover, S. H., and Dienstbier, R. A., 2002. 'What do we assess when we assess a Big 5 trait? A content analysis of the affective, behavioral, and cognitive processes represented in Big 5 personality inventories'. *Personality and Social Psychology Bulletin* 28(6): 847–58.

Ziv, A., 1976. 'Measuring aspects of morality'. *Journal of Moral Education* 5(2): 189–201.

Zuckerman, M., Kuhlman, D. M., Joireman, J., Teta, P., and Kraft, M., 1993. 'A comparison of three structural models for personality: the big three, the big five, and the alternative five'. *Journal of Personality and Social Psychology* 65(4): 757–68.

INDEX

Absentee ballot, (see remote voting)
Advance voting, (see remote voting)
Atmosphere, (electoral) xii–xii, xx, 8–9, 15, 18–22, 24, 29–31, 36–37, 46, 54–55, 59, 62–67, 74, 77, 106, 108–109, 117, 153, 156, 162, 169, 172–174, 179, 186, 201, 211, 223, 240, 247, 252, 262, 263–265, 268–274, 287–289, 293–295, 306, 315, 317, 324

Ballot, xx, 14–17, 40, 54–55, 62–63, 74, 81, 90, 94, 97, 102, 155, 174, 215, 237–244, 255–259, 319–320
'Brexit' Referendum on European Union Membership, xi, xx, 21, 26, 57, 83, 87, 123, 132, 217, 264, 269–270, 277–280, 285, 287, 290, 307, 312, 322, 328

Choice (electoral), xi–xii, xvi, xx, 5, 7, 10–12, 20, 26, 29, 32, 36, 40–42, 51–52, 54, 61, 76, 96, 114, 120, 133–136, 138, 149, 175, 180–181, 191, 204, 207–208, 214, 244, 247, 252–253, 258–261, 275, 297, 299–303, 308–309, 318–319, 324
Context, xiii, xix, 9, 15, 19–20, 25, 33, 34–40, 52, 118, 265, 268, 291, 295, 315–316, 319, 323, 334
Cycle (electoral), xi–xii, xx–xxi, 8, 11, 14, 17–20, 31, 36, 38, 48–50, 67, 109, 114–117, 121, 180, 192, 196–198, 205–206, 213–214, 227, 263–265, 268, 272–277, 289, 292–293, 296, 306–307, 313, 316, 320–321, 324, 327–328, 333
Cyclical (see cycle)

Efficacy (see projected efficacy)
Election Day, xiv–xv, 15–17, 22, 44, 46, 53, 59–60, 62, 64, 66–70, 106–109, 114, 117, 136, 152, 169, 202, 211, 215, 219, 238, 242–243, 246–248, 251–256, 268, 272–274, 293–294, 304–307, 316, 317, 320, 324, 326, 331–332

Election Night, xiv–xv, 17, 29–31, 36, 53, 58–59, 64–68, 106, 109–117, 122, 169, 184, 189–191, 201, 205–207, 215, 239, 268, 274–277, 289, 306–307, 317–318
Electoral ergonomics, xii–xiii, xix–xx, 17–22, 24, 36–37, 40, 48, 52–55, 79, 136, 219, 239, 240–262, 268, 272–273, 294, 300, 302, 315–316, 319–320, 324, 326–327, 332, 335
Electoral identity (incl. contrast with partisan identity, referees and supporters), xiii, xvii–xviii, 5, 19–24, 26, 28, 42, 44–45, 52–53, 59, 69, 103–105, 116, 135–136, 139–142, 145, 147, 150–153, 184–211, 262, 272, 293296, 301, 305, 311, 314, 322–323, 326–327, 331
Electoral psychology, xiii, 19, 22, 24–27, 33, 64, 130, 303, 316, 319–320, 324
Emotions, xii–xiii, xviii–xx, 2–3, 5, 9–12, 14, 17–18, 20–23, 24–27, 30–36, 41, 46–47, 51–54, 58–62, 68–69, 71, 74, 77, 81–83, 95, 103–106, 112–117, 121–122, 131, 136, 142–144, 148, 152–153, 159–161, 164, 167–169, 174, 182–185, 188, 191–193, 202, 209–211, 212–239, 240, 248–255, 261–262, 267, 270, 272–274, 282–283, 288–289, 293–303, 305–308, 311, 315, 317–321, 324–334
Empathic displacement, xviii, 6–7, 19–20, 42, 44, 77–78, 84, 94–96, 105, 108, 121–122, 136, 139–142, 145, 147, 150–153, 176, 178, 185, 187, 203–209, 246, 294, 300–301, 308, 317–318, 326,
Experience (electoral), xii, xiv, xvi–xxi, 11–13, 15–21, 25, 29, 36, 38, 43, 49, 51, 53, 58–59, 68–71, 94, 109, 117, 119–121, 123, 142–144, 146, 148–149, 166, 171, 176, 178–179, 181–183, 186, 204, 209–211, 212–214, 218, 227, 233, 238–240, 248, 255, 259, 262, 269, 274–275, 295–296, 300–303, 305–306, 308, 320–321, 325–326, 333

345

346 INDEX

First time voter, 19, 145, 160–169, 225, 301
France, xv, 14–15, 21, 30, 37, 52–63, 67, 70–80, 83, 86–93, 99, 102–109, 113–116, 123–130, 135–137, 140–143, 146–148, 151, 155, 159, 162, 165, 168, 171–177, 180–181, 194–195, 199, 205–210, 215–227, 230, 243–245, 248, 250, 253, 256, 259, 264–267, 272–273, 278, 299–300, 307, 313+online appendix
Function (of elections), xi, xiii, xviii-xix, xxi, 1–5, 14, 20, 38–40, 43–44, 48, 53, 70, 88, 119, 132, 185–188, 193–194, 196, 241, 267, 275, 305, 308–310, 320, 322–323, 327

Georgia, 14, 21, 52–58, 63, 70, 73, 155, 162, 165, 168–169, 172–173, 176–177, 194–195, 199–202, 205–206, 217, 220–227, 230, 243, 266, 279, 307, 312+online appendix
Germany, 14–15, 21, 37, 52–58, 62, 73, 105–106, 108, 113–116, 123–126, 128–130, 136–137, 140–143, 146, 148, 151, 155, 162, 165, 168–169, 172, 176–177, 180–182, 189, 194–195, 199–202, 205–210, 215, 217, 220–222, 224–227, 230, 235, 243, 248, 251, 256, 266, 278, 300, 307+online appendix

Homo Suffragator, 1–23, 24, 291, 327–328
Honeymooon (electoral), xx–xxi, 5, 20, 117, 265, 268, 274–277, 280, 304, 310, 316, 321–325
Hope, xii, xx–xxii, 4, 11, 17–18, 20, 22, 36, 46, 51, 54, 77, 79–83, 90, 97–98, 100, 108, 109, 116–117, 204, 233–234, 265, 268, 270, 274–275, 278–279, 286–289, 295–296, 304, 308, 312, 314, 321, 324–325, 328
Hopelessness, xii–xiii, xx-xxii, 22, 46–47, 79–83, 102, 204, 223, 233–234, 265, 268, 270–271, 274, 277–279, 286–289, 295, 324–325, 328–329
Hostility (electoral), xii–xiii, xvi, xx–xxii, 3, 6–7, 11–12, 17–18, 20–22. 24, 46–47, 51, 54–55, 64, 94, 99–101, 116–117, 130, 135, 185, 235, 262, 265–269, 274, 279, 280–289. 292, 294–296, 308–314, 321–325, 329

Internalization, xvii, xxi, 11–12, 17, 35, 51, 54, 104–105, 152–153, 156–158, 166–173, 178–179, 272–274, 293, 301, 304–305, 323, 326, 329,

Kinesics (see subconscious)

Memory (electoral), xii, xvi–xvii, 17, 19–20, 22, 28–31, 52–53, 58, 136, 149, 152–183, 225, 296, 298, 301, 323–324, 326–327, 329
Moral (Morality, moral hierarchization), xii–xiii, xv–xvi, xxii, 2, 4, 17, 19–20, 22, 34–35, 54, 58–59, 103, 117, 119, 127–131, 135–151, 162, 201, 193, 298–301, 309–311, 314, 322, 324, 329–330

Personality (traits), xii, xv–xvi, xxi, 2, 9–10, 17–21, 24–25, 32–36, 52, 54, 58, 60, 64–65, 117–118, 119–127, 131, 134–149, 179–180, 183, 199–201, 207, 213, 240, 261, 293, 296–301, 309, 320, 324, 330, 333,
Polling booth, viii, xiv-xv, xvii, xix, 13, 15, 21, 28, 36, 44, 48–56, 59–66, 68, 73–106, 159–160, 163, 169, 184, 186, 212, 214–215, 219, 231, 235–239, 257–261, 275, 314, 317
Polling station, xiv–xv, xx, 17, 13, 15, 21–22, 29–31, 36, 41, 49, 51–56, 60, 62–64, 67–75, 91–105, 106, 108, 122, 136–138, 143–144, 149–151, 158–163, 169, 172–174, 178, 180–183, 201, 207–210, 214–215, 219–225, 231–232, 236, 238, 240–260, 294–300, 306, 317, 319–320, 323, 326, 331–332
Postal voting (see remote voting)
Projected efficacy, xii–xiii, xviii, 7, 21, 42, 45, 89–90, 94, 118, 139–151, 153, 176–178, 203–209, 246, 261, 294, 296, 299–301, 326, 330–331,
Projection (including longitudinal and generational projection), xii, xvi–xvii, xxi, 6–7, 19–20, 34, 42–44, 46, 52, 78, 94, 98–99, 104–105, 118, 123, 131, 134–135, 139–151, 174–175, 187–188, 193, 202–204, 207–211, 247, 272–274, 279, 287–289, 294, 299–301, 308, 314, 323, 328, 331,
Proxy (see remote voting)

Resolution (electoral), xi–xii, xvi, xx–xxi, 2–3, 7, 11–12, 16–23, 36, 46–48, 51, 54, 63, 114, 116–117, 123, 135, 148–153, 179, 182–183, 186, 207, 210–211, 214, 219–222, 229–230, 239, 248–252, 259, 262, 263–268, 272, 275, 286–289, 292, 295–304, 306, 308, 312–313, 315–318, 320–321, 324–327, 331–333
Remote voting, xiv, xx, 7, 14–17, 36, 40–41, 48, 50, 52–55, 64, 69, 75–76, 93, 104–105, 112–114, 149, 191, 215, 219–222, 225, 240–256, 260, 272, 295–296, 300, 307, 317, 320, 331–332
Role of the voter (see Electoral Identity)

INDEX 347

Sociotropism and egocentrism, xiii, xv–xvi, xviii, xxi–xxii, 6, 8, 19–20, 39, 42–43, 52, 64, 90–91, 103–104, 118, 131–135, 139–153, 157–158, 169–171, 185, 193, 202, 246–247, 273–274, 289, 294–295, 298–301, 308, 310, 318, 322–323, 330, 332–333

South Africa, 14, 30, 52, 55–58, 77, 79–80, 82–84, 92, 95, 99, 101, 105, 106, 109, 124, 128–129, 135, 137, 140–143, 146, 148–149, 151, 155, 162, 164–165, 168, 172–173, 175–177, 180–182, 194–195, 199, 201–202, 205, 207–210, 215, 217, 221, 224–227, 233, 266, 278+online appendix

Subconscious (incl. methodology—implicit questions, visual experiment, kinesics), xii, xvii, xix, 3, 13, 16–19, 25, 28–32, 36, 45, 47, 50–51, 59, 69, 120, 127, 130–131, 135–136, 183–189, 194, 202, 207, 212, 215–216, 232–237, 239, 261, 292–295, 305, 308, 323–326, 333

Tears, xix, 112, 117, 157, 202, 212–219, 222, 293, 304–305, 320, 333–334

United Kingdom, viii–xi, xx, 14–15, 21, 26, 31, 35–39, 41, 50–59, 62–63, 70–73, 76–88, 90–95, 98–99, 101–109, 113–117, 123–137, 142–143, 146, 148–149, 151, 155–156, 164–165, 168, 170–173, 176–183, 189, 195–202, 205–210, 215–230, 233–237, 243, 248–250, 253–259, 264–265, 267–271, 277–286, 293, 296, 298–300, 307, 312–313, 316, 333–334 + online appendix

United States, xxi, 7, 13–15, 21, 26, 30–32, 36–37, 50, 52–59, 63, 65, 70–73, 76–109, 113,-117, 123–144, 148–150, 155–156, 162–168, 170–173, 176–178, 180–183, 187, 192–202, 205–210, 215, 217, 220–235, 243–251, 256–258, 264–265, 267–268, 273, 276–278, 280, 285, 296–302, 307, 312–313, 333 + online appendix

A NOTE ON THE TYPE

This book has been composed in Adobe Text and Gotham. Adobe Text, designed by Robert Slimbach for Adobe, bridges the gap between fifteenth- and sixteenth-century calligraphic and eighteenth-century Modern styles. Gotham, inspired by New York street signs, was designed by Tobias Frere-Jones for Hoefler & Co.